The State as a Work of Art

The State as a Work of Art

The Cultural Origins of the Constitution

ERIC SLAUTER

THE UNIVERSITY OF CHICAGO PRESS   CHICAGO AND LONDON

The University of Chicago Press, Chicago 60637
The University of Chicago Press, Ltd., London
© 2009 by The University of Chicago
All rights reserved. Published 2009.
Paperback edition 2011
Printed in the United States of America

20 19 18 17 16 15 14 13 12 11   2 3 4 5 6

ISBN-13: 978-0-226-76195-4 (cloth)
ISBN-13: 978-0-226-76196-1 (paper)
ISBN-10: 0-226-76195-9 (cloth)
ISBN-10: 0-226-76196-7 (paper)

PUBLICATION OF THIS BOOK HAS BEEN AIDED BY A GRANT FROM
THE BEVINGTON FUND.

Library of Congress Cataloging-in-Publication Data
Slauter, Eric Thomas.
    The state as a work of art : the cultural origins of the constitution / Eric Slauter.
      p. cm.
    Includes bibliographical references and index.
    ISBN-13: 978-0-226-76195-4 (cloth : alk. paper)
    ISBN-10: 0-226-76195-9 (cloth : alk. paper)
      1. Constitutional law—United States—Philosophy. 2. Constitutional history—United
States. 3. State, The—Philosophy. I. Title.
    KF4550.S54 2009
    342.7302'9—dc22

                                                          2008035898

♾ This paper meets the requirements of ANSI/NISO Z39.48-1992 (Permanence of Paper).

TO STEPHANIE BROOKS

Contents

Acknowledgments   ix

Introduction: Culture and Constitutionalism   1

A Note on Constitutional Interpretation   18

Prologue: The Fools' Contest   27

I. The State as a Work of Art

CHAPTER 1.   Making a Government of Laws   39

CHAPTER 2.   Aesthetics and the Science of Politics   87

CHAPTER 3.   The Matter and Meaning of Representation   123

II. The Culture of Natural Rights

CHAPTER 4.   Slavery and the Language of Rights   169

CHAPTER 5.   Being Alone in the Age of the Social Contract   215

CHAPTER 6.   The Godless Constitution and the Sacred Rights
of Man   241

Epilogue: The Age of Constitutions   297

Notes   303

Index   357

Acknowledgments

Like the Constitution, this book results from collaboration: archivists and librarians shared knowledge about sources; friends and colleagues refined the argument; and a few individuals inspired me to attempt to combine their ways of seeing the world with my own.

And like the Constitution, this book is a compromise, a balance struck between the examples of extraordinary teachers. Timothy Breen first exposed me to the pleasures of archival research and extensive reading; he taught me that historians, if they wish to explain the relation between ideas and events (and they should), should read everything. Jay Fliegelman taught me that historians should read anything—books, chairs, punctuation marks—intensively, working slowly to reveal unseen networks of ideas and to question which facts are relevant for the interpretation of events.

As the project took shape, George Dekker and Al Gelpi helped me recognize the literary stakes of seemingly nonliterary sources. Jack Rakove provided a model for thinking about ideas and politics or, as he would probably prefer, politics and ideas. And, though never formally my teachers, in person and in print Alfred Young and Richard Dunn pushed me to see intersections between social and intellectual history and taught me how to appreciate and even partially access the intellectual history of ordinary people.

Two special communities nurtured the book. The McNeil Center for Early American Studies at the University of Pennsylvania and the Newberry Library in Chicago provided time, space, support, and supporters. I thank Richard Dunn, Daniel Richter, and the McNeil community for their example and for enabling me see what the book could be; and I thank James Grossman, Sara Austin, and the Newberry fellows for suffering with me as I tried to realize it.

The staffs at the Newberry Library, the Library Company of Philadelphia, the Henry E. Huntington Library, the Special Collections Research Center at the University of Chicago, and the Library of Congress
provided me with leads I would never have discovered on my own. Robert Ritchie made my stay in San Marino possible. In a world of digital archives the knowledge research librarians possess has only become more
important, a fact I am reminded of whenever I talk to James Green or
Alice Schreyer. I turned to the online catalog of the American Antiquarian Society, with its unparalleled annotations, almost every day
while researching this book and years before I finally walked through
the door in Worcester. I acknowledge many scholars in the notes, but
University of Chicago Press style prevents me from giving bibliographic
credit there to John P. Kaminski and Gaspare J. Saladino, whose long-
standing efforts with *The Documentary History of the Ratification of the
Constitution* are masked by "et al."

Over the last decade I presented parts of the book at the Newberry
Seminar in Early American History, the School of Architecture at Princeton University, the International Seminar on the History of the Atlantic World at Harvard University, the McNeil Center at the University of
Pennsylvania, the Faculty Works in Progress Seminar at the Law School
of the University of Chicago, the American Studies Seminar at the University of Illinois at Champaign-Urbana, the Colloquium of the Omo-
hundro Institute of Early American History and Culture at the College
of William and Mary, the annual American Studies lecture at Kalama-
zoo College, a conference sponsored by the Program in the History of
the Book at the American Antiquarian Society, and a conference organized jointly by the Research Center for Cultural Theory (Konstanz)
and the Max Planck Institute for European Legal History (Frankfurt
am Main). Portions of the book were also delivered at meetings of the
American Society for Eighteenth-Century Studies, the Association for
the Study of Law, Culture, and the Humanities, the Modern Language
Association, the Society for the History of the Early American Republic, and the Society of Early Americanists. For formal responses I am
especially grateful to Bernard Bailyn, David Brion Davis, Christopher
Looby, and Michael Warner. For comments or other help, I thank Akhil
Reed Amar, David Armitage, Nancy Armstrong, Ralph Bauer, Wendy
Bellion, George Boudreau, Joanna Brooks, Kathleen Brown, Martin
Brückner, Christopher Castiglia, Joyce Chaplin, James Delbourgo, Ra-
chel De Lue, Karie Diethorn, Elizabeth Maddock Dillon, Paul Downes,

Carolyn Eastman, Paul Erickson, Betsy Erkkila, Nicole Eustace, Robert Ferguson, Jonathan Field, Philip Gould, Christopher Grasso, Sandra Gustafson, Evan Haefeli, David Hall, Philip Hamburger, Jill Hasday, Kate Haulman, Bernard Herman, Ronald Hoffman, Woody Holton, Greg Jackson, Calvin Johnson, Jane Kamensky, Suvir Kaul, Sean Keilen, Catherine E. Kelly, Sarah Knott, Albrecht Koschorke, Ed Larkin, Charlene Boyer Lewis, James Lewis, Agnes Lugo-Ortiz, Martha McNamera, Franco Moretti, Carla Mulford, John Murrin, Dana Nelson, Susan Scott Parrish, Sarah Pearsall, Yvette Piggush, Rosalind Remer, Sarah Rivett, Martha Elena Rojas, David S. Shields, Frank Shuffelton, Caroline Sloat, Doris Summer, Peter Stallybrass, Robert Blair St. George, John Wood Sweet, Len Tennehouse, Fredrika Teute, Dror Wahrman, David Waldstricher, Brian Waterman, Jim Williams, Karin Wulf, and Michael Zuckerman.

Early versions of chapters 4 and 5 first appeared in "Neoclassical Culture in a Society with Slaves: Race and Rights in the Age of Wheatley," *Early American Studies* 2, no. 1 (Spring 2004): 81–122, and in "Being Alone in the Age of the Social Contract," *William and Mary Quarterly*, 3d ser., 62, no. 1 (January 2005): 31–66. I am grateful to Daniel Richter and Christopher Grasso for permission to reprint material here and to Ruth Bloch, John Brooke, and David Waldstreicher for their responses in the *William and Mary Quarterly*.

This book has taken a long time to finish and I have incurred many personal debts. For helping me navigate through the University of Chicago Press, I thank Alan Thomas, master editor, and I thank Randy Petilos for helping the book do the same. Richard Audet showed exemplary care with the copyediting. Deans Janel Mueller and Danielle S. Allen made it possible to accept fellowships to research and write. At the University of Chicago, Lauren Berlant, Jim Chandler, Bradin Cormack, Raúl Coronado, Jacqueline Goldsby, Oren Izenberg, Janice Knight, Sandra Macpherson, Carla Mazzio, Jacqueline Stewart, Richard Strier, and Lisa Voigt all generously commented on parts of the manuscript. Nobody read this book so often, or so carefully, as Bill Brown. His own first book was the first thing Jay Fliegelman recommended I read when I began this project, and I am grateful to Bill for the care he took with this one.

My family—Stephanie, George, and Nora Brooks; George, Joan, Jennifer, and Sarah Brooks; Barbara, Will, and Ryan Slauter; and Larry and Nida Slauter—sustained me, supported me, put me up, put up with me, fed me, and often excused me while I worked.

Stephanie, George, and Nora lived with this book too long. One of them knows the book's unglamorous origins, two have never known me when I wasn't working on it, and all three provided the best incentive I can imagine for finishing it.

Stephanie Brooks changed my life and thought more than anyone else. The impact of her mind on mine can be seen on many pages of this book, and she made all of them possible. Her love for Nora and George as well as her work and rigor provide me with constant sources of inspiration. I am and will be forever grateful for her example, her support, and her love.

Introduction

Culture and Constitutionalism

On September 17, 1787, or shortly thereafter, James Madison recorded a final speech on the last page of his remarkable manuscript notes of the debates at the convention that framed the Constitution of the United States, a closing aside in which the oldest delegate, Benjamin Franklin, compared the result of that summer's deliberations to a half-eclipsed sun painted on George Washington's chair. Madison explained that Franklin made his remarks while the "last members," probably the delegates from the deep South who had won powerful constitutional protections for slavery that summer, were signing the Constitution in a chamber on the first floor of the Pennsylvania State House in Philadelphia. Looking toward the chair Washington often occupied as president of the convention, "at the back of which a rising sun happened to be painted," Franklin "observed to a few members near him, that Painters had found it difficult to distinguish in their art a rising from a setting sun." Madison rarely tried to capture speakers at the convention in their own voices, but for this final "speech" of the meeting, though uttered after debate had ended, Madison let Franklin speak for himself: "I have," Franklin apparently said, "often and often in the course of the session, and the vicissitudes of my hopes and fears as to its issue, looked at that behind the President without being able to tell whether it was rising or setting: But now at length I have the happiness to know that it is a rising and not a setting sun."[1] Franklin offered a perfect closing for the convention and for Madison's notes, a gesture later historians have relished in retelling the story of the framing of the Constitution. Indeed, when Congress purchased Madison's papers from his widow fifty years after the convention and finally arranged for their publication, the editor of the first letterpress edition selected the page with Franklin's clos-

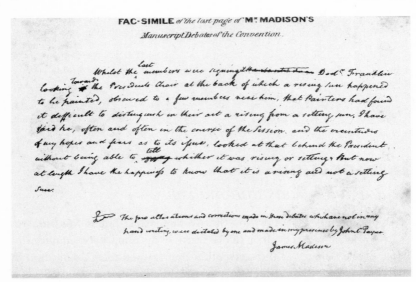

FIGURE I. "Fac-simile of the last page of Mr. Madison's Manuscript," from *The Papers of James Madison: purchased by order of the Congress, being his correspondence and reports of debates during the Congress of the Confederation . . .* (Washington, D.C., 1840). Courtesy of the University of Chicago Library.

ing remark as the only one to reproduce in facsimile (fig. 1); readers in 1840 thus gained both a feel for the manuscript, with its minor verbal revisions (Madison had substituted "tell" for "judge" in this passage), and a sense of the self-assurance of the framers at the dawn of a government that, with the expansion of slavery and sectionalism enabled by the Constitution, seemed to many to be fading into twilight.

The painting that attracted Franklin's attention, located near the top of an elaborately carved mahogany armchair, was meant to be an unambiguous materialization of revolutionary hope and ideology. Produced in the midst of war by Philadelphia artisan John Folwell for the Speaker of Pennsylvania's unicameral state legislature, the chair was part of an expensive redecoration in 1778 and 1779 of the second floor of the Pennsylvania State House, where the Pennsylvania legislature met while the Continental Congress occupied the rooms downstairs. The radically democratic Pennsylvania Constitution of 1776 enhanced the power and significance of the legislative branch, and, unlike other states, Pennsylvania dispensed with a single chief executive in the person of a governor. Instead, Pennsylvania's executive branch consisted of a council with an individual annually elected to preside over its meetings. In 1787 this person, the president, was Benjamin Franklin, though it is unlikely the physical chair he occupied in that role could rival the one Folwell made for the head of the legislature. A member of the state's radical or "Constitutionalist" party, the party that hoped to stave off more conservative calls for revision to the Pennsylvania Constitution, Folwell almost certainly designed the chair to celebrate and cement the revolutionary elevation of legislative authority.

Described in contemporary records as a carver, joiner, and cabinet-maker, Folwell had even been elected to the state legislature for a single term in 1777, though no records indicate he actually served; helping to fight the war probably kept him too busy. Perhaps because of his close ties to the government Folwell donated his work on the chair to the state, for the bill for £200 he presented in December 1779 was merely for the "materials for the speaker's chair" and not for his labor. Even in inflated wartime currency, this was a princely sum: only a year earlier the state had paid chairmaker Francis Trumble £60 for twenty Windsor chairs for ordinary representatives.[2] Though it is unclear if Folwell started or finished the chair in late 1779, the Speaker may have occupied it during the complicated debates and negotiations that resulted on March 1, 1780, in the Pennsylvania Act for the Gradual Abolition of Slavery, the preamble of which (sometimes ascribed to the radical writer Thomas Paine, who served as a clerk to the legislature) drew an analogy between the condition of enslaved blacks to white masters and the former condition of the colonies to Great Britain. "We rejoice that it is in our power," the legislators declared in this, the first abolitionist law of the new nation, "to extend a portion of that freedom to others, which has been extended to us."[3]

John Folwell's "speaker's chair" (fig. 2) blended English pattern-book style and revolutionary iconography.[4] Folwell flanked the gilded carving of a sun at the center of the crest-rail with two cornucopias signifying plenty. On the gothic arches of the back splat, he carved grains of wheat and military banners; and at the top of the outer uprights of the back he placed two shields. In a gesture almost unique for this period (a furniture historian has identified only one other contemporary example), Folwell connected the back splat horizontally with the uprights at the very center of the chair, a move that reinforced the structure and may have reminded contemporary viewers of the leveling ideology of the Pennsylvania Constitution.[5] The sun near the top of the chair, with thirteen

FIGURE 2. John Folwell, "Rising Sun" armchair made for the Speaker of the Pennsylvania House of Representatives, ca. 1779. INDE 11826, http://www.cr.nps.gov/museum/exhibits/revwar/image_gal/indeimg/armchair.html. Courtesy National Park Service, Museum Management Program, and Independence National Historical Park.

rays signifying the thirteen states, served as a symbol of enlightenment, union, and new national beginnings, a visual analogue of one of Paine's most famous phrases: "We have it in our power," Paine famously wrote in *Common Sense* in early 1776, "to begin the world over again." Folwell rendered the top half of the sun only, thus providing Franklin with the occasion for his remarks, and he gave the sun a human face. Viewers can detect the sun's eyes and nose but not yet the mouth, perhaps alluding to the Speaker's limited function—he observes and directs but does not himself participate in debate. (Washington remained silent while he presided over the Philadelphia Convention from the "speaker's chair"; he was free to speak, but chose not to, when the Convention became a committee of the whole and he sat with his state's delegation.) At the very top of the chair, just behind and immediately above the sun, Folwell carved what may have been the most important symbol: a thin pole supporting a liberty cap, the classical symbol of an emancipated slave and a hallmark of American revolutionary iconography. That Folwell fashioned this symbol of liberty from a wood harvested by slaves in Central America and the West Indies was a material fact that would not have registered with many contemporary viewers, black or white, who found themselves in the Pennsylvania State House.[6] To them, the chair would have symbolized the revolutionary promise that the rise of liberty could be as natural as the rising of the sun.

Signing the proposed Constitution, the activity delegates were engaged in when Franklin made his remarks about the pictorial problem of sunsets and sunrises, was an act fraught with difficulty, one that Franklin tried to render more easy by proposing that delegates consider their signatures not as personal endorsements of the text but simply as witnessing that the Constitution had been, as an addendum to Article VII made that day phrased it, "done in Convention by the Unanimous Consent of the States present." Not all states were present, and not all delegates approved of the text. Rhode Island refused to appoint a delegation. Robert Yates and John Lansing, two of New York's three delegates, departed in protest in early July. Their colleague Alexander Hamilton had left in late June; though he returned in September, he lacked authority to vote on motions. (Incredibly, the other delegates allowed Hamilton to sign the Constitution, even without authorization from his state, and Washington joked in his diary that night that the Constitution "received the unanimous assent of 11 States and Colo. Hamilton's from New York.")[7] In all, for one reason or another, almost a quarter of the members had left the Convention, and only four states still possessed their full delegations. Though the motion for this form of signing came from Franklin, and though Franklin offered a rousing speech (delivered by his colleague James Wilson) stressing the importance of unanimity, it was not his idea. "This ambiguous form," Madison observed in his notes, had been drawn up by another of Franklin's colleagues, Gouverneur Morris, the delegate most responsible for the "style" of the Constitution, "in order to gain the dissenting members, and put into the hands of Docr. Franklin that

it might have the better chance of success."[8] Morris and Franklin hoped
to persuade dissenting delegates that they could still attest that the proposed Constitution had the unanimous support of the remaining states,
even if some delegates did not approve of the text.

It is remarkable (yet much overlooked) that the final debate of the
Convention turned on what signing the Constitution would really mean
if delegates accepted Franklin's proposal: Was a delegate's signature
equivalent to a fundamental approval of the text, a claim in a share of
corporate authorship, a pledge that one would unambiguously support
the text during ratification, a mere recommendation to the Continental Congress, or simply (as the "ambiguous form" of Franklin's proposal
would have it) an agreement that the Constitution had been produced
not by the unanimous consent of the individuals at the Convention but
the "Unanimous Consent of the States present"? What Franklin offered
delegates, in other words, was precisely the kind of unsettled ambiguity
he subsequently returned to in his remark about the painted sun.

Franklin's final motion passed, but in the end Elbridge Gerry of Massachusetts and the Virginians Edmund Randolph and George Mason refused to see their signatures as anything but an endorsement of the text
and did not sign. Madison duly recorded as much in the final sentence of
his manuscript notes, immediately below the note he made about Franklin's reflection on the "rising sun": "The Constitution being signed by all
the Members except Mr Randolph, Mr Mason, and Mr. Gerry who declined giving it the sanction of their names," Madison wrote, "the Convention dissolved itself by an Adjournment sine die—" (fig. 3). Perhaps
because the reality of dissent at the founding moment struck the wrong
note among those who would prefer to see "a rising and not a setting
sun" at the conclusion of the Constitutional Convention, the editor of
Madison's papers in 1840 silently removed this final line when he reproduced the final page in facsimile. In retelling a sunny story of Franklin's
final remarks, generations of subsequent popular narratives have also
failed to appreciate the context in which those remarks were made—the
signing of the text by the delegates of the deep South, Franklin's political maneuvering about what signing meant, and Franklin's ultimate failure to transform the dissent of three delegates into an endorsement of
the Constitution.

It is easy for modern readers to forget the lack of unanimity during
the "founding period," to ignore strategies of compromise that framers
like Franklin employed to produce a veneer of consensus, or to over-

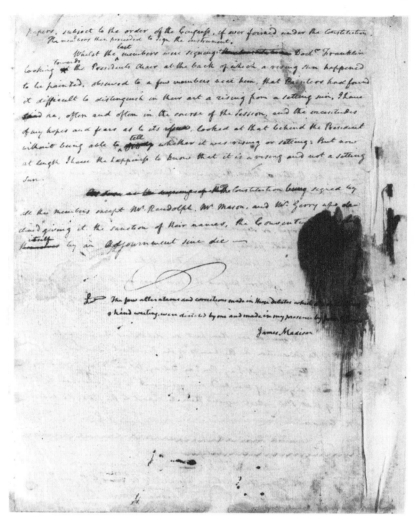

FIGURE 3. The final page of James Madison's "Notes of Debates in the Convention of 1787," with the final sentence left out of the 1840 facsimile. James Madison Papers, Manuscripts Division, Library of Congress.

look the lengths to which historians such as Madison's first editor have sometimes gone to cover over dissent. It has certainly proven easier for modern historians to describe the Constitution as either a rising or a setting sun—that is, to see the Constitution as the fulfillment of the American Revolution or as a counter-revolutionary reversal of the Revolution's democratic promise—than to hold onto the unsettled ambiguity that Franklin's final remarks at the Convention raise and only apparently settle.[9] Taken seriously, those remarks connect us to a revolutionary political culture that in its verbal, material, and social manifestations was layered with utopian optimism and political realism, with fantasies of unanimity and the compromises and bargains that sometimes enabled those fantasies to remain viable, with liberty and slavery. As Franklin's remarks about the uncertain sun suggest, it is only in the chosen perspective of the beholder, rather than in the object itself, that one can finally settle on one of the poles of revolutionary political culture to the exclusion of the other.

This book explores the vibrant political culture of the American Revolution, attending to both its unifying themes and its tensions and limits, and in doing so offers a new account of the origins of the Constitution. In the following chapters I tap neglected and overlooked sources and explore a series of topics historians have largely ignored in narrating the Constitution's immediate and distant backgrounds. Readers will find an examination of the revolutionary call for a government of laws and not of men in the context of a larger transformation in conceptions of statehood; a sketch of the simultaneous and linked rise of political science and philosophical aesthetics; an analysis of the objects and practices that informed competing ideas about political representation; a narrative about the role of antislavery agitation in transforming the revolutionary language of rights; a study of the cultural fascination, during a moment obsessed with the fiction of the social contract, with literary figures who left society; and a consideration of the rise of political secularization during an age in which many commentators came to describe the rights of man as sacred. As I hope to show, all of these disparate contexts provide crucial clues to help us understand the constitutionalism of the revolutionary period in new ways, but they are not as disconnected as any inventory is likely to suggest. Indeed, they are connected to each other by two overarching concepts that have not attracted sufficient attention from constitutional scholars.

The "state as a work of art" and the "cultural origins of the Constitution" are the central topics of this book. These topics dominated the constitutionalism of the early United States, and they hold the seemingly disparate strands of my argument together. Politicians and ordinary people in the early United States considered the state as a work of art. They believed that governments were fashioned by humans and subject to their control. They also believed that successful political constitutions should emerge from the manners, customs, tastes, and genius of the people being constituted. As one framer in Philadelphia put it, constitutions should ideally "grow out of" these cultural elements.[10] At a certain level, the revolutionary beliefs in the state as a work of art and the cultural origins of constitutions sat in tension with each other. How could law be both an artificial imposition on and a natural outgrowth of society? But, at a deeper level, it was exactly this tension that made the task of the legislator so difficult and the process of constitution-making so important, for the task as many saw it was for humans to organize politics in such a way that the state would both reflect the population and reform it.

Though the colonial charters and the documents produced during the English Civil War of the seventeenth century provided important models, American revolutionaries largely invented the genre of the written constitution. To them, as this book will illustrate at length, the political state was a work of art, a distinctly artificial entity created (some said founded upon or framed) from rights that had been surrendered by people in a state of nature and constructed to protect others that simply could not be given up. Some revolutionary writers and politicians described constitutions as collective works of art designed to reflect the culture of a people; others said that constitutions should reform a people and, if possible, make them more natural. Many revolutionaries came to think of constitutions in both of these ways at once. They described constitutions as products of their people and people as the products of their constitutions. It is in the rich terrain of the period's shifting desire to see politics as an effect of culture and culture as an effect of politics that it makes sense to consider, as I do in this book, the state as a work of art and the cultural origins of the Constitution of the United States.

The "state as a work of art" may be a familiar phrase to readers of Jacob Burckhardt's famous study of the Renaissance, but I do not take my title directly from him. In 1860 this Swiss historian discovered in the republican and despotic city-states of thirteenth-century Italy something he described as a "new fact" in history: "the State as the outcome of reflection and calculation, the State as a work of art."[11] Burckhardt was among the first professional historians to consider political history as a branch of cultural history, a development of the practice of historical writing that had its origins in Voltaire's histories of civilizations, written in the middle of the eighteenth century. The history Burckhardt described corresponded with his own ideas about the rise of individualism and contrasted with the theory endorsed by many of his academic peers in political science, the idea of the state as a living and evolving organism superior to the individuals who composed it. Though scholars debate precisely what Burckhardt meant by his phrase, he clearly did not intend to celebrate the development of "the state as a work of art" but instead (as a recent biographer notes) to offer a historical reflection on the European states of his own time, states that "no longer rested on historical tradition but on modern principles of administrative rationality and efficiency."[12] Whatever the historian might have meant, the concept of the state as a work of art had a long history in political thought and was not a product of Burckhardt's particular historical moment. Indeed, Jean-Jacques Rousseau, another Swiss writer, employed a similar phrase nearly a century before Burckhardt's essay appeared.

Drawing on a common comparison between human bodies and political bodies, one that found perhaps its greatest convergence in the word "constitution" itself, Rousseau observed in a section of his 1762 treatise *On the Social Contract* entitled "Of the Dissolution of the Body Politic" that "the constitution of man is the work of nature; that of the state is the work of art."[13] This notion of the state as a work of art was made possible in part by the secularization of political thought in the wake of the religious reformations of the sixteenth century. The idea was not uniquely Swiss. Rousseau borrowed the distinction between human constitutions and political constitutions from European social compact theorists of the seventeenth and early eighteenth centuries. While seventeenth-century English political writers like Thomas Hobbes or John Locke (as well as their contemporaries in the colonies in America) may have argued that the human constitution was a work of God rather than nature, they structured their political theories on the assumption that the constitution of the state was a work of human art, the very antithesis of what they sometimes termed the "state of nature."

This conception of the state as a non-natural entity formed one of the cornerstones of American revolutionary ideology. Revolutionaries in advance and in the wake of the Declaration of Independence celebrated their good luck in living at a moment (the first, some said, in human history) when people could create governments for themselves. By governments, they meant works of human art rather than of nature, God, or time. The right to institute, alter, and abolish these works was the central right claimed in the Declaration, though modern readers are more likely to attend to the unalienable rights of individuals barely enumerated in the second paragraph ("among these are Life, Liberty, and the Pursuit of Happiness") or to the rights of national sovereignty (the power to do all "Acts and Things which Independent States may of right do") that Congress claimed in the concluding resolution of that document. People fashioned governments out of the rights they had alienated, and though these rights were said to be "natural" and of divine origin (they had been endowed by a Creator), the governments fashioned from them were neither natural nor sacred. They were artificial constructions.[14]

But even among those who agreed that government was artificial, some said that certain forms of government were more "natural" than others, by which they meant one of two things. On the one hand, political writers sometimes argued that certain political forms allowed people universally to be more natural, to behave more naturally than other forms did. On the other hand, they argued that certain forms more naturally (that is, more relatively) suited a particular population. Then, as now, people differed in their understanding of what was truly natural. And so some writers praised certain forms of government as more "natural," others railed against forms that failed to correct artificial divisions between citizens, and still others rebuked politicians for trying to use the law to produce unnatural adjustments in the existing social order.[15] At stake in such debates was the question of how the recognized artifice of law and politics could be used to help people be more natural, to have the blessings of government while avoiding its burdens, and to help citizens see their lives under a political state as if politics was simply an extension of nature.

While the major statements in the political thought of the second half of the seventeenth century (that of, say, Hobbes and Locke) had been devoted to theoretical accounts of the founding of legitimate states, writers in the eighteenth century created a science of politics that took as a central tenet that the empirical manners, customs, taste, and genius—in a word, what I have called the "culture"—of a people must be taken into account in determining what constituted the most "natural" government for that people. The modern analytic meaning of the word "culture" would not be entirely lost on late eighteenth-century speakers and writers, but it is not their word. I have adopted it as a simple way to refer to the vortex of words and concepts they did use when they referred, as they frequently did in the late eighteenth century, to manners, morals, beliefs, opinions, customs, genius, and tastes. It was in this moment that the political theory of the previous age gave way to political science. Though the idea that states should suit populations had an ancient genealogy, its major publicist in the Enlightenment was Montesquieu. In an important passage at the opening of his *Spirit of the Laws*, one of the most widely invoked political books during the American Revolution, Montesquieu disputed that any one form of government was more natural than any other. A committed relativist, he was emphatic that laws "should be adapted in such a manner to the people for whom they are framed that it should be a great chance if those of one nation suit another." To him, the "government most conformable to nature is that which best agrees with the humor and disposition of the people in whose favor it is established."[16] To say that a government was natural was to show that it fit the culture of a people.

To many Americans at the end of the eighteenth century, the most natural and legitimate government was precisely the one that could claim cultural origins. In a series of lectures on moral and political philosophy delivered in the late eighteenth and early nineteenth centuries, for instance, President Samuel Stanhope Smith of Princeton told students that political science was founded on the principle that governments should conform to the manners, customs, and genius of the people governed. Smith related an anecdote that circulated widely in the early United States, one that had been invoked several times during the Convention at Philadelphia in 1787 as well as during debates in the South Carolina legislature and at the ratifying convention in Massachusetts. When the classical lawgiver Solon "was asked if he had given the Athenians the best civil institutions, he replied," Smith noted, "*that he had given them the best they were able to bear.*" For Smith, Solon's answer pointed to "a principle which lies at the foundation of political science; that the forms of civil government ought to be varied according to the character and manners of the people for whom they are designed" and should take into account any environmental and other circumstances that directly influenced those manners. This led Smith to a simple conclusion: that "no single form of government is to be considered as absolutely, and universally best: but that the perfection of any civil institution is wholly a relative idea to the state of the nation to which it is adapted."[17] The best political institutions, the best form of government, the best constitution for any people was the one that best fit their manners, customs, tastes, and genius—in a word, what Smith's modern counterparts might call the culture of a people. Like many college professors, Smith drew his lectures from unacknowledged sources. The most important in this case was Montesquieu's chapter "Of Laws in Relation to the Principles Which Form the General Spirit, Morals, and Customs of a Nation," which provided President Smith both with his general thesis and his particular anecdote. For Montesquieu, Solon's remark was "a fine expression," one "that ought to be perfectly understood by all legislators."[18]

By the end of the eighteenth century many American commentators followed Montesquieu and suggested that the best form of government was whatever was best for the particular nation, though they sometimes also claimed that objective standards could be produced upon which to judge which forms were absolutely or universally best for the accomplishments of certain ends. If one was speaking about a particular people, then the government that fit the people was the best; if one was speaking more abstractly about the preservation of liberty or the happiness of society, then a different set of criteria existed. Then as now, some writers sat uneasily between an acknowledged relativism and a chauvinistic universalism, claiming that what was best for a certain people was best for everyone.

And, then as now, some writers debated a question at the center of revolutionary constitutionalism: Did people make constitutions or did constitutions make people? At its simplest, this central question was of the chicken-and-egg variety. At its most complex, the question concerned the direction of the relationship between culture and politics: Does political form determine cultural life, or is it the other way around? Different voices answered the question in different ways. Political determinists said that a republican form of government would produce the right kind of citizens and that political republicanism could be placed atop a culture steeped in monarchism. In this view, people were a product of their governments. Cultural determinists replied that no form of government could work unless it corresponded to the actually existing social and cultural life of the people. To them, governments were products of a people, and a people could only support a government that fit them. The Constitution of the United States emerged from the context of this debate, a debate that erupted in the late eighteenth century but remains alive whenever people come together to revise or to create constitutions. This book, then, deals both with a set of historical problems and with a question that continues to have relevance—indeed, with a question that has taken on increased relevance in the last twenty years, as (just as in the late eighteenth and early nineteenth centuries) the breakup of empires and revolutions within already independent states have led people all over the globe to draft or revise constitutions.

* * *

This study of culture and constitutionalism builds on a vast literature of legal and political history, but I have tried to shed light on little-noticed practices and preoccupations, to draw on sources that may not be well known, and to tell the stories of unfamiliar figures.[19] Students of the age of the American Revolution are blessed with an abundance of primary material for understanding politics—so blessed, in fact, that they can be forgiven for sometimes segregating political thought from political reality or for focusing their understandings of politics on a narrow, if extraordinarily complex and deep, archive of newspaper essays, pamphlets, political correspondence, and the records of legislative debates. We could never do without these sources. Indeed, I believe this narrow archive should be read in some cases with more care and sensitivity, especially to the material conditions that made it possible, than it has been. I explain why this matters at different parts of my story and in the note that concludes this Introduction. But I also believe, as do many others, that the wider verbal, visual, material, and performative cultures of the revolutionary period must be taken into account, and in the chapters that follow I offer explanations of the politics of the period that incorporate rather than ignore this wider context.

I have approached different aspects of this study in different ways—sometimes by reading one text very closely, at other times by trying to reconstruct the larger and smaller contexts that made ideas meaningful. In telling my story, I have drawn on the full range of both domestic and imported texts produced and consumed in the period, and have tried to use new technologies (such as searchable digital texts, which allow scholars to follow the career of words) in ways that open up new interpretive possibilities. I take seriously what was in fact written, what might have been spoken and written down, and I even speculate on what might have been thought, but I do not ignore the material realities that led people to say or think things, and I have followed Robert A. Ferguson's call to listen to crucial silences during an age in which print culture expanded and oratory reigned. Readers will find qualitative accounts of individual texts side by side with quantitative analysis of long-term trends, explorations of metaphors beside analysis of the material objects that gave the metaphors meaning, and treatments of the best-known figures of the period enhanced by explorations of the intellectual histories of ordinary people.

My account of constitutional origins turns frequently to the ideas of John Adams, Thomas Jefferson, James Madison, Thomas Paine, Benjamin Franklin, and James Wilson, among others, but I have also peopled the book with a cast of other players whose political thought or importance is rarely considered. This includes the Massachusetts poet Phillis Wheatley, an enslaved African who learned to speak the colonial language of rights; Joseph Thomson, a Vermont Baptist who became so upset when his cows were confiscated and sold to support another religion that he decided to alter, publish, and sell John Locke's century-old *Letter Concerning Toleration*; a Philadelphia patron of the arts and tax collector, John Swanwick, who wrote the longest rebuttal to Jefferson's famous Statute for Religious Freedom; enslaved black men and women whose condition gave content to the idea of political slavery and who argued for freedom by invoking and critiquing revolutionary declarations of rights; miniature painters who set up shop in communities across the United States providing ordinary people with images of loved ones as well as Anti-Federalists with a potent metaphor about identity and political representation; entrepreneurial shorthand newspaper reporters whose ability to summarize the voice of political representatives provided Federalists with a counter-metaphor and a standard for summarizing the voice of the people; and printers who made stories about hermits and people who abandoned civil society some of the most popular narratives to circulate during the framing and ratification of the Constitution.

I have organized the book topically rather than chronologically. The two main sections of the book mimic the division of many books on politics written in the eighteenth century though in reverse order, with chapters on rights following chapters on government. And the topics I treat are ones that were central to political thought in the late eighteenth century: state and society, liberty and slavery, the individual and the community, the divine and the human. The early chapters consider constitutionalism as a branch of cultural history (in the sense of the fine arts) but the final chapters demonstrate how cultural history (in the sense of customs, manners, mores, and tastes) presented a problem for American constitutionalism.

The first chapter charts long-term shifts in emphasis between metaphors for the state grounded in nature and human anatomy and meta-

phors grounded in culture. As part of a gradual change in the identification of political bodies with human bodies, new ideas about race,
gender, and governance in the second half of the eighteenth century
contributed to a devaluation of the popular seventeenth-century metaphor of the "body politic." At the same time, American writers increasingly depicted the state as a work of art and even artifice, an object at
once beautiful and potentially deceitful. This change in metaphors re-
cast politicians as cultural producers, government as a cultural product,
and citizens (and noncitizens alike) as spectators and cultural consumers
of politics. By examining these metaphors in the context of their material referents, this chapter reinterprets why Thomas Paine called constitutions the "property of a nation" and why certain groups began to claim
that the nation belonged to them.

The increasing significance of the concept of the state as a work of art
in the late eighteenth century should be understood within the context
of the contemporaneous rise of modern political science and philosophical aesthetics. As I argue in chapter 2, both these nascent disciplines
addressed the problem of building consensus by reconciling individual
judgments with the authority of experts, while culture—customs, manners, morals, and tastes—presented a seemingly insurmountable obstacle to a science of either politics or aesthetics. The Constitution itself
could not have been ratified without an appeal to its total beauty and
a strategic refashioning of political consent on the model of aesthetic
"taste." Supporters like Noah Webster compared the proposed Constitution to a painting that should be appreciated for its overall design; his
opponents argued that constitutions should be judged by reason and understanding rather than taste. Nevertheless, the meaning of the text and
the possibilities for interpreting it were bound up for many with a particularly aesthetic way of thinking about its overall design. Even more, the
emerging concept of "constitutional taste"—the proper fit between cultural life and political form—allowed Americans to consider the Constitution as simultaneously an artificial creation and an outgrowth of the
culture of the people.

The third chapter closely examines the material foundations for two
models of political representation articulated during the ratification debates. Arguing that the legislative branches proposed by the Constitution were too small to be representative, opponents of ratification in 1787
and 1788 appropriated a phrase from John Adams and held that Congress should be "a portrait in miniature of the people at large." Supporters countered that a representative body should not necessarily look like

the people but should instead be a "transcript" of the voice or the mind of the people. The Anti-Federalist ideal of "likeness" drew upon the colonial and revolutionary consumption of miniature portraits. The Federalist preference for metaphors of transcription was rooted in the cultural practices of note-taking, practices that informed key revolutionary texts from Thomas Jefferson's *Notes on the State of Virginia* and James Madison's *Notes of Debates in the Federal Convention of 1787* to the genre of the written constitution itself. By reconnecting language with material culture, this chapter explores the growing schism between a revolutionary politics based in identity and a fading deferential politics of expertise.

The revolutionary era gave rise to a modern language of rights and to modern forms of racism. The fourth chapter examines the naturalization of concepts of race in the face of ideas about the artificiality of government and new claims for and about rights. The language of American rights in the debates leading to the American Revolution drew strength by pointing to the condition of black slaves and by describing imperial policy as political "slavery." In turn, black writers like Phillis Wheatley and Jupiter Hammon embraced the language of the imperial debate to describe the situation of unfree blacks in America. But when blacks petitioned for freedom and compensation for slavery, many whites were reluctant to see the analogy between America and unfree blacks. Instead of drawing a direct (if temporally deferred) line of causality from the rhetoric of political slavery and liberty to black emancipation, this chapter argues that we should look to that rhetoric to help us explain why justifications of black slavery based on the supposed mental and cultural inferiority of black people began to emerge precisely in this period, and why black writers in turn worked to shift rights discourse away from its new groundings in ideas about mental equality.

The narrative of the social contract, I argue in chapter 5, competed in revolutionary America with a vogue for solitude and with narratives of individuals who voluntarily chose to leave the protections of both government and society. Social contract theorists (from James Otis in the 1760s, to Thomas Paine in the 1770s, to James Wilson in the 1790s) described solitude as unnatural and government as inevitable, but the hermits described in almanacs, elite periodicals, and cheap chapbooks and featured in traveling wax exhibits prompted readers and viewers to think differently about the artificiality of both government and society. Episodes in the anxious origins of individualism and modern notions of privacy in the United States, popular stories of postpolitical and postsocial

solitary beings allowed Americans to reflect on the most significant political questions of the day: Was society natural? Did people make better
decisions in private or in public? Did rights originate in a state of nature,
or were they really created by governments? Ultimately, was it better to
consider states as artificial products of individuals or the individual as an
artificial product of the state?

Since the eighteenth century, commentators have described the Constitution as "godless," by which they have meant not only that the text
does not include the word "God" but also that the document represents
(for better or worse) a moment of political secularization. The sixth chapter, beginning with an account of the rises and falls of the word "God"
in the eighteenth century, teases out the forces of both secularization
and sacralization at work in the American Revolution. Despite dramatic
changes in religious vocabulary and a marked drop in references to God
in the period of the Revolution, it was next to impossible for Americans who employed arguments rooted in natural rights to dispense with
God (both the word and the concept) as a foundation for rights, but the
sacralization of rights as God-given in the revolutionary age was an effect rather than a cause of the increased conception of government as an
artificial, man-made creation. The proper relation of culture to politics
remains an open question, and in a brief Epilogue I offer a bridge between the concerns of the first age of constitutions and our own times.

One final point: this book is a work of intellectual, cultural, and literary history, and not of political theory or constitutional law. Nevertheless, by describing the ways in which culture posed a problem (and
for some, a solution) for politics in the period of the American Revolution I hope that the book can shed light on a major legacy of the Enlightenment: the attempt, ever since the eighteenth century, to reconcile the
demands of cultural particularity with the desire for universal constitutional principles. If I have turned to topics that seem distant from the
concerns of legal or political historians, it is out of a conviction I share
with many of the eighteenth-century thinkers I treat that cultural and
constitutional history can and should be mutually illuminating.

A Note on Constitutional Interpretation

Though this book is a contribution to cultural history rather than law,
its chapters reflect on the nature and sources of several current schools

of constitutional interpretation. Readers interested in learning how the cultural history of constitutionalism might impact interpretation should read this note now; other readers may wish to enter the book and return later to the next few pages.

Over the last two decades, the project of determining the original intention, meaning, or understanding of the individuals who framed and ratified the Constitution has achieved a remarkable prominence in public and academic debates. Often concerned more with ends than means, scholars, lawyers, and judges of very different political persuasions have sometimes proceeded as if the philosophical question of whether original meanings should guide current efforts to interpret the Constitution could be set aside in order to take up pragmatic questions about how to determine those meanings or about whose meanings should count as original. At moments of hyper-reflexivity, some scholars have looked to the revolutionary period in order to understand the original understanding of original understanding or to determine the framers' intentions about the framers' intentions. Such ingenious exercises in intellectual history tell us how real-world demands for interpretation sat side by side with abstract musings about epistemology and intentionality in the late eighteenth century; but even when these studies reveal that the framers rejected "originalist" interpretive stances, they are really versions of originalism rather than answers to it. Modern interpreters have a right to their own abstract musings, of course, and scholars and judges have revealed that there are now many ways to be an originalist.[20]

The book that follows might be read as another self-reflexive study, for I have taken the idea of origins itself as one of my central topics. I have also tried to show that the modern interpretive divide between those who see the Constitution as a static document and those who see it as a living organism was present in the revolutionary era. My point in doing so is not to promote one side of the modern debate at the expense of the other but to reveal a history of complexity, tension, and conflict. Nevertheless, for readers whose main concern is with interpreting the Constitution, this study speaks to the smaller sphere of practical questions about the kinds of evidence structuralist, intentionalist, and textualist interpreters employ to determine original meanings.

Modern interpreters who emphasize the structure of the text will benefit not simply from a more refined awareness of the exigencies of ratification and of the debates in newspapers and pamphlets, but from the kind of attention I pay in this book to the period's own ideas about structure. Though a product of compromise and designed to accommodate various interests represented by the delegates in Philadelphia, the Constitution was barely ratified by the state conventions to which it was sent in 1787 and 1788. The Constitution's Preamble promised a "more perfect union" than the Articles of Confederation, but no supporter of the text in 1787 or 1788 believed the Constitution itself was perfect. To be sure, the thirty delegates at the state convention of Delaware, the first of the ratifying conventions, voted unanimously in favor of the proposed Constitution, as did delegates in New Jersey and Georgia, but a third of the sixty-nine delegates to the second state convention, in Pennsylvania, voted against the text. The same percentage voted against ratification in South Carolina. Fifteen percent of delegates dissented in Maryland, and just under a quarter of delegates said no in Connecticut. Both North Carolina and Rhode Island formally rejected the Constitution in 1788. Forty-five percent of delegates in New Hampshire voted against the Constitution, but more significantly 47 percent of delegates in each of the conventions in Massachusetts, New York, and Virginia opposed it. The margins of victory in these key states were truly miniscule. Ten votes in Massachusetts, six votes in Virginia, and two votes in New York were the difference between ratification and rejection of the Constitution. And in each of these three cases supporters of the text were forced to make concessions to opponents: the official forms of ratification in those states all make clear that the Constitution being ratified was not perfect and that it should be immediately amended to address perceived structural problems.

In newspaper essays, pamphlets, and broadsides, supporters and opponents of the Constitution routinely talked over rather than to each other in an effort to capture the attention of undecided members of the public. By tracking the circulation and appropriation of different commentaries on the Constitution, John Kaminski and Gaspare Saladino, the current editors of the magnificent *Documentary History of the Ratification of the Constitution*, have revealed a still too little understood and appreciated world of print. Newspapers did not offer equal advantages and opportunities to all writers. In locations where they had difficulty placing essays in gazettes, Anti-Federalists pursued other options, which helps explain the curious fact that printers issued many more broadsides and pamphlets against the proposed Constitution than for it in late 1787. By imagining ratification as a "great national discussion," to adopt Hamilton's phrase in the first essay of *The Federalist*, interpreters have overlooked the very local ways in which editors and writers employed and recycled pieces in support or opposition to the Constitution as well as the ways in which the disputants often avoided discussing the same points. Anti-Federalists in New York sometimes reprinted Federalist pieces, letting Federalists "speak for themselves" on the assumption that readers would see the weaknesses on their own. Virginia Federalists believed they could make use of out-of-state writings by Anti-Federalists, especially when opponents fixated on the advantages that the Constitution might give to large states like Virginia. Newspaper editors in Connecticut seem to have run bogus, purposefully weak Anti-Federalist essays to allow Federalists the chance to demolish them; inevitably, some readers found the concocted pieces persuasive and expanded on them in other forums.

Supporters and opponents of ratification in each city and state addressed the public on different topics, and sometimes simply ignored the arguments of the other side. When "Publius" of *The Federalist* delayed discussing the proposed Constitution until he treated what he took to be the impending breakup of the Union into smaller confederacies, an idea that seems to have had very few proponents, Anti-Federalists charged that this was simply a "spectre . . . raised to terrify and alarm the people out of the exercise of their judgment," a "hobgoblin . . . sprung from the deranged brain of Publius" designed to "force conviction by a torrent of misplaced words." To waste so much time and energy on a fiction was a sure sign to Anti-Federalists that the Constitution could not be defended on its own merits; to modern interpreters it might serve as evidence that no "great national discussion" really took place.[21]

The realities of the print marketplace structured argumentation during ratification, but interpreters who look to the structure of the Constitution for the meaning of particular clauses should also attend to ideas about structure in the period. As I argue in the second chapter, supporters of the Constitution in 1787 and 1788 sometimes emphasized what they took to be the beauty of the whole document over the putative deformities of certain clauses. They obviously did so strategically, for the Constitution could only be ratified or rejected, and they wished to ward off calls for a second constitutional convention. This strategy dovetailed with a public ratification campaign that more frequently focused on the total design of the text than on individual parts. The result is a documentary record often silent on the meaning of now controversial clauses and sometimes contradictory on the contemporary understanding of the

larger structure. Structuralist interpreters should thus pay attention to
the period's concepts of structure, but they should also be aware of how
competing concepts of structure can directly preclude modern attempts
to understand the meaning of parts of the text.

Interpreters who care about the intentions of the Constitution's framers and ratifiers derive their understandings of those intentions from the
records of debates in the Philadelphia Convention and the state ratifying conventions. These documents also require more sensitivity and cultural contextualization than interpreters usually give them. Though legal scholars debate the relevance of his records for an understanding of
the ratified Constitution, James Madison's longhand notes of debates in
the Federal Convention provide an essential window into the proceedings of the Constitution's framing, but these notes are rarely consulted
in anything but an edited form. In this study I have relied on and cited
the standard edition of Madison's notes prepared by Max Farrand and
published as part of his *Records of the Federal Convention* in 1911, but
I have also found it necessary to return to the manuscript notes themselves. Although Farrand was careful in cases he deemed significant to
record changes Madison made to the manuscript—sometimes immediately, as when Madison crossed one word out and wrote another; at other
times more distantly, as when Madison added the exact wording of resolutions from other manuscript and printed sources—Farrand did not attempt to include all minor changes. An edition prepared by an archivist
at the Department of State and published a few years before Farrand's
edition, but rarely cited today, attempted to reproduce more of the feel
of the manuscript by including cross-outs, carets for insertions, and different type sizes for revisions. That edition, despite its many faults (some
pointed out by Farrand), is probably the closest to the manuscript one
can come in print, but no letterpress edition could ever fully convey certain details of the manuscript. My use of Madison's notes sometimes
turns on precisely the kind of details that printed editions conceal (that,
for instance, the longest revised speech in the notes concerned slavery).
And so while I make use of Farrand's edition, I also refer readers to the
original manuscripts in the Madison Papers at the Library of Congress;
though almost never cited by interpreters of the Constitution, photo-
graphic reproductions of these papers have been available on microfilm
since the 1960s, and the Library has recently made a digital version of
the microfilm available online.

Beyond Madison's notes, we are fortunate to have the records of debates at state conventions, but modern interpreters almost never situate these texts in their proper historical context. A new conception of representation materialized during the American Revolution. Starting in the 1760s, legislatures began to open their doors to the public and to build gallery spaces to accommodate spectators; by the middle of the 1780s, newspaper editors were printing legislative debates with far more detail than the sparse official printed journals ever had, and some entrepreneurial shorthand reporters began to see a market for even more fulsome coverage of the debates in statehouses. The transcripts of debates during the state ratifying conventions, made with the permission of the conventions but not supported by them, partake of a new culture of legislative transparency, accountability, and publicity, one that in the material form of reported debates was only two or three years old in the United States. We should not romanticize the transcripts or see them as transparent texts that provide us with unmediated access to the intentions of speakers at the state conventions. Some of them were clearly partisan documents. The transcripts drawn from the Pennsylvania Convention, made by Thomas Lloyd, were not "debates" in any sense of the term; they included only the speeches of supporters of the Constitution and were most likely prepared and published as briefs for circulation to like-minded delegates at other state conventions. Many reporters of course aimed for a more complete record, but no method of shorthand reporting could yet fully capture a speaker's words verbatim, not all speakers could be heard equally, and not all conventions resulted in the publication of edited transcripts. Indeed, it is telling that the states where printers believed a market for such an item might exist were often the states where ratification was most close: Massachusetts, New York, and Virginia. The records for these states are a hodgepodge of good-faith attempts to record some speeches in the first person, summaries of other speeches, and synopses of positions taken without attribution to particular speakers.

In arguing from the notes of debates in the individual state ratifying conventions, some of the major sources for originalist interpretation, interpreters often conflate transcribed reports of speeches with what delegates actually said and do not attend to the cultural and legal practices that governed the transcription of speech. As I describe them in chapter 3, these practices assigned authorship and ownership of transcribed speech to the reporter rather than the speaker, and as such tend to mitigate the textualization of intention. Setting aside the reliability of the reporters, transcribing speech in the late eighteenth century—even for the most talented shorthand reporters—inevitably led to compression, a necessity that made a transcript a recognizably subjective product of the transcriber. Supporters of the Constitution sometimes tried to imagine written constitutions and bills of rights as themselves summary "transcripts" of the voice of the people, but the contemporary cultural meanings of transcription detach convention speakers from what we have come to think of as their speech. Understanding these practices complicates (and in some ways, compromises) any attempt to derive the intentions and understandings of the speakers from these sources.[22]

Finally, in response to textualist interpreters, my book argues that engaging broader cultural contexts and unfamiliar texts is a necessary precondition for any sincere attempt to recover the public meaning of the words of the text in 1787. Interpreters who call themselves "textualists" prefer to know the public meaning of words rather than what the framers or ratifiers intended, but they often look to the same narrow set of sources as originalists. More often than not, textualists and intentionalists discover common ground in choosing *The Federalist* as a fitting place to discover both intention and public meaning. But in granting "Publius" authoritative status intentionalist interpreters routinely ignore the irony that both James Madison and Alexander Hamilton were disappointed with important aspects of the product they marketed. On the other hand, in looking to "Publius" for the public meaning of words formalists can downplay the New York state context for which the papers were written. These admittedly significant papers, especially the early ones, circulated far beyond New York, but interpreters have overestimated what we now know was an uneven circulation and have fantasized into existence a homogeneous national "public" for "Publius."[23]

Textualists face another unacknowledged problem with *The Federalist*: the surprising degree to which all three of its authors avoided sustained reflection on the actual words of the Constitution. "Publius" began his series of essays in October 1787 but only first cited a specific piece of the text of the Constitution in January 1788, after more than thirty essays. In total, citations of the language of the Constitution appear in only a quarter of the eighty-five essays, and some of these citations are really paraphrases of the text placed within quotation marks, suggesting the relatively loose commitment to what was known as the "style" and "arrangement" (as opposed to the "detail" or substance) of the text. Opponents of the proposed Constitution spent much more time parsing clauses and fearing the worst from ambiguous expressions; their writings teem with critical citations of the actual text. Of course "Publius" and other Federalists sometimes responded to these charges, perhaps most vehemently in explaining the "necessary and proper" clause. But on the whole defenders of the proposed Constitution were not as committed to defending the language of the text as their opponents were to attacking that language. Writers like "Publius" were not, in other words, committed textualists. Part of their reticence was strategic, but some of it related to how Federalists understood the genre of the written constitution itself.

Framers of constitutions in the revolutionary period put faith in written documents, to be sure, but they never imagined that words themselves made for well-built constitutions. It is worth recalling James Madison's claims in *The Federalist* that "parchment barriers," "mere declarations in the written constitution," or "a mere demarcation on parchment" served as insufficient safeguards for either the rights of citizens or the powers of particular branches of government.[24] Constitutions had to be considered not as mere texts but as texts that created the conditions for their own preservation. That is, written constitutions created governments that would guarantee the various rights declared on paper not simply because they were on paper but because the texts had explicitly created mechanisms for protecting those rights (a government that checked itself) or because the constitution had created conditions under which citizens could rely on extratextual protections (such as the scale of the republic). These were the topics that James Madison treated in the two essays that modern readers of *The Federalist* perhaps know best, papers 10 and 51. In neither of these now famous essays did Madison invoke the specific language of the Constitution itself.

My study has aimed to reach a broader understanding of the contemporary meanings associated with the text by situating the Constitution within a larger cultural context. Attending to the use of the words in the Constitution in the world of almanacs, sermons, novels, children's books, poems, and nonpolitical pamphlets could potentially democratize textualism, which (some have argued) is the method of historical interpretation with the most democratic potential. But honoring the linguistic complexity and cacophony of the founding period will necessarily frustrate the quest for common or unitary meaning at the heart of the textualist enterprise. While the "cultural study of law" has emerged as a distinctive intellectual project in the recent past, the kinds of evidence that count for understanding the place of law in culture continue to be circumscribed by older ideas of relevance.[25] This book has been written as much from a firm belief that we need to read familiar texts in unfamiliar ways as from a conviction that we need to expand the domain of documents considered relevant for the interpretation of democratic texts.

Prologue
The Fools' Contest

American revolutionaries debated momentous political questions: How should power be organized? What makes one form of government better than another? And who has the right to say? Since politicians and ordinary people believed these were practical rather than theoretical questions, perhaps no political maxim was more cited or more censured than a couplet written in 1733 by the English poet Alexander Pope:

> For Forms of Government let fools contest;
> Whate'er is best administer'd is best.[1]

Pope's lines irritated an international audience, from the philosophers David Hume and Immanuel Kant in Europe to the politicians John Adams and Alexander Hamilton in America. Political writers invoked and answered them, often in the early paragraphs of essays, pamphlets, or books. Following the thread of responses to Pope's couplet leads into the heart of late eighteenth-century politics, for what Pope saw as a contest among fools was the great debate of the age, and his lines constituted an assault on one of its cherished ideals: the creation of a government of laws and not of men.

Pope's lines appeared in one of the most popular works of the century, his *Essay on Man*. A conservative meditation on the ordering of the world addressed to the Tory political writer Henry St. John, Lord Bolingbroke, this may have been the best-known poem of a disordered, revolutionary age. It is hard to find a major figure in late colonial British America or the early United States unfamiliar with at least some of its verses. Printer Benjamin Franklin sold and President George Wash-

ington owned the *Essay*. Abigail Adams cited it in letters to friends and
family. Pennsylvania botanist John Bartram carved a couplet from it
above the door of his greenhouse in 1761 and transmitted an appreciation for the poem to his son, traveler and naturalist William Bartram.
Sometime before he turned twenty in 1763, Thomas Jefferson made ex-
tracts from it in a commonplace book; on the book-scarce Virginia frontier, future Chief Justice John Marshall transcribed the entire poem by
age twelve. John Dickinson cited it three times in *Letters from a Farmer
in Pennsylvania*, the most reprinted political pamphlet of the late 1760s.
While a student at Princeton in the early 1770s, James Madison was able
to identify an echo of it in verses by another writer. In London in 1773,
the African-American slave and poet Phillis Wheatley bought an or-
nately bound nine-volume set of Pope's works (volume 3 included the
Essay), probably the first books she purchased for herself. On the eve of
Independence physician Benjamin Rush placed a copy in the bedroom
library he prepared for fiancée Julia Stockton, but she probably knew
the poem from her mother, a published poet. In 1779 Ethan Allen dis-
rupted a Vermont court proceeding by citing the irritating lines about
form and administration; in 1781, while negotiating an exchange of prisoners, Allen's brother Ira sent a copy to a loyalist friend. John Adams
referred to the poem throughout his published writings, choosing one
line ("All nature's difference keeps all nature's peace") for the title page
of his 1787 *Defense of the Constitutions of the United States of America*. Framer James Wilson often alluded to the text in the law lectures
he delivered to women and men in Philadelphia in 1790. George Mason, the primary author of the Virginia Declaration of Rights (which influenced the Declaration of Independence and the French Declaration
of the Rights of Man), quoted a snippet of the *Essay* ("Whatever is, is
right") to future President James Monroe in one of the last letters of
his life. At the turn of the nineteenth century novelist Charles Brockden Brown offered to buy an elegant edition of the *Essay* for his beloved
and to mark the passages that most pleased him. When the future senator's father brought home a cheap pamphlet copy of the *Essay* sometime
around 1794, Daniel Webster (he was not yet a teenager) committed the
poem to memory: "I read, reread, and then commenced again," he later
noted, "nor did I give up the book till I could recite every word of it from
beginning to end."[2] As influential as it was for these figures, surviving
copies also bear marks of proud possession from women and men who
left behind few other traces.

Commonly published in the size and length of a political pamphlet, and designed by its author to seduce readers into retaining its moral precepts, the *Essay* may have been the most internalized work of social and political thought of the eighteenth century. It is impossible to know just how many copies circulated, but presses in Britain and America reprinted the poem over ninety times between 1750 and 1800. In the fifteen years following the Declaration of Independence, printers and booksellers in the new United States offered even more editions than their counterparts in the former mother country, who nevertheless continued to supply American readers. The irritating couplet appeared in the third section of the poem, where Pope conducted a tour of the mythical state of nature, and explained the origins, extent, and ends of government. But, then as now, readers did not need to know the poem in full to have encountered its well-wrought phrases in almanacs, anthologies, and schoolbooks. The couplet about form and administration was cited in letters and diaries, preserved in commonplace books, and jotted on blank pages of printed political treatises by those anxious about a world in which government was reducible to the men who governed.[3]

Perhaps it did not matter what Pope really meant, though editors often tried to explain Pope's intentions. Did the poet truly believe forms of government were irrelevant—that, for instance, an absolutist state could be preferable to a limited monarchy? In the late 1730s the Reverend William Warburton of England defended Pope from such charges. Careful readers saw that one target in this poetic exchange between two Tories was the current administration of Whig leader Robert Walpole, but Warburton claimed that Pope alluded to now-distant debates of the middle of the last century, debates about political form that overturned the constitution of England and brought about civil war. Pope did not endorse the divine right of kings or tyranny; in fact, his defender noted, he favored the mixed form of the contemporary British state and simply wanted to skewer anyone who would rather engage "in a speculative Contest for the superior Excellence of one of these Forms to the rest, than in promoting the good Administration of that settled Form to which he is a subject."[4] After Pope's death Warburton became the poet's literary executor and in 1751 produced a new, heavily annotated edition of the poem that included "the Poet's own apology" for the lines. "The author of these lines," Pope had apparently scribbled in the margins of a book by a writer who misread his couplet, "was far from meaning that no one form of Government is, in itself, better than another (as, that mixed or limited Monarchy, for example, is not preferable to absolute) but that no form of Government, however excellent or preferable in itself, can be sufficient to make a people happy, unless it be administered with integrity." "On the contrary," he added, meaning to suggest what he took to be Walpole's corruption of the British state, "the best sort of Government, when the *form* of it is preserved, and the *administration* corrupt, is most dangerous." Though Warburton's notes and Pope's "apology" frequently appeared with late eighteenth-century reprints of the poem in Britain and America, political writers had already severed the couplet from its poetic context prior to either Walpole's fall in 1742 or Pope's death three years later.

That so many who made it their business to think seriously about politics felt obliged to refute a couplet testifies to the popularity of poetry and the power of Pope's phrasing, but it also suggests the obstacle faced by political writers who wanted to create a new science of depersonalized politics. The most important early critique came from Scottish philosopher David Hume, who condemned Pope's maxim in the opening paragraph of his 1741 essay "That Politics May Be Reduced to a Science." Hume despaired that stability in government should depend entirely on the "humours and characters of particular men." To make administration more important than the form of government was to concede the impossibility of either a science of politics, as Hume remarked in this essay, or of "a government of Laws, not of Men," as he famously paraphrased the seventeenth-century English political writer James Harrington in another essay published the same year.[5] Near the end of the century, Prussian philosopher Immanuel Kant subjected the couplet to greater scrutiny. In a footnote to his 1795 essay on perpetual peace Kant remarked that if Pope meant for the second line to stand alone and to suggest that "the best-administered government is the best administered," then the poet was guilty of tautology. But if Pope meant to connect the first and second lines and to say that the best-administered government "is the best mode of government, that is, constitution of state," then he had committed an error: anecdotal or empirical examples of well-administered governments proved nothing about which political form was theoretically the best.[6] By the time Kant made his remarks, in the wake of the American and French Revolutions, many who commented on the couplet had come to similar conclusions. They insisted, though never as memorably as the poet they critiqued, that administration was a product of political form.[7] The best form of government was the one that assured the best administration, no matter who administered it.

Committed to the construction of governments of laws rather than governments of men, and directing aim at the maladministration of the

British Empire, American revolutionaries insisted on the primacy of political form and described Pope's couplet as heresy. In early 1776 John Adams dismissed Pope in the opening paragraphs of *Thoughts on Government*, his blueprint for building republican governments in the southern colonies. Adams, then a member of the Second Continental Congress, charged that Pope "flattered tyrants too much," for nothing was "more fallacious" than these lines or "more certain, from the history of nations and the nature of man, than that some forms of government are better fitted for being well administered than others." But what should one expect from poets? After all, "poets read history to collect flowers, not fruits—they attend to fanciful images, not the effects of social institutions." And effects had to be attended to, for the only way to judge the best form of government was by having a sense of the end of government. For Adams, that was the "happiness of society"; hence Adams argued, "the form of government, which communicates ease, comfort, security, or in one word happiness to the greatest number of persons, and in the greatest degree, is the best." Adams was inclined to side with a host of seventeenth- and early eighteenth-century writers in believing that a republic, which he defined as "an Empire of Laws, and not of Men," was the best form of government.[8] In a letter written in March 1776 to fellow congressman William Hooper of North Carolina, a precursor to *Thoughts*, Adams noted that this "puerile famous couplet of a very great poet" stated the matter backwards since "the Rectitude of Administration depends upon the Form; Some Species of Governments being always well administered, others never."[9] His point, one he shared with many framers of the early state constitutions, was that governments had to be built in such a way that they ensured good administrations. Adams made the point again in drafting the Massachusetts Constitution of 1780, the oldest written constitution still operating and the closest model for the Constitution of the United States of any of the state constitutions crafted during the American Revolution. In the final article of the Declaration of Rights that prefaced this constitution, the people of Massachusetts (borrowing a phrase from Harrington by way of Hume and Adams) declared that by ensuring that legislatures could not exercise executive or judicial powers, that executives could not legislate or judge, and that judges could not draft or execute laws, a constitution could create "a government of laws and not of men."[10] The real fools were citizens or subjects who put faith in specific individuals rather than in institutions.

But who could say which institutions were most sound? Who should be allowed to judge forms of government? These were questions raised by the radically popular nature of politics in the aftermath of independence, and ones the anonymous author of a series of "Maxims for Republics" tried to answer in the first issue of the *United States Magazine*, a literary and political monthly published in Philadelphia in January 1779. The author called himself "Sidney," but his opinions overlap with and bear the marks of the physician and sometime politician Benjamin Rush. Though he theoretically addressed a national audience, his obvious concern was the Pennsylvania Constitution of 1776, the most "democratic" of the early state constitutions. "Sidney" drew a distinction between the principles of a government and its form, arguing that only a select few were truly prepared to judge the latter. "We judge of the principles of a government by our *feelings*," he explained, and "of its form by our *reason*." This division of faculties of judgment in individuals was, for "Sidney," indicative of a larger social division, for while feelings were equally distributed, reason was not. This meant that the "bulk of mankind are judges of the *principles* of a government, whether it be free and happy," but that "men of education and reflection only, are judges of the *form* of a government, whether it be calculated to promote the happiness of society by restraining arbitrary power and licentiousness—by excluding corruption—and by giving the utmost possible *duration* to the enjoyment of liberty, or otherwise." "Forms *in* government," he concluded, "are essential to the very existence of freedom in a government." Hence "Mr. Pope's position, that that 'form of government is best which is best administered'" was a great mistake.

Whereas Adams described a government of laws in opposition to a government of men, "Sidney" put the matter differently; he held that "*Laws* and not *opinions* should govern in all free countries." This was the problem in another direction—not a fear of governors, but of the governed—for which the solution was again an appeal to a disembodied ideal of government and a culture of political expertise. By "opinions," this writer meant the faulty reasoning of most people on political matters or what was coming to be known as "public opinion." For while the "feelings" of the people at large were generally right, their "opinions" were often erroneous. (This was an early articulation of a position Benjamin Rush would argue more fully in 1787: that rights were understood by all, but government only by a few.) Feelings were clearly foundational; they could not be ignored, but they could be directed. In a later maxim, one that also sounds much like Rush, "Sidney" held that correct feelings about political principles could be taught (though felt, they were not simply innate), and it was of "the utmost importance, that the women should be well instructed in the principles of liberty in a republic."[11] But despite the suggested expansion of political instruction or affective enfranchisement to women, "Sidney" believed only a few men were truly capable of reflecting on political forms. This vision of a feeling multitude and a reflecting few, and the opposing vision of a multitude capable of reflecting on political form it was meant to redress, suggests the stakes of the new political thought and thinkers in the age of the Revolution.

During the framing of state constitutions in the second half of the 1770s few would have endorsed the idea that administration was more important than the form of a government, but as war gave way to peace, positions began to shift. Even the well-built constitution John Adams drafted for Massachusetts could not, it seemed to his spouse Abigail Adams in late 1782, ensure a good administration. Taxes in Massachusetts were so "exceeding heavy," she wrote to John Thaxter, her husband's private secretary in London, that certain counties had ignored them for two years. "Tis said by Pope," she noted, "that that government which is best administered, is best." "I mean not to discuss this point," she explained, but "a good government ill administered is injurious to every member of the community."[12] In July 1783, Arthur Lee of Virginia, preparing to step down as a delegate to the Continental Congress, resumed correspondence with his friend the Earl of Shelburne, who had recently assumed the role of British secretary of state. Lee told Shelburne that he looked forward to "the satisfaction of dwelling under that constitution which I have laboured to assist in rearing to liberty, virtue and public happiness." But as good as the Virginia Constitution was, the experience of living with it for six years taught him that "politicians have been too sanguine in their expectations from systems of government," for "corruption and intrigue seem inseparable from them all." Lee believed that such features were "promoted or restrained more by the genius of the people, than by forms of government, or the operation of laws." Indeed, he added, "it does not seem so unwise now, as it once did, in Mr. Pope, to say, 'For forms of government let fools contest; That which is best administer'd, is best.'"[13]

What was beginning to matter most to Lee was not the form of government but what he called the "genius of the people," by which he meant the prevailing character, spirit, inclination, or taste of the population. The concept was hardly novel, but it took on increased importance in the revolutionary period as politicians broadly debated the relation of the "genius of the people" to the form of government. How, exactly, did the form of government influence the "genius of the people"? Must political forms reflect the manners, customs, and taste of a population, such that what was best for one people might be worst for another, and such that it would be difficult to give an established population a new form of government? Inevitably the broad debates were played out over much smaller institutional arrangements. Was the "genius of the people" in favor of annual elections, or would it allow elections every two years?

The question of form and administration remained a compelling one in the post-revolutionary United States. Although John Adams had thought he answered the question definitively in early 1776, a decade later, as his son John Quincy Adams sat in the audience, two graduating students at the Harvard College commencement in July 1786 performed a forensic debate on the question "Whether the happiness of a People depends upon the Constitution, or upon the administration of it?"[14] The question was not an abstract exercise among the elite, but one of supreme importance in Massachusetts that summer. Impromptu conventions consisting of indebted farmers and others in the western counties of the state were beginning to call for radical revisions to government, including an elimination of the senate and the Court of Common Pleas, a widening of the franchise, and an alteration in the structure of taxation. By the end of August the government faced an armed uprising. Reports of "Shays' Rebellion" frightened Abigail and John Adams in London; it prompted John Adams to address his *Defense of the Constitutions of the United States of America*, a work nominally designed to refute the criticisms of European writers on the state constitutions, to one of the central constitutional desires of the Shaysite rebels: the reduction of the two legislative chambers in Massachusetts into a single chamber. These issues were not confined to Massachusetts. When the reports of Shays' rebellion circulated in other states, they helped galvanize calls for a stronger central government and for a convention in Philadelphia to revise the form of the federal government.

On the final day of that convention in 1787, as the proposed Constitution of the United States was about to emerge from behind the closed doors of the Pennsylvania State House, delegate Benjamin Franklin reflected on the question of form and administration. Expressing some of his reservations about the text the delegates were about to sign, Franklin alluded to Pope's maxim when he noted that "there is no *Form* of

Government but what may be a Blessing to the People if well administered." Perhaps gesturing to George Washington across the room, or
flattering the forty other delegates who remained, Franklin evinced confidence that the proposed form was "likely to be well administered for a
Course of Years."[15] Starting in December 1787, as the individual states
began to hold conventions to debate the Constitution, and continuing
well into 1788, newspapers printed and reprinted Franklin's speech. The
reprintings, numbering at least fifty, made Franklin's one of the most
widely disseminated and read of all the pieces in support of the Constitution. Carrying the authority of his name during a campaign in which few
other Federalists signed their pieces; pragmatically admitting to what he
saw as imperfections in the text; and taking readers for a brief moment
behind those closed doors at the Federal Convention, Franklin's speech
was one of the pieces most helpful in winning support for the adoption
of the text among moderate or undecided members of the public.

But Franklin's claim that any form of government could be a blessing
if well administered met a wall of protest from opponents to the Constitution. "Are we to accept a form of government which we do not entirely
approve, merely in the hopes that it will be well administered?" one Boston Anti-Federalist asked on the eve of the Massachusetts ratifying convention.[16] Another writer wondered if Franklin was too old to be trusted:
he was a great man, but was it "surprising, that when the body is debili-
tated, and the mind worn out, in philosophical, theological and political
researches, that the enfeebled sage should wish to rid himself of the trouble of thinking deeply on the fatal consequences of the *assumed powers*
and *bold designs* of the *system makers* in Philadelphia"?[17] In pointing
to the Constitution's makers this writer charged that those men had designed a government that fit their own rather than the people's needs.
They had violated a central tenet of the American Revolution: the framers had produced a government of men rather than of laws.

Despite detractors ever ready to point out the dangers of any appeal
to administration over form, numerous supporters of the Constitution
followed Franklin and emphasized the potentially meliorating effects of
good administration on any form. At the Pennsylvania ratifying convention in late October 1787, Thomas McKean, the chief justice of the state,
allegedly went so far as to say that despotism, "if wisely administered,
is the best form of government invented by the ingenuity of man." Anti-
Federalists ridiculed McKean in the press, and they burned him in effigy
in western Pennsylvania (James Wilson went up in smoke beside him).[18]

In late 1787 "The Federal Farmer," one of the most eloquent opponents
of the Constitution in New York, told readers that he was "much convinced of the truth of Pope's maxim"; he did not want to seem a fool and
contend too much about political forms, but he nevertheless launched
into a strong critique of the Constitution's form, and lesser writers copied his criticisms.[19] The Anti-Federalist "Poplicola" believed he put his
finger on the intent of the Federalist strategy: Federalists knew that the
proposed Constitution "will not endure a strict scrutiny; they wish . . .
that the people would adopt it in its present form, and depend upon a
wise administration."[20] But how could citizens of the United States accept such a hard and uncertain bargain?

Amid such charges, and sensing there was no way to win support for
an unpopular form of government by pointing to the possibility of a good
administration, Alexander Hamilton, writing in March 1788 as "Publius," called Pope's couplet a "political heresy." "The true test of a good
government," he noted, echoing John Adams in 1776, "is its aptitude and
tendency to produce a good administration."[21] To the Anti-Federalist
"Cornelius" the problem was that Federalists did not want to have a discussion about the best political form for the United States; they simply
wanted their way. As "Cornelius" observed, also echoing Adams, any
society that chose the uncertainty of administration over the certainty of
form necessarily chose a "government of *Men* and not of *Laws*."[22]

The rhetorical unanimity about the preference for a government of
laws over a government of men covered over larger divisions. The responses to Pope's couplet took it as axiomatic that certain forms were inherently better than others, and thus contending about forms was not a
fools' contest. But the nature of the best government was the real subject
of dispute. Could political writers really say what form of government
was best—that is, best for everyone? Shouldn't governments ultimately
fit the people who frame them? As we will see, the way individuals understood the relation of culture to politics formed the basis for answering such questions. That relation is the subject of this book.

PART I

The State as a Work of Art

CHAPTER ONE

Making a Government of Laws

The anonymous author (it may have been Thomas Paine) of a pamphlet published in Philadelphia in 1776 contended that "constitution" was a word often "bandied about" but rarely defined. For him, a constitution meant a "written Charter" that stipulated how a government would be erected. Absent such a document a nation might have a "government" but not a constitution. The English Constitution, so lauded in the previous decade of colonial unrest, was not really a "constitution" at all; England had a government of men and not of laws.[1] A decade and a half later, in the wake of the French Revolution and a dozen written constitutions, Edmund Burke and Thomas Paine debated this very issue, with Burke contending that a constitution was the accumulated body of practices and laws that each generation inherited from the last while Paine insisted that a constitution was a text a man could pull out of his pocket and that each generation had the right to change it.

Though in 1791 Paine was nominally defending the federal and state constitutions produced in the United States and the French Constitution, British readers knew he desired radical change at home. In December 1792 Paine was convicted in absentia for a seditious libel in the second part of *The Rights of Man*, and a few weeks later a London printmaker depicted "Thomas Pain" as a revolutionary tailor—Paine had in fact been a corsetmaker—who wished to sacrifice the British body politic to fantastical French fashions and to reshape Britannia's constitution in ways that were uncomfortable and unnatural (fig. 4). Cartoonist James

FIGURE 4. James Gilray, "Fashion before Ease," London, 1793. Prints and Photographs Division, Library of Congress (LC-USZC4-3146).

Gillray failed to sign his name or initials to the print and instead claimed that it had been designed by "G.W.," likely a reference to George Washington. Paine had dedicated the first part of *The Rights of Man* to Washington, praying that the president would live to see the rights of man become universally recognized and that he would "enjoy the happiness of seeing the New World regenerate the Old."[2] (The seditious book itself appeared in the print in the form of a tape measure, a signal that the constitutional tailoring would be done to suit that standard.) Republicanism as Paine spoke it was a language saturated with the idea of returning to men their natural rights as men and (as Paine wished) of regenerating corrupt nations. But to his opponents it was an unnatural imposition; no wonder, then, that the figure of Britannia in Gillray's print clung to a

sturdy oak tree while "Pain" appeared framed by a humble cottage below a sign advertising his services: this was a tug of war between nature
and culture. Even as Paine was trying to reform the meaning of the word
"constitution," his opponents understood him to be a threat to the embodied life of politics and to the shape of the nation.

Despite celebrations of the naturalness of republicanism in the United
States, artists and writers rarely equated the body of the nation with an
allegorical figure like Britannia or described political constitutions as
bodies at all. In the verbal and visual culture of late eighteenth-century
America depictions of government that reference the human body gave
way to depictions of a depersonalized political apparatus identified most
often in architectural constructions. In 1802 an American engraver produced a similar satire on the political designs of Thomas Paine, "Mad
Tom in a Rage" (fig. 5), but this one embodied the particular understanding of governments as architectural erections. Here Paine, assisted by
the Devil and a bottle of brandy, attempts to bring down the federal government, which the artist represents not as a body but as an architectural
monument. The image played on the idea of the state as a work of physical art, and on an ingrained idea that Paine (as John Adams claimed
after reading *Common Sense*) was better at tearing down governments
than in building them. Adams and his generation believed constitutions
were founded or framed like buildings; constitutions were not the products of time or of organic growth but works of human art.

In late eighteenth-century America the concept of the state shed
most of the bodily associations of the older ideas of the state as the name
for an artificial moral person. This transformation is best understood
as a contested and long-term transition away from ideas about the living constitution of the state and toward a notion of the constitution of
a state as a static work of legislative art, an imagined object that could
and should be appreciated in terms of its formal beauties. It is important not to overstate the transition, to fail to recognize the lasting power
of images of the body politic, or to imagine that the images did not com-
pete with each other; nevertheless, the very different understanding of
what a constitution *is* and *was* stems from this larger change. This transition was contemporaneous with the rise of modern notions of an "impersonal" state, a state autonomous and equally independent from its rulers
and its citizens. Indeed, the aestheticization of the state—the creation
of a state that should be viewed from a proper distance—was simultaneously a cause and an effect of this modern notion of statehood.[3]

FIGURE 5. "Mad Tom in a Rage," ca. 1802. Reproduced by permission of The Huntington Library, San Marino, California.

The State as a Person

In a sermon delivered in April 1781 Joseph Huntington described for his parishioners in Coventry, Connecticut, the similarities between the general government of the tribes of ancient Israel and the government of the American states. "We have our Sanhedrim, *i.e.* our General Congress," Huntington noted, "answering for substance to the seventy elders of Israel that were over all the tribes as their supreme council; we have our distinct states as they had their distinct tribes, and it is really worthy of notice that our number should be exactly the same, even in the first establishment of our independency." His listeners, familiar with the traditional descriptions of New England as a New Canaan, were probably not used to hearing the other states described in biblical terms. The analogy was not readily apparent. Huntington had to remind his audience that, counting the subdivision of the tribe of Joseph, *thirteen* tribes descended from Jacob's twelve sons, not the customary twelve. Against a tradition of political biblical interpretation that claimed that God had not mandated one particular form of civil government over another, Huntington maintained that God had "given us the sum and substance of the most perfect form of civil government in his word" as witnessed by "that ancient plan of civil policy, delineated for the chosen tribes of Israel." Like the United States of America, the "Thirteen United States or tribes of Israel" had "no king, no despot, no emperor, no tyrant, no perpetual dictator" but had instead "by divine appointment a general congress, with a president at their head; Moses was the first, Joshua succeeded him, so on till the days of Samuel, when the constitution was subverted." Huntington probably did not need to remind his audience (for it was a moment constantly alluded to in the political sermons of the day) that the wise judge Samuel had unsuccessfully protested against the creation of a monarchy for Israel, but the voices of the people had overwhelmed him, precipitating the appointment and anointment of King Saul and the end of the Mosaic theocracy.[4] Given all the similarities, auditors paying attention may have asked, wouldn't a monarchy inevitably sprout up in America?

Huntington's typology stopped short of predicting the monarchical subversion of the Confederation, but the reference to Samuel was perhaps comically irresistible to the minister, whose older brother, Samuel Huntington, was an associate justice of the Superior Court of Connecticut and the current president of the Continental Congress. In any

event, comparisons between the "president" of ancient Israel and the
head of the Continental Congress stretched the analogy and exposed
the real differences between the United States of Israel and of America.
The Confederation was obviously not a theocracy. Peyton Randolph, the
first president of the First Continental Congress in 1774 and hence the
American equivalent of Moses, had been elected by the other delegates
in Congress, not appointed by God. And Huntington did not mention
that Article IX of the Articles of Confederation, which had been drafted
in 1777 but ratified only a month before the minister spoke in 1781, stipulated that the person selected to preside over Congress could serve only
one year out of every three. Although the delegates had returned Huntington's brother to the office of president for two years in a row, this was
no indication that the constitution of the Confederation had been subverted; it attested instead both to the political inexpediency of adopting
such term limits while the Articles remained unratified and to the difficulty of finding someone willing to take the job.

The analogy between the United States and ancient Israel bestowed
legitimacy on a confederated national government, but the bulk of Huntington's sermon was devoted to expounding an analogy between the
civil nation-state and the human body. When he came to publish the sermon later that year in Hartford he entitled it *A Discourse . . . on the
Health and Happiness, or Misery and Ruin of the Body Politic, In Si-
militude to that of the Natural Body.* In a sense, the Bible and the body
were intimately connected, for Huntington argued that "we of this nation have now for substance, that very same plan of government, which
infinite wisdom and goodness pointed out to the chosen the much beloved tribes of Israel, in the constitution of which we see a political man
perfect, [showing] how the community ought to be organized and regulated, as clearly as we see in the formation of the human body."[5]

Huntington used the word "constitution" in its older, bodily sense
rather than in the sense of the textual organization and limitation of
power that the term had acquired during the previous half-decade, the
years when eleven states framed constitutions. (Rhode Island and Huntington's own state of Connecticut had been the only states not to draft
new constitutions; they simply enacted their colonial charters as fundamental law.) Huntington's "political man" consisted of separate and distinct members, each representing part of the national commonwealth.
The head (the "seat of thought, council, and understanding") was a perfect analogy for the legislative powers, the arms and hands stood for ex-

ecutive powers, religious ministers like Huntington resembled the heart or "inward parts" as well as the "prevailing spirit," and the human frame in general and the legs in particular represented "the body of the people of which a nation is composed."

Delivered during the American Revolution, Huntington's sermon was one of the last sustained accounts of the civil state as a "political man." For Huntington, the Revolution itself could be read in bodily terms, since "all tories and traitors . . . all mal-contents that would stir up rebellion, anarchy, and confusion in the bowels" of the body politic were not really part of the body so much as "the very excrement of the body politic," who might also be compared to "a gangrene, or to a baneful putrefaction which calls for the instruments of incision, that it may be discharged; or to any nauseous infection which must be purged out, or distemper that must be subdued, before perfect health can return."[6]

Head, heart, arms, legs, and excrement did not constitute a fully anatomized body, at least by the standards of late eighteenth-century medicine; nor, by the standards of late eighteenth-century political thought, did they describe a fully formed state. Huntington's state supported religion, and so it was easy to find an imaginative place for religious ministers like himself in the body politic. But in separating powers, Huntington failed to locate the anatomical equivalent of the judiciary—a bizarre oversight for the brother of a sometime judge. But that oversight may have had more to do with contemporary conceptions about the structure of the Confederation and the powers of the Continental Congress itself, a body whose principal function (was it legislative, executive, or diplomatic?) confused even John Adams and Thomas Jefferson.[7] And, aside from the claim that all should "act in perfect union and concert, guided and actuated by the same soul, the same will," he had ignored completely the vexing subject of sovereignty.[8] His listeners must have seen in this performance a kind of throwback to older ways of thinking at odds with contemporary politics.

And it was. He described a fantasy of corporate solidarity, a body that had more to fear from internal disorder than from the external threats from other political bodies. Huntington's thesis is easily summarized: "in the political man, the commonwealth, the head and every member must keep their respective places or it becomes a hideous and horrid monster." Throughout his sermon Huntington contrasted the unanimity of a healthy body with a monstrous image of bodily disorder. "What a wretched thing would the human body be," he asked, "if the head and vitals, limbs, organs and members were alternately to changes their places, and assume the offices of each other?" "What man is there that wishes to have his head and feet change places with each other?" he asked, "Or to have his breast and his back transposed? Who wishes to see with his ears, or hear with his eyes, or to taste with his nose, and smell with his mouth?" If we "set the arms to hear and see and direct, and the head to strike the blow for the execution, . . . what then would ever come to pass?" "[P]lace the heart where the head is," he said, describing ministers and magistrates, "and the head where the heart is, and the man would not survive the exchange."[9] For officers to change places was bad, but by far the greatest danger involved usurpations by the people: "it is altogether as monstrous to see the legs where the arms should be, as the arms where the legs should be; it is as great an evil to have the feet growing on the head as the head growing on one of the feet." "For people in general to turn guides and counsellors, and refuse to be guided and counselled by rulers, to say what ought, and what ought not to be done, in the highest and most important concerns of the state, of which, indeed, most people are utterly ignorant, is just as if a madman should endeavor to pluck his eyes from his head, and place them in sockets made in his feet for that purpose, or with his ears grafted on either leg, and the senses which are seated in the head removed to the lower parts of his body."[10]

Huntington's metaphor of the body politic belonged to a tradition of political metaphorics stretching back to the classical period. The political philosophies of Plato and Aristotle developed limited organic conceptions of the state, theories resting on the primary division between head and members but lacking any real anatomical specificity.[11] But the kind of thinking that Huntington articulated in the 1780s was more medieval than classical. Truly intricate analogies between government and the body first began to appear in the twelfth century, particularly in John of Salisbury's *Policraticus* (1159). Here a prince is said to rule a city in the same way a head rules a body, but the image is fuller: a senate is like a heart; judges and sheriffs are likened to the senses; financial officers resemble stomach and intestines; hands are fitting analogues for both tax collectors and soldiers; the feet are the peasantry; and clerics are like the soul, not really a part of the body and hence separate in some sense from the city. As it developed after *Policraticus* the organic metaphor allowed for differentiation with order, reconciling disparate interests by stressing not only hierarchy but also mutual dependence.[12] The notion that republican governments are themselves living beings, with their own life expectancies and cycles, can be found in the writings of Machiavelli in the sixteenth century.[13] Such conceptions helped to distinguish the state from the person of its ruler, but the separation was never really complete, and it is only with the political writing surrounding the English Civil War of the seventeenth century that the metaphor begins to assume the kind of emphases that Huntington gave it in 1781.[14]

Hobbes's *Leviathan,* published in London in 1651, provided the most memorable image of the state as a body politic in the early modern period. Like other seventeenth-century political writers, Hobbes described government as an artificial construction. But unlike others, Hobbes consistently elevated art over nature, going so far as to define "Nature" itself as "the Art whereby God hath made and governes the World." The human art of government and absolute subjection to the artificial person of the sovereign were infinitely more appealing to Hobbes than a life lived in the "naturall condition of mankind," the condition that others called the "state of nature." "[B]y Art is created that great LEVIATHAN called a COMMON-WEALTH, or STATE," Hobbes wrote, "which is but an Artificiall Man; though of greater stature and strength than the Natural." In Hobbes's revision of the metaphor of the political body, sovereignty was the soul, magistrates were joints, rewards and punishments were nerves, counselors of state were memory, equity and laws were artificial reason and will, and money was blood.[15] This was an image of a state apparatus produced by its subjects but essentially detached from them, an image both strikingly similar and sufficiently different from the one elaborated by Joseph Huntington in Connecticut 130 years later.

But how could such a body be pictured? At least since John of Salisbury's analogy between the parts of a political constitution and the internal parts of a physiological or anatomical constitution, it had been difficult to give a detailed visual representation of the body politic. The body politic was really a verbal analogy. It was perhaps hopeless to try to capture graphically Hobbes's description of a body politic, with its emphasis on internal anatomy (joints, nerves, blood) and abstract entities (soul, memory, reason, will). The artist who engraved the title page of *Leviathan,* an image of a sovereign whose arms and torso are covered with individual subjects who seem to gaze at him in adoration, visualized one aspect of the metaphor of the body politic (fig. 6, taken from James Madison's copy). The illustration represents not Hobbes's description but the more traditional idea that the sovereign was the head and the people the body. The illustrator depicts Hobbes's idea of the sovereign as the "Artificiall Man" constituted by and representing (or acting for) his subjects,

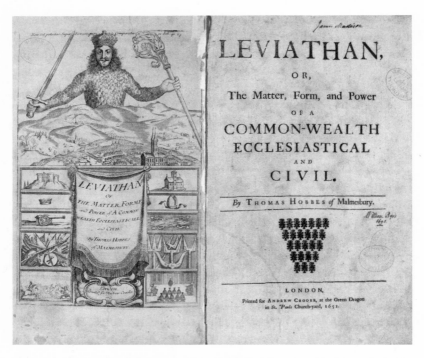

FIGURE 6. Short on cash, Congressman James Madison purchased Hobbes's *Leviathan* from a Philadelphia book seller in 1782 and sent the charge to his father, complaining that unless the Virginia Assembly made liberal provisions and compensation for its delegates in Congress, he would be "under the necessity of selling a negro." He sold a twenty-four-year-old man named Billey the next year. Frontispiece from Madison's copy of *Leviathan*. Courtesy of The Historical Society of Pennsylvania (Am 1651 Hob AqM18, file 1151).

but the illustration implies things the text would seem to dispel, like the suggestion that the sovereign is not so much constituted by his subjects but clothed with them. The sovereign appears almost to wear his subjects as a protective suit of armor (the reverse of the idea that the sovereign lives to protect the lives of his subjects), but other commentators have argued that the sovereign has devoured his subjects, swallowing them up in the act of state incorporation.[16] The "Artificiall Man" described in Hobbes's text is perhaps most intriguing in the way it seems both to include and exclude its subjects, to alienate them from the body politic at the same time it claims them as constituent parts.

Although they disagreed vehemently with the nature of government that Hobbes proposed, Puritan writers in New England shared with the contractual absolutist a vision of government and society as bodily in character.[17] The idea that institutions were best described as "societies" and that societies were best described as "bodies" had been disseminated by writers in old and New England in the half-century leading up to the English Civil War. This latter image above all combined the competing demands of the social reality of diversity (or inequality) and the social necessity of corporate unity, especially for those colonial Puritans who feared being labeled as "separatists." Near the end of the sixteenth century, the English Puritan divine William Perkins explained in a treatise on callings that in "mans body there be sundry parts and members, and every one hath his severall use and office, which it performeth not for it selfe, but for the good of the whole bodie; as the office of the eye is to see, of the eare to heare, and of the foote to goe." All "societies of men," Perkins contended, "are bodies, a family is a bodie, and so is every particular Church a bodie, and the common-wealth also."[18]

Early Puritan colonists like John Winthrop brought the conceptions of Perkins with them to New England. Winthrop's lay sermon delivered aboard the *Arabella* in 1630, "A Model of Christian Charity," constructed the community of Massachusetts colonists as "members of the same body" who "must be knitt together as one man" by love. Winthrop's ideas about bodies were fairly standard: "There is noe body but consistes of partes and that which knitts these partes together gives the body its perfeccion, because it makes each parte soe contiguous to others as thereby they doe mutually participate with eache other, both in strength and infirmity in pleasure and pain, to instance in the most perfect of all bodies, Christ and his church make one body." The anatomical metaphor, as limited as it was in Winthrop's presentation, allowed for a conception of society as a regulated system. In the only extended use of the body metaphor in his sermon, Winthrop argued that rich persons were like mouths and that they should remember that in "the natural body the mouth is at all the paines to receive, and mince the foode which serves for the nourishment of all the other partes of the body, yet it hath noe cause to complaine; for first, the other partes send backe by secret passages a due proporcion of the same nourishment in a better forme for the strengthening and comforteing the mouthe. [And secondly] the labour of the mouthe is accompanied with such pleasure and content as farre exceeds the paines it takes."[19] The mouth's labor, in other words, was compensated by the duties "the other partes" returned to it and by the sheer pleasure in doing its job.

Perkins and Winthrop (and much later, Huntington) derived their im-

agery from the statements of Paul in 1 Corinthians 12 that compared
Christ to a body made up of many members. These members are necessarily differentiated, and must be so, for the image of a single-organed
body was monstrous: "If the whole body were an eye," Paul asked,
"where were the hearing?" (1 Cor. 12:17). Any attempts to claim alien-
ation from the body were as ridiculous as "if the foot shall say, Because
I am not the hand, I am not of the body" (1 Cor. 12:15). Organs speak in
Paul's analogy because they are each imagined as individuals comprising
a social, political, and religious body in which the members must take
care of each other so that there is "no schism in the body" but in which
each must keep its proper place. Revisions of this question—and its to-
pos of speaking "parts"—could be found in New England sermons as
late as Huntington's in 1781.

Paul, Perkins, and Winthrop celebrated what they called "diversity"
over homogeneity, inequality over equality, and this commitment to diversity is the main impulse behind the image of the body politic as it developed in New England. The image offered a way of ordering social
classes that granted a nominal meaning and significance to even the lowest in society. "Naturalists tells us," William Hubbard argued in a 1676
Massachusetts election sermon, "that beauty in the body arises from an
exact symmetry or proportion of contrary humours, equally mixed one
with another: so doth an orderly and artificial distribution of diverse
materials, make a comely Building, while homogeneous bodyes (as the
depths of waters in the Sea, and heaps of sand on the Shore) run into confused heaps, as bodyes uncapable to maintain an order in themselves."
The conclusion for Hubbard was obvious: "whoever is for a parity in any
Society, will . . . reduce things into an heap of confusion."[20] Such sentiments retained power almost one hundred years after Hubbard uttered
them. As Abraham Williams put it in an election sermon in Boston in
1762, "The natural Body consists of various Members, connected and
subservient one to the other, each serving some valuable purpose and
the most perfect and happy State of the Body results from all the Members regularly performing their natural Offices; so collective Bodies, or
Societies, are composed of various Individuals connected together, related and subservient to each other. Every Person has his proper Sphere,
and is of Importance to the whole; and the public Peace and Welfare is
best secured and promoted, by every Member attending to the proper
Business of his particular Station."[21] The same appreciation of the non-
leveling effects of diversity animated Huntington's "political man."

Like Hobbes's "Artificiall Man," the Puritan state was regarded as a work of human art. Election-day preachers often expounded the idea that government was a collaboration between God and human beings that left political form to humans. John Higginson explained in his 1663 Massachusetts election sermon that "Civill Government in *Genere* is an Ordinance of God, (*the higher powers are Ordained by God, Rom. 13.1.*) but in *Specie*, it is an Ordinace of man, though every form of Civill Government is to be subservient unto Religion, as its ultimate end; yet . . . this or that particular forme of Civil Government is an Ordinance of man, it is . . . a humane Creature." Higginson cited 1 Peter 2:13—"Submit your selves to every ordinance of man for the Lords sake, whether to the King as Supream, or unto Governours sent by him"—a passage that would be cited over and over for the next hundred years.[22] There was no real question about the best kind of state for Higginson: it was a state that was above all an instrument to combat the toleration of religious difference. While a degree of toleration in Massachusetts developed with the denominational culture of the eighteenth century, the idea that the form of the state was left up to men was widely accepted throughout that century.

The older ideas of Puritan covenant and body politic could find reanimation when blended with social compact thought, and the view that governmental form was human-made rather than God-given left great latitude to the people to form and reform government. In the eighteenth century this went hand in hand with Lockean contractualism, as when John Barnard noted in 1734 that "as every People are left to their Liberty to constitute what Form of Civil Government, all things considered, may appear best to them, . . . so doubtless it remains with any civil Society to alter, and change, the Form of their Government, when they see just Reason for it, and all Parties are consenting to it."[23] What men had made they could remake. But such statements could sometimes lead to a renewed insistence on God's role. "Government is a natural and a divine Ordinance," Abraham Williams noted in his 1762 Massachusetts election sermon. Williams had to remind his listeners and readers that "Government is a divine Constitution, founded in the Nature and Relation of Things,—Agreeable to the will of God." "And when Men enter into civil Societies, and agree upon rational Forms of Government, they act right, conformable to the Will of God, by the Concurrence of whose Providence, Rulers are appointed. Thus the origin of Government is from God, tho' it be an *human Ordinance* or *Creature*, (1 Pet. 2, 13) and immediately proceeds from Men; as all other Blessings and Things advantageous to Mankind, proceed from him, tho' visibly effected by second Causes."[24]

Williams's insistence on God as the first cause of government was a response to the current of political thought that often removed God from human politics. John Wise in 1717 claimed that "it is certain Civil Government in General, is a very Admirable Result of Providence, and an Incomparable Benefit to Man-kind, yet must needs be acknowledged to be the Effect of Humane Free Compacts and not of Divine Institution; it is the Produce of Mans Reason, of Humane and Rationale Combinations, and not from any direct Orders of Infinite Wisdom, in any positive Law wherein is drawn up this or that Scheme of Government." For Wise, government was not a divine ordinance, since "nothing can be Gods Ordinance, but what he has particularly Declared to be such; there is no particular Form of Civil Government described in Gods Word, neither does nature prompt it."[25] Against such statements Charles Chauncy in a 1747 election sermon solicited by the Massachusetts House of Representatives reiterated that government was not a "mere human constitution" but was "essentially founded on the will of God." For Chauncy, this meant that government was founded in reason, for "the voice of reason is the voice of God." It was, however, important to distinguish between government "in its *general notion*" and the "*particular form* and *manner of administration*." While government itself was a divinely mandated moral necessity, Chauncy maintained that "it cannot be affirmed, that this or that particular form of government is made necessary by the will of God and the reason of things." This explained why governments had been different in different nations and even why the same nation changed forms over time. The logical conclusion of Chauncy's relativism was that the mode of government that was best for one people was not necessarily best for another: it was "left to the wisdom of particular communities to determine what form of government shall take place among them; and so long as the general ends of society are provided for and secured, the determination may be various, according to the various circumstances, policies, tempers and interests."[26]

This left open an important political question, perhaps the most important of the age: "If there be no particular Form of Civil Government appointed by God, and every Nation and People are left to their own Prudence to establish what Form they please," John Barnard asked in a 1734 election sermon, then "which Form or Scheme is best?" Barnard's answer was unusually equivocal. If the question was to be "considered absolutely" it was an "improper Question," since it suggested that government could be imagined without reference to subjects: but "there can be no Government without a People, or Subject of it," so "the Circumstances of a particular People must come into consideration, to determine what is best." If the question means "what Form is relatively best?" then the answer was similarly "that which will suit the People best: which requires a thorow Knowledge of them, their Scituation, Produce, Genius, and the like, to resolve." If the question was asked particularly about the people of Massachusetts in 1734, and provided they were "absolutely free to choose for themselves," then "it must be left to the wisest Heads, the greatest Politicians among us, and those best acquainted with the People, and Country, to advise upon it." But, Barnard admitted, "we are not at liberty now to choose," and so the best form of government for Massachusetts was the one they were currently under: "I mean the *British Constitution*."[27] After the Revolution, the question of what form of government was best became more pressing, and ministers like Samuel Huntington felt no compunction in claiming, contrary to the Puritan tradition, that God had in fact sketched "the most perfect form of civil government in his word," and that the United States assembled in Congress currently embodied it.

The state may have been left to men to form, but it should be, as Winthrop argued in 1630 and as John Higginson reiterated in a 1663 election sermon, considered as "one Man."[28] This notion of the state as a single being incorporated contemporary contractualism. During a religious controversy in 1717, John Wise argued that the covenant between rulers and subjects included "that Submission and Union of Wills, by which a State may be conceived to be but one Person." For Wise, "the most proper Definition of a Civil State, is this. *viz.* A Civil State is a Compound Moral Person, whose Will (United by those Covenants before passed) is the Will of all; to the end that it may Use, and Apply the strength and riches of Private Persons toward maintaining the Common Peace, Security, and Well-being of all." It was, Wise declared, as "tho' the whole State was now become but one Man; in which the aforesaid Covenants may be supposed under Gods Providence, to be the Divine *Fiat*, Pronounced by God, let us make Man. And by way of resemblance the aforesaid Being may be thus Anatomized":

1. The Sovereign Power is the Soul infused, giving Life and Motion to the whole Body.
2. Subordinate Officers are the Joynts by which the Body moves.
3. Wealth and Riches are the Strength.

4. Equity and Laws are the Reason.
5. Councellors the Memory.
6. *Salus Populi*, or the Happiness of the People, is the End of its Being; or main Business to be attended and done.
7. Concord amongst the Members, and all Estates, is the Health.
8. Sedition is Sickness, and Civil War Death.[29]

Wise's anatomization (which was reprinted twice in the 1770s) was little more than an enumeration of the "Artificiall Man" described in the introduction to *Leviathan*, by way of the English translation in 1703 of Samuel Pufendorf's *Law of Nature and Nations*. Pufendorf had maintained that "the most proper Definition of a civil State seems to be this, 'It is a compound moral Person, whose Will, . . . is deemed the Will of All,'" and had cited the opening paragraphs of *Leviathan* with admiration.[30] Pufendorf and Hobbes shared a vision of the state as one will, incorporating ruler and ruled but independent of them, and Wise had followed this thinking almost word for word.[31] Indeed, the only significant variation between Hobbes's 1651 description and Wise's 1717 copy was that Hobbes and Pufendorf had glossed "*Salus Populi*" as "the *peoples safety*" while Wise had rendered it "the Happiness of the People." This change, seemingly minor, was important, for it aligned Wise with a tradition of Puritan political thought that focused on the happiness of subjects.[32] The state was a body with one will, but what kind of body was it in which the feet could reform the head in order to promote their own happiness? The image of government as a body politic simply made little sense within the contractual logic of the eighteenth century.

The figure of the body politic declined in both use and conceptual value over the course of the seventeenth and eighteenth centuries. Never especially prevalent in the middle or southern colonies, it had come to seem relatively meaningless even in New England by the time Huntington gave his *Discourse*—indeed, he was actively trying to vivify the idea. The published election sermons in Massachusetts and Connecticut provide one way to chart the declining significance of the phrase, but it seems to have lingered longer in Massachusetts than elsewhere. Ministers in the eighteenth century certainly used the metaphor less often and developed it less imaginatively. While colonial patents, royal charters, and impromptu political combinations found the idea of a body politic useful, the phrase seemed to disappear in the technical prose of the revolutionary era. Those "loyal subjects of our dread soverigne Lord, King

James," who in 1620 subscribed their names to a document off the coast of what became Plymouth, agreed to "covenant and combine ourselves together in a civill Body Politick." This covenant would then give them the authority "to enacte, constitute, and frame such just and equall laws, ordinances, acts, constitutions, and offices . . . as shall be thought most meete and convenient for the generall good of the Colonie."[33] In narrating this event in 1787, the author of "A Short Description of New-England" published in a Boston almanac noted that the 1620 Plymouth settlement had "formed themselves into 'a civil body politic' for the purposes of government," placing quotation marks around the phrase either to mark its historical accuracy or to suggest a continuity with the Massachusetts Constitution of 1780, the only state constitution written in the revolutionary era that found the phrase useful enough to include.[34]

"The end of the institution, maintenance and administration of Government," the preamble of the Massachusetts Constitution of 1780 asserted, "is to secure the existence of the body-politic; and to furnish the individuals who compose it, with the power of enjoying, in safety and tranquillity, their natural rights and the blessings of life." But what did the framers and ratifiers of the Massachusetts Constitution mean by "body politic"? For those unfamiliar with the concept, the phrase was glossed this way: "The body politic is formed by a voluntary association of individuals: It is a social compact, by which the whole people covenants with each citizen, and each citizen with the whole people, that all shall be governed by certain laws for the common good."[35] This, then, was not the image of government rendered as a body, with a legislative head and executive arms, but a simple revision of the social contract with no anatomical differentiation. And while the Massachusetts Constitution provided an important model for the Constitution of the United States, the phrase significantly did not appear there.

From Body Politic to Nation-State

The word "congress" in the eighteenth century signified a social or political gathering, but it could also describe the sexual union of bodies considered either unnaturally similar or exceptionally different: the "incestuous congress" of persons related by blood, for instance, or the "congress of black and white persons."[36] The designer of a title-page emblem for the *Journal of the Proceedings of the Congress*, printed in Philadel-

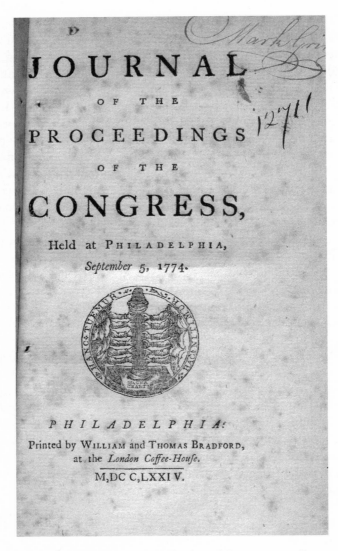

FIGURE 7. Title page of the *Journal* of the Continental Congress, 1774. Courtesy of The Library Company of Philadelphia.

phia in 1774, may have played on this double meaning, fashioning a symbol for the First Continental Congress that embodied the tensions at play in the extraordinary political mixing in Philadelphia of male delegates from twelve different colonial polities, each of which claimed descent from a common parent state (fig. 7). To read the image at all is to risk interpretation beyond the boundaries of meaning contemporary historical agents may have assigned to it. Like so many of the statements within the political documents of the period, the intentions and motivations behind the title-page image remain largely unavailable to us.

Only a few circumstances surrounding the production of the emblem are known. The text of the *Journal* itself tells us that on October 22, 1774, Congress ordered a group of three Pennsylvanians (two delegates and the secretary who had kept the official manuscript account of the proceedings) to oversee the printing.[37] The Philadelphia printers Thomas and William Bradford produced the 132-page document mostly or perhaps entirely at their firm's own expense. They completed the job in late November, nearly a month after most of the delegates had returned to their home colonies, and then shipped hundreds of copies to a few of those delegates who had—for political and commercial reasons—agreed to help the Bradfords distribute the *Journal* to booksellers in markets beyond the printers' immediate reach.[38]

It is not clear who designed the emblem, whether it was the autonomous idea of someone within the Bradfords' printshop or a collaboration between an engraver and a member from the congressional delegation. In any event, we know nothing of what contemporaries thought of the image. Delegates to Congress did not remark upon it in their surviving private letters, nor did they mention it in any of the formal documents of the Second Continental Congress that met in Philadelphia in 1775, documents printed by John Dunlap rather than the Bradfords. Congress did not officially adopt the emblem, and it did not reappear in subsequent publications or in reprints and translations of the 1774 *Journal* published elsewhere, which would seem to testify either to a general antipathy or a muted ambivalence about the design. The emblem did not emerge as a candidate when Congress organized a committee in August 1776 to propose an official great seal for the United States, which is one indication that it failed to achieve popularity among members of Congress. If this early image of continental political unity was unremarkable (or unworthy of remark) to contemporaries, it has fared little better among historians, earning no attention in the historiography of the Continental Congress and, aside from a few derogatory remarks, little in the way of critical commentary by scholars of political iconography.[39]

Absent contemporary discussion, we can only speculate about the meaning of the title-page emblem, but it is worth speculating because the image represents one step in a transformation of ideas about government itself, a transformation from depictions of government that reference the human body to depictions of a depersonalized political apparatus embodied most often in architectural constructions. The device shows twelve arms clasping a single pillar. The arms symbolize the twelve colonies that sent delegates to Philadelphia, but they emerge like twelve divine hands from the heavens—a striking and perhaps atavistic image for a monotheistic and secularizing culture that found such imagined providential intrusions less and less meaningful.[40] The pillar sits above an unfurled piece of parchment or paper imprinted with the words "MAGNA CHARTA," a suggestion perhaps that the pillar should be interpreted as an extension (like the British Constitution itself) of the thirteenth-century textual enumeration of the rights of English barons that had come to signify in the late colonial British popular imagination, maybe wrongly, the fundamental basis for British liberties.

Such an interpretation would not have been uncontroversial. In a 1764 pamphlet directed against Parliament's attempts to raise revenue from the colonies by taxing sugar, the Boston lawyer James Otis complained that political writers too often described rights as "rising out" of or "spring[ing]" from textual foundations like the Magna Charta rather than stemming from human nature or from God; nevertheless, the action of springing or rising seems to describe fairly well one possible contemporary understanding of the relation between the document and the pillar in the emblem.[41] The association between the pillar and some concept of liberty or rights is further advanced by the pilleus, the classical Roman "liberty cap" that symbolized the emancipated status of a former slave, which sits atop the pillar. But the image leaves ambiguous the precise relationship between the pillar and the Magna Charta, a document never itself mentioned in the text of the *Journal* or appealed to in any of the formal statements of rights expressed in the letters this Congress sent to the king, to the people of Great Britain, and to the inhabitants of the British colonies.

If liberty derived from the Magna Charta, how could it be—as so many British radical opposition writers and colonial Whigs maintained—an "unalienable" right"?[42] The suggestion that liberty was granted by government and that it rested in documents was perhaps one of the problems with the image, one clue to its transience. Rights may be textual in nature, a young Alexander Hamilton observed in February 1775, but they were "written, as with a sun beam, in the whole *volume* of human nature, by the hand of the divinity itself," and were "not to be rummaged for, among old parchments, or musty records."[43] In any event, the written text of the Magna Charta in this image appears as little more than a paper-thin foundation for the pillar, which in turn protects the document like an oversized paperweight, implying simultaneously that the pillar would fall without the paper's foundation and that the paper would blow away without the pillar's mass. This theme of strength coupled with fragility, this confusion between the source of authority and its protection, is repeated in the relationship between the arms and the pillar. The Latin motto encircling the device and broken by the tip of the pilleus ("HANC TUEMUR . . . HAC NITIMUR," or roughly "we protect this and we lean on this") places the pillar in a symbiotic relationship with the arms and the Magna Charta: they support it even as it supports them. In one of the documents printed in the *Journal*, a letter to the British general Thomas Gage who served as the military governor of Massachusetts, Congress claimed that the individual colonies had appointed the delegates to be "the guardians of their rights and liberties." The emblem literalizes this guardianship, equating the preservation of British rights and liberties with upholding a fragile pillar in its erect state.[44]

The 1774 emblem belonged to a political culture that sometimes explicitly identified political liberty more with the erection and consecration of vertical and even phallic images (the liberty pole, the liberty tree) than with the well-known allegorical female figure of Liberty, and so the resemblance between the pillar and pilleus motif and representations of erect male sexual organs by contemporary European medical illustrators and pornographers is probably not coincidental.[45] "The Liberty Cap is the head of the Penis, an emblem of Liberty," the Connecticut poet and U.S. diplomat Joel Barlow bluntly explained in an unpublished manuscript on the mythical and historical "Genealogy of the Tree of Liberty" written in Paris in the 1790s. The "Phallus became the emblem of *Libertas*" in Rome and was carried "in a posture of strong erection" in Egypt, but its meaning had been obscured and its dimensions altered as the symbol circulated to England and to America. Barlow observed that in the modern era "the *Phallus* has lost its *testicles*, and has been for many centuries reduced to a simple pole, in some countries carried on a sort of bier pointing up in the air, in others inserted in the ground."[46] Barlow's learned essay was a late and admittedly comic manifestation of the connection between liberty and phallus.

Within the context of a popular generative association between liberty and male sexual organs, strong government was often figured as an instrument of especially localized confinement. The character of a hood-

winked Anti-Federalist husband in a widely reprinted 1788 allegorical
essay satirizing this particular vein of liberty rhetoric, for instance, described the proposed Constitution as a tight pair of new breeches that
"*conspired* against the liberty of my thighs, knees, and loins," a pair of
pants so narrowly tailored by Federalists that to wear them would be
to "enslave my thighs" and to "lay restraints upon my *free-born* members, which are utterly incompatible with our republican form of government."[47] This was satire aimed at ridiculing the political position of
Anti-Federalists, but the exaggerated conception of liberty in such accounts shared with more serious descriptions an understanding of liberty
as essentially a private, personal, unseen, and secret thing rather than a
public or communal one, the terms "secrets" and "privates" themselves
being common euphemisms for the male genitals whose "government"
was described in the astrological charts included in nearly every almanac published in the period.[48]

The purpose of government, in the logic of this rhetoric, was to protect privacy without suffocating liberty. Alluding specifically to the post-
lapsarian coverings for Adam and Eve's nakedness, Thomas Paine in
Common Sense (1776) compared government to dress—"the badge of
lost innocence." Or, as Columbia explained in a poem written by the
Federalist Francis Hopkinson, a thousand copies of which were printed
on a parade float during the Fourth of July Federal Procession in Philadelphia in 1788 and distributed by a man dressed as Mercury, "the god
of intelligence":

> My Sons for *Freedom* fought, nor fought in vain;
> But found a naked goddess was their gain;
> *Good government* alone, can show the Maid,
> In robes of SOCIAL HAPPINESS array'd.[49]

In Hopkinson's view, freedom was not opposed to government; government was what allowed freedom to be seen in society. For Paine, government was (like dress) a necessary article that provided the twin advantages of protection for private property and the restraint of vice in a
world where men could not be expected to behave like angels.

This was a view Paine shared both with his more conservative contemporaries and (to some degree) with a tradition of political thought
articulated by Puritans in seventeenth-century England and New England.[50] Paine himself drew a fundamental distinction between the terms

"society" and "government" by observing that while society promotes happiness "*positively*" by uniting affections, government does so "*negatively* by restraining our vices," an open admission of the perfect compatibility of happiness and restraint.[51] "The necessity of having civil governments arises from the moral corruptions of mankind," one writer observed in late 1786. "If all men would conform to the rules of virtue, or the moral government of God, civil government would be unnecessary. They might then all continue in a state of nature."[52] Or, as James Madison famously noted in 1788, the necessity of government itself was the "greatest of all reflections on human nature," for "if men were angels, no government would be necessary."[53] The vices alluded to by Paine and by Madison found realization in the secular sins of "libertinism" and "licentiousness," crimes that described not excesses of private liberty but liberty unrestrained by government, whether that word was understood as the government of the self or of the state.[54] The definition of "libertinism" by Noah Webster as "looseness," and "licentiousness" as a lack of restraint, helps us situate the erotics of firmness and manual maintenance in the 1774 device: liberty always inclines to looseness, and in order to protect the rights of the subject it must be restrained and held in place by the agents of state power.[55] Governors—or governments themselves—uphold liberty in a physical sense.

The contemporary association between liberty and male sexual organs can be seen more obliquely in a modified version of the 1774 emblem reproduced on the dedication page of *A Collection of Designs in Architecture* printed in Philadelphia in 1775, the first architecture book published in the colonies. Engraved by John Norman and printed by Robert Bell, the central motif of the image derived from the 1774 *Journal* title page, with the addition of a thirteenth arm to signify the admission of Georgia to the Second Continental Congress. "Magna Charta," rather than a testicular documentary reservoir resting beneath the pillar, has here become a de facto titular inscription on the base of a sculptural monument. The Latin motto has been replaced by a looping snake imprinted with the text "UNITED NOW ALIVE AND FREE . . . FIRM ON THIS BASIS LIBERTY SHALL STAND . . . AND THUS SUPPORTED EVER BLESS OUR LAND . . . TILL TIME BECOME ETERNITY." The book, based on the house patterns for upper middle-class Britons in Abraham Swan's *British Architect* (1745), was "respectfully addressed" to John Hancock, the president of the Continental Congress, and to "all the MEMBERS, of that HONOURABLE

and AUGUST BODY." This was an appeal for patronage, predicated
perhaps on the hope that the Congress would cancel its association with
the Bradfords and opt to print with Bell, the publisher of the first American edition of Blackstone in the early 1770s, an agitator for the repeal
of local restrictions against book auctions starting in 1773, and later a
self-described purveyor of books "for legislators, and for sentimentalists."[56] The members of Congress are described as "the SELECT REP-
RESENTATIVES, of the PEOPLE," and, according to Bell, it follows
that they "therefore are the PATRONS of the LIBERAL, USEFUL,
AND ORNAMENTAL ARTS." Like the designs in the book, they are
"EXALTED PATTERNS, of every PATRIOTIC VIRTUE."[57] Bell
and Norman may have known that congressmen like John Adams sometimes spoke of "political architects," but the image and the dedication
may have encoded language that was as playfully mocking as it was respectfully deferential.

The congressional *Journal* itself formally referred to individual partic-
ipants in Congress as "delegates" and "deputies," but "member" had become both a customary term for the constituents of a legislative "body"
as well as an established pun for penis in the culture of eighteenth-
century male social clubs, a parodic world modeled and governed to a
large degree on the forms and proceedings of legitimate colonial legislatures. Dr. Alexander Hamilton, for one, never seemed to tire of jokes
about "longstanding members" in his mock-history of one such club in
midcentury Maryland. It is not necessarily a stretch to imagine that the
printer and engraver alluded to this culture when they placed the term
beneath the image and referred to liberty as something that "stand[s]"
"firm" on the basis of "union" (a synonym for sexual intercourse); and
perhaps (who knows?) they also intended a gentle pun on "Han[d]
cock."[58] Whatever may have been encoded into the dedication and image, it is worth noting that such clubs were as often training grounds and
sources for legitimate political culture as they were perverse mirrors of
or refuges from it. Hancock's title of "President," to cite one of the most
telling examples, derived more immediately from the practices of non-
governmental organizations and clubs like Dr. Hamilton's than from the
precedents of colonial political administration.

The great significance of these images lies less in their stale coffee-
house wit than in their erotic conception of liberty and their representation and understanding of government itself. Government here resem-
bles a divine but nevertheless bodily intervention into human affairs,

while rights and liberty are rendered as a fragile and statuesque monument, part abstract embodiment of liberty and part castrated but consecrated phallus.[59] In this petrified understanding of what government is designed to safeguard and uphold, it is the document that animates the monument, whether we see the document as the prescriptive source of alienable rights and liberties or the descriptive acknowledgment of unalienable ones. This image of government as arising from a document represented one step in a shift in emphasis from the conception of the state as a living being—a moral person or a "body politic"—to a conception, frequently elaborated during the debates over the Constitution in 1787 and 1788, that the state resembled a work of art. The transition from the Articles of Confederation to the Constitution was regularly figured in contemporary rhetoric and imagery as the abandonment of an "impotent" Congress and the "erection" of a new piece of architecture, an edifice designed to shelter the law and liberties of the United States. The rhetoric of the constitutional discourse of the period, in other words, entrenched one notion of bodily government even as it seemed explicitly to abandon the idea of the personal state. But the notion of government as an "erection" represented an unstable middle ground, a fantasy of architectural fixedness that masked a fear about the body's insurgency, its potential for eruption and inevitable detumescence.

The Impotence of the Confederation and the Erection of the Constitution

The Massachusetts Constitution of 1780 described the government of distinct and separated powers it created as "a government of laws, and not of men," an echo—if he did not in fact draft the phrase here—of John Adams's concise definition of a republic.[60] This was an explicit attempt to depersonalize the state, an act similar to the coronation scene described in Thomas Paine's *Common Sense*. "Let a day be solemnly set apart for proclaiming the charter," Paine wrote in 1776, referring to his own proposed continental constitution, and "let it be brought forth placed on the divine law, the Word of God; let a crown be placed thereon, by which the world may know, that so far as we approve of monarchy, that in America the law is king. For as in absolute governments the king is law, so in free countries the law ought to be king; and there ought to be no other. But lest any ill use should afterwards arise, let the crown at the conclusion of the ceremony be demolished, and scattered among the people whose right it is."[61] Placing the charter, the words of the people, on the Bible, the "Word of God," would help cement in the minds of readers the differences between "divine law" and human-made law. A revolution against the latter was not, Paine implied in *Common Sense*, a revolution against God. But if crowning the law would serve as the official succession from the personal rule of kings to the impersonal rule of charters, the chiasmus of law and king, king and law also acknowledged the concept of a living constitution. In 1787 Adams himself described the state constitutions as analogous to buildings for a sovereign. The authors of these texts, having been called upon "to erect suddenly new systems of laws for their future government, they adopted the method of a wise architect, in erecting a new palace for the residence of his sovereign. They determined to consult Vitruvius, Palladio, and all other writers of reputation in the art; to examine the most celebrated buildings, whether they remain entire or in ruins."[62] Adams's phrasing left it somewhat ambiguous, but he suggested that it was not the people themselves but the law that inhabited the newly erected building. If Adams's images served to create the idea of a depersonalized state, a government of laws and not of men, it was a strangely living law that was housed like a sovereign in the palace of government.

When Alexander Hamilton wrote in 1788 of the "erection of a new government," he also imagined politics by analogy to architecture.[63] During the ratification debates of 1787 and 1788 supporters and opponents of the Constitution described government in a new language that was not directly grounded in older figures like the "body politic." For politicians and for the public, the term "constitution" began to lose its primary association with the physical body and came to signify the textual (and architectural) organization and limitation of political power.[64] The tendency to think of governments in this architectural way is largely a product of the eighteenth century. But what did they mean by "erection"? The word "erection" functions in *The Federalist* as part of a largely unnoticed but nevertheless radical shift in the language political writers and ordinary people used to define the relationship between state and society in the second half of the eighteenth century. The physiological meaning of "erection" was certainly available to the authors of *The Federalist*, but when Alexander Hamilton called for "the erection of a new government," he spoke as a "political architect."[65] Hamilton's metaphor—and the contemporary visual representations of pillars of the "great National Dome" or "Federal Edifice"—helped inaugurate in American constitutionalism the persistent metaphor of government as architecture and the state as a work of art. But, for all of the attempts to remove political thinking from its old reliance on the body, the pillars and even the word "erection" could still signify within that older discourse. Architectural and physiological vocabularies overlapped in 1787, and the original understanding of the American constitutional state was intimately linked to the word "erection" in both senses. This section locates the erection of the republic on the cusp of a transformation from metaphors for the state grounded in the body to metaphors grounded in culture, a transformation that remained incomplete in the late eighteenth century but nevertheless had lingering consequences for American constitutionalism.

The conception of government as an erection is intimately linked to modern consent-based theories of politics. We find the word first gaining prominence in contract theory and practice in the seventeenth century. In 1650 Hobbes described the "erection of a Common-wealth," using the word "erection" to signify that sovereign power was elevated over the people, even if the people were the erectors.[66] In 1690 Locke invoked architectural metaphors to opposite ends, using "erecting" to signify the process by which a people could create a new legislative power for themselves if ever an old one became oppressive.[67] A hundred years after Hobbes, it was conventional for speculative political writers to refer (as Hume did in his "Idea of a Perfect Commonwealth," published in 1752) to "the erection of commonwealths."[68] Outside the airy realms of political theory, the common trope of government as an "erection" appeared often in seventeenth-century colonial documents. In 1639 a group of Puritans in what is now Exeter, New Hampshire, agreed "to erect & set up amongst us such government as shall be to our best discerning, [and] agreeable to the will of god."[69] The language of the Exeter agreement was typical of expressed social contracts, documents that represented the explicit invention of a "people" prior to the erection of a government. The language of seventeenth-century theory and practice acknowledged the human-made quality of government, but even still, the prevailing metaphor for government in the seventeenth century—for Hobbes and Locke, as for the Exeter settlers—remained the "body politic."

Given the link between erection and consent, the American Revolution itself could be imagined as architectural in nature. In June 1775, John Adams lamented that the Continental Congress were not "good architects."[70] Later that year, Adams offered Richard Henry Lee a sketch of government that could be erected in a single month. "[H]uman Nature would appear in its proper Glory," Adams explained, "pulling down Tyrannies, at a single Exertion and erecting such new Fabricks, as it thinks best calculated to promote its Happiness."[71] "Fabricks" here signified as architectural constructions rather than textiles.[72] When he read Paine's *Common Sense*, Adams noted that Paine "has a better hand in pulling down than building"; claiming to be unflattered by the suggestion that he was the author of the popular pamphlet, Adams grumbled that he himself would have "made a more respectable figure as an architect."[73] His own *Thoughts on Government,* written in the wake of the success of Paine's pamphlet, was designed to do what he thought Paine could not. In *Four Letters on Interesting Subjects*, a pamphlet published in Philadelphia later in 1776, the author (perhaps Paine himself), observed that "individuals by agreeing to erect forms of government, (for the better security of themselves) must give up some part of their liberty for that purpose," and it was a constitution that stipulated just how much.[74] The Massachusetts Constitution (drafted largely by Adams) was itself divided into a Declaration of the Rights of the Inhabitants and a Frame of Government, and the architectural language of frames and framers reflected colonial experience at least as far back as William Penn's 1682 "Frame of Government of the Province of Pennsylvania."

The association between erection and consent could be found, in a different register, in contemporary discussions of the physiological erection of male sexual organs. Erections had to be willful and above all voluntary. A treatise on venereal disease from 1787 abridged by a Philadelphia physician described the progress of gonorrhea as producing unnatural effects: "In men the erections become painful and involuntary, and are more frequent and lasting than when natural."[75] But not all erections were sexually motivated. As the Virginia author of another pamphlet on venereal disease in 1787 observed, "children of three, four, or five years old, are known to have frequent erections," and the author warned that white parents who raised children in a slave society needed to make sure that the black women who supervised their children did not take advantage of these erections for their own lascivious pleasure.[76]

In New England election sermons the language of government as an architectural erection sat side by side with the image of the body politic. Benjamin Colman offered one of the most sustained meditations on the relationship between architecture and the state in his *Govern-*

ment the Pillar of the Earth, a sermon preached in 1730 before the governor of Massachusetts. Interpreting 1 Samuel 2:8—"For the Pillars of the Earth are the Lord's, and He hath set the World upon them"—Colman observed that the "metaphor is plainly taken from architecture; as in stately, spacious and magnificent structures we often see rows of pillars, to sustain the roof and lofty towers." The "princes and rulers of [the earth] are called it's pillars," Colman explained, "because the affairs of the world ly upon their shoulders." But Colman preferred to transfer the metaphor from individual rulers to the concept of government itself: "by pillars we are to understand governours and rulers among men; but not the persons that bear rule, so much as the order it self, government and magistracy." For Colman, the metaphor of architecture offered a parallel to the metaphor of the body politic, for "as the legs are to a body, comely in it's goings: Such are pillars in a stately structure for beauty to the eye." And like the body that revolts against itself, without unity the "house totters, the high arches above cleave asunder, and the roof falls in."[77]

New England ministers in 1787 followed Colman in describing government as architectural. The Rev. Joseph Buckminster told the assembled government of New Hampshire in 1787 that he would not amuse them with "a dissertation upon the nature of civil government, the character of civil rulers, the dignity of their office, and its importance to the world," the traditional fare of election-day sermons. The times were desperate ones, the "infant empire" was in danger, and Buckminster delivered his sermon while the Federal Convention met in Philadelphia. He argued that when "a beautiful edifice stands firm on its foundation, the spectator may justly amuse himself in contemplating its symmetry, proportions, ornaments, and prospects; but, if it were tottering to its fall, he would be unpardonable to be thus employed, and neglect every effort to sustain and restore it." Buckminster did not speak exclusively in terms of architecture; at times he read the present constitutional crisis as an antitype to "the mariners with Jonah"—the people must cast their sins overboard "or the ship will sink." But he mentioned the "beautiful edifice" enough to establish it as the operative metaphor of his sermon, envisioning God as the architect who would "bring order out of our confusion, and establish and complete the fair political edifice, whose foundation he has so happily laid."[78] The image of God "the SUPREME ARCHITECT"—as a Massachusetts orator reminded an assembly of Masons—was omnipresent.[79] The Rev. Joseph Pilmore of Philadelphia told the Freemasons of Pennsylvania that "THE GREAT BUILDER of this vast and beauteous fabric of universal nature, is love—pure, essential, eternal love," but that "by the malice of the devil, the very *masterpiece* of the GRAND ARCHITECT was utterly ruined." Even still, "the *out-lines* of the GREAT BUILDER's glorious PLAN" remained, with "JESUS CHRIST himself being the CHIEF CORNER STONE."[80]

Isaac Backus, a Massachusetts Baptist, resorted to similar imagery to lament that "instead of being the light of the world, and the pillar and ground of the truth, as those are that obey Him . . . what a stumbling block are we to other nations, who have their eyes fixed upon us."[81] Joel Barlow told the Connecticut Society of the Cincinnati that "FRIENDSHIP and CHARITY" were "the great pillars of their Institution."[82] A broadside addressed to Quakers in Pennsylvania in November 1787 stated that "we have lately passed through a day of great commotion and distress, wherein the foundations of many were tried and shaken."[83] A poem printed in both German and English and read at the dedication of Franklin College in Lancaster, Pennsylvania, in 1787 used architectural metaphors:

By JEHOVAH's Care protected
The Fabric gains a Height sublime . . .
All in the glorious Work assisting
We build on Christ, the Corner-Stone,
The Walls may bear diverse Directions.
The Building still shall be but One . . .
While Time remains, the Work shall stand.[84]

The rhetoric of the erection of a political edifice could be seen more explicitly in the election sermon in Connecticut in May 1787. The Reverend Elizur Goodrich took as his text Psalm 122:3, "Jerusalem is builded, as a city that is compact together." Goodrich offered his discourse as a commentary on "the great principles and maxims, which are the foundation and cement of civil union and society," under the conviction that "every builder should well understand the best position of firmness and strength, when he is about to erect an edifice." Goodrich hoped that "the foundations of our Jerusalem would be laid with polished stones, and the city of our habitation be built up without the noise of saws and hammers." With respect to the Federal Convention about to commence in Philadelphia, Goodrich asked "whether to neglect the great interest of the whole, and to imagine that each state can singly preserve and defend itself, be not as absurd, as if several men, at an amazing cost, should lay a costly foundation, and erect the mighty frame of a most magnificent palace; and then, before the expence be paid, from a fondness for finishing, each one, his own room, and of enjoying the pleasures of his separate apartment, they should fall into such contention and division, as not only to leave the frame neglected, uncovered and exposed to continual decay and ruin." Like Buckminster in New Hampshire, Goodrich stressed God's role: "Human art in order to produce certain effects, must conform to the principles and laws, which the Almighty Creator has established in the natural world."[85]

As Joseph Huntington's 1781 sermon attests, the image of the Confederation as a body politic found some adherents. George Washington, in his 1783 Circular Letter to the states (reprinted in Philadelphia in 1787), observed that an "indissoluble union of the States under one fedral [*sic*] head" was essential to the well-being of the United States, but he chiefly used architectural metaphors to describe the federal government: "These are the pillars on which the glorious fabric of our independency and national character must be supported. —Liberty is the basis—and whoever would dare to sap the foundation, or overturn the structure, . . . will merit the bitterest execration."[86] Early in 1787 an association of ministers in New England remarked that "the present situation of the *Congress* fills us with painfull sensations; for though it is the head, the federal head of the nation, yet it is greatly in want of necessary powers from its constituents to preserve the faith of the nation inviolate." The ministers called for a concerted national prayer "that all the states in the *Federal Union*, and all the citizens of each *state*, may have not only true moral and christian, but also true political virtue; even *that patriotic benevolence*, which shall cause all the members of the national body, whether as citizens or states, *to feel and care for, and to exert their several powers in promoting the good of the whole*; even as the several members of the human body—[promote] the good of the whole body." Individuals should pray "that there may be no delay in clothing the *Congress* with all necessary powers to act in character as the *Federal Head* of a *sovereign independent nation*."[87] The metaphors may have been mixed— Congress as a naked body and a head—but the idea of the government as a body remained. The idea of a "Federal Head" with constituent "members" was fairly widespread.[88] The chief bodily trope in 1787, the watchword of the early papers of *The Federalist*, was the dissolution of union imagined as the dismemberment of a body. In the words of one anony-

mous pamphlet printed in Philadelphia in May 1787, "the minds of the
people are less disposed to a dismemberment of the Union, than an improvement in the Foederal Constitution."[89] But who were the members,
the states or the citizens within the states?

The distinction and tension between the metaphor of the body politic
and the metaphor of government as an architectural erection figured in
an anonymously authored political pamphlet entitled *Anecdote for Great
Men* (1787), published in Hartford a month before the Federal Convention met and addressed to "the Supreme Council of the Nation, and the
whole Legislature, in all the United States of America." The *Anecdote*
offered an extended allegory about the aftermath of the American Revolution. The action was set on "the large new manor called Doveland"
owned by "Publicus" and inhabited by 1,000 tenants. Publicus has suc-
cessfully resisted the efforts of his older brother "Britannus" to enslave
him by appealing to the mercy of "Gallus," an uncle, and by borrowing
money from approximately one out of every thirty or forty of his tenants.
The *Anecdote* largely centers on the politics of reimbursing those tenants. In one scene, set in a thinly veiled version of Congress, some characters suggest that those who provided funds at the revolutionary moment should consider them more as gifts than loans. As the particularly
public-spirited tenant "Philanthropos" argues, recalling the sentiments
of John Winthrop in 1630, "in all communities, individuals must suffer
in their turns, and such is the imperfection of all human affairs it cannot be otherwise; however, on the whole, they who suffer the most, by a
necessary connection with the body politic, gain a thousand times more
than they lose, by the same connection." In the allegory Philanthropos's
claims find more favor in the legislative chamber than in the homes of
the tenants. The female tenant "Puritana," for instance, narrates to her
husband a nightmare she has had about his "necessary connection with
the body politic":

> I was, methought in the midst of the manor, and you and all the tenents were
> there; you were raising the largest and grandest fabrick I ever saw; all seemed
> well engaged at first, but soon most of them stood off, or set down, went to
> eating, and drinking, and smoaking, as if they had nothing more to do, but
> to mind their own pleasure: I saw you, my husband, and about thirty more
> with your shoulders under a huge beam, the heaviest piece of timber I ever
> saw, and the main piller of the great house, in which all were interested alike;
> you that were under it reeled and staggered, and I thought in my soul it would

have crushed you all under it, and I most earnestly called on the rest to go
and help you, but had as good called on so many stumps.

Puritana's dream had a simple moral: "it was as much the duty of the rest
to build the house as yours, and all for the common interest."[90] The *Anecdote* blended the social ideal of body-politic thinking with the idea of
government as a work of architecture: the country was embodied by the
landlord figure of Publicus, and the government was embodied by the
image of the manor house. But could the nation really be seen as a unanimous social and political body? The preamble to the 1787 *Rules of the
Society of St. George* in New York, a charitable society for the benefit of
"Natives of England or Descendants of Englishmen," claimed that even
though Americans were now "blended in one political Body, they are
still distinguished by the Places from which they sprang." Such distinctions were given force in Rule II: "That no Person who is not an Englishman, or the Descendent of an Englishman, shall be admitted a Member
of this Society."[91]

The division between nation as a social body and government as architecture could be found often in 1787. Noah Webster observed that
"nations are often compared to individuals and to vegetables, in their
progress from their origin to maturity and decay," but urged ratification
of the Constitution based on an analogy with architecture.[92] Some suggested that Americans had not been covered by the British Constitution as colonial subjects. An orator in Boston in July 1787 proclaimed,
the "English Constitution was erected before America was born, and its
gates were not open to the younger offspring."[93] Of course, some claimed
that there really was no English Constitution. The author of *Observations on Government* (1787) observed that "our governments are universally founded on ORIGINAL COMPACT; they are the result of pre-
concerted plan, and calm deliberation. In vain have Englishmen boasted
of a constitution; in vain shall we search their records for an original
compact. No one part of the government can be said to be unalterably
fixed and established."[94] Paine made a similar claim in *Rights of Man*
(1791). And, responding to Paine's quip that there was no British Constitution, John Quincy Adams in 1791 maintained that it was a building
nonetheless: "The constitution of Great Britain is a constitution of *principles*, not of *articles*; and however frequently it may have been violated
by tyrants, monarchical, aristocratical, or democratical, the people have
always found it expedient to restore the original foundations, while from

time to time they have been successful in improving and ornamenting the building."[95]

The issue of whether there really was a British "Constitution" was intimately related to the question of parliamentary omnipotence. The English jurist Blackstone argued in 1765 that Parliament had "sovereign and uncontrollable authority in making, confirming, restraining, abrogating, repealing, reviving, and expounding of laws, concerning matters of all possible denominations, ecclesiastical, or temporal, civil, military, maritime, or criminal: this being the place where that absolute despotic power, which must in all governments reside somewhere, is entrusted by the constitution of these kingdoms." This power was evident in acts that had changed the succession of the crown, altered the established religion of the land, created a union with Scotland, and modified the length of terms of members of the House of Commons. "It can, in short, do everything that is not naturally impossible; and therefore some have not scrupled to call it's power, by a figure rather too bold, the omnipotence of parliament."[96]

Only a written constitution, numerous writers argued, could counter legislative omnipotence. "The truth is," the author of *Four Letters on Interesting Subjects* explained in 1776, "the English have no fixed Constitution." With the sole exception of trial by jury, legislative power was unlimited. There was nothing to prevent Parliament from passing laws to allow members of the House of Commons to sit for life, or from permanently disenfranchising counties, cities, or towns. "In short, an act of parliament, to use a court phrase, can do any thing but make a man a woman."[97] By 1787, in criticizing the writings of Adams and Jean Louis de Lolme, John Stevens of New Jersey felt compelled to use scare quotes when describing "the constitution of England." Prefiguring Paine's attack on Burke in *The Rights of Man*, Stevens observed that no constitution could be said to exist if it could not be produced in a textual form. "In vain have Englishmen boasted of a constitution; in vain shall we search their records for an original compact. No one part of the government can be said to be unalterably fixed and established. The parliament are without any controul whatever; they are, in the language of their lawyers OMNIPOTENT; and I think Coke tells us they can do every thing except making a man a woman."[98]

The revolting idea of legislatures' omnipotence was frequently predicated on their unanimity as "bodies."[99] Some protested that this conception of unanimity gave a false impression of the power of legislative assemblies: "supposing the [North Carolina] Assembly to be [an] omnipotent" body, one critic in North Carolina noted, evoked the idea that "the superior power of the state is vested in their hands as *one person*," a purely "imaginary" notion. Against this idea of government as a man, this writer asserted that the state constitution was a "Gothic structure" of great antiquity and that "great strides have been made most ILLEGALLY and UNCONSTITUTIONALLY, to overturn this Gothic structure, contrary to the Great Charters of our forefathers, contrary to the declaration of rights by the convention of the people and contrary to repeated acts of Assembly." This same writer imagined that the North Carolina "*Constitution* was permanently established as a sacred temple."[100] The notion of a "temple" for Liberty was widespread in period iconography.[101]

In 1787 those who agitated for a revision of the Articles of Confederation cited the impotence of the national government as ruled by a weak and plural executive power vested in Congress. "Weak in itself, a variety of causes have conspired to render it weaker" said Chancellor Livingston of New York of "the debility of our federal constitution."[102] Another New York critic drew attention to what he called "the lameness of the Articles."[103] Noah Webster described Congress as a "*useless body*, a mere expense."[104] Charles Pinckney of South Carolina believed that this was a structural problem: "The Confederation seems to have lost sight of [a] wise distribution of the powers of government, and to have concentrated the whole in a single un-operative body, where none of them could be used with advantage or effect"[105] But the most frequently used term was "impotent." James Madison worried to Jefferson about the "impotency in the foederal Govt.," to James Monroe about the "impotency in the federal system," and in a memo to himself about the "Impotence of the laws of the States."[106] During the drafting of the Constitution, Pennsylvania delegate James Wilson deplored the "impotent condition" of the Confederation. The charge of impotence contended with "imbecility" as the major term in the campaign against the Articles of Confederation.[107] A Fourth of July orator in New Haven in 1787 reminded listeners of "the singular firmness" of the Congress that had voted independence, and sadly contrasted it with the "impotency" of the current congress under the Confederation. Because the Federal Convention was then sitting, some felt encouraged to hope they would soon see "a government firmly established over us."[108] Edmund Randolph of Virginia did not support the Constitution, but even still he claimed in 1787 that "the confederation was tottering from its own weakness" brought about by its "wretched impotency."[109] David Humphreys, the author of a rejected draft of George Washington's 1789 First Inaugural Address, wanted Washington to remind his auditors (the assembled Congress) that it was "well known, that the impotence of Congress under the former Confederation" had led to its overhaul.[110]

Why was "impotence" a common word in the Federalist attack on the Articles of Confederation?[111] "Impotence" in 1787 meant weakness generally, and it is this weakness that most constitutional historians cite as the occasion for revising the Articles of Confederation. But "impotence" also specifically connoted a lack of sexual potency, "a natural inability to coition" as one authority defined it in 1771.[112] Sexual impotence carried legal ramifications and was traditionally grounds for suit in high-profile divorce cases in Britain.[113] Federalists who worried about the extralegal character of the proceedings in Philadelphia may have invoked impotence as a defense when supporters of the Confederation dismissed their breach-of-treaty claim that the misbehaviors of certain states (particularly Rhode Island) had annulled the contract, enabling the people of other states to negotiate a new constitution as if they were in a state of nature.[114]

Impotence as grounds for divorce or annulment of the Confederation may have found meaning within the larger metaphor of politics as marriage. From the mid-seventeenth century to the Revolution, the notion that government represented a marriage between politicians and constituents helped structure colonial American political discourse. Reconfiguring the same-sex relationship between a male electorate and male politicians on the model of a voluntary heterosexual union, the metaphor of government as marriage established political legitimacy in the language of the consensual contract. The meaning of this metaphor was by no means static or stable over the course of two centuries. Its force changed as the assumptions behind the terms being compared changed and as different groups appropriated it to serve different ends.

Modern ideas about representative democracy in England and America emerged almost simultaneously with ideas about the legality of divorce. Puritans in seventeenth-century Massachusetts, for instance, regularly made an analogy between the relationships of governors to governed and husband to wife. At his impeachment trial in 1645, Deputy Governor John Winthrop provided the classic statement of the metaphor. Just as a woman was free to choose a husband, Winthrop reasoned, so citizens were free to select their representatives. But once the choice was made, wives and citizens must submit themselves to the authority of their chosen rulers. Annual elections made political marriages short-term contracts, but the force of the metaphor was to promote political stability. Within the parameters of Winthrop's logic, impeachment was the political equivalent of divorce. New England ministers periodically repeated Winthrop's antidemocratic analogy at election sermons throughout the seventeenth and well into the eighteenth century, long after the Massachusetts charter was revoked and positions like Winthrop's became crown appointments rather than elective offices. The metaphor gained currency, especially among politicians, because it linked rulers and ruled in a way that seemed to naturalize the duties each party owed to the other and because, in a patriarchal society, it subordinated the all-male electorate by feminizing it.[115]

In the eighteenth century a current of antipatriarchal thought transformed the meaning of the metaphor of government as marriage, but the metaphor itself proved hard to abandon. As the electorate broadened (remaining, of course, all male), as new ideas about the legitimacy of divorce circulated, and as philosophers questioned the naturalness of monogamy for humans and animals, the metaphor itself shifted. On the eve of the Declaration of Independence, some politicians remarked on the similarities between courting women and courting votes. "Popularity," grumbled one ousted Virginia politician in April 1776, is "an adulteress of the first order." It made no difference if a candidate "kissed the arses of the people," since no matter how "sacredly wedded" to one officeholder she might appear she will always be scouting for someone better, someone newer, someone different. Popularity may have been fickle and mythically unfaithful, but the metaphor of politics as marriage now recognized the radical power of the electorate rather than its necessary submission.[116] In such a context "impotence" may have found new political significance, especially as a justification for overriding the procedural barriers of amendment that made the Articles of Confederation a "Perpetual Union."

The language of politics as marriage—of the Constitution as a bride—occasionally surfaced in relation to the Constitution itself. Stating that "Allegory [has] been much exhausted, in explaining and discussing this grand, National Question," William Stuart of New York nevertheless described the proposed Federal Constitution in July 1788 as "our *In-*

tended." "Critics," Stuart noted in a private letter to a friend in Pennsylvania, "might perhaps sneer at this Phrase and ask how can it mean the New Constitution," but Stuart proposed that "the great Body of the People in every Free Government, must always be considered as the Husband of the Constitution thereof." Stuart was a learned man; he peppered his letter to Griffith Evans with allusions to Shakespeare's *Othello* and Alexander Pope's "Eloisa to Abelard." Although it was uncommon in 1788, his allegory was not exactly as "unhackneyed" as he imagined. Stuart's allegory extended the language of heterosexual marriage contracts and the Lockean language of political contracts into the sphere of constitutionalism. "[A]s long as such Constitution performs the duties of Love Honor and Obedience to Her great Constituent Body, or Political Husband, She is entitled to be Kept both in sickness and in Health, with all possible Love and Fidelity by such her said Husband and that on a breach of her Duty she must expect to incur the Pains and Penalties of *Divorce.*"[117]

Contractualism, the dominant language of marriage and politics, offered recognizable rights and obligations. The Constitution, like a wife, was "entitled" to be kept if it performed its duty; and the people, like a husband, had a right to revolt (divorce) if the Constitution breached its duty. Stuart elaborated his allegory, dividing it into two scenarios that we might call the story of weak people and the story of weak government. Stuart claimed that "the *Anti-Federals*, are a train of Hen-pecked Husbands, who having surrendered the Breeches to their dear Domestic *Ribs*, through want either of skill, or Courage, to Know or defend their own Rights; are led to suppose that the great Body of the People, like unto themselves, will surrender the political Breeches, and suffer themselves to be *Beaten, scolded & Cuckolded* . . . I have a better opinion of the Understanding & spirit of my Country men, and rather fear, that instead of suffering their Political *Rib* to *Attalantus* them— they on their Part will sometimes Play the Infidel, and scold and Cuckold their faithful Wife, which should She at any time attempt to retaliate, They deaf to the doctrine of *Lex Talionis*, would instantly tear her in Pieces!"[118] In the first story, the people/husband ends beaten and scolded, deprived of rights; in the second story, the law (*Lex Talionis*) is subverted, and the Constitution/wife is torn to pieces by an unfaithful people/husband.[119]

For whatever reason, "impotence" found a place alongside and against "firmness" and "rectitude," watchwords of republican ideology that frequently carried implicit references to the phallus.[120] The key word in this change was "firmness," one that appears over and over in the political vocabulary of the period. The Resolution of Congress of February 21, 1787, declared that a Federal Convention was the "most probable mean[s] of establishing in these states a firm national government."[121] As Charles Pinckney of South Carolina argued, "the true intention of the States in uniting, is to have a firm national Government."[122] Even in deciding not to sign the Constitution, Edmund Randolph claimed that "the most fervent prayer of my soul is the establishment of a firm, energetic government."[123] In place of an impotent corporate executive in Congress, the Federalists championed a single executive who would be vigorous, efficient, energetic, and above all "firm."[124] The connection between male virtue and rectitude was emblematized by the column and motto ("EX RECTO DECUS") on the title page of the English translation of Montesquieu's *Spirit of the Laws*, a book constantly invoked in 1787 and 1788. The column on the title page (unlike the text itself, or even the Latin motto) seemed to hold out the promise of a state of erection that could be maintained without reference to outside props (the virtue of the citizenry or the administration); unlike the early images of Confederation, which made the column's fate dependent on the states, this column stands on its own.

Firmness was an especially significant part of republican vocabulary. The association of New England ministers proposing a concerted national prayer in early 1787 suggested readers should pray "that the nation may always be blessed with men of understanding, prudence and integrity, in every department of power and government; that all now invested with the powers of government may have wisdom, firmness and fortitude to play the man."[125] "Our character and consequence, as a people, depend," an orator in Carlisle, Pennsylvania, observed in 1787, "on the firm union of these States, now called United."[126] Effeminacy posed a serious threat. The argument of "The Sofa," the first book of British poet William Cowper's *The Task* (the best-selling volume in the United States in 1787), described "the fatal effects of dissipation and effeminacy upon our public measures."[127] Constitutions, both physical and political, should be "firm." The Methodist founders of Cokesbury College in 1787 designed their syllabus around the idea that a "bad Constitution" was the result of "softness and effeminacy of Manners" and proximity to vice.[128] But firmness was a prerequisite for union, even if union was imagined to be a female allegory. In a "Cantata for the Fourth of July, 1788" appearing in the *Pennsylvania Packet* on July 17, 1788, "The Goddess of Union" concluded:

> Let firm union defend,
> With her powerful hand,
> And the building shall stand,
> Forever, forever—Amen.[129]

But as much as republican political culture disparaged impotence and celebrated erection, it also described reproduction as politically dangerous. In 1789 George Washington's speechwriter suggested he should emphasize his own sterility as an example of his republicanism. He had no children to succeed him.[130] It was largely the inclusion of such personal and private information in a public speech that led James Madison to draft a shorter, less confessional First Inaugural. Nevertheless, filial issue remained an issue for republicanism. When Washington stepped down in 1796, a caucus of Democratic Republicans who favored Jefferson as the next president and considered John Adams a monarchist told the people of Pennsylvania that "*Adams* has Sons who might aim to succeed their father; *Jefferson*, like Washington, has no Son."[131] Outside of political discourse, the word "constitution" retained its status as synonym for the body. Two manuals for the treatment of venereal disease published in 1787, for example, described gonorrhea as a "constitutional" problem.[132]

The language of firmness and impotence made a certain sense to a political culture on guard against the seduction of the people by ambitious politicians. As Washington's speechwriter put it, "Should, hereafter, those who are entrusted with the management of this government, incited by the lust of power and prompted by the supiness and venality of their constituents, overlap the known barriers of this Constitution and violate the unalienable rights of humanity; it will only serve to show, that no compact among men . . . can be pronounced everlasting and inviolable." Given lustful politicians and ambivalent constituents, "no wall of words, . . . no mound of parchment, can be so formed as to stand against the sweeping torrent of boundless ambition on one side, aided by the sapping current of corrupted morals on the other." The Constitution, in other words, was not a prophylactic (or, for that matter, a chastity belt). James Madison's version of the First Inaugural was more optimistic; he stressed that the Constitution could be "impregnably fortified" with amendments. Whether or not the Constitution and its early amendments provided protection against the "violation" of rights, the erotic characterization of the relationship between politics and the people continued to permeate most political discourse of the day.[133]

Given this context, it is probably no accident then that the icon for the ratification of the Constitution by the states was the image of individual pillars brought to erection by a divine hand, sometimes accompanied by the slogan "it will yet rise." While historians have used such images to illustrate the period, they have not focused on the career of the column as a symbol for the state or nation. It warrants investigation, however, both for what it might tell us about how the Constitution was understood and for what it says about the cultural and gendered origins of the modern nation-state. This notion of nation-building is a legacy of the eighteenth century, and the early icons and rhetoric—some of which persist today—can help us comprehend something about the process of nation-making. In these popular images for ratification, the bodies of the states have hardened; the states are no longer hands supporting a single national pillar, but concrete supports for a larger federal superstructure. Here also the whiteness of the columns takes on new significance with respect to the place of black persons in the new nation; we can see this especially in the way Rhode Island—the last of the original states to ratify—was represented: in 1788 as a cracked white pillar equal in political magnitude to the others, and in 1789 as a small black pillar that sags outside of the new federal edifice. In the same vein, one orator in 1787 described Rhode Island as "an unruly member of the political body."[134]

Constitutional discourse in 1787 often figured the revision of the Articles of Confederation as architectural renovations. As James Campbell told members of the Society of the Cincinnati in Philadelphia in 1787, the Federal Convention had been assembled "to supply the defects of our confederation—to prop the tottering fabric of our union, and to lay the foundations of national safety and happiness." Campbell claimed he could "already see the stately fabric of a free and vigourous government rising out of the wisdom of the FOEDERAL CONVENTION."[135] The meaning of the passage from Articles to the Constitution was debated in the Pennsylvania General Assembly in September 1787 by analogy to the transition from a "humble cabbin" to a "new house." One member argued that the Assembly should not condemn the Articles as "rotten" until the "new house" is "finished and furnished." But another, the future novelist Hugh Henry Brackenridge, argued that the Articles had already been condemned and that the states were then in a "state of nature": "we are not now forsaking our tenement, it is already been forsaken." To wait until "the new house is furnished" could mean watching the "old cabbin" collapse over them.[136] Francis Hopkinson's prose allegory "The New Roof" published in a Philadelphia newspaper in late 1787 suggested that the Confederation was a house with a bad roof.[137] As if to clinch the architectural dimensions of the document, in several early broadside printings the text of the Constitution could itself appear as pillars or "columns" supporting the "roof" of the Preamble.[138]

But where did "We the people" fit into all of this? What, ultimately, did the new architectural images mean for them? One Massachusetts Federalist stressed that the people should stop thinking of themselves as the feet of the body politic and instead consider themselves the foundation of a new federal edifice. The writer asked, "Can a Palladio erect a palace, that shall be the wonder of the ages, with untempered mortar, soft bricks and rotten timbers?" The answer was obvious:

> In the republican edifice the people are not inanimate materials, but *living stones*. They must not only be sound and proper, but also willing to lie, to stand, *to join* as the architect wishes, nay to go into their proper places: . . . [but] The very stones of the foundation can, if they please, begin to fight, and like a fatal earthquake shake the whole fabrick, into a heap of rubbish.[139]

The conception that the people formed the foundation of a structure was a great change from the late seventeenth-century idea that the rulers were the foundation. It strikes us as modern, but this Massachusetts Federalist was in a minority in thinking about the people in this particular, architectural way.

Francis Hopkinson's musical adaptation of "The New Roof," variously published as "The Raising" and "The New Roof: A New Song for Federal Mechanics," was the most extended attempt to translate the extended metaphorics of the body politic into the new language of architecture. He achieved a new level of specificity: the people at large were like "Plates . . . the Ground-work of all" (a plate is a horizontal piece of timber used to support a structure); senators were "the Girders" and the representatives were like "Joists"; judges were "King-Posts" and laws were "Braces"; and each of the states was a frame to the rafters. It was an odd piece, especially since in enumerating a one-to-one relationship between the Constitution and the imagined edifice Hopkinson had omitted any mention of the most controversial figure, the president. Hopkinson imagined the new roof as "a Federal head o'er a people still free," but though foundational the mass of people are primarily described as supporters and spectators: "The Sons of *Columbia* shall view with Delight / It's Pillars, and Arches, and Towering Height."[140] A "Cantata for the Fourth of July, 1788" from Philadelphia also imagined the Constitution as a building, but made no mention of the people.[141] The essays in *The Federalist* mentioned "foundation" thirty-five times, but never in direct reference to the people. And, while the essayists frequently invoked the idea that the Constitution was a "structure," a "building," or an "edifice," they never suggested that the people were a part of this structure; instead, they talked about the "structure of the edifice which we are invited to erect."[142] In other words, they considered the people as erectors rather than as part of the erection, as builders rather than component parts. But most of all they considered the structure as an object not composed of but removed from the people.

It was above all this sense of a sublime but distant object that was enshrined in the Grand Federal Procession of 1788, when a 36-foot high "grand federal edifice" was pulled through the streets of Philadelphia by ten white horses. Designed by the painter Charles Willson Peale, the "federal edifice" consisted of a "dome supported by thirteen Corinthian columns, raised on pedestals proper to that order . . . ten of the columns complete, and three left unfinished . . . On the top of the dome, a handsome cupola . . . Round the pedestal of the edifice were these words, '*in union the fabric stands firm.*'" One observer fluent in the vocabulary of eighteenth-century taste marveled at the "sublimity of the sight" of this edifice. As the parade marshals made clear, the federal edifice was to be entered by the people's representatives, not by the people themselves. (Perhaps this occurred to the 450 "architects and house-carpenters" who walked behind the float and horses.)[143]

The idea that the Constitution created an edifice separate both from the people and the politicians dominated the verbal and visual descriptions of the new government. At the end of 1788, after the ratification of the Constitution by eleven of the thirteen states, a Philadelphia engraver named James Trenchard generated his own idea of what the government looked like (fig. 8). He represented the government as "A PLAIN BUT STATELY EDIFICE, in a durable style of architecture: Its portico, seen entire, is composed of thirteen columns of the Tuscan order, supporting a pediment decorated with the armorial insignia

FIGURE 8. James Trenchard, "Behold! A Fabric now to Freedom rear'd," *Columbian Magazine,* frontispiece for bound volume of 1788. Prints and Photographs Division, Library of Congress (LC-USZ62-45513).

of the United States . . . Two of the columns are cracked—in allusion to the non-concurring states."[144] The edifice was probably more stately than plain. The fear of ornate architecture was expressed well in a guidebook to Methodism published in New York in 1787. In a section "On Building Churches, and on the Order to be observed therein," the authors observed, "Let all our Churches be built plain and decent; but not more expensively than is absolutely unavoidable: Otherwise the Necessity of raising Money will make Rich Men necessary to us. But if so, we must be dependent on them, yea, and governed by them."[145] The design of the edifice in Trenchard's engraving differed from Peale's design for the float in the Philadelphia parade—Trenchard's had Tuscan columns, Peale's Corinthian; this one had a portico, the other did not. The two structures may have belonged to two architectural orders but they communicated the same message.

Or did they? Trenchard's illustration served as the frontispiece to the second volume of the *Columbian Magazine*. Though this periodical is often associated with literary nationalism, the editor was an Anti-Federalist named Alexander James Dallas. In printing the Constitution itself in the pages of the magazine in October 1787, Dallas had made a sly commentary on the text by juxtaposing an anecdote about a man who chooses Turkish slavery in order to be with his captured wife with George Washington's letter transmitting the Constitution from the Constitutional Convention to the Continental Congress. Washington's letter (he had signed it but had not written it) stressed that it was "obviously impracticable in the federal government of these States, to secure all rights of independent sovereignty to each, and yet provide for the interest and safety of all—Individuals entering into society, must give up a share of liberty to preserve the rest," and "the magnitude of the sacrifice must depend as well on the situation and circumstance, as on the object to be obtained." The anecdote that Dallas placed next to this letter shared the language of sacrifice, but placed it in the register of voluntary slavery.

On closer inspection, Trenchard's drawing and the poem printed beneath it offer a more ambiguous message about the Constitution. Trenchard has accentuated the foundation of the building far more than other representations in the period, and has placed Liberty with a pole and cap at the very apex of the building. And it may be no accident that the winged boy holding a scroll that reads "Constitution" is pointing specifically to one of the cracked pillars representing the states that had not ratified the Constitution by the end of 1788 (Rhode Island and North Carolina). The poem similarly gives the impression that unity is a fabrication:

Behold a Fabric now to *Freedom* rear'd,
Approv'd by friends, and e'en by Foes rever'd.
Where *Justice*, too, and *Peace*, by us ador'd,
Shall heal each Wrong and keep ensheathed the Sword

Approach then Concord, fair Columbia's Son;
And faithful Clio, write that *"WE ARE ONE."*

The muse of history Clio, kneeling with quill in hand, has been called to
the scene to produce a text that will offer a counterbalance to the reality described in the poem: the world of friends and foes, of wrongs and
swords. Indeed, history is on hand to record unity in the face of obvious discord, and the text she will produce and the voice she will assume
("WE ARE ONE") will be a fitting analogue to the text of the Constitution itself, where "We the People" speak the language of consensus in
the face of obvious fissure and dissent.

Anti-Federalists quickly learned to speak the lingua franca of politics as architecture, finding in it a way to point out that the Federalists
had built something for themselves but not for the people. As one Anti-
Federalist in Boston put it on the eve of the Massachusetts ratifying convention, after Delaware, Pennsylvania, and New Jersey had all agreed to
the document:

> The three pillars lately erected at the southward, are like the hanging towers
> of Pisa, to be propped up and cemented by the blood of posterity, if ever they
> stand at all; for the present generation have too strong a sense of the rights of
> nature, of the sufferings experienced from their re-establishment, to set down
> passively under a tottering pile, erected on pillars of porcelain—and if half a
> dozen others should yet be added to the guilded dome, it will still be astonish-
> ingly defective; as the artificers have hurried it through for their own present
> accommodation, without one solid heart of oak to support an edifice, whose
> wings extend to embrace the territory from the Mississippi, to the chain of
> lakes, and from the inland seas to the eastern shore.[146]

The icons and verbal representations for the state that proliferated in
the late eighteenth century inaugurate a movement away from the body
as an analogy for government. As I have suggested, the movement was
not completely successful. The older concept insinuated itself into the
new representations, and the pillar functioned as a sign of somatic state
power as well as an emblem of the distance between old and new conceptions of the state. As part of a long-term change in ideas about the state,
the use of architectural metaphors highlighted the human creativity of
legislators and implied that government was more permanent than when
it was grounded in the body, but the metaphors and the phallocentric im-

ages intimated that the body metaphor had not been abandoned but re-configured. In 1787–88, the Federalists used architectural metaphors to teach the people to think of themselves as spectators present at the erection of the new government, part of the foundation but not the building. Anti-Federalists took a different view. To them the structure was shaky at best.

CHAPTER TWO

Aesthetics and the Science of Politics

The idea of the state as a work of art developed in the context of the contemporaneous rise of modern political science and philosophical aesthetics. These nascent disciplines both emerged in the second half of the eighteenth century, and they shared a common vocabulary that included terms like "consent," "disinterestedness," and even "voting." For European and American writers and readers the most prominent topic of aesthetic debates, the question of taste, addressed a central political problem, especially for governments based on the consent of the governed. How, political and critical writers asked, could the subjective judgments of individuals be reconciled with or even subordinated to the authority of experts? How could—and why should—one opinion count more than another?

For European and American writers in both nascent disciplines, taste represented a central problem for the successful integration of individuals into communal life. For certain writers, theorizing about taste was an offshoot of thinking about public opinion; for others it was related to understanding the way certain political forms seemed to suit some nations but not others. Ultimately, the growing recognition of the centrality of taste in politics marked a significant turning point in the history of political thought, a turn brought about by an attempt to describe the subject-centered, consent-based character of modern politics and to account for the significance of those subjects, especially women, whose consent remained politically unrecognizable. This chapter traces the intellectual history of the connection between government and taste in the eighteenth century and ends with an examination of the place of taste in debates over the ratification of the Constitution. The Constitution itself might not have been ratified if supporters of the text had not strategically and routinely appealed to the total beauty of the document. That strategy involved refashioning political consent on the model of aesthetic taste, but it was simply one aspect of a much larger development that brought taste to the center of discussions of politics in an array of settings in the late eighteenth century.

Constitutional Tastes

One of those settings was Belchertown, Massachusetts, a town that had participated in the agrarian revolt known as Shays's Rebellion and had joined with most of the other towns in its county in voting against ratification of the Constitution.[1] On July 4, 1797, a young law student, Samuel Fowler Dickinson, delivered an oration on "The Connection of Civil Government with Manners and Taste." The relationship between manners, taste, and government was an odd subject for a Fourth of July oration. Though the genre was only two decades old it had already become formalized; audiences knew what to expect. Often pointing to local veterans, orators generally reminded audiences of the public virtue of the heroes of the Revolution, cast scorn on British villains, predicted the impact the assertion of rights and sovereignty would have worldwide, and (in the aftermath of the French Revolution) celebrated the extension of the philosophy of the Revolution to other nations or censured what the speaker took to be a mistaken application of one nation's philosophy to a completely foreign situation. But the speaker, Dickinson, was barely older than the genre itself; he was a child during and of the Revolution. Born in 1775, the aspiring lawyer from nearby Amherst was part of a rising generation of orators whose reflections on the Revolution dispensed quickly with accounts of British tyranny and American heroism. Even still, hearing the title his audience must have worried that they were going to get a misplaced lecture in political science on a day that should be devoted to festivity.

They had reason to worry. Dickinson had given a similar speech two years before, in Latin, as the salutatory address at the Dartmouth College commencement. On that day his thesis was *De administrationis civilis et morum natura; atque momento eorum mutae relationis:* that is, the "Nature of Civil government & manners; their mutual relation & influence in society." Dartmouth had been established by Eleazor Wheelock in 1770 to educate and evangelize American Indians, but by the 1790s all of Dickinson's classmates were white and few were preparing for the ministry. (The position of Professor of Divinity was vacant between 1787 and 1804.) Indeed, though the commencement ceremonies in 1795 had opened with a prayer and had taken place in a church, the topics of the other speeches on the program that day give the temperature of the school: in addition to a poem in English and a Greek oration (both on unknown subjects) and an oration on thunderstorms, the audience was treated to a forensic dispute on the question "Is the political establishment of a uniform system of Education advantageous to a community?"; to a dialogue on "Constitutional Freedom"; to a syllogistic dispute (like Dickinson's, in Latin) on the question "Is there an original difference in the mental faculties of mankind?"; to a dialogue on the state of Poland; to another forensic dispute, this one on a question that may have been the only reference to the original college mission, "Have Savage Nations an exclusive right to the territory which they occupy as hunting ground?"; and, finally, an oration on "The connection of Morals with political Society."[2] It was a long program, almost certainly an exhausting day, but these were the great issues and terms of the times: freedom, rights, constitutions, educational uniformity, the original equality of minds, and the relation of manners and morals to politics.

Though no record of the curriculum of what we would call political science at Dartmouth exists before 1796, and then just a bare notice that seniors were required to learn the elements of natural and physical law, the topics that Samuel Dickinson and his classmates discussed were no doubt promoted by the college's president John Wheelock. Wheelock, who had taken over after his father's death in 1779, was the professor of history and (after 1796) the professor of politic law, and shortly after assuming the presidency he had devoted his scholarly attentions to political history and political theory. The result, twenty years in the making, was a massive manuscript he called "A Philosophical History of the Advancement of Nations; with an Inquiry into their Rise and Decline." To understand modern nations, Wheelock needed "to go back to their origin." It was not sufficient merely to familiarize himself with the "spirit of human institutions"; he had to "interrogate the very legislators themselves, develop their principles, and analyze the various relations of the laws to themselves, to those they govern, and to every thing that is or belongs to man as connected in civil society." It was clearly a big undertaking, requiring "great political research" in the habits, customs, and political forms of nations; and it was a "philosophical" history because Wheelock was forced to go beyond the documentary record and "to supply the silence of historians by judicious conjectures, and to extract, as it were, truth from probabilities."[3]

A publisher in Boston who bravely thought subscribers might be willing to pay five dollars for the distillation of twenty years of Wheelock's drudgery, estimated that the manuscript would fill a thousand printed pages in three octavo volumes; but though the publisher tried to stoke interest by referring to Wheelock as a kind of American equivalent to Montesquieu, subscribers were not forthcoming. And when the publisher then decided that it might be better to print in London anyway, the reports of the London readers described the manuscript as "a confused mass of facts, assertions, quotations and stories totally distinct in the points they were to establish, irrelevant in their objects to each other and to any common established opinion, principle or sentiment." The reviewers of the manuscript thought the style was "bad and ancient," "not that of any man who could ever have written anything for the press." And most crucially, as the Boston publisher reported, the readers couldn't tell what the main subject of the book was or even what Wheelock's political views about modern nations were. Whatever Wheelock's politics might be, and whatever his book might be about, the readers cringed that the author had spent twenty years working on his book but had failed to cite the principal recent works in the fields he touched upon. The book was simply unpublishable. The readers destroyed his chances of becoming a *philosophe,* an American Montesquieu; and in turn, Wheelock may have destroyed the manuscript: only two of what must have been thousands of pages of "A Philosophical History" survive.[4]

Wheelock's students may have had similar problems understanding what exactly he meant when he taught history and politics, but Samuel Dickinson's speech was on a topic that Wheelock clearly relished, the "mutual relation" of manners and government. Dickinson's topic, in its broad scope, was typical of the kind of thinking that Wheelock's college fostered, for so many of the speakers at Dickinson's commencement and at others in the period took up similar topics: in 1794, when Dickinson was a junior, four seniors debated "Whether legislators have a right to enact laws which are not founded on moral principles?" while two others performed a dialogue on the question of "Whether the difference in the political state of nations depends more on physical, or on moral causes."[5] And in 1801 Dartmouth's most famous graduate of the period, the future senator Daniel Webster, offered an oration on "The Influence of Opinion," a subject that the speaker admitted was "not entirely new." Indeed, the treatment of opinion as a (even *the*) governing force in politics was at least sixty years old, though the reactionary Webster wished to harness that political fact in order to show that if the opinion of the divine right of kings had supported tyranny in the seventeenth century, it was the opinion of the "imprescriptible rights of man" that was licensing new but comparable forms of tyranny at the dawn of the nineteenth century.[6]

The telegrammatic table of contents of Wheelock's unpublished manuscript (which had been included in his Boston publisher's failed subscription proposal) shows that Wheelock probably had much to say about most of the topics that emerged as orations, disputations, and dialogues at his college. And he had much to say in particular about manners, which was the final topic he was to treat in a chapter on the "Spirit of Freedom" that was to close volume one. In an early chapter on "The Influence of Causes that form the Character of the Mind," Wheelock was to discuss the "revolution of manners—Improvement of manners—Customs—The empire of manners." The other topics he was to treat in the chapter—education, the influence of religion on the mind and on the state—suggest that he clearly understood a great deal to be contained by the term "manners."

In the great midcentury work of Enlightenment political theory to which Wheelock was obviously indebted, *The Spirit of the Laws,* Montesquieu had drawn a distinction between the terms *manières* (often translated in the eighteenth century as customs or behavior) and *moeurs* (manners or morals), though both were understood to be opposed to *lois* (laws). In a section devoted to "Laws in Relation to the Principles Which Form the General Spirit, the Morals, and Customs of a Nation," Montesquieu explained that *moeurs* and *manières* (the earliest English translator, Thomas Nugent in 1750, said "manners and customs") were "those habits which are not established by legislators, either because they were not able or were not willing to establish them." Montesquieu explained that laws were directed at men's actions as political subjects whereas *moeurs* (Nugent said "manners") regulated men's actions as men. *Manières* (Nugent said "customs") also concerned nonlegal regulation, but with this difference: *moeurs* ("manners") concerned the internal regulation of conduct, and *manières* ("customs") concerned external pressures on conduct.[7] Too often, Montesquieu noted, legislators confounded laws, customs, and manners (this had happened in Sparta and China, for instance). Despite his attempts to be distinct and technical, many of his readers inevitably did too.

For Wheelock, as for many in the period, manners was a catchall term meaning morals, customs, religious beliefs and practices, tastes, mental attitudes, and perhaps much more. Indeed, manners seemed to signify for him that category of "every thing that is or belongs to man," which took him twenty years to root out, if he ever did. Though he would not have used the word in this sense, a fitting modern cognate might be the flexible analytical term "culture." Wheelock and his students would certainly have understood the mind as something cultured or cultivated—acted on and influenced by causes that formed a person or a people's mental character.

And so it was not surprising that Wheelock's discussion of religion would be considered under the larger rubric of what he called the "empire of manners." He was not said to be a successful teacher. He seems to have stressed the acquisition of factual knowledge more than its application; he was, as a member of the class of 1800 put it, "confined to the book." Nevertheless, if he shared his scholarship with his students, they must have been delighted (or perhaps scandalized) by the questions he apparently answered in his book manuscript: for instance, "Is atheism or superstition most unfavourable to civil government?" The questions were not simply abstract. The constitution of the state of New Hampshire held the "rights of conscience" to be an unalienable right, and had said that individuals had a natural right to worship God as they saw fit. But it had also said that "morality and piety, rightly grounded on evangelical principles, will give the best and greatest security to government," that public worship of the Deity and public instruction in religion was the best way to propagate morality and piety, and that therefore the state had a right to tax citizens to support and maintain Protestant teachers of piety, religion, and morality.[8] Wheelock's discussion of the relation of religion to government must have broached this point of the local proximity of church and state, for he promised a "solution of a problem" of how religion was "to be restrained." It was heady and complicated stuff, and it was easy to see why readers were confused, for Wheelock believed in the influence of physical and moral causes on the structure of government, and reciprocally he believed that a philosophical historian could learn a lot about the morality of certain societies simply by considering their political forms and their legislation.[9] He must have made quite an impression on his students, and especially on Samuel Dickinson.

But Samuel Dickinson was not just a student of political theory; he had witnessed popular politics firsthand in his native Amherst. When Dickinson was eleven or twelve, his town and family had been caught up in the large-scale agrarian revolt now known as Shays's Rebellion, when roughly two thousand angry farmers took up arms against the state. In part the uprising was about taxes and representation, the classic sources of protest in the age of the American Revolution. The farmers suffered—they faced debtor's prison and foreclosures on the mortgages for their farms—because taxes were high and money was in short supply; they believed that the senate and governor didn't care. This issue was acute in Amherst, and a significant number of Dickinson's relatives were involved: a historian has recently estimated that thirty members of the extended Dickinson family took up arms against the state government; they represented about 25 percent of the rebels in Amherst. Almost half of the town joined the insurgency, and Dickinson's father, Nathan Dickinson, Jr., a successful farmer who had been educated at Harvard and was in the top fifth of property owners in the community, was one of the insurgents; so were two of Dickinson's older brothers.

The insurgency had actually started with a convention of delegates from the towns in Hampshire County who met on August 22, 1786, and drew up a list of grievances calling for a revision of the state's constitution. Such conventions were a legacy of revolutionary practice, and they were the targets of verbal and graphic satire. One image produced in Boston in late 1786 for a 1787 almanac depicted a "County Convention for the Redress of Grievances of Courts," a group of men drinking from punch bowls and talking around a table while one stands and holds a sign that says "No Courts or Lawyers." The delegates in Hampshire County did not say anything about lawyers, but they wanted to eliminate the senate and the Court of Common Pleas; they desired changes in the mode of representation (suffrage was tied to property holding) and the mode of taxation; and they wanted more money to circulate. In the document they produced the delegates stressed that inhabitants should "abstain from all mobs and unlawful assemblies, until a constitutional method of redress be obtained." But almost immediately armed insurgents began to close courthouses across the state, impeding debt-related trials; the government mustered militias and hired mercenaries, and the insurgency was put down in early 1787. Though on a national level conservatives' fear of similar uprisings helped bring about the revision of the Articles of Confederation that resulted in the U.S. Constitution, no constitutional change came about in Massachusetts. Nevertheless, the annual elections in early 1787 brought candidates sympathetic to the insurgency into the state legislature, and these men liberalized debt laws.[10] Constitutional change did not come, but the rebels changed politics in the state. It was no wonder that a year after the insurgency was put down that Amherst and Belchertown (and many other towns in the county) instructed the men they sent to Boston to discuss the proposed Constitution to vote against its ratification.

The ordinary insurgents, including Dickinson's father along with 120 others, were forced to appear before a justice of the peace in February or March 1787 and to subscribe to an oath of allegiance to the state of Massachusetts. Six men were tried for high treason, and of this group only Moses Dickinson of Northfield was not sentenced to death. In the end, after a wave of petitions, the governor pardoned all the insurgents. Moses and the other men were represented in part by a lawyer named Simeon Strong, a wealthy landholder in Amherst whose loyalism during the Revolution had not hurt his social standing, though no doubt his political views made him obnoxious to the Dickinsons, the chief patriot family of Amherst. The populist agrarianism of the rebellion had gone hand in hand with a current of antilawyer sentiment. The same almanac that mocked the county conventions reserved its real scorn (and its title-page illustration) for an attack on gluttonous and inebriated lawyers who fed themselves on debt litigation. Lawyers were an "order" of men, one essayist put it in 1786, who were "daily growing rich, while the community in generall are rapidly becoming impoverished."[11] After graduating from Dartmouth, Samuel Dickinson—son of one rebel and relative to twenty-nine others—taught school for a year, and during that time he converted to Christianity. He decided to become a minister, but almost as quickly changed his mind and began to read law under the direction of Simeon Strong in his native Amherst.[12] This was what he was doing when he made his Fourth of July oration in nearby Belchertown on the connection of civil government with manners and taste.

The thesis Dickinson put forward in Belchertown was simple, even if it may have sounded counter-intuitive or even blasphemous to an audience used to celebrations of republican simplicity. "Government," Dick-

inson argued, "being connected with the constitutional taste and manners of a people, improves with the progress of refinement." Dickinson
invoked, though given the audience he wisely didn't drop names, most
of the touchstone theories of modern constitutionalism: John Locke's
narrative of the social compact and the origin of delegated power and
legislative supremacy; Montesquieu's theory about the effect of climate
on national laws; and the ideas about the influence of social stage on
governmental form that had been articulated by Adam Ferguson and
Adam Smith. These were the topics he had learned at Dartmouth. To all
of these theories Dickinson added an aesthetic dimension, an explora-
tion of the way in which "taste" (the master noun of eighteenth-century
aesthetic thought) and "government" (the master noun of eighteenth-
century political thought) were intimately connected. Taste was a hot
topic, one he may have learned about in college as well: the year after
Dickinson left Dartmouth, four graduating students disputed the question "Is Taste the standard of Beauty?," that is, whether there were universal laws of beauty or whether everything was relative and depended
on personal or cultural preferences.[13] And the question of taste was also
said to relate to social stage. Everyone could be said to have taste—
indeed, the naturalist Bernard Romans published in New York in 1775
an engraving of a "Painting in the Creek Taste" (fig. 9)—but whether or
not standards should and did fluctuate remained an exciting topic for the
philosophically inclined.

Dickinson's audience may have been bored, but it is just as likely that
this young law student spoke a language that farmers and pardoned insurgents could understand: they too believed that constitutions and governments needed to accommodate people and not the other way around.
Dickinson's was certainly an unusual performance, but perhaps most
surprising (especially for someone who had converted to Christianity recently) was the absence of the traditional emphasis of Fourth of July orators on virtue, a key word in the vocabularies of religion and republicanism. In fact, while the words "manners" and "taste" appeared on nearly
every page of the printed version of his oration, "virtue" did not figure
prominently as either a term or a concept.[14]

Is it significant that this young orator chose to focus on taste and manners rather than virtue? One way to make sense of Dickinson's oration
is to invoke J. G. A. Pocock's compelling explanation for the period. As
commercial humanism replaced civic humanism at the end of the eighteenth century in Britain, Pocock has argued, "virtue" was redefined as

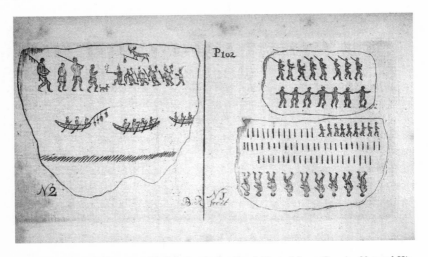

FIGURE 9. Bernard Romans, "A Painting in the Creek Taste," from *Concise Natural History of East and West Florida* (New York, 1775). Courtesy of the Edward E. Ayer Collection, The Newberry Library, Chicago.

the refinement of manners. This explanation has much to recommend it, as do many of the applications of Pocock's thesis to the American context. Most scholars who study the materials Pocock has surveyed observe some shift in American political discourse in the late eighteenth century. Isaac Kramnick, for instance, describes a privatization of virtue in this period. In Kramnick's revision of Pocock, the disinterested attachment to public good characteristic of classical republican virtue was overwhelmed by a latent Protestant tradition emphasizing private self-reformation. On the other hand, Gordon Wood has set forth a Madisonian view of the period, arguing that the neoclassical politics of virtue ended around 1790, just as the analysis of interest groups replaced the older vocabularies of politics. According to Wood, American politics after 1790 was as likely to acknowledge vice as to assume virtue. Ruth Bloch has shown that the shift Wood and Pocock describe looks radically different from the perspective of women, especially since republican virtue was a gendered discourse that increasingly redefined the private acts of women as forms of public virtue. Rather than giving way to private manners, Bloch has shown, female virtue emerged as a public issue in the late eighteenth century. Similarly, Richard Bushman has made a case that the redefinition of virtue as manners was inherently based in class. For Bushman, 1790 was a turning point in the history of the refinement of American manners, a moment when conduct books and primers on gentility began to reach middle-class rural and even lower-class urban readers.[15] The wealth of historiographical accounts of the transformation of thought in the late eighteenth century suggests that debates over the founding period have evolved beyond generalizations about liberalism and republicanism, but these interpretations explain only half of the provincial orator's thesis. For Samuel Dickinson, "taste" was as crucial and distinct a term as "manners," and for all of our accounts of the redefinition of virtue as manners in the period, we still have little explanation for the other term.

What did "taste" signify to a provincial orator or audience? And what did Dickinson mean when he said that laws and government were connected to the "constitutional taste" of a nation? Answering these questions can illuminate new connections between political and aesthetic thought and help us understand better the shift in the way the relationship between state and society was described and understood at the moment of the writing of the U.S. Constitution. In many ways we are in a better position now to understand why an aesthetic idea like taste found its way into a political oration than when Pocock first formulated his thesis. In addition to the extensions of Pocock's thesis that take virtue as the key term, a wealth of recent scholarship makes manners its central object of inquiry.[16] Critical trends in literary scholarship have combined with renewed interest in questions of aesthetics, leading to investigations of both the place of politics in aesthetic discourse and of aesthetics in political discourse.[17] The entry of "taste" into American political discourse coincided with the shift in the language political writers and ordinary people used to define the connection between American government and society. As I argued in the first chapter, conceptions of government in the late eighteenth century shed the bodily character of classical republican theory, with its attendant discourse of inevitable decay, corruption, and revivification. The new cultural metaphors for government imagined citizens (and noncitizens alike) not as parts of a political body, or as physicians monitoring the constitutional "health" of the republic, but as cultural consumers and spectators. In such an environment, taste was a significant constitutional issue.

Taste and Politics

"Taste" was a relatively new term in the American political vocabulary in 1797, but it had a genealogy in European political writing dat-

ing back to the 1740s and 1750s. While neither political science nor aesthetics achieved the status of an autonomous discipline in the eighteenth
century, theorists of politics—including the writers most influential to
American constitutional thought—frequently felt compelled to produce
accounts of aesthetic experience. In the 1750s political writers such as
Montesquieu, David Hume, and Edmund Burke all produced studies of
what would later be called "aesthetic" experience, each acknowledging
if not always concentrating (as Samuel Dickinson would a half-century
later) on the connections between national or individual tastes and the
forms of government that seemed simultaneously and paradoxically to
generate and to rely on that taste. Modern political science and philosophical aesthetics both emerged during this period, and for European
writers taste was a problem with obvious political analogies. How could
the subjective judgments of individuals be reconciled with (or subordinated to) the authority of experts in order to produce consensus? This
was a question that preoccupied both politicians and aestheticians. The
relationship between political and critical thought in the eighteenth century can be seen in the conjunction of the ideas of "taste" and "consent."
Debates about whose opinion counted, about who was qualified to pass
judgment (or, in the language of some aestheticians, "to vote") on aesthetic and political issues reflected radically similar concerns.[18]

Political thought not only coincided with aesthetic theory, sharing a
few crucial terms like "disinterestedness," the self-negating stance of
tasteful spectators before an art object and the proper posture of enlightened representatives in the face of party zeal: in the eighteenth century, political thought and aesthetic theory were mutually constitutive.[19]
Aesthetics was hardly the depoliticized activity it was putatively to become in the nineteenth century's division of intellectual labor. If anything, unified taste and common sentiments seemed to be what held societies together, and descriptions of how to render sentiments common
and how to neutralize subjective tastes preoccupied midcentury political thinkers (many of them emerging, significantly, from the provincial
peripheries of metropolitan culture) who produced important aesthetic
statements, texts we are only now beginning to appreciate (if sometimes for the wrong reasons) as "ideological." Given that prominent
seventeenth-century predecessors to Hume, Burke, and Montesquieu
felt no need to render an account of what we now call aesthetics, the
critical writings of Enlightenment political theorists mark a significant
turning point in the history of modern political thought, a turn brought

about in an attempt to describe new developments in the character of political experience.

Eighteenth-century European political writers believed that individual taste had to be accounted for, especially in governments based on the consent of the governed; and they slowly began to describe all governments—whether despotisms or democracies—as de facto products of consent. "Nothing appears more surprising to those, who consider human affairs with a philosophical eye, than the easiness with which the many are governed by the few; and the implicit submission, with which men resign their own sentiments and passions to those of their rulers," David Hume wrote in an essay "Of the First Principles of Government" (1741). Yet "when we enquire by what means this wonder is effected, we shall find, that, as FORCE is always on the side of the governed, the governors have nothing to support them but opinion."[20] The opinion of fear kept despotic governments alive, while love supported republics—this was in essence the old line that Daniel Webster would tow in his 1801 address on the "Influence of Opinion." But how were such opinions to be generated and, more important, how were they to be governed? This was a question Hume left primarily to his "literary" essays, opening his discussion "Of the Standard of Taste" (1757) by acknowledging that the "great variety of Taste, as well as of opinion, which prevails in the world, is too obvious not to have fallen under every one's observation." Taste, for Hume, was both like opinion in its variousness, "even where the persons have been educated under the same government, and have early imbibed the same prejudices," and unlike opinion, in that disputes over opinion tend to be disagreements over general principles (easily resolved if the disputants can come to an agreement about the meaning of terms), whereas disputes about taste were almost always based on distinctions about particulars and about the applicability of terms to certain objects: *this* poem is elegant, for instance, or *that* one is cold and affected. And hence Hume proposed that it is "natural for us to seek a *Standard of Taste;* a rule, by which the various sentiments of men may be reconciled; [or] at least, a decision, afforded, confirming one sentiment, and condemning another." Some order must be imposed on a world where the clash of opinions frustrated the creation of a common culture or at least the criteriology that would allow one to decide what parts of a diverse culture were the best.

Hume bemoaned the variations in the physical constitutions of men that rendered their sentiments relative and discordant despite that prin-

ciples of taste could be said to be universal, and consequently Hume's
rule for taste tends to be absolutist or "authoritarian" in nature. Persons
who have "no opportunity of comparing the different kinds of beauty"
may of course form a personal opinion about an object but they are "totally unqualified to pronounce an opinion with regard to any object"
presented to them. Instead, they must defer to the authority of others,
and Hume concludes that "though the principles of taste be universal,
and nearly, if not entirely the same in all men; yet few are qualified to
give judgment on any work of art, or establish their own sentiment as the
standard of beauty." Hume's theory of taste, in other words, reinscribed
the "many" and the "few" of his theory of politics from 1741. It is no longer surprising that the many "resign their own sentiments and passions"
to the few: it is necessary.[21] As Mary Poovey has observed, Hume's statements on taste focused more on social interaction than on the psychology of individual likes and dislikes, and they should be read primarily as
"contributions to a theory of government."[22] It is, no doubt, the political dimension of Hume's aesthetic that produces the tension between the
radical empiricism, or even relativism, that pervades most of his writings
and the universalist conclusions of this particular essay.[23]

Hume's authoritarian standard of taste found sympathetic agreement
in the work of the young Edmund Burke, who added an introductory essay on taste to the second edition (1759) of his influential *Philosophical
Enquiry into the Origin of our Ideas of the Sublime and Beautiful* (originally published in London in 1757). Burke's essay was little more than a
synthesis of the more rigorous thinking of his contemporaries. The Irish
author maintained that it was "probable that the standard both of reason
and Taste is the same in all human creatures," and that differences in
taste should be attributed to defects in judgment. Without a standard of
taste, Burke argued in a particularly tautological passage, what was the
point of writing a treatise like the *Philosophical Enquiry*? For "if Taste
has no fixed principles, if the imagination is not affected according to
some invariable and certain laws, our labour is like to be employed to
very little purpose; as it must be judged an useless, if not an absurd undertaking, to lay down rules for caprice, and to set up for a legislator of
whims and fancies." As his remark indicates, Burke shared with Hume
an understanding of the connection between critical rule-giving and political law-giving. But to legislate a standard of taste was to invite an inevitable criticism: that the rules handed down were merely personal and
not truly "philosophical." This was precisely the charge Burke encountered from Oliver Goldsmith, a fellow Irishman who objected in a review

of the first edition of Burke's book that its author mistakenly "founds his philosophy on his own particular feelings."[24] But even if Burke's aesthetics seemed idiosyncratic, the young writer labored to make them fit within a familiar political framework. In the body of his text Burke described the origins of feelings about sublime and beautiful objects through a narrative of the social compact, the sort of narrative he sometimes mocked in his *Vindication of Natural Society,* published the year before the first edition of the *Philosophical Enquiry.* While Burke traced ideas of the sublime back (in an almost Hobbesian sense) to passions for self-preservation, he claimed that ideas of beauty stemmed from passions for society, passions lodged primarily but not exclusively in sexual attraction. Burke's book, in other words, offered a history of social affections that made beauty the core component of civil society.[25]

But did the preservation of civil society necessarily depend on an agreement about what constituted a beautiful object? This was a question taken up, in a limited fashion, in an unfinished essay on taste by Montesquieu. The French political writer whose meditations on the English Constitution profoundly influenced both Federalists and Anti-Federalists declined to write the articles on "Democracy" and "Despotism" for the *Encyclopédie,* opting instead for the article on "Taste." Montesquieu's "Essay on taste in matters of nature and of art," first published posthumously in French in volume 7 of the *Encyclopedie* in 1757, found readers in Britain and America following its translation and inclusion as an appendix to the first two editions of the most extensive and popular British treatment of the subject, Alexander Gerard's *Essay on Taste* (1759).[26] Montesquieu's incomplete essay was not a synthesis of contemporary theories but rather a set of fragments attempting to articulate a new psychology of taste. He did not explicitly argue for a standard of taste, treating taste instead as a set of manipulable preferences that might be employed to political advantage. "Taste in its most general definition is whatever forms a bond based on feeling between us and an object," Montesquieu wrote, emptying the term of the connotations of good or bad judgments. It was exactly these kinds of bonds and feelings that he described in his more exclusively political writings. Despotic governments were held together by bonds based in feelings of fear, democratic and republican governments by bonds based in feelings of love.[27] His theory of taste reflected as well the interest in comparative cultural psychology he developed in *Spirit of the Laws.* "Low style is the sublime of the common people," Montesquieu wrote, for "they love to see something which is made for them and which they can understand."[28] At their heart statements such as this in Montesquieu's aesthetics paralleled the cultural relativism of his *Spirit of the Laws,* especially the idea that political measures appropriate for one form of government or one society are inappropriate for another. Political and civil laws, Montesquieu wrote, "should be adapted in such a manner to the people for whom they are framed that it should be a great chance if those of one nation suit another."[29] And tastes, always multiple, derived from the various gradations among a people.

What was "taste," after all? Writing in *The Spectator,* a British text "almost as likely to be present as the Bible" on late colonial bookshelves, Joseph Addison in 1712 defined taste in writing as "that faculty of the soul, which discerns the beauties of an author with pleasure, and the imperfections with dislike." The degree of taste a person possessed could be accurately measured by that person's pleasurable agreement not with the authors of certain texts so much as with the opinions of others, whether this was the opinion of "different ages and countries" that had led to the canonization of ancient writers or "the sanction of the politer part of our contemporaries" that had enshrined certain modern writers. In an age in which the doctrine of innate ideas met with fierce attack by Locke and others, taste seemed to Addison to be as close as one could get to an inborn quality. It was this innateness that led the French critic the Abbé DuBos to redefine taste as a "sixth sense" in 1719, and caused the Scottish philosopher Francis Hutcheson to call taste an "inner sense" in 1725.[30] But this did not mean that taste could not be improved. "The faculty must in some degree be born with us," Addison noted, but he offered his remarks as a preface to a series of essays "On the Pleasures of the Imagination" specifically designed to help educate the taste of his readers.

In its appeal to cultural authorities and in its promise that tastes could be improved, Addison's brief statement on taste was typical of a great deal of early eighteenth-century critical writing. Over the century, the essays of *The Spectator* had an unusually wide impact, especially with those provincial readers for whom the text offered a limited cultural enfranchisement within the polite metropolitan world described in so many of the papers. Benjamin Franklin famously modeled his own periodical writing on *The Spectator,* recalling in his memoirs how in the late 1710s he had imitated the language of the original so well he sometimes improved upon it.[31] In the 1750s John Adams similarly copied passages from the papers into his commonplace book, and sometimes chided himself for spending more time with *The Spectator* than with his legal stud-ies.[32] Late in his life, James Madison recalled *The Spectator* as a text that had instilled in him "a taste for the improvement of the mind and man-ners" back in the early 1760s. It was, in fact, the only book he mentioned by name in his autobiography.[33] For these American readers, *The Spec-tator* offered a style of reflective engagement and a license to reflect aes-thetically on topics ranging from high art to low life.

The disparate essays, treatises, and primers on taste written in eighteenth-century Europe often seem directed specifically at read-ers conscious of and anxious about their peripheral position to the po-lite centers of metropolitan culture, that is, to people like Franklin, Ad-ams, and Madison. Like Addison, many writers argued that taste was inborn, but even still they seemed to find a common theme in the idea of the educability of opinion. Taste could be taught. "We have all within us the seeds of taste," Daniel Webb wrote in his *Inquiry into the Beau-ties of Painting* (1760), one of the most widely available aesthetic trea-tises in America, "and are capable, if we exercise our powers, of improv-ing them into a sufficient knowledge of the polite arts."[34] This was not necessarily easy work. In a prefatory "Essay on Taste" to his 1734 guide-book to the cultural attractions of London, the expatriate Pennsylvanian James Ralph observed that "true taste is not to be acquir'd without infi-nite toil and study; and we are generally too indolent to accept of an ad-vantage on such terms. This is the real occasion, why a false one is so apt to prevail, and, on a division of mankind, would number three to one in its own favour." This was a task, Ralph noted, even for those who had the advantage of unlimited access to culture and "are distinguis'd by so many perfections as almost elevate them above the Rank of their Fellow-Creatures, and set them at an awful Distance for the Vulgar of Mankind to wonder at."[35] Ralph, who abandoned his family and moved from Phil-adelphia to London with Benjamin Franklin in 1724, was able by 1728 to pass himself off on the title pages of his publications as "a Person of some Taste," generating guidebooks to London culture for uninitiated tourists.

Ralph was so successful in selling himself as a man of taste that his up-lifting remarks on taste—uplifting because of their insistence that taste could be acquired—were republished in Boston in the *American Maga-zine and Historical Chronicle* in 1744, a decade after they appeared in London and with no indication that the author of the remarks was a for-mer colonist.[36] But even if taste was learned rather than inborn, the real test was to educate your acquired opinion to the point where it could counterfeit for natural. For Voltaire in 1757, taste "anticipates thought," and one must train oneself so that "nothing must escape instantaneous perception." The connoisseur is the person who can "discern in a rapid glance" between good and bad: "Practice and reflection alone will make it possible for him to experience immediate pleasure from elements that formerly he could not distinguish at all."[37] Montesquieu also stressed that taste was best measured by speed, defining taste as "only another word for the gift of subtly and rapidly discovering the degree of pleasure men can derive from any object."[38] It was chiefly this acquired immediacy that the various guidebooks and primers on taste like Ralph's promised to help readers learn.

But there was always a danger that what the guidebooks taught was not really taste, and there were always critics who described the facility as a natural faculty. In a series of essays on taste published in 1787, one Connecticut writer observed that "a good taste is an aptitude to discern instinctively" those objects that cause pleasure.[39] But too often those who read treatises on taste became "accurate critics" without ever transforming themselves into "persons of taste": "Their judgment of the objects of taste proceeds from mere learning, or reasoning, and not from any relish, or real perception of the beauties, about which they write." While Addison was a person of taste, this Connecticut writer argued, Dr. Johnson remained merely a critic.[40] For all of the invitations to culture and promise of participation in the polite world, the discourse on taste often remained a world based on exclusion. Alexander Gerard in his *Essay on Taste,* for instance, followed Hume's appeals to a common standard of taste. For Gerard, taste was composed of natural and cultivated elements: "It derives its origin from certain powers natural to the mind; but these powers cannot attain their full perfection, unless they be assisted by proper culture."[41] Henry Home, Lord Kames articulated a theory of taste similar to Hume's and Gerard's but emphasized that most were excluded from "voting" on taste. Kames had no difficulty arguing that taste rested on a universal standard that only a few could appreciate.[42] Hugh Blair's *Lectures on Rhetoric* (1783), widely imported, reprinted, and abridged in the United States in the 1780s, began with a chapter on taste that argued against this authoritarian idea. But it was rare to find someone who claimed, as Blair did, that "the common feelings of men carry the same authority" as the judgments of the experts.[43]

The "taste" of the experts, of course, always had its satirists, and the competition between individual likes and dislikes and authoritarian standards ran throughout the discourse on taste. "Taste is now the fashionable Word of the fashionable World," a writer in the *American Magazine and Historical Chronicle* observed in 1745, but what did it really mean? Taste was "a metaphor to express that Judgment each man forms to himself of those Things, which are not contain'd in any certain Rules," a metaphor based in the physical palate. Thus circles themselves "allow of no taste," but the colors they are drawn with depended on "personal" choice. But this did not seem to be the idea of taste that prompted the printing of this writer's remarks, almost certainly a reprint or paraphrasing of a contemporary British essay. After "all the Pains I have taken to find out what was meant by the Word," this author noted, "and whether those who use it oftenest had any clear Idea annex'd to it, I have only been able negatively to discover, that they do not mean their own natural Taste; but on the contrary, that they have sacrificed it to an imaginary one of which they can give no account. They build Houses in Taste, which they can't live with in Conveniency; they suffer with Impatience the Musick they pretend to hear with Rapture; and they even eat nothing they like, for the Sake of eating in Taste." In sum, this author bemoaned, the "Right of tasting for one's self, is now totally surrender'd."[44] "We constantly hear Talk of good and bad *Taste,* without well understanding the Meaning of such Terms," an article printed in the first issue of the *New England Magazine of Knowledge and Pleasure* observed in a similar vein in 1758. "A *good Taste* seems to be little else than *right Reason,* which we otherwise express by the Word *Judgment.*" But those who have earned the title of "men of taste" seem to lack this reason or judgment, enjoying things or claiming to enjoy them based not on personal liking but out of a social desire to seem tasteful, and so it would seem "a Man of TASTE is a Man of DIS-TASTE."[45] These were critiques of taste specifically articulated in the political language of the surrender of personal "rights" and "natural" judgments to the artificial and authoritarian standards of socially fashionable architects, composers, and chefs.

In its British manifestation the discourse on taste was dominated by provincial writers. Almost without fail, the aesthetic treatises imported into the colonies in the third quarter of the eighteenth century evinced a marked sense of British cultural inferiority relative to other European peoples (especially the French and Italians); the treatises were written to help compensate for and correct those feelings and to spur interest in the arts. One wonders how the perceived British inferiority played in a place like colonial America. But the relation between place and taste was crucial. Indeed, we should probably wonder why some of the most elaborate and systematic discussions of taste in the English-speaking world—by Hume, Burke, Gerard, Kames, and Blair—came from writers born outside or living outside of England. Quite often (but not always) these theories were the most rigid in their adherence to the cultural authority of a standard of taste, in their belief that—as Blair put it, in a book reprinted ten times in the United States between 1783 and 1800—it was absurd to think that "the Taste of a Hottentot or a Laplander is as delicate and as correct as that of a Longinus or an Addison."[46] The discourse on taste indirectly confronted the problems of provincial, national, and imperial unity, and this is one reason why taste may have been an interesting concept for political thinkers who came of age on the eve of the American Revolution.[47]

Why was the midcentury discourse of taste dominated by provincials? The question is tough to answer since it was never directly addressed. But one clue comes in the frequent appeal by some of these writers to the notion of the arts as a space for agreement and for the elimination of social and cultural difference. Writers who emerged from England's "cultural provinces" saw standards of taste and culture as a way of unifying a disparate imperial society, and this may have been an especially appealing notion during the period in which the key texts by Hume, Gerard, and Blair were written: the late 1750s, the moment of the Seven Years War.[48] Lord Kames, a Scottish jurist whose *Elements of Criticism* (1762) was widely available from booksellers in the American colonies, saw culture as the unifying arena for different classes within a state: "The separation of men into different classes, by birth, office, or occupation, however necessary, tends to relax the connection that ought to be among members of the same state; which bad effect is in some measure prevented by the access all ranks of people have to public spectacles, and to amusements that are best enjoyed in company. Such meetings, where every one partakes of the same pleasures in common, are no slight support to the social affections."[49] For James Ralph, agreement about culture could heal the divisions caused by political and theological controversy. "As we cannot reasonably expect to be ever all of a Mind, as to the Principles of Religion or Politicks," Ralph wrote in 1728, "I should be glad, we might in some Respect, be look'd upon as an united People; that we may at least agree in Singing and Dancing."[50] John Swanwick's "POEM, On the Prospect of seeing the fine ARTS flourish in AMERICA," included as an appendix to his *Thoughts on Education, Addressed to the Visitors of the Young Ladies' Academy in Philadelphia, October 31, 1787,* de-

scribed culture as unifying political parties. Swanwick looked forward
to the day when "all the arts that minister to life,/ Expell for ever, party
feuds, and strife," and he specifically described women as agents in the
creation of consensus through art and culture.[51]

Fashion and Faction

The anxiety over the union of tastes in culture may indeed have been
prompted by an anxiety about the strained possibility of union in an imperial polity, especially in the context and aftermath of the Seven Years
War, but both worries revealed a similar preoccupation with consensus.
These anxieties and this preoccupation, in turn, rested on a still more
foundational political uncertainty: the relationship between society and
the state. Do political constitutions conform to people, or people to political constitutions? This was the implicit question of Samuel Dickinson's 1797 oration as well as countless statements by other writers in the
last decades of the eighteenth century. Dickinson's answer was as typical as it was unsatisfying: there must be a balance between government
and social manners and taste; when one progresses or declines too rapidly, constitutional crisis ensues.[52] The suitability of the document for the
people was a constant theme of the Constitutional Convention.[53] During the debates over the ratification of the Constitution, Anti-Federalists
often quoted Montesquieu to the same effect: "The excellent Montesquieu himself observes, that 'the manners and customs of the people
have an intimate connection with their laws,'" one Pennsylvanian Anti-
Federalist wrote in October 1787. Hence the "question which should be
agitated is not whether the proposed constitution be better or worse than
those that have from time to time existed; but whether it be in every respect adapted to secure our liberty and happiness at the *present stage* of
the world."[54]

The connection between social refinement and "constitutional taste"
was a common theme. In an oration in July 1787, just as the Constitutional Convention was meeting in Philadelphia, the poet Joel Barlow
told an audience in Hartford, Connecticut, that all previous constitutions had failed because they had not adapted the government to the corresponding "state of social refinement." Barlow made a similar point in
a prose digression on the Peruvian lawgiver Manco Capac in his long
poem *The Vision of Columbus* (also published in 1787), when he criti-

cized ancient constitution writers for thinking that a constitution alone could civilize a barbarous people.[55] And the poet had even written his legal dissertation in 1786 on this very subject: the connection of the law to the state of society. Others in 1787, such as a Baltimore poet who published under the pseudonym "Augustus Chatterton," thought that "refinements of Art" should go hand in hand with "refinements of Government." Americans, he claimed, deserved a culture and society as refined as their politics.[56] Reciprocally, John Adams in London in 1787 wondered how modern European civilization had become as refined as it had, since it clearly knew nothing about political refinement.[57] Still others celebrated the relatively unrefined state of America. "In the present age, our Country is in a medium between Barbarity and Refinement," one Massachusetts minister remarked in 1787. "In such an age, the minds of men are strong and vigorous, being neither enfeebled by luxury, nor shackled by authority."[58] But even if a state of refinement seemed desirable to some politicians and poets, "refinement" was primarily a pejorative term in 1787 and 1788. Whenever the word appears in *The Federalist* papers, to measure one political barometer, the intent is generally to malign some "erroneous theory" by questioning its utility: refinement means overrefinement.[59]

The word "refine" carries a positive meaning only once in *The Federalist,* in Madison's famous analysis of the relationship between faction and geographic space. The positive connotation of "refine" in *Federalist* no. 10 highlights the significance of expertise in the Federalist conception of the national government. Madison argues that representation forms the chief difference between a democracy and a republic. In a democracy the people speak for themselves. But in a republic the effect of representation is to "refine and enlarge the public views" by mediating them through enlightened statesmen. "Under such a regulation," Madison suggests, "it may well happen that the public voice pronounced by the representatives of the people, will be more consonant to the public good, than if pronounced by the people themselves convened for the purpose." But Madison acknowledged that it was equally probable that the public voice would be mispronounced, and hence other safeguards were necessary. While no constitution could guarantee the election of enlightened statesmen, an extensive geographic territory could ensure a diversity of interests, and it was this diversity that made it probable that a representative assembly would never be composed of potentially tyrannous majorities eager to invade the rights of minorities.[60] Madison's theory mediated between two notions of taste and politics: it embraced the older authoritarian ideas about enlightened standards for judgment even as it repudiated received ideas about the blessings of consensus.

In a society in which fashions changed rapidly, Madison would later argue, diversity was as necessary in taste as it was in government. As Madison observed in a 1792 newspaper article on "Fashion," a unified taste led to unity in manufacturing, leaving whole sections of the economy dependent on changes in fashion. Madison specifically described the suffering of a group of bucklemakers in Birmingham, England, after the market for shoe buckles had suddenly collapsed in 1786, the result of a craze for slippers and shoes tied with laces. Madison wrote in partial sympathy for the 20,000 Birmingham bucklemakers who had petitioned the prince in 1791 for redress, but the moral he drew from their plight was that American cities should not base their entire economies on a single frivolous item.[61] Madison's "Fashion" essay was hardly novel in its theoretical assumptions about the politics of personal and social preferences. It built on at least two decades' worth of remarks in the press about the political effects of imported British fashions, remarks that specifically theorized the political dimensions of female consumption.

The discourse of refinement was as politicized as it was politicizing, bringing new agents into politics by investing their tastes with an immediate political dimension. In 1787 the Federalist Noah Webster worried about the "pernicious effects of introducing foreign manners" and "false taste." "By attaching ourselves to foreign manners," he argued, "we counteract the good effects of the revolution, or rather render them incomplete. A revolution in the form of government, is but a revolution in name; unless attended with a change of principles and manners, which are the springs of government." Although changes in British fashion might seem like mere whimsy to outsiders, Webster explained them as "highly political," part of a "wise systematic policy" that allowed British manufacturers to continue to eat by continuing to produce for an ever-unsatisfied market. It made no sense, then, for Americans to purchase British products, and Webster specifically called upon American women to forgo foreign fashion. "Have the ladies of America . . . no taste?" he asked. Writing at the moment of the framing of the Constitution, Webster granted women the role of supreme legislator and lawgiver. "When the ladies shall exercise the rights of their sex, and say, we will give the laws of fashion to our *own nation,* instead of receiving them from *another,*" Webster concluded, the United States would realize "a new species of independence."[62] Or as David Daggett of New Haven put it to the women present at his Fourth of July oration in 1787: "You can establish fashions, or destroy them, by a single smile or a frown. It is with you to promote oeconomy and industry, or luxury and extravagance at your pleasure.—By attending to the former, you will yield an essential service to your country."[63]

Fashion was a tyrant that could only be overthrown by women. In August 1787, Tench Coxe told the nascent Society for the Encouragement of Manufactures and the Useful Arts that the United States needed to be rescued from "the tyranny of foreign fashions, and the destructive torrent of luxury."[64] In the rhetoric of the day, the importation of luxury items had made Americans "slaves to foreign masters."[65] Instead of paying debts, Joseph Lyman told the Massachusetts government in 1787, we have bought "exotic dress" and "the expensive productions of foreign regions, and thus are become the servants of foreigners, and strangers rule over us." We are now, Lyman concluded, in "a state of servility and dependence."[66] The narrator of Peter Markoe's *Algerine Spy in Pennsylvania* (1787) observed that "there are three sorts of tyranny; the first civil; the second ecclesiastical; the third I shall call the tyranny of *fashion*. . . . The Pennsylvanians have known but little of the first, and nothing of the second; but the greater part of them is grievously oppressed by the last." The "origin of fashion" might be traced to Eve, the spy continued, but it crept into all societies who chose to "dismiss simplicity and call in art."[67] *The Virginia Almanack* for 1788 carried two brief anecdotes in which Solon, the Athenian lawgiver, and Alexander the Great both traced fashion to its source: "The art of dress did ne'er begin, / Till Eve our mother learnt to sin."[68] Not all of the discourse on the politics of fashion was directed at women, as an article on "a Beau's Dressing Room" in the *Columbian Magazine* made clear, but most of it was.[69] In a poem addressed to young women republished in Philadelphia in 1787, the British poet John Fry asked, "How can you ever be at ease,/ When no invented mode can please/ When once it's common grown?"[70] An almanac from New Jersey for 1788 advised women and men to "never be either the first or the last to follow the fashions."[71] And Benjamin Rush in 1787 argued that fashion was a tool for the subjection of women created specifically by men. "I have sometimes been led to ascribe the invention of ridiculous and expensive fashions in female dress entirely to the gentlemen, in order to divert the ladies from improving their minds, and thereby to secure a more arbitrary and unlimited authority over them." "The very expensive prints of female dresses which are published annually in France," he noted in a conspiratorial aside, "are invented and executed wholly by GENTLEMEN."[72]

Short print pieces suggested that the attempts to police or politicize fashions were no better than the laughable idea of medieval-style sumptuary laws, but orators frequently stressed that women earned a part in politics through acts of self-denial.[73] Women were an especially sensitive gauge of a society's standing. In his *Thoughts upon Female Education* (1787), Benjamin Rush noted that "in the ordinary course of human affairs, we shall probably too soon follow the footsteps of the nations of Europe in manners and vices. The first marks we shall perceive of our declension, will appear among our women."[74] And as Robert Davidson, a minister and professor of history and belles lettres at Dickinson College, told "a brilliant circle of patriotic ladies, and a number of gentlemen" on July 4, 1787, in Carlisle, Pennsylvania, "the daughters of America . . . deny themselves many things, the produce of foreign climes, which custom had taught them to consider as part of the necessaries of life."[75] In May 1787 the Reverend Elizur Goodrich reported to Connecticut lawmakers that "the necessity of the times has begun to work its own relief. . . . the distaff, the wheel and loom are becoming more fashionable—the shops of trifling baubles and gewgaws are less crouded."[76] Or as another Philadelphia writer observed in respect to the ratification of the proposed Constitution in October 1787, "Ye mothers, wives, daughters and sisters of America! . . . your influence in every civilized society is like the vernal sun, and the gentle rains of May. Your prudence, frugality and taste are of peculiar importance in the present exigency."[77]

The question of female cultural consumption was debated by Benjamin Rush and John Swanwick in separately published discourses delivered at the Young Ladies Academy in Philadelphia in 1787. Rush's *Thoughts upon Female Education, Accommodated to the Present State of Society, Manners, and Government, In the United States of America,* published that same year, argued against novel reading, since most British novels described an overly refined social state, and against music education, since it was costly and tended to distract from other studies. Instrumental music was "by no means accommodated to the present state of society and manners in America. The price of musical instruments, and the extravagant fees demanded by the teachers of instrumental music, form but a small part of my objections to it. To perform well, upon a musical instrument, requires much time and long practice. From two to four hours in a day, for three or four years . . . How many useful ideas might be picked up in these hours from history, philosophy, poetry, and the numerous moral essays." And how many harpsichords had become sideboards for their parlors after marriage?[78]

Arguing against Rush's *Thoughts* at the same school three months later, John Swanwick claimed that the academy should "add to the useful, the ornamental endowments of the mind," especially music. Swanwick dedicated his own *Thoughts on Education* (1787) to Benjamin Franklin, who had invented the glass armonica and was "the proper patron of the Fine Arts in Pennsylvania." In late 1786 Charles Willson Peale described Swanwick himself as "a friend to the arts"; and Swanwick financed Peale's exhibition of a collection of Italian paintings (the first in the country) in Philadelphia during the summer of 1787. Swanwick was a successful merchant and investor in the Bank of the United States. Though he lacked formal education himself, he had little trouble prescribing it for others. Swanwick believed young women should be able to play a few tunes on the guitar without great expense, and that they should be taught to dance, draw, and speak French, all of which Rush had defined in opposition to the present state of society in the United States.[79] In the "POEM, On the Prospect of seeing the fine ARTS flourish in AMERICA" appended to his essay, Swanwick wrote that it was:

> [C]hiefly you, ye fair! whom heav'n decrees,
> To charm, to soften, captivate, and please;
> To you belongs the pencil, and the lyre,
> The taste to fashion, and the soul t' inspire,
> The sad to chear, the thoughtless to restrain,
> To urge the timid, and to check the vain;
> Great is the pow'r of these engaging arts,
> To guide the passions, and to conquer hearts.

"These are the spheres of your supreme controul," Swanwick concluded.[80]

If women did not participate in politics directly, their political influence was often celebrated as an extension of their good taste. "How often," James Fordyce noted in *Sermons to Young Women* (1787), "have I seen a company of men who were disposed to be riotous, checked all at once into decency, by the accidental entrance of an amiable woman."[81] "It is the conversation of Women," the author of *The Polite Philosopher*

(1787) argued, "that gives a proper bias to our inclinations, and, by abating the Ferocity of our passions, engages us to that Gentleness of deportment which we stile Humanity."[82] The lawyer and Rhode Island congressman James Mitchell Varnum, in a 1787 preface to his plea in *Trevett v. Weeden,* observed: "It is customary, in some countries, for the ladies to attend upon the trial of popular causes. What an excellent practice, and how admirably calculated to produce elegance of sentiment, delicacy of expression, and a polite address!—It is true, the presence of the fair sex may excite diffidence in the young practicioner; but how amiable is diffidence, how charming is modesty, in opposition to those ridiculous airs, which give to impudence an appearance of knowledge, and to pertness of speech the resemblance of elocution." Currently, trial speech was full of inaccuracy, absurdity and "scurrility itself."[83] In his *Thoughts upon Female Education,* Benjamin Rush noted that a "philosopher once said 'let me make all the ballads of a country and I care not who makes the laws.' He might with more propriety have said, let the ladies of a country be educated properly, and they will not only make and administer its laws, but form its manners and character."[84] Education held out the promise of female equality in politics, but Rush's analogy to the significance of ballads over laws suggested that the primary duties of the female legislator would be to codify the laws of manners and taste.

Taste and the Ratification of the Constitution

"There is a taste in government as well as the polite arts," the narrator of Peter Markoe's *The Algerine Spy in Pennsylvania* observed in 1787. Noting that American political practice too often stretched itself to apply the models of European political theory, he observed that Americans were "too often captivated by the brilliancy of the colours." After all, "Who is not soothed by the splendid dreams of Plato and Rousseau? Who is not roused by the thunder of Demosthenes and Cicero?" "But in all matters, which involve the welfare of nations," the spy insisted, "fancy should be restrained and judgment alone consulted."[85] Ratification of the Constitution often involved an appeal to fancy, a refashioning of political consent on the model of aesthetic consent. In the final section of this chapter, I turn to consider one example of the entry of taste into the debates over the Constitution. The Constitution may not have been ratified without certain appeals to taste, but the effect of this strategy renders it difficult to make specific claims about the understanding of the Constitution at the moment of its adoption.

In October 1787, Noah Webster wrote a pamphlet in favor of the proposed Federal Constitution that brought the issue of constitutional taste to the center of debates over ratification. Webster—a lawyer by training, a schoolteacher and author by profession—had personal economic reasons for supporting the Constitution: the clause empowering Congress to protect the rights of authors and inventors (Article I, section 8) would help secure his "literary property" from legal piracy by unifying and nationalizing copyright laws.[86] Webster did not mention the copyright clause, and (following custom) he did not credit himself as the author of his *Examination into the Leading Principles of the Federal Constitution*. Instead, publishing under the pseudonym "A Citizen of America," Webster made the common argument that republican citizens should cancel out personal interests when reflecting on political matters. He modeled this for readers by supporting the text as a whole despite claiming to have reservations about one particular clause. It was, he argued, "absurd for a man to oppose the adoption of this constitution, because *he* thinks some part of it defective or exceptionable." "Let every man be at liberty to expunge what *he* judges exceptionable," the "Citizen" predicted, "and not a syllable of the constitution will survive the scrutiny." In fact, Webster argued, criticism of parts of the Constitution should yield to a consideration of the aesthetic totality of the text, and he offered an anecdote illustrating this concept:

A painter, after executing a masterly piece, requested every spectator to draw a pencil over the part that did not please him; but to his surprise, he soon found the *whole piece* defaced. Let every man examine the most perfect building by his *own* taste, and like some microscopic critics, condemn the whole for small deviations from the rules of architecture, and not a part of the *best* constructed fabric would escape. But let *any* man take a *comprehensive view* of the whole, and he will be pleased with the general beauty and proportions, and admire the structure.

"The same remarks," Webster concluded, "apply to the new constitution."[87]

Paintings and buildings may seem like odd sites for national consensus, especially given the state of American cultural production in 1787, but Webster was hardly alone in appealing to the beauty of the text in

1787 and 1788. It is, however, slightly ironic that it was Webster who advocated a "comprehensive view" of the written document. The "Citizen of America" may have been a Federalist, but Webster made a living as a "microscopic critic." He was not the kind of reader to pass over a piece of writing uncorrected or uncondemned. In editions of his textbooks published in Hartford and Philadelphia in 1787 (textbooks calculated to "refine the Taste" by exposing young readers to the writings of moralists and statesmen) he showed—far beyond the point of pedantry—how the style of any sentence could be improved. If Addison's prose could be more polished, if Swift's syntax could be smoother, then surely Webster must have struggled to keep from criticizing the infelicitous and ambiguous phrasings within the text of the Constitution.[88] Webster perhaps withheld such judgments because he knew that critics of the Constitution objected to certain clauses in the text not because they disliked the literary style in itself, but because they disliked the political implications of the Constitution's literary style, or rather because they worried that the Constitution's purposefully ambiguous statements ("necessary and proper," "general welfare") would generate powers for the federal government as potentially limitless as if no textual boundaries existed at all.

What exactly governed Webster's choice of metaphors? Why did he ask readers to consider the text of the Constitution as if it were a painting or a piece of architecture? On the most basic level, Webster may have been led by the linguistic association of terms like "frame" and "framing," words that signified in architecture and painting as well as constitutional politics. As one Pennsylvanian constitutional theorist in 1776 explained, "Men entrusted with the formation of civil constitutions should remember they are *painting for eternity;* that the smallest defect or redundancy in the system they frame may prove the destruction of millions."[89] Bombastic statements like these—could a "defect" in a painting *really* prove the destruction of millions?—took the static and permanent (or antievolutionary) nature of constitutions as their starting point, but they also consciously figured the framers of constitutions as creative artists. While the word "frame" had a long history in colonial charters and compacts (where it sometimes explicitly referenced the "frame" of a body) and multiple meanings in the second half of the eighteenth century, it almost always signified culturally rather than legally.[90] In weaving, a frame was the support of a loom over which and by which a fabric was created; in painting, a frame might be both the hidden support of a canvas and the decorative border surrounding the finished product; in architecture, a frame was both the supporting structure (or "skeleton") of a building and a synonym for the exterior of a wood building itself. In other words, the term was usefully ambiguous, describing at once the means of production as well as the interior beginnings and exterior endings of a cultural product. Webster's description of the Constitution as a visual object, then, would not have been incomprehensible to his audience, even to readers in Pennsylvania who had (by Section 15 of the Pennsylvania Constitution of 1776, which declared that bills would be "printed for consideration by the people" before being passed into law by the legislature) functioned more or less as the kind of critics described in Webster's anecdote.

Webster's move from verbal Constitution to visual object transformed citizens into "spectators," a category of being in the eighteenth century that did not necessarily imply passive disengagement but often involved an active and conscious distancing of oneself from the object to be contemplated. As an unattributed maxim in an almanac published in New York state in late 1787 put it: "To be a spectator one must not be in a bustle of the world, but at a certain distance; as to observe a regiment march, one must be on a line where they file off, not in the ranks."[91] It is important to note that Webster wants his reader to become not just a spectator, but a reverential beholder: a beholder who can recognize a "masterly piece" and treat it with distant reverence instead of physical defacement or carping microscopic condemnations. He is not calling for the creation of the citizen as connoisseur, if connoisseurship implies anything beyond an appreciation of "the general beauty and proportions" and "the structure" of an object. Webster's citizen-spectator should avoid criticizing objects of aesthetic contemplation on the basis of either systematic "rules" of art or "his own taste." To judge objects this way would be to prejudge them.

Webster's appeal to a sense of beauty available to anyone and based in common consent paralleled a decline in appeals to theoretical authorities for legitimacy in political argumentation. If we compare the number of footnotes, for instance, in the revolutionary pamphlets of the 1760s with similar essays on the Constitution, we find a decrease in citations and a corresponding increase in reliance on ideas of "experience," whether that concept was understood as national or personal.[92] Webster himself claimed in his pamphlet that "experience is the best instructor—it is better than a thousand theories," and the sentiment was shared with many other writers in the period.[93] But, above all, Webster's male citizen-spectator, like republicans generally, should be able to cancel out or suppress subjective judgments (what *"he* thinks . . . defective" or what *"he* judges exceptionable") and take pleasure in a *"comprehensive view"* of the total object. The use of "masterly" paintings or "perfect buildings" as analogues to the Constitution raises empirical questions beyond both the immediate concerns of this chapter and the present limits of historical knowledge: How available were original paintings or examples of perfect architecture in 1787? Who had seen them and where?[94] It also prompts theoretical questions more pertinent here: What was involved in the commodification suggested by Webster's analogy between constitutions and art objects? And, more significantly, is aesthetic pleasure the proper response to a political document?

It is not ultimately surprising that Webster adopted a rhetorical ratification strategy that compared the Constitution to paintings and buildings, aesthetic totalities that could only be appreciated or dismissed from a "comprehensive view" of their overall effect. To the great dismay of its critics and some of its framers, the Constitution itself could only be ratified or rejected as a whole, which can make determining the original meaning or understanding of specific clauses an imprecise exercise at best.[95] Edmund Randolph, the governor of Virginia and one of the few delegates to the Constitutional Convention who declined to sign the document, objected that the state ratifying conventions "must either adopt the constitution in the whole, or reject it in the whole," contending that "the criticism of the world" should be able to contribute to the finished product, not simply reflect on it as it stood.[96] But like Webster's painting and building, the Constitution had to be appreciated or condemned as a totality; citizens were not free, like the critical spectators in Webster's anecdote, to perform revisionary acts of defacement. Readers, Webster's anecdote suggested, should encounter the text without pencils in their hands. They should consider themselves, in other words, as readers rather than writers. For its supporters—who often claimed that the document was not perfect, but merely a "more perfect" version of the Articles of Confederation—the Constitution had to be considered at a level of generality, as a total object greater than the sum of its parts. To dwell on this or that clause, to subject it to "deviations from the rules" of political science (rules that stated that republics could exist only within a limited geographic space), meant losing the chance to take a more pleasing "comprehensive view" of the whole.

The idea that works of art should be considered as rounded wholes was currently being enshrined in such contemporary European aesthetic treatises as Karl Philipp Moritz's 1788 *On the Plastic Imitation of the Beautiful* (*Uber die bildende Nachahmung des Schönen*), and would reach its apex in Kantian aesthetics after 1790, but the conception of art and architecture as objects that should be appreciated at a level of generality was widespread.[97] The author of *The Polite Philosopher,* a moral essay reprinted in Boston in 1787, insisted that "Behaviour is like architecture; the Symmetry of the whole pleases us so much, that we examine not into its parts."[98] "Beauty, in architecture, painting, and other arts," the editors of the *Encyclopedia Britannica* wrote in 1771, summarizing received wisdom, "is the harmony and justness of the whole composition taken together."[99] Palladian architecture, comparing buildings to organic bodies, stressed that "beauty will result from the form and correspondence of the whole, with respect to the several parts, of the parts with regard to each other, and again to the whole; that the structure may appear an entire and compleat body, wherein each member agrees with the other."[100] While Alexander Hamilton would argue in 1788 that it was "time only that can mature and perfect so compound a system, can liquidate the meaning of all the parts, and can adjust them to each other in a harmonious and consistent whole," Webster announced in 1787 that it was only by reflecting on the whole that the work could and should be appreciated or even understood.[101]

Aestheticization of the document may have been a necessary and strategic effect of the process of ratification, but it was not an uncontested one. Webster's comparison of the Constitution with works of art did not go unnoticed by "microscopic critics" of the proposed Constitution. In a November 1787 pamphlet, a "Federal Republican" in Philadelphia (the author remains unidentified) charged that many Federalist arguments lacked reason. The "Federal Republican" described one glib Federalist essay as patently "ridiculous," suggesting that the author was "no doubt a friend to Shaftsbury's position, and feels that it is easier to *laugh* than to *reason*." And as for Webster:

> The good natured simularity which the citizen of America discovered between this constitution and a piece of painting, is perfectly erroneous. All painting is addressed to the *sense* and relished by *taste* which is various and fluctuating—but this constitution is addressed to the *understanding,* and judged of by *reason* which is fixed and true.

The "Federal Republican" opposed the Constitution as it existed on paper at that time, and proposed that the state ratifying conventions be

allowed to revise, correct, and amend the text before sending it to another general convention. But curiously, while the "Federal Republican"
rejected Webster's art analogy as "erroneous," he saw no such error in
thinking about the proposed government as a body. "If a perfect con-
solidation of the States is to take place, if the people are to become the
source of power, and if Congress is to represent them as the head of this
grand body politic," he suggested, "in the name of all that is dear to freemen, permit not the veins through which the life of government itself is
to flow from the *heart* to the *head,* be any way obstructed—let the passages be free & open [so] that *vital* heat may *animate* every *limb.*"[102] If
head (Congress) and heart (We the People) were ever to be reconciled,
this writer argued in the older body-politic thinking, the Constitution
would have to provide a better circulatory system, not be a better building or a finer painting.

The critique of Webster's "good natured simularity" by the "Federal
Republican" rested on standard, if sometimes contested, philosophical distinctions. Objects as different as constitutions and paintings demanded the use of different critical faculties. The Constitution, as a rational abstraction, could be said to bypass sense and operate directly
on the understanding. (An engraving from 1795 entitled "Taste under
the Influence of Wisdom" [fig. 10] in which Minerva towers over a bare-
breasted allegorical figure suggested that the conflict of the faculties was
acute, especially in a world in which sense and sensuality were the primary inlet to the understanding.) Although Webster had specifically argued against anyone judging on the basis of "his own taste," the "Federal Republican" maintained that considering the Constitution as a work
of art meant accepting or rejecting it on the "various and fluctuating"
whimsy of taste, and the "Federal Republican" believed taste rested on
the unstable ground of individual particularity. So explained the anonymous author of "TRUTH and TASTE," a brief article published in the
same October 1787 issue of the *Columbian Magazine* as the proposed
Constitution and the same month as the exchange between Webster and
the "Federal Republican":

> TRUTH is disputable, not taste: what exist[s] in the nature of things is the
> standard of our judgment; what each man feels within himself is the standard
> of sentiment. Propositions in geometry may be proved, systems in physic may
> be controverted; but the harmony of verse, the tenderness of passion, the bril-
> liancy of wit, must give immediate pleasure. No man reasons concerning an-
> other man's beauty.[103]

TASTE *under the* INFLUENCE *of* WISDOM.

FIGURE 10. James Thackara, "Taste under the Influence of Wisdom," from *The Literary Miscellany* (Philadelphia, 1795). Courtesy of the Historical Society of Pennsylvania (Am 1795 Lit Api795 W74).

For the "Federal Republican," the Constitution was like geometry, but for Webster the document was more like an art object, an object that should give "immediate pleasure."

But could beauty be the foundation for national politics? And, if it could, who would judge it? Personal beauty—beauty reified—was described as dangerous and seductive to the observer, and potentially ruinous to the possessor, as in the 1787 poem "The Fate of Beauty; or the Involuntary Prostitute, A True Story."[104] Madison admitted that the Constitution lacked the perfect "beauty of form" characteristic of Montesquieu's theories, but he argued that the latter had been based on the mistaken assumption that the British Constitution was a "perfect model" rather than simply one example.[105] The Constitution announced that it would form a "more perfect" union than the Articles had, but the lack of perfection in the document itself was routinely conceded. "Perfection is not the lot of humanity," Webster admitted.[106] And as a New York Federalist observed, "I will not presume to say, that a more perfect system might not have been fabricated;—but who expects perfection at once?— And it may be asked, *who are judges of it*? Few, I believe, who have leisure to study the nature of Government scientifically."[107] That government, like art, was a discourse closed off from most people was amply argued in 1787. "The *rights* of mankind are simple," Benjamin Rush argued in May 1787. "They require no learning to unfold them. They are better *felt*, than explained. Hence, in matters that relate to *liberty*, the mechanic and the philosopher, the farmer and the scholar, are all upon a footing. But the case is widely different with respect to *government*. It is a complicated science, and requires abilities and knowledge of a variety of other subjects, to understand it."[108] Some maintained that feeling always trumped reason, at least for the mass of the people. As one orator told the Massachusetts Society of the Cincinnati in July 1787, "mankind at large do not always reason: they are prone to imitation, are susceptible of injuries, and in their political conduct are generally, governed by their feelings."[109]

The mass of people were routinely described by their absence of thought and their malleability in the hands of artful statesmen. One almanac astrologer predicted that a 1787 eclipse would cause "designing factious knaves" to "persuade the unthinking to rise in opposition to the government, despising Rulers, Magistrates, and Judges."[110] This difference between political feeling and political reasoning meant that the choices of many counted for little. John Quincy Adams, for instance, accused Paine in 1791 of mistaking "power" for "right," pure choice for moral decision-making. Paine's contention in *Rights of Man* that "that which a whole nation chooses to do, it has a right to do" was clearly wrong since the "eternal and immutable laws of justice and of morality, are paramount to all human legislation." Governments could be dismantled and reformed only when they were judged to be incompetent. But "Who is to judge of this incompetency"? It was, Adams conceded, the people who should judge, but they must act from "principle" and not from "passion."[111] If government was to be a product of "reflection and choice," as Alexander Hamilton put it in the first number of *The Federalist,* it was important that people be able to choose others who knew how to reflect and choose better than they could themselves.[112]

CHAPTER THREE

The Matter and Meaning
of Representation

What exactly should political representatives represent? James Wilson offered one answer to this perennial question in a speech on June 6, 1787, at the Constitutional Convention in Philadelphia. Wilson, a member of the Convention from Pennsylvania, addressed the immediate issue of who should elect representatives to the first (or "popular") branch of a national government: the people themselves or their state legislatures? The election of representatives in the "popular" branch went to the heart of attempts to revise the Articles of Confederation because it embraced a larger question of whether the national government would represent the states or the people. In 1787, under the Articles of Confederation, each state legislature annually appointed (and had the power to recall) between two and seven "delegates" to the Continental Congress; and each state delegation in Congress, regardless of the number of delegates or the size of the state, had one vote. Individual state legislatures had also appointed Wilson and his colleagues (who were more frequently called "deputies" than "delegates") to the Constitutional Convention itself.[1] The debate on June 6 began when Charles Pinckney of South Carolina proposed that the state legislatures should select what he termed (following British practice) the "members" of the "Commons." The "Virginia Plan" currently under consideration on June 6 proposed election by the people, but Pinckney and his supporters argued that the people were simply unfit to make such decisions and that

the states would never ratify a new constitution that so radically compromised their powers. In response to Pinckney's motion, the moderate nationalist Elbridge Gerry of Massachusetts proposed a compromise
scheme in which the state legislatures would "elect" the actual members
of the House after the people had selected double the number of representatives required. But Wilson argued that it would be wrong to leave
the election to the states even in a partial way. Since the states would be
rivals for both the power and the attachment of the people, state legislatures would inevitably elect representatives they could control. While
on other occasions James Wilson voiced the written sentiments of his
colleague, the ailing Benjamin Franklin, he spoke as and for himself on
June 6. But what, precisely, did he say?

Narrative histories of the Convention often blend the notes of individual members, producing a false coherence from fragmentary records
as well as a sense that the words preserved in those records represent the
voices (or even the intentions) of the speakers rather than the recorders. The notes from Wilson's speech of June 6 reveal that members of
the Convention employed different practices of notation, practices that
speak to their differing ideas about the concept of representation itself.
Three of the members present that day attempted to capture Wilson's
speech on paper. Rufus King of Massachusetts took down the first part
of Wilson's speech this way:

> Wilson contra—they shd. be appointed by the people you will then come
> nearer to the will or sense of the majority—the protrait [*sic*] is excellent in
> proportion to its being a good likeness.[2]

Robert Yates of New York recorded this part of the speech differently:

> Mr. Wilson is of opinion that the national legislative powers ought to flow im-
> mediately from the people, so as to contain all their understanding, and to be
> an exact transcript of their minds.[3]

And James Madison from Virginia took a longer note on Wilson's
speech:

> Mr. Wilson. He wished for vigor in the Govt. but he wished that vigourous au-
> thority to flow immediately from the legitimate source of all authority. Govt.
> ought to possess not only 1st. the *force*, but 2dly the *mind or sense* of the

people at large. The Legislature ought to be the most exact transcript of the whole Society. Representation is made necessary only because it is impossible for the people to act collectively.[4]

The debate notes for June 6 taken by three other members survive, but they tell us nothing about the substance of Wilson's speech. Alexander Hamilton of New York and William Pierce of Georgia (who made a speech supporting Wilson's position) made no mention of Wilson's speech on representation.[5] John Lansing, yet another New York member, did not attempt to record Wilson's speech but instead summarized the debate in this way:

> 4th Resolve—C. Pinkney [*sic*] moves—dele *People* and insert *Legislature*. Messrs. Wilson, Gerry, Sherman spoke in Favor of Amendment. Mr. Mason, Mr. Read, Mr. Dickinson and Mr. Maddison [*sic*] against it.[6]

Lansing may not have been listening, he may have made a clerical error, or Wilson's speech itself may have been ambiguous and confusing. In any event, Lansing's summary notes construed Wilson's speech as favoring the motion of "Pinkney" when the other recorders aligned him with "Maddison" and the opposition.[7]

Perhaps we can infer what Wilson meant more than we can know what he actually said about political representation. From the spare *Journal* of the Convention made by the official secretary William Jackson, we know the outcome of the vote on Pinckney's motion. While Pinckney found support primarily from other delegates from South Carolina (and from the delegations of the small states of Connecticut and New Jersey), Wilson mustered speeches from some of the most prominent delegates: John Dickinson of Delaware, famous for his pre-revolutionary *Letters from a Farmer in Pennsylvania* (1767); George Mason of Virginia, the chief author of the widely acclaimed Virginia Declaration of Rights (1776); and James Madison, the author of the "Virginia Plan" that Pinckney had challenged. If the notes he took of his own speech are accurate, Madison used Pinckney's motion to test an early version of the arguments he would publish in November as *Federalist* no. 10.[8] In any event, Pinckney's motion to have the state legislatures elect representatives failed in a vote of 8 states to 3 (Connecticut, New Jersey, and South Carolina). The final draft of Article I, section 2 of the Constitution expressed the outcome of this debate, and Pinckney remained bitter about his defeated motion. During the popular elections for the first House of Representatives in January 1789, Pinckney wrote to Rufus King that this method of election was "the greatest blot in the constitution." In a letter to Madison two months later, just before Pinckney became governor of South Carolina, he restated his opinion that the claim that the people would be better represented by representatives of their own choosing was "theoretical nonsense."[9]

Wilson's speech and the ensuing vote settled the issue of who would be represented ("the people" rather than the states) but left open the question of what exactly about the people would be represented in the House of Representatives. The notetakers who recorded Wilson's speech all belonged to delegations that sided with him in the vote. As the brief examples from their notes show, each had a different idea about how best to represent speech, and each produced a slightly different account. The notes by King, Yates, and Madison suggest that Wilson may have used at least two primary metaphors for the representation of the people, or that these notetakers summarized Wilson with the metaphors for popular representation that each found most persuasive. King recorded that a representative assembly should represent the "will" or "sense" of the people in the way an excellent "portrait" is a good "likeness." On the other hand, Yates wrote down that a representative assembly should be an "exact transcript" of the "minds" of the people, and Madison wrote down that the House of Representatives should be an "exact transcript of the whole Society." It was variously an abstraction—the "will," the "sense," the "understanding," or the "mind(s)" of the people— that was to be represented, but the models for representation and for representatives themselves referenced material objects: portraits and transcripts.

Was there any real difference between imagining the House of Representatives as a portrait or a transcript of the people? If he did use both metaphors on June 6 (and we obviously cannot know for sure), Wilson may have been trying to build consensus among members by evoking two radically different conceptions of popular political representation. While Wilson may have used both (or possibly neither) of these metaphors in defending the idea of popular election during the Federal Convention, Federalists and Anti-Federalists employed these metaphors in divergent ways during the debates over ratification of the Constitution. On the most general and binary level, Anti-Federalists viewed representation as a poor substitute for the assembly of the body of the people themselves. Anti-Federalists tended to use metaphors based on pictorial ideas about "likeness," describing representative assemblies as "miniature portraits" of the people at large. Even as their rhetoric constructed the ideal representative assembly as a material object, Anti-Federalists also celebrated the potential for sympathetic identification between representative and represented, especially by members of the same classes or occupations. Federalists, on the other hand, saw representation as an opportunity for legislative excellence of a kind that would be impossible if the whole body of the people assembled—or even if a large number of representatives assembled. Federalists regularly dismissed the Anti-Federalist call for representatives who sympathized with their constituents or who resembled the different classes of the people. Their metaphors for representation highlighted the mental expertise of the representative not just in making laws but in taking a transcript of the "public mind" and in pronouncing the "public voice" (as Madison put it in *Federalist* no. 10) better than "if pronounced by the people themselves" in person.[10]

Neither of these ideas about representation was encoded into the language of Article I of the Constitution, but to understand the original meanings of representation we need to know what and how these metaphors signified in 1787 and 1788. This chapter considers the material referents behind the metaphors of image and voice in political representation, looking especially at miniature painting and shorthand transcription. The political metaphors may have competed in 1787 and 1788, but they are not perhaps as fundamentally different as they first appear or as political historians have sometimes made them out to be. The material referents of transcripts and portrait miniatures shared a common language of eighteenth-century representation—the language of "taking"—as well as an aesthetics of smallness. In advertising their services, miniature painters promised to "take" a likeness of a sitter; writing masters similarly offered to teach anyone how to "take" down the words of a speaker, and the title pages of published transcriptions often mentioned that they had been "taken in shorthand." Whatever the idea of representing the mind(s), sense, understanding, or will of the people may have meant, capturing voice and capturing image were not radically different projects. Those who wished to represent image and those who tried to represent voice shared a cultural obsession about the best way to take down their original, an obsession that was encoded in the framers' attempts to produce and reproduce the people.

Portraits in Miniature

In his brief pamphlet *Thoughts on Government, Applicable to the Present State of the American Colonies. In a Letter from a Gentleman to a Friend* printed in Philadelphia and Boston in 1776, John Adams argued that an ideal representative assembly "should be in miniature, an exact portrait of the people at large. It should think, feel, reason, and act like them."[11] Whatever Adams may have meant in the immediate context of advising his friends in southern colonies on drafting new state constitutions, his metaphor of representation as miniature portrait has achieved an emblematic status in modern theoretical discussions of political representation. Political scientist Hanna Pitkin cites Adams's remark as typical of what she calls "descriptive representation." This category of representation privileges the resemblance or correspondence between a representative, considered as a copy, and the original thing represented. In Pitkin's account, descriptive representatives "stand for" their constituents rather than "act for" them. In descriptive representation, form trumps function; that is, people who desire resemblance between representative and represented believe a representative assembly is more important for how it is composed than for what it does.[12] Following Pitkin, historian and narrative theorist F. R. Ankersmit has recently invoked Adams's remark as an example of what he calls the "mimetic theory" of representation, a theory in which the identity of the representative and the person represented is the ideal. Ankersmit contrasts mimetic representation unfavorably with "aesthetic representation," a theory that acknowledges the difference of identity or the aesthetic "gap" between representative and represented. According to Ankersmit, the aesthetic theory of representation supplanted the mimetic theory in Europe and America around 1800. While the aesthetic theory holds the most promise for healthy states, Ankersmit argues, the mimetic theory has led (in the hands of the Nazis) to totalitarianism.[13]

Neither Pitkin nor Ankersmit are particularly interested in Adams or American political philosophy, and both regard his statement with more than a hint of distaste. But both cite his miniature portrait metaphor as the first (and hence most representative?) example of their categories. Pitkin goes further than Ankersmit, construing Adams's metaphor as both typical of American political thought during the late eighteenth century and as representative of the thought of the framers of the Constitution. We should question, however, both the status of Adams's remark as representative of his period and the status of Adams as someone for whom Pitkin's and Ankersmit's categories are entirely appropriate. Significantly, both Pitkin and Ankersmit focus on the first half of Adams's remark, specifically on the invocation of miniature painting as a model for political representation, but neither problematize the status of painting in the eighteenth century as a vehicle for realist representation. More important, neither theorist fully relates the second half of his remark (that representatives should "think, feel, reason, and act like" the people) to the first.

Studies focusing more specifically on American ideas of representation have also tended to use Adams's sentences as an example of one side of two competing ideas about political representation. In this case Adams's miniature portrait metaphor functions not as an instance of "mimetic" or "descriptive" representation, but as the best example of "actual" representation. The linguistic distinction between "actual" representation and "virtual" representation originated in the immediate constitutional conflict of the American Revolution. Apologists for the British Parliament argued that the American colonists were virtually represented by Parliament in the same way that British subjects who did not actually elect members of Parliament were represented.[14] Political historians have suggested that the miniature portrait metaphor was both an innovative and, in a sense, representative maxim of American political thought, but they have been hard-pressed to explain the cultural motivations behind Adams's metaphor.[15] Adams's remarks may have reflected long-held assumptions about political representation, particularly in Massachusetts, but his metaphor of miniature portrait cast these assumptions in a relatively new language of aesthetic likeness.

The connection between aesthetic and political representation has become both an object and a commonplace of contemporary critical thought. Beyond a shared vocabulary, however, this connection can sometimes seem overly clever or unconvincing, a structural homology with little real substance to offer social historians or students of political thought.[16] But Adams's metaphor provides an opportunity to examine the relationship between aesthetic and political representation at a particular historical and social moment. I will argue that Adams's metaphor was more than an offhand or eccentric way of conceiving the relationship between a representative assembly and its constituency. By scrutinizing the ideologies inhering in the persistent analogy between visual and political representation in the period, I intend to show that certain aesthetic assumptions about likeness, resemblance, and form structured American political thought at its foundational moment. The issues cluster around a set of basic questions: What made painting a model for political representation? What did Adams and others mean by comparing dynamic political assemblies to static visual images? What did the specific terms "portrait" and "miniature" signify in the period? Were miniature portraits "aesthetic" objects, and for whom? What did "likeness" really mean? And how, ultimately, was a politics based on "likeness" understood?

Adams felt no need to elaborate precisely what he meant by the metaphor, and it is difficult to interpret it from the immediate context of his 1776 pamphlet. Adams began his discussion of representation in a fashion that would become typical, by acknowledging that in a large society "it is impossible that the whole should assemble, to make laws." Before the publication of *Thoughts* in April 1776, Adams sent slightly different versions of his remarks to William Hooper and John Penn, fellow delegates to the Continental Congress who were to be involved in drafting the North Carolina state constitution. Both of these letters use the miniature portrait metaphor but contextualize it in slightly different ways. In the letter sent to Hooper, Adams uses the miniature metaphor as a contrast to his explanation of why the "whole Body" of the people could never assemble—"They would be too numerous. They could not afford the Time or Expense."[17] To Penn he explained that the "most natural Substitute for an Assembly of the whole, is a Delegation of Power, from the Many, to a few of the most wise and virtuous."[18] And, in the published version, Adams argued that the first step in forming a representative assembly was "to depute power from the many, to a few of the most wise and good."[19] In its elevation of the artifice of republicanism over the naturalness of democracy, the metaphor of miniature portrait functioned first, as we have seen elsewhere, as an explicit contrast to the idea of government as a body.

But in its original context, the miniature portrait metaphor was paradoxical: Adams wanted representatives who would both resemble the people (and who would be able to "think, feel, reason, and act like them") and who would also be better than the people ("a few of the most wise and good"). The tension between resemblance and wisdom in Adams's metaphorics here points to a fault line in his thinking about representation. Had Adams offered only his miniature portrait metaphor, we might have less difficulty categorizing his thought. Coupled with his call

for enlightened, virtuous statesmen, Adams's metaphors of exact portrait and perfect likeness epitomized the tensions between two competing models of political representation. Adams was torn between the desire of constituents for representatives who resembled themselves and
articulated their local interests ("actual representation") and the charms
of high republican theory in which the wills of the many (as well as the
interests of all those persons said to lack wills of their own: children,
slaves, women, white men without property, American Indians, free African Americans) were deputed to the wise and good ("virtual representation"). While the future (and perhaps the past) of American political
thought lay with actual representation, in 1776 Adams held the two in
precarious balance.[20] But the seeming paradox of representatives who
were both like the people and better than the people was probably an
effect of Adams's attempts to assuage his intended political audiences
rather than an unresolved personal contradiction. Adams told numerous correspondents that *Thoughts* was meant only for the southern colonies, and that it would probably be appreciated in neither the South
nor the North: "In New England, the 'Thoughts on Government' will be
disdained, because they are not popular enough. In the Southern Colonies, they will be despised and dissected, because too popular."[21] Adams's *Thoughts* offered something for everyone: the miniature metaphor
and the idea of representatives resembling constituents would make his
friends in Massachusetts happy, and the high republican theory of virtual representation was intended for the slave societies of the southern
colonies.

But the aesthetics of smallness in Adams's thought reflected still
other political aims and tensions. At a general level, the miniature portrait metaphor served as an acknowledgment that representation had
to be reductive. But Adams probably also intended the metaphor as a
specific critique of the idea—put forth a few months earlier in Thomas
Paine's *Common Sense* (1776)—that a representative body composed of
a large number of representatives was more representative than a representative body with a small number of representatives.[22] Adams may
have found Paine's proposal for a national legislature consisting of
390 members impractical, but could anything compact or miniature possibly express or represent one's thoughts as well as something large? In
his correspondence about *Thoughts*, Adams often apologized for the
brevity of the pamphlet he sometimes denigrated as merely "a Sketch."
Adams told his friend James Warren in Boston that the copy published

was regrettably shorter than some of the versions he had sent as private letters. He contrasted the public version—"a little Pamphlet" that was "very incorrect, and not truly printed"—with the manuscript originals—"Ten Sheets of Paper, pretty full and in a fine Hand."[23] Another Massachusetts correspondent told him that "I have seen your pamphlet" and "I lament its littleness."[24] Josiah Quincy complimented Adams on the little pamphlet, observing that "it is difficult to contract, within the Limits of a Sheet of Paper, ones Thoughts upon such *a copious Subject.*" Nevertheless, Quincy spent the rest of his letter to Adams pointing out that Adams's "Sketch" had been so brief that it failed to answer the most important question about selecting a few of the most wise and good to be representatives: "By what *Criterion* are these *rare Geniuses* to be distinguished?"[25] Adams did eventually flesh out his sketchy ideas about selecting the most wise representatives, but it is arguable if he ever fully answered Quincy's question. Quincy's anxiety that the contraction of Adams's thoughts to Adams's *Thoughts* had forced Adams to omit a consideration of the most important subject paralleled contemporary anxieties about what was lost when society itself was contracted "within the Limits of a Sheet of Paper."

On the eve of the Constitutional Convention in 1787, Adams revised the metaphor of the miniature portrait in the first volume of his *Defence of the Constitutions of Government of the United States of America* published in London (where he served as a minister from the United States), in Philadelphia, and in New York. "The end to be aimed at in the formation of a representative assembly," Adams now argued, "seems to be the sense of the people, the public voice. The perfection of the portrait consists in its likeness."[26] Adams retained the portrait analogy but removed the issue of miniaturization. Completely absent is the 1776 idea that representatives should be like or look like their constituents, and in its place is the idea of representation as the "sense" or "voice" of the people. It was no doubt a citation of some version of this sentiment that James Wilson repeated at the Convention (or that Rufus King recalled as Wilson spoke) in the June 6, 1787 debate over representation that opens this chapter.

By 1787, however, Adams's visual analogy was most often made by opponents of the proposed Constitution. Melancton Smith, a New York Anti-Federalist, defined "representative" at the ratifying convention in New York in June 1788 in a way that echoed Adams in 1776: "The idea that naturally suggests itself to our minds, when we speak of rep-

resentatives, is, that they resemble those they represent." But Smith suffered from none of Adams's ambivalence and cast the metaphor in a far
more literal mode, calling for representatives who would be a "true picture" and who could "possess a knowledge of their [constituents'] circumstances and their wants, sympathize in all their distresses, and be
disposed to seek their true interests."[27] By late 1787 Anti-Federalists in
Massachusetts were reading Adams against the proposed Constitution.
"Who are this House of Representatives?" asked an Anti-Federalist
known only as "John DeWitt." He let Adams answer: "A representative Assembly, says the celebrated Mr. Adams, is the sense of the people, and the perfection of the portrait, consists in the likeness." But "De-
Witt" then asked: "Can this Assembly be said to contain the sense of
the people?—Do they resemble the people in any one single feature?"[28]
Anti-Federalists argued that they did not and could not, and routinely
complained that the proposed number of representatives in the House
(sixty-five) "could not resemble the people, or possess their sentiments
and dispositions." True resemblance demanded a large number of representatives. For, as "Brutus" in New York saw it:

> [T]hose who are placed instead of the people, should possess their sentiments
> and feelings, and be governed by their interests, or in other words, should
> bear the strongest resemblance of those in whose room they are substituted.
> It is obvious, that for an assembly to be a true likeness of the people of any
> country, they must be considerably numerous.—One man, or a few men,
> cannot possibly represent the feelings, opinions, and characters of a great
> multitude.[29]

There's no need to multiply quotations: Anti-Federalists shared a common vocabulary on this issue. But why, we should ask, did "Brutus" and
others express their dissatisfaction with the Constitution in the peculiarly
aesthetic vocabulary of feelings, sympathy, and especially likeness?

For Anti-Federalists, resemblance compensated for lack of full assembly, and the concept of representation itself was a begrudgingly accepted surrogate for the always imagined (if always dismissed) fantasy
of assembling the whole population.[30] As the "Federal Farmer," one of
the most articulate (and consequently one of the most plagiarized) Anti-
Federalists defined it, a "full and equal representation" was one "which
possesses the same interests, feelings, opinions, and views the people
themselves would were they all assembled."[31] The anxiety that repre-

sentatives might possess different interests, feelings, opinions, and views could be partially mitigated by an extended franchise, a large number of representatives, and frequent elections, but it never went away. "Do you represent your wants, your grievances, your wishes, in person?" Anti-Federalists like "John DeWitt" asked. "If that is impracticable, have you a right to send one of your townsmen for that purpose?"[32] If the concept of virtual representation was a theoretical and consensual shell game concealing the fact that some interests could never be represented, actual representation involved another set of anxieties centering not on nonrepresentation but on misrepresentation.

The metaphors of representation as miniaturization expressed a desire to diminish the power of the representative and a fantasy about the amalgamation of the propertied white-male bodies of constituents. In revolutionary America the legislature was the most important element of government, since there (in Locke's phrase) "the members of a Commonwealth are united, and combined together into one coherent, living Body."[33] Echoing John Adams, the author of the Essex *Result* of 1778, a critique of the unratified Massachusetts Constitution, offered the most detailed description of the logic of political miniaturization:

> The rights of representation should be so equally and impartially distributed, that the representatives should have the same views, and interests with the people at large. They should think, feel, and act like them, and in fine, should be an exact miniature of their constituents. They should be (if we may use the expression) the whole body politic, with all it's property, rights, and priviledges, reduced to a smaller scale, every part being diminished in just proportion. To pursue the metaphor. If in adjusting the representation of freemen, any ten are reduced into one, all the other tens should be alike reduced: or if any hundred should be reduced to one, all the other hundreds should have just the same reduction.[34]

The political commonplace that a legislative assembly was like an individual underwrote this Swiftian fantasy of reductive miniaturization. The social compact (or social contract) was itself an exercise of reduction, a making small. The passage from the Essex *Result* is perhaps most noteworthy because it borrows from Adams everything but the explicit idea of representation as portraiture, although the term "miniature" could certainly signify a miniature portrait. Arguments about miniaturization that were not tied directly to the miniature portrait were as rare as arguments still couched, as the Essex *Result* was, in the metaphor of the body politic.

This fantasy of a miniaturized population somehow inhering in a representative assembly and the desire for an unmediated, transparent relationship between representative and represented led Anti-Federalists to a semiotic conception of political representation. As "Brutus" defined it in 1787, the "term, representative, implies that the person or body chosen for this purpose, should resemble those who appoint them—a representation of the people of America, if it be a true one, must be like the people." "It ought to be so constituted, that a person, who is a stranger to the country, might be able to form a just idea of their character, by knowing that of their representatives," "Brutus" continued, since "they are the sign—the people are the thing signified."[35] The latter assertion played to the standard Anti-Federalist tendency to talk about representatives as a group rather than as individuals (significantly, saying that an assembly of representatives is a sign is not the same as saying that a single representative is a sign), but as much as "Brutus's" vocabulary startles post-structuralist sensibilities with its modernity, we should immediately recognize that "Brutus's" "sign" and "thing signified" do not easily correspond to mainstream twentieth-century semiotics. "Brutus's" sign is not Saussure's, if by Saussure we understand the sign as a physical entity composed of a material signifier and a nonmaterial signified. Certainly, "Brutus" did not imagine that the people were immaterial. If anything, the people were somehow present in the sign(ifier).[36] Hanna Pitkin's discussion of representation recognizes a great difference between "standing for" and "acting for," and we should perhaps observe her distinction here.[37] But if the Federalists saw representatives as acting for the people, Anti-Federalists only begrudgingly allowed representatives to stand for them and frequently saw representatives as a passive sign under the control of its referent, the people.

Federalists certainly gave their opponents plenty to worry about, for they argued that legislation demanded enlarged views, not localism, and they privileged a nationalist perspective. Noah Webster insisted that "John DeWitt's" idea that representatives should represent only the interests of their particular town was "a false principle" and a "vulgar idea." For Webster, a member of the legislature from any particular town was a representative of the whole state. It was ultimately a matter of views. While Anti-Federalists worried that representatives would neither possess the people's views nor be governed by their interests,

Federalists like Webster shifted the focus and worried that representatives would be too shortsighted. On the state level, a representative must "view the whole collective interest of the state, and act from that view." On a national level, "the design of representation is to bring the collective interest into view." Only by electing a group of men who were "less local and dependent" could the House of Representatives hope to mitigate the factional jealousy that local interests excited.[38] Anti-Federalists like "The Impartial Examiner" of Virginia stressed that constituents had "views" too, and argued that representation should be so *ample, that amongst the members* there may be a competent knowledge of the constituents[,] their sentiments, connections, views and habits."[39] Madison's response to such claims suggested that the Constitution's solutions to representation would "refine and enlarge the public views by passing them through the medium of a chosen body of citizens, whose wisdom may best discern the true interest of their country." Far from being the necessary evil Anti-Federalists described as a mere substitute for public assembly, representation was a chance for amplification and eloquent articulation. "It may well happen that the public voice, pronounced by the representatives of the people, will be more consonant to the public good," Madison argued in *Federalist* no. 10, "than if pronounced by the people themselves, convened for the purpose."[40] Federalists like Madison favored metaphors that privileged voice over image or likeness, but Federalists like Webster who argued in visual terms stressed that representation demanded not an exact portrait of the people but an enlarged, enlightened view.

Anti-Federalists attacked the mimetic presumptions behind Madison's defense of enlightened statesmen who could ventriloquize what they imagined to be the public voice, and argued that the most articulate members of each order of society should be allowed to represent themselves. Samuel Chase, a Maryland Anti-Federalist, objected that representatives (presumably a few rich men) could never represent the people at large and he invoked the familiar visual metaphor: "A representative should be the image of those he represents. He should know their sentiments and their wants and desires—he should possess their feelings—he should be governed by their interests with which his own should be inseparably connected." The debate centered not just on representation but on "true" representation. As Chase put it, to "form a proper and true representation each order ought to have an opportunity of choosing from each a person as their representative."[41] Federalists, by contrast, spoke in terms of "natural" rather than "true representation," mocking the Anti-Federalist idea of choosing a person from each class or order. As Hamilton scoffed in *Federalist* no. 35, the "idea of an actual representation of all classes of the people by persons of each class is altogether visionary." Whatever its theoretical merits, it could never happen in reality, since certain socially dependent groups (mechanics and manufacturers) would always be inclined to give their votes to merchants "in preference to persons of their own professions." Thus, Hamilton argues, we should consider merchants as the "natural representatives of all these classes of the community."[42] But Hamilton's un-"visionary" "natural representative" was a far cry from Chase's concept of "true representation" as the "image" of the thing it represents, and it was even more distant from Adams's original metaphor of a political assembly as a miniature portrait. On the most rudimentary level, Federalists and Anti-Federalists disagreed about whether representatives were subjects or objects: Federalists like Hamilton and Webster constructed representatives as subjects with enlarged views and comprehensive gazes, while Anti-Federalists wanted representatives to be the objects of a collective gaze, miniature portraits chained to and contemplated by the people.

The Meanings of Likeness

What material ideologies underwrote this persistent analogy between visual and political representation? On the most basic level, miniatures were not simply reduced portraits, since the smaller size also seemed (at least materially) to connote a reduction in what could be represented: most miniatures of the period show head and shoulders only while portraits might represent persons at half-length, three-quarter length, or even full-length. That miniatures, more than other forms of painting, focused on the face and head rather than the body is a telling fact of the distance from and revisions of older metaphors of the body politic. While representation was the most important political concept of the revolutionary era and was, as one contemporary phrased it, "the feet on which a free government stands," miniatures always eliminated the feet and focused exclusively on the head.[43] Conventional interpretations of colonial portraiture have suggested that eighteenth-century Americans preferred "realism" to idealistic renderings. We have traditionally viewed these objects from the point of view of the artists, as evidence of provincial artistic efforts, and as examples of the transfer of ideas from painters in London to their provincial counterparts in the colonies.[44] Social and cultural historians, however, have recently begun to treat these paintings as part of a larger pattern of Anglo-American material consumption, focusing attention on the complex interactions between portraitist and subject.[45] "Likeness" was above all a social construction, and we can begin to see what the terms "portrait" and "miniature" meant in the political discourse by examining some of Adams's own portraits and miniatures.

While we tend to identify individual eighteenth-century paintings today as fully independent objects, contemporary American portrait painters and sitters often grouped separate portraits as complementary pendants. On at least two occasions, Adams sat for a paired portrait. In 1766 John and Abigail Adams had their likenesses taken in pastels by Benjamin Blyth, a Salem portraitist. Blyth's decision to produce two separate bust-size portraits may have been motivated by the sitters, or by a desire to make a life-sized picture on the dimensions of paper he had, or may have simply reflected his own artistic insecurities about the compositional difficulties of grouping two figures in a single portrait. In any event Blyth's portraits reflected the visual and conjugal ideology of the dependent pair. While portraits could theoretically stand alone (as they frequently do in modern museums), their contemporary meaning inhered in their complementarity, in the incompleteness of both the individual object and subject.

For Adams large portraits were also a means of exchange with others and tokens of absence and affection. The only other surviving pendant portrait of Adams was done by the expatriate American painter Mather Brown as a complement to Brown's painting of Thomas Jefferson. Jefferson posed for Brown during a trip to England in 1786, most likely at the request of Adams. The members of the Adams family in London had one by one sat for Brown who made (in the words of Adams's daughter) a "tasty" picture "whether a likeness or not." Hung in the Adams's residence, the portrait of Jefferson was seen as a substitute for Jefferson himself. When Jefferson returned to France, Abigail Adams wrote him that his "portrait dignifies a part of our room, tho it is but a poor substitute for those pleasures we enjoy'd some months past." Soon Jefferson wanted a portrait of Adams for himself and asked Adams's son-in-law to see to it that Adams sit for Brown again, apparently dissatisfied with a previous likeness taken in 1785. John Adams was unhappy with any portraits of himself then in his possession. Abigail Adams wrote to Jefferson: "He has not a portrait that he likes to send you. Mr. Trumble [sic] talks of taking one. If he succeeds better than his [painting] Brethren, Mr. Adams will ask your acceptance of it." Adams's son-in-law sent word in early 1788 that Adams had agreed to sit for the American painter John Trumbull, but Jefferson again insisted that Brown do the portrait, citing scale as the determining argument against Trumbull, "because Trumbul [sic] does not paint of the size of the life."

This was certainly not a personal attack on Trumbull, whom Jefferson engaged to oversee Brown's work, but it tells us that Jefferson clearly felt that someone who usually produced small paintings might have difficulty rendering a life-size likeness. But "likeness" as a category of representation necessarily had a different meaning during a period in which the artist now known as John "Trumbull" might be recognized (as in the above quotations) as both "Trumbul" or "Trumble" depending on the writer. In any event, on March 6, 1788, Trumbull wrote to Jefferson that "Brown is busy about the pictures. Mr. Adams's is like. Yours I do not think so well of." Jefferson wrote back to Trumbull nervously, "You say mine does not resemble. Is it a copy? Because he agreed that the original should be mine."[46] It's hard to say if Jefferson received the originals he wanted or the copies he feared. In the end Brown painted four portraits of Adams and Jefferson to serve as two pendant sets in a new national and deliberately homosocial political family, and he showed these paintings to great success in London.[47]

In using the metaphor of the portrait in 1787, Adams also recognized the power of a painting to express both power itself and proportionality. John Singleton Copley painted a full-length portrait of Adams in London in 1783, shortly after the peace negotiations ending the Revolutionary War. Abigail Adams, who had not seen her husband in four and a half years and who saw the painting in Copley's studio in London, remarked: "I have been to see a very Elegant picture of Mr. Adams which belongs to Mr. Copely [sic], and was taken by him. . . . It is said to be an admirable likeness." Although Adams paid for the massive portrait and had it framed, the portrait remained with Copley (who showed it in 1796 at the Royal Academy annual exhibition, in honor of Adams's election as president) until after the artist's death in 1815. Aristocratic in style and scale, the portrait became something of an embarrassment to Adams, even a political liability. When asked by a London bookseller in 1793 if the Copley portrait could be engraved and placed as a frontis-

piece to a new edition of Adams's *Defence* (where Adams had argued
for the pictorial resemblance of representative and represented), Adams
replied that he should be "much mortified to see such a Bijou affixed to
those Republican volumes." In the end, the bookseller chose to engrave
only Adams's bust for the frontispiece. In a telling remembrance that
speaks to the founding generation's attention to proportionality in representation, John Quincy Adams later recalled specifically that Copley
had used a compass to measure his father's head, face, arms, and legs.[48]
Copley's small sketch for this painting shows a matrix of horizontal and
vertical lines, a grid used to assure exact proportions both in making the
sketch itself and in transferring the sketch to the larger canvas.

But if a life-size portrait sometimes originated in a small sketch, a
miniature was by no means a reduced portrait. Portraits and miniatures
differed in form and function. When Abigail Adams wrote to John from
America in 1780 to request a new miniature, she revealed much about
the purposes of the object:

> I have a request to you which I hope you will not disappoint me of, a minia-
> ture of Him I best Love. Indulge me the pleasing melancholy of contemplat-
> ing a likeness. The attempt here faild, and was more the resemblance of a
> cloisterd Monk, than the Smileing Image of my Friend. I could not endure the
> sight of it.—By Sampson will be a good opportunity [of delivering it], should
> he be taken none but a Savage would rob a Lady, of what could be of no value,
> but to her.[49]

Worn in a locket, secreted on a person's body, the miniature was a token
of affection as absence. Possessing one bespoke an intimacy between the
wearer or holder and the absent subject represented, an intimacy that
rendered the miniature (unlike the large oil painting) worthless to anyone unfamiliar with the subject or unaffected by the likeness. In a Protestant colonial society, Abigail Adams's remarks suggest that the miniature allowed for secular idolatry and even "fetishism."[50] Unlike an
oil painting, a miniature's "value" was divorced from its sheer materi-
ality and depended (as any non-"Savage" could recognize) on its "likeness" to its subject. Portrait and miniature might thus serve opposite
functions. The portrait was meant for public exhibition and personal
consumption and was often retained by the sitter; the miniature was private and exchanged.[51] Or, in the case of Blyth's pastel pendants of the
Adamses or Mather Brown's oils of Adams and Jefferson, portrait and

miniature were terms that split not public and private but two versions of privacy.

Miniature painting required changes in materials, in expense, and in production. While practiced most often by men and worn as jewelry by men and women, miniature painting was a field open to women in a way that large-scale oil painting was generally not. Unlike silhouettes, which gave white sitters a black profile, miniatures in this period capitalized on the qualities of the ivory ground they were painted on to give translucent sheen to a sitter's hair and a natural foundation for white skin.[52] The back of the miniature supposed to be of John Adams and by Copley (both attributions are questionable) included a braided lock of Adams's hair twisted into an artist's signature ("Copley"). The representational strategy of "hair work" attempted to close the gap between the artificial and authentic representation of the sitter but ultimately offered a double representation: the actual but partial representation of the sitter's hair that bespoke its own authenticity, and the painted image that was subject, as Abigail Adams suggested, to misrepresentations of likeness.

But what, exactly, was the meaning of "likeness"? Some colonial patrons of the arts seemed to have prized likeness above all other qualities in art. In 1765 John Singleton Copley wrote from Boston to an English engraver and mezzotinter with a request to print a portrait of the Rev. Joseph Sewall, asking the engraver to take "perticular care in the preservation of the likeness that being a main part of the excellency of a portrait in the oppinion of our New England Conoseurs."[53] If Copley's remark suggests discomfort with the overvaluation by local connoisseurs of the face, his portraits done in the period show little ambivalence. Copley often went far beyond his contemporaries in Europe in the representation of the facial blemishes of what another colonial painter referred to as his "patients."[54] In the language of contemporary advertising, likeness was equated with the skill of the artist. One week after the Federal Convention closed in Philadelphia, Charles Willson Peale advertised "A Mezzotint Print of His Excellency General Washington, . . . from a portrait which he has painted since the sitting of the Convention, . . . the likeness is esteemed the best that has been executed in a print."[55] But Peale left open the obvious question: esteemed by whom? In most cases the idea of likeness reflected a complicated negotiation between the sitter, the artist, and ultimately the consumer.

Americans became consumers and subjects of miniature portraits in the late eighteenth century. Starting around 1750, miniature painters advertised with increasing frequency and regularity in the newspapers of Boston, Charleston, Baltimore, New York, Trenton, and Philadelphia. With a few exceptions, like the "very ingenious Miniature Paintress" Hetty Sage Benbridge, the artists were men.[56] Frequently, their brief advertisements mention both their foreignness and their metropolitan successes. They seem always to have just arrived from somewhere else: from London, Paris, Glasgow, Lausanne.[57] Some claimed to have given satisfaction to "Gentlemen and Ladies in London."[58] Others claimed "the honour of taking off the Profiles of many of the Nobility in England and Ireland."[59] Less often, they invoked the names of their teachers in Britain, painters like Joshua Reynolds and Benjamin West, and they rarely reference other artists who are not their teachers.[60] One wonders how many readers in Charleston in 1773 knew what a miniature painter named Stevenson meant when he advertised his ability to paint larger works "in the Stile of Zoffani."[61] These advertisements often stress the smallness of the price, and frequently make claims that their products were "equal to any in Europe."[62] The artists offered to wait on their customers, or invited them to their studios. To supplement income, miniature painters sometimes offered to instruct students on how to paint miniatures on their own.[63]

In advertisements for their services, painters used the term "likeness" more frequently than the word "portrait." A limner in New York in the 1750s sold what he called a "true Likeness."[64] Reports in American papers of the London successes of American painter Mather Brown noted that he had produced a "strong likeness" of one of his English subjects.[65] An artist in Philadelphia in 1785 claimed to paint the "most forcible likeness of every subject."[66] An artist in New York in 1791 guaranteed "the most correct Likenesses in Miniature."[67] In the 1780s painters in Philadelphia, New York, and Baltimore regularly promised "striking likenesses," and this language remained in advertisements at least through the turn of the century.[68] The meaning of likeness, then, was intimately associated with its strikingness—with the idea of the violent but pleasurable moment at which beholders were struck by the resemblance between the stippled marks and the sitter.

If the artists described the effect on the beholder as an act of "striking," their advertisements described the act of painting as the physical "taking" of the subject's likeness. Likenesses were sometimes "drawn" or "executed," but—like modern photographs—they were more often simply "taken." Lawrence Kilburn, a London "Limner" in New York in

1754, promised to please by "taking a true Likeness, and finishing the Drapery in a proper Manner."[69] An artist in South Carolina in 1770 advertised that "Ladies and Gentlemen inclinable to have their pictures taken, will be immediately waited upon."[70] A painting teacher in South Carolina promised in 1774 to teach students to become "capable of taking their own, or any Person's likeness with Crayons in less than three months."[71] An article in a New York paper in 1786 reported that Charles Willson Peale had come from Philadelphia "to take the likeness of his Excellency the President of Congress, and some other public characters."[72] Miniature painters especially referred to their art as a process of "taking." In 1784 a painter traveled in Philadelphia and Maryland and advertised "Miniature Painting, in all its various branches, and the most striking likenesses taken, at three guineas each."[73] That same year one Philadelphia miniature painter (from France) promised that "no money [will be] demanded if a good Likeness is not Taken."[74] A miniature painter in Charleston—possibly the same itinerant painter from Philadelphia—noted that "if I fail in taking the Likeness, I do not make any charge, but hope to be permitted to draw until I do."[75] A Mr. Mack in Philadelphia in 1785 bragged that he was "so fortunate as scarce ever to fail taking the most forcible likeness of every subject he attempts."[76] By the end of the next decade, artists frequently described their likenesses as "warranted to be undeniably striking."[77] And by 1800, Raphaelle Peale had formulated the miniature portraitist's equivalent of "no taxation without representation": "No likeness, no pay."[78]

During the price-sensitive years following the Revolution, miniature painters often emphasized the reasonable cost of their products. John Walters, a Philadelphia miniature painter, charged two dollars for miniatures in 1782, but painted children under six for half that price. The lower price for children was perhaps a lure for multiple commissions, an acknowledgment that the likenesses of young people soon became obsolete, or perhaps even an incentive for parents to make pre-death mementos in a society with a significant infant and child-mortality rate.[79] Walters's price also reflected that he would remain stationary in his studio and clients would have to come to him. He explained in 1783 that his "utter inability to wait on his employers at their own houses, he would wish to be an apology for the low price he charges." By 1784 his workplace in Philadelphia also sold items associated with miniatures: "lockets, rings, hair pins and other articles in the jewelry way, at a much lower rate than those imported."[80] Walters faced stiff competition in 1784 from a studio in Philadelphia called Cooke and Co., artists from London who specialized in miniature painting as well as jewelry and silversmithing. Cooke and Co. offered parents an even better deal than Walters, promising "Miniature Painting, in all its various branches, and the most striking likenesses taken, at three guineas each, children ditto at one guinea, exclusive of the setting."[81]

What, ultimately, was represented by and in a miniature? An encyclopedia article on miniature paintings from 1771 defined them in this way: "MINIATURE, a delicate kind of painting, distinguished from all others by the smallness of the figures, its being performed with dots or points instead of lines; by the faintness of the colouring; its requiring to be viewed very near; and by its being usually done on vellum. This is the nicest and most tedious of all kinds of painting, being performed wholly with the point of the pencil."[82] More often than not portrait miniatures involved shifts in focus as well as scale. A few advertisements mentioned that customers were paying for an image of "head and bust," but most didn't need to specify.[83] As the art historian Harold Dickson has observed: "It was commonly held that good miniatures should be susceptible to enlargement to full portrait size, though more commonly in practice it was the large picture that was copied in reduction."[84] At least one miniature painter in New York advertised in 1780 that "he has [a] few instruments made on an entire new plan, for reducing of likenesses, &c. which he will sell at Two Guineas each, with which he will instruct the purchaser [in] the use of them, and the whole art of reducing figures of any size."[85] Reducing figures may have been an "art" in a technical sense, but some contemporary critics argued that miniature painting was not exactly painting (so much as dotting) any more than it was an art.

Miniatures demanded close viewing, but Americans in 1787 may not have considered miniatures as objects of particularly aesthetic contemplation. One of Charles Willson Peale's Maryland sponsors wrote to the painter in London in 1767, insisting that he abandon the lowly business of miniature painting in favor of large-scale portraiture, a move that would better suit the elevated "Taste of the People with us."[86] Comprehensive how-to books like *The School of Wisdom, or Repository of The most valuable Curiosities of Art* (1787) included sections on drawing, painting in water and oil colors, etching, engraving, painting on glass, bronzing, and staining glass but remained silent on the techniques of painting miniatures.[87] Modern art historians have noted that the presence of portrait miniatures in colonial America suggested "evidence of the concern for the intimate, individual portrait."[88] But, looking back from the 1830s, William Dunlap offered a brief "History of Miniature Painting," in which he argued that "this department of art, from its reduced scale, and consequent minuteness, does not fill the eye, or dazzle the imagination, so as to come in competition with the higher order of historic composition," or even with regular portraiture.[89] Despite the presence of miniature painters in the colonies in the 1750s, Dunlap could name no miniaturists before John Ramage, who worked in Boston in the 1770s. And the obscurity and anonymity of the men and women who advertised their services—often failing to provide their names in their advertisements—should perhaps be read as a function of the way in which miniatures were valued, much the same way that portraits were themselves valued in this period: as objects appreciated for their association with the sitter rather than the artist.[90]

But if miniatures were not objects for aesthetic contemplation, they nevertheless served as portable, wearable, and exchangeable devotional objects. In 1774 William Birchall Tetley, a New York painter from London, advertised his ability to take likenesses "in miniature for the bracelet, or so small as to be set in a ring."[91] Many miniature painters advertised their skill as jewelers and their ability to fashion bracelets out of hair ("Hair Work").[92] In 1784 a Philadelphia shop specializing in miniature painting advertised "hair worked in any device to the greatest perfection, and set in gold on the most reasonable terms."[93] While men tended to conceal miniatures from public view, emphasizing the privacy of the sentimental object, women can be seen in portraits from the 1780s and 1790s wearing miniatures from ribbons and chains around their necks. The chains formed by the combination of hair and gold served, as one art historian has recently observed, as a decorous way to emphasize female dependency.[94] But the dependency evoked by the wearing of a miniature could be a dependency on a departed loved one. As one poem written in the 1760s suggests, "To wear the looks of those we value most" was to "Reflect the image which the faithful mind / Holds dearest, when the real form is lost."[95] In American novels of the 1790s, miniatures function as what one recent critic has called "fetish objects endowed with great affective significance," an "artistic form meant, like letters, to promote sympathy between private individuals—to bridge distance, absence, and even death."[96] The idea that miniature portraits preserved what the artist had "taken"—the presence of the absent—made them objects that should not and perhaps could not be appreciated from a purely aesthetic standpoint.

Miniatures seemed to generate their primary public meanings by an association with women. An 1800 advertisement addressed "To the Ladies" described miniature paintings as objects exclusively for women:

> LADIES, As it is under the warm and effulgent rays of your powerfully creative influence that all the arts, and especially the Fine Arts, have received their birth and acquired their present degree of perfection, it is reasonable to expect that considering them as your darling offsprings, you will continue to feel for them that tenderness and interest without which they must certainly die away; they have a natural and indisputable claim to your immediate protection and among them, that of Miniature Painting, being intirely devoted to you, has an exclusive right to your fostering solicitude.[97]

Painters who made larger portraits of women sometimes highlighted the sentimental and fashionable functions of miniature portraits. James Peale's 1803 portrait *Mrs. Edmond (Jane) Rouvert* represents a woman cradling the likeness of her husband in a particularly infantilizing way. Ralph Earl's *Mrs. Jared (Apphia Ruggles) Lane* (1796) shows a woman wearing a closed locket near her heart, calling attention to absence even as the absent subject (husband? friend? child?) remains unidentified. If the locket frequently signified an absent husband, then a similar closed miniature in Earl's *Mrs. Elijah (Mary Anna) Boardman and Son* (ca. 1796) perhaps served as a way of incorporating the presence (but not the image) of Elijah Boardman himself into the picture—a family portrait of mother, son, and miniaturized absent father.

Charles Willson Peale's painting of his brother *James Peale Painting a Miniature* (ca. 1795) (fig. 11) offers a complicated image of the relationship between representation and women as the subjects and consumers of miniature painting. James Peale sits at a desk, staring out from the painting even as he dabs his quill on his tiny palette. James's likeness has been taken at a moment in the process of painting the image of a woman onto a piece of paper, but Charles's finished painting portrays a fundamental ambiguity to its beholder: Is James Peale looking away from the female subject of his unfinished miniature in order to meet the eye of the male painter, or is the viewer of Charles's finished painting in some sense constructed as the subject of James's miniature? The ambiguity is perhaps a function of Charles's self-promoting attempt to advertise his

FIGURE 11. Charles Willson Peale, *James Peale Painting a Miniature,* ca. 1795. Courtesy of the Mead Art Museum, Amherst College, Amherst, Massachusetts. Bequest of Herbert L. Pratt (Class of 1895).

skill at both mediums. Charles could "take" a female likeness in miniature, but he could also handle the compositional demands of a complicated half-length life-size painting of a man. But *James Peale Painting a Miniature* encodes an additional commentary about the representative status of miniature painting. Had Charles painted a miniature of James, he could never have included the crucial signs that construct the miniature portraitist as a writer rather than a painter: the chair, the writing desk, the paper, and the quill itself. The meaning of likeness was, Peale's painting suggests, perhaps as dependent on ideas about the miniaturist's practices of writing as it was on the image of the subject or the utility of the object for a consumer.

Representation as Transcription

If Anti-Federalists drew on the material culture of miniature painting as a model for political representation, constructing a representative assembly as an absent or even deceased loved one and the electorate as a (female) consumer, what material and cultural practices informed Federalist metaphors of representation as an "exact transcript"? On the one hand, a transcript was merely a copy. In election sermons like the one Ebenezer Pemberton gave in Boston in 1710, ministers had argued that rulers must "endeavour that their Rule may be a fair Copy and Transcript of the Justice and Equity of the divine Government."[98] But when Federalists called for representatives who could transcribe the minds and voices of the public, they used the term in a way that reflected developments in notetaking over the eighteenth century and perhaps specifically the practice of recording the speeches of members of Parliament in Britain. "Notes" was one of the key words of American culture in the 1780s, figuring prominently in the title of Jefferson's *Notes on the State of Virginia*—a title frequently shortened in textual citations and on leather bookspines to *Notes on Virginia* but not to *On the State of Virginia* or even *Jefferson's Virginia*—and evident elsewhere. The "notes" James Madison kept of debates in the Constitutional Convention shared with Jefferson's *Notes* a common descriptive (and non-narrative) agenda. But what conventions governed the practice of "taking" notes or of transcribing speech in 1787?

An advertisement promising to teach students how to record a "deliberate speaker" appeared in a Philadelphia newspaper while the Constitutional Convention deliberated at the Pennsylvania State House:

> MR. LLOYD having nearly completed his Subscription, proposes on Monday next to begin Teaching his Method of Writing SHORT-HAND. . . . Gentlemen who are desirous of being enabled to *use* this Art, will be pleased to call at his house in Cherry Street, above Fifth Street. The simplicity of his

method renders the acquisition so easy, that persons of but common capacity will write it with sagacity enough to follow a deliberate speaker after one
week's application at an hour each day.[99]

Shorthand transcription was one of the great arts of eighteenth-century
culture. While seventeenth-century English authors and publishers issued dozens of shorthand manuals, the number of self-help guides to
what was variously called "tachygraphy," "brachygraphy," and "stenography" proliferated in the late eighteenth century.[100] The first edition of
the Scottish *Encyclopedia Britannica* (1771) devoted as much space to
an article on "the Art of Short-hand Writing" as it gave to "Religion and
Theology," suggesting the importance contemporaries placed in dissem-
inating the cultural practices that would allow passive listeners of even
"common capacity" to convert themselves into active transcribers and to
capture and represent the words and thoughts of "deliberate" and delib-
erating speakers.[101] "The principal advantage . . . which speech has over
writing," one shorthand manual argued, "is the communicating our notions with greater speed, and with less trouble," but the practice of short-
hand could "bring the art of writing as near to speech in these respects,
as the nature of things will permit."[102] If, as Charles Brockden Brown argued in a magazine article in 1800, "the movements of the hand are necessarily much more tardy than those of the imagination or the tongue,"
shorthand promised to synchronize the physical act of writing both with
"the speed of utterance" and the speed of thought itself.[103]

But the practice of recording speech exactly—particularly the speech
of political representatives—was at least as controversial as it was exciting. An essay signed "Queritus" in the *New-York Daily Gazette* in
April 1789 argued against that newspaper's proposal to publish the debates of the new House of Representatives as recorded by shorthand
writers. The practice, "Queritus" argued, "would not comport with the
present situation of public affairs, and the dignity of Congress":

[I]t is one thing to make marks and numbers, by which naked words may afterwards be recollected and arranged; and another, to transfuse the soul of a
Speaker into a transcript of his speech. . . . [T]o have the various and different
modes of address which may distinguish and adorn the public speaking of the
respectable members of the house, blended, confused and lost, in a plain un-
eccentrick, un-adorned narration of their speeches, is what they will hardly
consent to; it is unprecedented, and cannot reasonably be expected.[104]

"Queritus" articulated the fear—a fear held by many representatives themselves—that those who represented representatives would inevitably misrepresent them. But his claim that attempts to "transfuse the soul of a Speaker into a transcript of his speech" were "unprecedented" was not exactly accurate. Colonial governments had published different accounts of their proceedings since the late seventeenth century. Massachusetts printed the records of its General Courts starting in 1685. The debates of the Pennsylvania legislature were considered confidential until 1764, but the 1776 Pennsylvania Constitutional Convention resolved to publish weekly proceedings in English and German, and the Pennsylvania Constitution of 1776 itself mandated the weekly publication of votes and proceedings. New York's Constitution of 1777 went further and provided for daily publication.[105] Most state legislatures published "journals" of their proceedings. But these records, proceedings, and journals were, as "Queritus" observed, little more than "marks and numbers"—bare documents recording the presence of members and the outcomes of votes without dialogue.

Colonial readers, ironically, were better informed about the petty everyday politics of the British Empire than about the activities of assemblymen they had elected. The London *Gentleman's Magazine* had published, both legally and illegally, the debates of Parliament since 1732, and colonial readers could find versions of these debates in their local papers. The practice of transcribing the voices of representatives in the United States began in the 1780s, and was by no means uniform in 1787. The *Charleston Evening Gazette* continued to carry the proceedings of the British Parliament, and in 1785 also began to print the proceedings of the South Carolina House of Representatives in the same style. Mathew Carey in Philadelphia transcribed the debates of the Pennsylvania Assembly, printing a single-issue pamphlet of speeches about the rechartering of the state bank in 1785; that same year, Carey began to publish selectively the debates of the Assembly in his *Pennsylvania Evening Herald*. By late 1787 entrepreneurs like Thomas Lloyd (who, as we have seen, taught the art of shorthand in Philadelphia) were securing copyrights for their transcriptions of legislative debates. Sometimes these transcriptions were little more than third-person summaries that told readers little about how politics worked: "Mr. Bee made an excellent speech on the general state of public affairs."[106] Nevertheless, readers like "Juvenis" wrote to the editor of the *Charleston Evening Gazette* with praise for the "utility" of "your intention of giving the substance of such debates, as shall be agitated in either house." For these debates served both as a political education for readers and a way for "the people" to control in some way the activities of those they authorized to speak on their behalf.[107]

Shorthand writing shared with miniature painting the language of "taking" and an aesthetics of smallness.[108] Transcripts, like likenesses, were "taken." The title pages of books of sermons as well as debates of legislative bodies announced that they were "Carefully Taken in Characters or Short-Hand, as they were delivered" or that the words had been "taken . . . from the Mouths" of the speakers.[109] Shorthand manuals regularly described the process as "taking down" a speaker, language that suggests the ideas of both reduction and control involved for the transcriber.[110] And, of course, shorthand was small. All systems celebrated the merits of contraction: the omission of vowels, the exclusion of duplicated letters, the contraction of syllables and whole words to symbols. How-to manuals promised to teach readers *"to minute down their own thoughts, or the sentiments of others, in as little time and room as possible."*[111] A "Minute" was "a short memoir, or sketch of a thing, taken in writing."[112] Transcripts were of course more expansive than what one shorthand recorder called "a bare minute of the proceedings."[113] Nevertheless, shorthand writing aimed to be as small as possible. As Mathew Carey's brother John observed in 1793, a stenography student should "make his short-hand characters as small as conveniently may be; since he cannot but know that small writing creates less motion and fatigue to the hand, less frequent occasion to take ink, change pens, turn leaves, &c." Carey himself claimed to average "five lines to every inch of paper" but mentioned that his teacher, Thomas Lloyd, wrote "much closer" (fig. 12).[114]

Painting and writing could find a common denominator in the eighteenth-century word "sketch," a term that suggested both the lack of finish of verbal transcripts and their link to drawing. In 1789 John Fenno, the editor of the *Gazette of the United States* (published in New York), promised "a succinct & impartial sketch of the Debates of Congress, by which the Characters, abilities & views of the members will be developed."[115] The London *Analytical Review* observed of the debates transcribed in Thomas Lloyd's *Congressional Register* (1789–90) that "upon the whole, more perfect sketches have perhaps never appeared in any country."[116] When Jonathan Elliot, the editor of the first collected edition of the transcripts from the state ratifying conventions, wanted

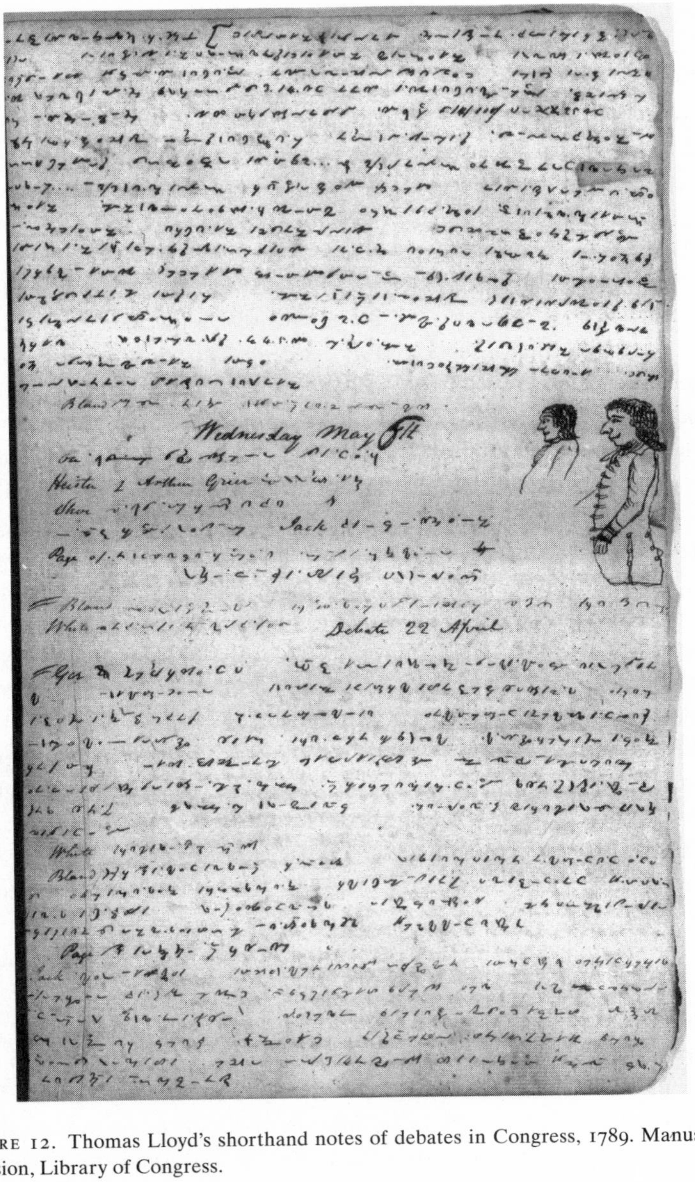

FIGURE 12. Thomas Lloyd's shorthand notes of debates in Congress, 1789. Manuscripts Division, Library of Congress.

to criticize the utility of some of the records, he described the notes as
"too faintly sketched."[117] The distinction between voice and image could
be slippery. One Pennsylvania Anti-Federalist maintained that a speech
made by James Wilson on October 6, 1787, in front of the Pennsylvania State House "delineates his true character, beyond the reach of the
pencil of a *West* or a *Peale*."[118] John Adams himself regularly equated
a verbal description with a painting. In responding in November 1775
to a letter from Mercy Otis Warren in which she described her dinner
with three generals of the Continental Army, including Washington,
Adams observed: "The Characters drawn in your last entertained me
very agreeably. They were taken off, by a nice and penetrating Eye. . . . I
wish I could draw a Number of Characters for your Inspection. I should
perhaps dawb on the Paint too thick—but the Features would be very
strong."[119] In early 1776 Adams wrote again to Warren about her letter,
flattering her that "Copeleys Pencil could not [have] touched off, with
more exquisite Finishings, the Faces of those Gentlemen." Adams then
suggested that he would "draw the Character of every new Personage
I have an opportunity of knowing, on Condition you will do the same.
My view will be to learn the Art of penetrating into Mens Bosoms, and
then the more difficult Art of painting what I shall see there. You Ladies
are the most infallible judges of Characters, I think."[120] The verbal description of a speaker—or in the case of Wilson, a representation of the
speaker's own words—could be as penetrating (or as striking) as a visual
image.

Nevertheless, shorthand manuals often emphasized that the language
of notation should be verbal rather than visual, and they constantly debated the desirability of what one textbook called "An Alphabet of
Words."[121] Some shorthand systematizers feared the introduction of "arbitrary marks" that might be forgotten by the stenographer, but many advocates for shorthand argued that "the doctrine of arbitrary signs" was
the only thing that could ensure improvement in the art.[122] Textbooks of
shorthand writing regularly distinguished between the "natural alphabet" and the "superfluous letters" and "complex marks established by
custom in our common alphabet." In "an alphabet according to nature,"
c, q, w, x, and *y* would have no place, since they reduplicated sounds.[123]
Some manuals demanded that the symbols used in shorthand should be
publicly legible, at least by others trained in the same methods. But other
manuals suggested the creation of a private language, noting that "every
practicioner will find it much easier to form his own particular abbrevia-

tions, than to adopt those of another." The stenograph "is to spell as he pronounces, without any regard to the ordinary rules of orthography." Hence the abbreviation "ality" over the letter *K,* the Congressional reporter John Carey noted, might signify "constitutionality," but *K* might also mean "Congress" or "Committee," depending upon the convention of the transcriber and the immediate context of the speech.[124]

Always, it seemed, the shorthand systematizers felt compelled to compare and contrast their vocabularies of notation with Hebrew and especially Chinese writing, a system that had "impracticably" converted words into marks. Carey observed that "the Chinese, with all their boasted acuteness and penetration, can hardly, during the course of the longest life, learn to decipher one half of the characters invented by the preposterous ingenuity of their writers; and the most learned man of their nation must, in the course of his reading, every day, meet with words, which he can neither understand, nor even read or spell: whereas, with us, the very children are, in a few days, taught to name and recognize all the characters used in our language, which being few in number, are easily remembered, and soon enable them to read every word, however difficult or new to them, and to express in writing, every sound, or combination of sounds, of which the language is susceptible." Nevertheless, Carey's system did recommend using certain letters only for certain words. Carey's system employed only "the consonants, which constitute the grand outlines of almost every word, and may be considered the bones and muscles in the body of a language." Vowels could be supplied by the reader, "as is the case in the Hebrew[,] when printed in its original form." And if, Carey reasoned, "the ancient Jews (who, by the way, were not very famous for accuteness or apprehension) could, without the assistance of vowels, read the writings of men who had lived hundreds of years before them, it is surely no very extravagant compliment to the present enlightened age, to suppose that a man of any tolerable education and understanding shall be able to supply the deficient vowels in his own writing, and to read, in the evening, a speech, that he himself has committed to paper in the morning."[125] The figural and literal children of the Western Enlightenment were much better off than the "ancient Jews" or modern Asians because they could distinguish between image and word.

That shorthand was thought to be an act of writing rather than picturing could be seen in the construction of the transcriber specifically as an author. Even while the Pennsylvania ratifying convention sat, the Philadelphia printer Thomas Bradford published *The Substance of a Speech Delivered by James Wilson, Esq. Explanatory of the general Principles of the Proposed Foederal Constitution; Upon a Motion made by the Honorable Thomas McKean, In the Convention of the State of Pennsylvania. On Saturday the 24th of November, 1787.* Although this was not an "authorized" publication, the printed text mimicked the genre of officially published debates: the title that appears on page three is simply "Proceedings in Convention, &c." A note on the final page suggests that Bradford (who held the state contract to print all laws) had tried to secure a copyright for the pamphlet, a move that would (if successful) potentially infringe upon and circumvent the rights of those printers who had won the contract to print the proceedings of the state convention.[126] The status of who owned Wilson's speech was ambiguous. Wilson, for one, could not be said to have authored the pamphlet. The speech was made in a public capacity, but it was not printed at the demand of the convention, so the official printers to the convention really had no right to it. Bradford could submit the pamphlet as his property as printer, but the "author" of Wilson's speech was ultimately Alexander Dallas, the shorthand reporter who had recorded the speech for Bradford's *Pennsylvania Herald*.

In the weeks that followed the publication of Wilson's speech, Federalists charged that Dallas had intentionally misrepresented Wilson, and that the speech was as much Dallas's as Wilson's. One Pennsylvania delegate sent the pamphlet to the governor of Massachusetts, complaining that the transcription was "very inaccurate, and not only parts are omitted and the leading points often lost for want of seizing the exact expression, but some parts are absolutely misstated."[127] Thomas Lloyd, who had also transcribed the speech for a planned book publication, issued a statement in early December, denying that the speech was his work and promising that his own future edition of the speech would be "without mutilation or misrepresentation."[128] Francis Hopkinson wrote to Jefferson in Paris that "Wilson exerted himself to the astonishment of all hearers. The powers of Demosthenes and Cicero seemed to be united in this able orator," but he declined to send Jefferson the Dallas version of the speech and promised to send Lloyd's version when it appeared.[129]

In a series of copyrights secured in 1787, the transcriber of debates emerged as the legal author of the speeches he transcribed. In that year the transcriber Thomas Lloyd and the publisher Daniel Humphreys obtained a copyright in Pennsylvania for the first volume of *Proceedings and Debates of the General Assembly of Pennsylvania. Taken in Short-Hand by Thomas Lloyd.*[130] Humphreys then transferred his partial ownership of the rights to another printer, Joseph James, who brought out the second volume of *Proceedings.* Lloyd also secured the copyright for his *Debates of the Convention, of the State of Pennsylvania, on the Constitution, Proposed for the Government of the United States. . . . Taken Accurately in Short-Hand, By Thomas Lloyd.*[131] Lloyd retailed this volume, observing in one advertisement in a Maryland paper that "the critical reviewers at New York, speak in the highest terms of this work, as the best treatise on government in general."[132] Modern bibliographers often list such texts as if they were the official publications of states (filing them under the state name as author); that reviewers could think of Lloyd's *Debates* as a treatise and also as Lloyd's suggests, however, the point at which transcription and authorship met in late eighteenth-century America.[133] There was no question that, when Lloyd wrote down what the state's representatives said, it was Lloyd who both authored and owned their speech.

Once transcription was imagined as a kind of authorship, and multiple transcribers and publishers competed to represent the speeches of representatives, charges of plagiarism sometimes followed. A notice in the New York *Daily Advertiser* on June 22, 1789, alerted readers to a theft of intellectual property:

> It is requested that a certain Printer, who copies the Debates of the House of Representatives, as published in this paper, would copy them literally and faithfully, and not attempt to disguise the transcript by dishonest interpolation, and disingenuous alterations of phrases, to give it the air of originality. Men of sense and observation will easily detect the ungenerous plagiarism through this thin veil of concealment; but many readers, who have not an opportunity or curiosity to make comparisons, may not see the mangled imitation.[134]

The text was pointed particularly at Lloyd, whose manuscript shorthand notes rarely correspond with the polished style of the debates he published in the *Congressional Register.* Lloyd, in fact, seems to have transcribed his published version of debates not from the debates themselves, but from the transcriptions of others, making slight changes in phrasing to avoid charges of theft.[135] Like the reporters he stole from, Lloyd had a

distinctive style of reporting speeches, a style that at once tried to offer
the best and most literary representations of the voices of the speakers
yet had to be distinguishable from the style of other reporters.

But what was the best way to represent a speaking subject? In October 1787, the New York publisher Francis Childs issued two editions
of *Observations on the Plan of Government submitted to the Federal
Convention, In Philadelphia, on the 28th of May, 1787. By Mr. Charles
Pinckney, Delegate from the State of South-Carolina.* Unlike most post-
Convention texts by delegates (which offered observations on the finished text of September 17), this pamphlet purported to give readers a
peek into the Convention by printing Pinckney's observations as they
were "*Delivered at different Times in the Course of their Discussions.*"
The speech concerned the "Virginia Plan" presented in May, a plan far
more radical in the power it granted the national government than the
Constitution signed in September. The text was presented as an address
(as was customary in the Constitutional Convention) to the president
of the Convention. Although it seems likely that Pinckney supplied the
printer with the text, Childs printed the speech as if it had been captured
in delivery at the Convention, presenting a Sternian prose punctuated
almost entirely by dashes:

> Our government is despised—our laws are robbed of their respected
> terrors—their inaction is a subject of ridicule—and their exertion, of abhor-
> rence and opposition—rank and office have lost their reverence and effect—
> our foreign policies are as much deranged, as our domestic economy—our
> friends are slackened in their affection—and our citizens loosened from their
> obedience. . . . To what, then, are we to attribute our embarrassments as a
> Nation? The answer is an obvious one.—To the weakness and impropriety
> of a government, founded in mistaken principles—incapable of combining
> the various interests it is intended to unite and support—and destitute of that
> force and energy, without which, no government can exist.[136]

The style of Pinckney's pamphlet was highly unusual in other respects,
especially since it offered a critique of a document that was not public and made no mention of the document that had been published. By
claiming to represent a speech made within the closed session of the
Constitutional Convention, Pinckney broke the vow of secrecy the members had imposed on themselves. Washington and Madison, on reading
the pamphlet, were disappointed that the young South Carolinian would

willfully compromise the proceedings of the Federal Convention simply for the sake of personal literary "fame."[137]

Pinckney's pamphlet was part of a general cultural movement to represent American voices in the action of eloquent speaking.[138] The lawyer and Rhode Island congressman James Mitchell Varnum, in a preface to his *The Case, Trevett against Weeden* (1787), explained that he would print his argument as he spoke it rather than relate it as a historical narrative. "BUT why should the author impose upon the reader a recital of his *own* tedious, indigested pleas?" he asked. "Why did he not content himself with a simple relation of facts?" The reason was simple: "the orators of Greece and Rome exhibited to the public, in the same way, their pleadings upon the most weighty occasions. And although the author hath not the vanity to compare himself to any the least of these orators, yet he feels a pleasure in *attempting* to imitate them, and to revive that part of ancient learning."[139] Noah Webster made much the same argument in selecting some American orations for his *American Selection of Lessons in Reading and Speaking*, arguing that the writings of the Revolution "are not inferior in any respect to the orations of Cicero and Demosthenes."[140] And when Jonathan Elliot published the debates of the state ratifying conventions in the late 1820s, he cited "the most bold and striking features of eloquence" in some of the speeches as one of the chief attractions of the work.[141] Samuel Lorenzo Knapp, in his *Lectures on American Literature* (1829), welcomed the publication of Jonathan Elliot's *Debates*, but cautioned that "at that time the art of reporting speeches was but little known; and it cannot be supposed that in cases where the speakers did not assist the reporters, that we have anything more than the skeletons of the speeches delivered." Even worse, after a "comparison of their different styles of speaking on other subjects," Knapp found "that the reporter's, not the speaker's style, is to be seen."[142]

The literary style of transcription varied from reporter to reporter. Some chose to represent speakers in the first person; others reported speech in the third person. Lloyd's transcripts of the September 4–29, 1787 debates in the Pennsylvania General Assembly are typical. Lloyd employed mostly short third-person summaries: "Mr. Brackenridge represented, that . . .," "Mr. Wright hoped . . .," and so on. But sometimes the voice of the speakers shifted dramatically to first person. When debating a call for a state ratifying convention, for instance, the voices were mostly in the first person: "Mr. D. Clymer. . . . Could it be expected that

Virginia (the dominion of Virginia, as some people in derision call it—though I say it is a land of liberty—a land of patriots, and the nurse of science)—I say will you expect, Sir, that Virginia and the southern states shall coincide with alterations made only for the benefit of Pennsylvania?"[143] The dashes represented Lloyd's attempts to take down and make sense of unpunctuated speech. The inclusion of first-person speech may have signaled that the speaker had collaborated with the transcriber after the fact (an occasional practice), or it could represent a self-conscious attempt to dramatize the often tedious debates.

In any event, the tension between first- and third-person voicing reflected the eighteenth-century history of reporting speech. The *Gentleman's Magazine* of London began carrying "PROCEEDINGS and DEBATES of the last Session of Parliament" in July 1732. The style in the first installment showed members (whose names had been typographically veiled) speaking in the third person: "Mr *D—rs* said, he wish'd he could tell his neighbours, on his Return into the Country, that Part of our Debts were paid off. . . ."[144] By August 1732, when the debates became the lead article, some voices had shifted to first person: "Mr *P—r*] If I thought there was an absolute Necessity of continuing a Standing Army . . ."; "Sir *R—t W—le*] Sir, I find the Gentlemen who oppose the Motion. . . ."[145] For legal reasons, first-person speeches were often explicitly identified as summaries produced by the transcriber: "Mr *O—pe* stood up, and spoke to the Effect following: I am persuaded that . . ."; "Capt. V—n rose up and spoke in Substance as follows, 'Mr. Speaker, I hope. . . .'"[146] Increasingly, the speeches in the *Gentleman's Magazine* become longer, so that by 1736 the monthly section of debates was often taken up with a single speech or reply to a speech. In 1737 it published a sixty-page supplement of "Proceedings," with a note at the end: "The candid Reader, who knows the Difficulty, and sometimes Danger, of publishing the Speeches in P—t, will easily conceive, that it is impossible to do it in the very words of the Speakers. With regard to the major Part, we pretend only to represent the Sense as near as may be expected in a summary Way." Most speeches appear in the supplement with tags like "To this it was answered in Substance as follows" or "The Reply was to the Effect as follows. . . ."[147] And this form was largely continued after the House of Commons passed a resolution in 1738 forbidding the reporting of parliamentary proceedings, including thinly veiled versions rendered as if they had taken place not in London but (referencing *Gulliver's Travels*) "in the Senate of MAGNA LILLIPUTIA."[148] After

1737, Samuel Johnson served as the person who put the illegal notes of others into a presentable literary style.

While parliamentary injunctions and threats of libel in Britain dictated some of the shifts between first-person speech and third-person reports, the authors of British shorthand manuals sometimes suggested that some transcribers were simply more capable than others. Similarly, John Carey of Philadelphia in 1793 contrasted "him who intends to take down entire speeches, as they are pronounced in public" with others who simply wished to record the "substance" of a speech, noting that "in this, as in every other art, the man of superior genius will, no doubt, be most successful; and may (like the accurate Mr. [David] Robertson, who has so faithfully published the Debates of the Virginia Convention) be able to take down every word, as it is uttered; whilst others, of inferior abilities must be content with the substance of a speech, without confining themselves to the exact words of the orator."[149] The opposition between "substance" and "every word" was perhaps a false one: no system of stenography developed in the eighteenth century allowed reporters to completely capture a fast-talking speaker. Alexander Dallas's transcript of Wilson's speech of November 1787 appeared in Philadelphia not as the speech itself but under the humble title of *The Substance of a Speech Delivered by James Wilson*. Even Lloyd himself never promised all the speeches of a given legislative session, merely "the most interesting Speeches."[150] Lloyd's system, one modern stenography expert has noted, was a sort of "longhand shorthand," incapable of recording a speech verbatim. And, of course, Lloyd also plagiarized some of the speeches from other newspapers, changing the voice from first person to third or from third to first in order to make the transcripts look like original products of his own pen.[151]

The tension between representing the exact words of debates rather than reporting their substance paralleled contemporary difficulties in the composition of fiction. The editor of a posthumously published novel by William Hill Brown (d. 1793) argued in 1807 that it was better to represent character in a novel through the speaker's sentiments rather than through a mimesis of voice. He contrasted the representational models of "English relation" and "French dialogue," claiming that Brown's was a "*COMPOSITE* style." But a composite style presented certain difficulties. It demanded that "the character be so strongly designated that the reader may know who is the speaker, not only by the insertion of *said he* and *said she*, but, in some small degree, by the uniformity of the speaker's sentiments." But most "modern novelists," the editor observed, "leaving both sentiment and person as above and beneath their comprehension, have endeavoured with bold attempt to make a *verbal* distinction of character . . . which is a difference known only by provincial accent; false English; favourite words; idiomatical barbarity; vernacular vulgarity; insipid tautaulogy; discordant technicals; disgusting prophanity; domestic prejudices, or foreign unintelligibility."[152] According to this critic, verbal distinctions like dialect and idiom held no real promise for characterization unless at the same time the writer was able to convey "the speaker's sentiments." Members of the House of Representatives were not characters in a novel, but transcribers faced similar literary problems of representing "sentiment" and "person."

But unlike novelists, transcribers had the power of representing or misrepresenting speakers who were themselves representatives. The homogenization and even confusion of voice in transcribed speeches sometimes offended the speakers. Transcribers and publishers regularly claimed to report speeches with "impartiality, and strict accuracy."[153] Manuals like Robert Graves and Samuel Ashton's *The Whole Art of Tachygraphy, or, Short-hand Writing Made Plain and Easy*, published in England in 1775, held out the promise of taking an objective, neutral account of any speech by any speaker. To take one example, the editors of the declarations or sermons of the Quaker Stephen Crisp published in 1694 (and republished in 1787) felt obliged to admit that the anonymous London transcriber was "of another [religious] persuasion," but explained that it was "the Art of Short-Writing" itself that kept the transcriber honest.[154] Shorthand might allow a writer's hand to move at the speed of a speaker's lips, but it could hardly correct for partisanship. Federalists like Benjamin Rush in 1788 complained of "the imprudent conduct of [the Anti-Federalist] Mr. Dallas in misrepresenting the proceedings and speeches in the Pennsylvania Convention."[155] Madison lamented in June 1789 that in the transcriptions of the House of Representatives "the reasonings on both sides are mutilated, often misapprehended, and not infrequently reversed."[156] To Jefferson in Paris, Madison sent the first number of Lloyd's *Congressional Register* in May 1789, noting it would give him "*some idea* of the discussions in the new Legislature" but also that "you will see at once the strongest evidences of mutilation & perversion, and of the illiteracy of the Editor."[157] Debates on the floor of the House of Representatives specifically took up the issue of "misrepresentation" by reporters in January 1790. A few months earlier,

Aedanus Burke of South Carolina proposed a resolution that would allow the House of Representatives to appoint an official reporter. Burke
resented the "misrepresentations," claiming that he did "not like that the
world should suppose these publications were authorized by the house."
But others like Madison found the unofficial quality of the publication
to be their greatest virtue, since representatives could always claim that
their speech had been mistaken or misconstrued. Congressionally sanc-
tioned publication would entail the responsibility of defending one's political speech out of the doors of the House.[158]

In the face of criticism of the "misrepresentation" of representatives,
newspaper editors remarked that transcripts were the only thing that assured that the people themselves would not be misrepresented. "This
method of laying open to the full view of the people the proceedings of
their political Fathers," one editor observed, "is productive of the hap-
piest effects: It prevents innumerable impositions arising from misrepresentation and falsehood; it unfolds principles, and exhibits characters
in a just point of light; the people learn to know whom to trust, and to
give honor to whom honor is due."[159] John Carey, in his 1793 summary of
Thomas Lloyd's system of shorthand, fantasized that the laws would be
better respected if every man was his own "stenograph," wishing

> that every man, capable of handling a pen, would be able to take down the
> substance of a speech, while he sits in the gallery, and to inform his fam-
> ily and neighbors, upon what principle Mr. A, B, or C, voted for such and
> such a measure; and upon what ground it was opposed by Messers. D, E, and
> F. Hence would, no doubt, result respect and obedience to the Laws of the
> Union, and grateful veneration for those who frame them; since their con-
> duct and their motives, in order to command the general approbation of their
> fellow-citizens, need but to be publicly known.[160]

Such statements couched the surveillance quality of transcription in the
language of patriotism and obedience, but there was always a hint that
the transcripts served as the best way for the people to control their representatives between elections.

As noted, the specter of partisanship haunted the concept of transcription in the period. How, after all, could a "warm and decided friend
to the new constitution" be expected to report the speeches of its opponents accurately?[161] The question remains a real one, especially as it relates to the most famous notes associated with the Constitution, those of

James Madison published in 1840. In an unfinished preface to these notes written late in his life (ca. 1835–36), Madison described his process:

> I chose a seat in front of the presiding member with the other members, on my right & left hand. In this favorable position for hearing all that passed, I noted in terms legible & in abbreviations & marks intelligible to myself what was read from the Chair or spoken by the members; and losing not a moment unnecessarily between the adjournment & reassembling of the Convention I was enabled to write out my daily notes during the session or within a few finishing days after its close in the extent and form preserved in my own hand on my files. In the labor and correctness of this I was not a little aided by practice, and by a familiarity with the style and the train of observation and reasoning which characterized the principal speakers. It happened, also, that I was not absent a single day, nor more than a casual fraction of an hour in any day, so that I could not have lost a single speech, unless a very short one. It may be proper to remark, that, with a very few exceptions, the speeches were neither furnished, nor revised, nor sanctioned, by the speakers, but were written out from my notes, aided by the freshness of my recollections.[162]

Madison constructs himself as the perfect reporter for the debates: he takes the ideal physical position for listening; he is familiar with the principal speakers; he attends constantly. But Madison also suggests that he is not a mere medium for the relay of information but a historical filter. His notes are not the product of capturing speech at the moment of articulation in the statehouse, but the result of time "between the adjournment & reassembling of the Convention"—a product of evening retrospection and reflection rather than immediacy. Madison did not practice shorthand writing. His longhand notes, the most extensive records of the activities of the Convention, fill hundreds of pages, but they are in no sense as long as they could have been. Madison was probably glad that they were not more extensive. His retrospective preface signaled his fear that the notes would represent the speaker Madison (or "Mr M" as he often referred to himself) as an explicit advocate for a strong national government, a position that had become a political embarrassment to him as early as the 1790s. He must have worried that the notes would (as they in fact did) lend support to those politicians and readers who wanted to construct the power of the federal government in the broadest terms imaginable. At the close of the above passage, Madison observes that certain "views of the subject might occasionally be presented, in the speeches and proceedings, with a latent reference to a compromise on some middle ground, by mutual concession." In other words, the expressions sometimes must be read with an understanding that certain speakers (including "Mr M") articulated positions they may not have agreed with in order to achieve political compromise.[163] For political reasons, Madison suggested, representatives sometimes expressed themselves in voices that were not really their own.

*   *   *

"Representatives . . . are the sign—the people are the thing signified," the Anti-Federalist "Brutus" remarked in a New York newspaper in November 1787. One week later, another New York paper published Madison's remark in *Federalist* no. 10 that representatives should be able to pronounce "the public voice" better than the people themselves.[164] In his conception of representatives as a passive sign of the people, "Brutus" suggested that the people were the substance to a representative assembly's form. For "Brutus," representatives did not express but were expressed, did not govern so much as they were governed by a sympathetic identity with their constituents. Madison's image of the representative as transcriber and mouthpiece reversed this conception: it was the people who were expressed by the representative, not the representative by the people.

This chapter has argued that any serious consideration of the political meanings for representation must engage with contemporary understandings of "likeness." Political writers in the period were by no means precise in their use of terms like "portrait" or "miniature," but they employed a common aesthetic language that figured political representation as a shifting problem of "views" and viewers. The novel genre of the written constitution and the older idea of the social contract or compact shared with miniature paintings and shorthand minutes an aesthetics of smallness. To "contract" or "compact" meant to reduce, to make small, as well as to pledge. In a larger sense, both the Anti-Federalist critique of the pretensions of Federalist representation and the reality of the cultural and material practices of eighteenth-century transcription pose lingering problems for the recovery of an original meaning of the Constitution through the transcripts of the Constitutional Convention and state ratifying conventions. Politics and transcription united in the idea of the "dictator," the eighteenth-century name that embraced both a person who told another what to write and a person whose word is law. But even if representatives were to take dictation from their constituents, as Federalists imagined, the people could not become dictators in the second sense. For transcription, as any shorthand writer knew, always meant contraction, omission, and the partial intrusion of the voice of the recorder. The conception of representatives as transcribers of a "public voice" that the people could not themselves articulate necessarily entailed the exclusion of irrelevant material and incoherent voices, and we can trace the difficulties involved in exactly representing another's voice in the variance of notes taken by the different members of the Constitutional Convention in the debate over representation described at the opening of this chapter. The disparity between these transcripts serves as an ironic parable of the pitfalls involved in defining representation as exact transcription.

But this disparity has often had the opposite effect. In the face of multiple and conflicting transcriptions, even the most sophisticated readings of the records of the Convention and the origins of the Constitution have privileged Madison's own notes as the most "exact transcript" of the proceedings. In imitation of the Federalist fantasy of refined views, historians of the Constitution have either refused to see Madison's perspective as evidence of representative failure and authorial control, or they have silently incorporated his notes and the various other transcripts into a seamless narrative. A more accurate narration of the writing of the Constitution must recognize the situated perspectives of the delegates, a belated reflection of the Anti-Federalist understanding that a small group of elite men could never represent the views of their social inferiors. But it should also acknowledge the inability of any of the reporters in Philadelphia or in the state ratifying conventions to produce a perfect transcript of the meanings and intentions at play in the moment of social contraction.

Even Madison felt the need to revise his manuscript notes, and he did so in a number of instances to clarify the views of his colleagues on the issue of slavery. That issue was intimately associated with representation, and the question of how to reconcile slave states with nonslave states and to provide equitable representation for each preoccupied much of the early part of the Convention. Madison himself argued that the difference between slave states and nonslave states was the fundamental difference in the nation; it was for him a geographical difference between the North and the South. But slavery existed in every state except Massachusetts. This fact was pointed out by Gouverneur Morris in what turns out to have been the largest single nonprocedural addition to Madison's notes. "Travel thro' ye whole Continent," Morris apparently said, "& you behold the prospect continually varying with the appearance & disappearance of slavery. The moment you leave ye E. Sts & enter N. York, the effects of the institution become visible: Passing thro' the Jerseys and entering Pa. every criterion of superior improvement witnesses the change. Proceed Southwdly & every step you take thro' ye great regions of slaves, presents a desert increasing with ye increasing proportion of these wretched beings." Max Farrand, the editor of the standard edition of Madison's notes, found it "difficult to account for this passage." The manuscript "seems to show fairly certainly that it was a later insertion." Almost certainly, however, the insertion was made sometime between 1787 and the early 1790s, when Madison provided Jefferson's nephew, John Wayles Eppes, with his notes. But Morris went further than simply suggesting that slavery was the fundamental difference between the states: he suggested that he would rather pay a tax and emancipate all the slaves than produce a Constitution that encouraged slavery. Morris was late in making his motion—that representation in the House of Representatives should be proportional only to free inhabitants, not slaves. This compromise had been made weeks earlier, when Morris was away from the Convention.[165] The clash between the right to liberty and to property, the cultural difference slavery made between the states, and the proposals sometimes put forward to solve these problems are the focus of the next chapter.

PART II

The Culture of Natural Rights

CHAPTER FOUR

Slavery and the Language of Rights

The revolutionary embrace of the state as a work of art went hand in hand with a conception of the naturalness of rights, for alienated natural rights were the building blocks of government. Slavery challenged the culture of natural rights that emerged in the 1770s and 1780s. Claims for the rights of persons sat uneasily with claims for rights in persons. But by bringing the claims so close together, the culture of natural rights also challenged the legitimacy of slavery.

Liberty and slavery sat in close proximity in revolutionary America. On July 2, 1776, the Continental Congress voted independence, and the printer Benjamin Towne of Philadelphia reported the news that same day on the back page of his *Pennsylvania Evening Post* (fig. 13). There, amid commercial advertisements for products from around the globe, the announcement that "the CONTINENTAL CONGRESS declared the UNITED COLONIES FREE and INDEPENDENT STATES" sat side by side with notices of three individuals who had declared their own form of independence. Simon Gibney, a thirty-year-old Irish servant, had taken flight from a baker. William Wright, "a bought apprentice lad" of eighteen, had broken his contract with a shoemaker, stealing himself and the tools of his master's trade. And Ishmael, "twenty-five years of age, above six feet high, strong made, his colour between a Mulatto and a Black," managed to run away from his owner despite his being "somewhat lame, occasioned by his having his thigh bone broke

Laſt Wedneſday the Fowey ſailed from Annapolis with Governor Eden on board.

The following Captains, belonging to this port, were at the bay of Honduras the 24th of laſt February, viz. Spain, John Green, Taylor, Philips; alſo Capt. Buchannan of Baltimore.

In CONGRESS, June 27, 1776.

Reſolved, That four companies of Germans be raiſed in Pennſylvania, and four companies in Maryland, for to compoſe the German battalion.

That it be recommended to the Committee of Safety of Pennſylvania immediately to appoint proper officers for, and direct the inliſtment of the four companies to be raiſed in that colony. By order of Congreſs,

JOHN HANCOCK, Preſident.

In COMMITTEE of SAFETY, July 1, 1776.

The Committee taking into conſideration the reſolution of Congreſs, and being of opinion that the public ſervice requires that it be carried into execution, without any delay, and the recruiting ſervice be entered on as ſoon as poſſible,

Reſolved, That this Board will on Friday the fifth inſtant appoint Captains, and on Friday the twelfth inſtant Lieutenants and Enſigns, for the four companies of Germans directed to be raiſed in this province by order of Congreſs, and that it is the opinion of this Board that, conſiſtent with the reſolve of Congreſs, no perſons but ſuch as are Germans born, or the ſons of Germans, ſhould hold any office in ſaid companies.

All ſuch gentlemen, who fall under the above deſcriptions, and are deſirous to enter into the ſervice, are requeſted to ſend in their applications as early as may be.

Extract from the minutes,

WILLIAM GOVETT, Secretary.

This day the CONTINENTAL CONGRESS declared the UNITED COLONIES FREE and INDEPENDENT STATES.

TO be SOLD, the brigantine TWO FRIENDS. She is a prime ſailor, but three years old, and carries nine hundred and fifty or a thouſand barrels of flour.

The ſchooner MARY ANN. She is a prime ſailor, but four years old, and carries four hundred and fifty barrels of flour.

The ſchooner is loaded and ready to go, and will be ſold with her cargo, or alone. She has an inventory ſuitable and complete. The brig may be fitted for ſea with a very ſmall expence, and the ſchooner requires none. Both veſſels are very good, but any gentleman inclining to purchaſe may have them viewed by proper perſons. Inquire for Mr. JOHN PARRY, on board the brig, at Vine-ſtreet wharf.

Philadelphia, July 2, 1776.

RAN away laſt Sunday week from the ſubſcriber, baker, in Second-ſtreet, an Iriſh ſervant man named SIMON GIBNEY, thirty years of age or upwards. He had on, when he went away, a blue coat, ſpotted ſtuff jacket, a pair of Wilton drilling breeches, white ſhirt, half worn beaver hat, thread ſtockings, a pair of pumps half worn, and pinchbeck buckles. He is ſuppoſed to be in or about Philadelphia.

Whoever takes up ſaid ſervant, and ſecures him ſo that his maſter gets him again, ſhall have TWENTY FIVE SHILLINGS reward, and reaſonable charges.

LAWRENCE POWEL.

Choice INDIGO to be ſold by John Hart.

Philadelphia, July 2, 1776.

THIRTY SHILLINGS Reward.

RAN away laſt Saturday night, from his maſter, a certain WILLIAM WRIGHT, a bought apprentice lad, by trade a ſhoemaker, about eighteen years of age, pale complexion, ſhort brown hair, to which he generally ties a falſe tail, is knock kneed, and very ſlovenly in his dreſs. He took with him the tools of his trade, and ſome clothes, in a bag made of old ſail cloth, drawn together at the mouth like a purſe, with a calf ſkin thong. He is with his mother, who is ſuſpected of having inticed him to abſcond. Any perſon ſecuring him in jail, ſhall receive the above reward and all reaſonable charges, by applying to his maſter between Market and Cheſnut ſtreets, in Front-ſtreet.

ANDREW HUCK.

FOR the accommodation of paſſengers going up and down to the FORT, a STAGE BOAT, well provided for that purpoſe, which will ſet off from Joſeph Price's wharf, oppoſite the ſign of St. Patrick, Southwark, three times a week, viz.

Sundays, Wedneſdays and Fridays, between eight and nine o'clock. Each perſon paying one ſhilling and ſixpence for going and coming the ſame day, or not returning one ſhilling. JAMES SLOAN and JOHN DONNAL.

THREE DOLLARS Reward.

RAN away the fifth inſtant, a Negro man named ISHMAEL, twenty-five years of age, above ſix feet high, ſtrong made, his colour between a Mulatto and a Black, rocks in his walk, or rather ſomewhat lame, occaſioned by his having his thigh bone broke when a boy. Had on when he went away a ſmall bimmmed hat, a brown cloth jacket without ſleeves, let cut in the back, new tow ſhirt and trouſers, old ſhoes. Whoever takes up and ſecures ſaid Negro in any jail, ſo as his maſter may have him again, ſhall have the above reward and reaſonable charges, paid by the ſubſcriber living in Second ſtreet, oppoſite the Swede's church in the diſtrict of Southwark.

WILLIAM THOMAS.

N. B. All maſters of veſſels and others are forbid to carry, take, or harbour him at their peril.

A QUANTITY of white and brown BUCKRAM to be ſold by Mary Flanagan, the corner of Front and Spruce ſtreets.

A FEW hogſheads of old Jamaica SPIRITS, very good green TEA in quarter cheſts, Goa ARRACK, and two CANNON, four pounders, to be ſold by Dominick Joyce, at Capt. John Sibbald's in Second-ſtreet, oppoſite the New Market. Philad. June 11.

STRAYED from the ſubſcriber, living near John Jones's, inn-keeper in Carnarvan townſhip, Berks county, a BAY MARE, one quarter blooded, a natural trotter, ſhod all round, remarkably bad to ſhoe behind, and difficult to catch when out of hand, between thirteen and fourteen hands high, ſix years old this ſummer, a few white hairs mixed with brown on her forehead, by way of a ſtar, a little roundiſh brand on her nigh ſhoulder. Whoever takes up ſaid Mare and brings her home, or gives notice where ſhe is, ſo that the owner gets her again, ſhall have FIVE POUNDS reward and reaſonable charges. ROBERT SMITH.

PHILADELPHIA: Printed by BENJAMIN TOWNE, in Front-ſtreet, near the London Coffee-Houſe.

FIGURE 13. Congressional resolution for independence and runaway slave notice, *Pennsylvania Evening Post*, July 2, 1776. Reproduced by permission of The Huntington Library, San Marino, California.

when a boy." William Thomas, who claimed to own Ishmael, was a recent graduate of the College of Philadelphia and had inherited the slave in 1775. Thomas's father may very well have abused Ishmael and broken his leg; given the description of the fugitive's complexion, it is possible that Ishmael's father was a free white person like Thomas's father, someone who had coerced Ishmael's unfree black mother into sex. The young master had probably grown up with the slightly older slave and knew him well, for Thomas waited an extraordinarily long time before advertising a reward for the return of his property, perhaps because he expected his slave to return on his own. Ishmael had been gone almost a month. He was one of many black slaves in Philadelphia and elsewhere who "stole" themselves in advance and in the wake of the formal Declaration of Independence.[1]

The newspapers and state papers of the American Revolution made impassioned claims about the rights of liberty and property, and in doing so set the stage for a civil war in the language of rights acted out by and upon unfree individuals like Ishmael. The Revolution divided what on July 2, 1776, officially became a new nation, and it also ushered in new forms of affiliation, identification, and political union. One wonders, though, if readers of the *Evening Post* would have identified a fugitive slave's flight with the resolution that passed Congress on July 2 or with the Declaration explaining that resolution that was dated July 4, published in Towne's newspaper on July 5, and publicly declared in Philadelphia and elsewhere on July 8. That Declaration, the Declaration of Independence, announced that Congress held that "all Men are created equal, that they are endowed by their Creator with certain unalienable Rights, that among these are Life, Liberty, and the Pursuit of Happiness."[2]

Though the phrasing was novel, the sentiment was not. Since the 1760s talk of natural rights had been omnipresent in pamphlets and newspapers; by the early 1770s, in Massachusetts and elsewhere, free and enslaved blacks made claims for their rights that built upon that talk. Ongoing military actions beginning in April 1775 also created a climate of instability in which more and more black slaves like Ishmael "stole" themselves, sometimes with the explicit intent of accepting Virginia governor Lord Dunmore's offer to trade military service with the British for freedom. Runaway notices in Philadelphia in this period sometimes explicitly mentioned that (as one slaveholder put it) "Negroes in general think that Lord Dunmore is contending for their liberty," and that run-

away slaves needed an "honest Whig" to disabuse them of that thought
and return them to their masters. It is therefore likely that some whites
read the notice of Ishmael's escape as further proof of a British conspiracy to rob the colonies of their liberty and property. Other readers, such
as the Quakers who had been manumitting slaves in large numbers or
the Philadelphia reformers who had founded the world's first abolition
society in 1775, perhaps identified Ishmael's cause with America's; they
routinely worried that Americans compromised claims for rights (and for
God's protection) by enslaving human beings. Loyalists and British sym-
pathizers may have thought so too, and may have joined with Dr. Samuel
Johnson in wondering why it was that slaveholders always seemed to yelp
loudest about liberty. It is of course impossible to know if or how readers
of this newspaper connected the report of political independence with
these other notices, or, more important, if Ishmael himself connected his
escape into freedom and his rights with the actions and rhetoric of revolutionary white leaders.[3]

To ask the question is to confront two powerful narratives: one about
how the original meaning of the Declaration of Independence changed
over time; and the other about the way in which the imperial debate between Britain and the colonies transformed debates over domestic social
issues and particularly slavery. At least since the 1960s, scholars have
forcefully contended that the Declaration's meaning to its earliest domestic and foreign readers was not centered in the self-evident truths
of equality and individual rights of the second paragraph. Indeed, a
wealth of evidence suggests that the earliest readers of the Declaration
largely ignored the second paragraph in favor of the long list of charges
against the king and the final paragraph, which reproduced (and in early
printed versions typographically emphasized) the Congressional resolution of July 2. This Declaration—what could be called the original
Declaration—declared that "these United Colonies are, and of Right
ought to be, FREE AND INDEPENDENT STATES; that they are ab-
solved from all Allegiance to the British Crown, and that all political
Connection between them and the State of Great-Britain, is and ought
to be totally dissolved; and that as FREE AND INDEPENDENT
STATES, they have full Power to levy War, conclude Peace, contract Al-
liances, establish Commerce, and to do all other Acts and Things which
INDEPENDENT STATES may of right do." The uppercase letters of
the final paragraph of the printed Declaration were the only ones in the
body of the text, which was, after all, a declaration of independence and
not a declaration of rights.[4]

Historians have persuasively demonstrated that later generations transformed the Declaration from an assertion of national sovereignty to a charter of individual rights and a central creed of American civil religion. From the 1790s through the second decade of the nineteenth century, the Declaration was embroiled in party politics, was negatively associated by Federalists with Thomas Paine's *Rights of Man* and the French Revolution, and was enthusiastically embraced by members of the Democratic Republican party—sometimes specifically as a text produced by one of their national leaders, Thomas Jefferson. It was only in the second quarter of the nineteenth century, as the Federalist party declined and as a wave of celebrations and decorative facsimiles made the text better known, that a recognizably modern reading of the Declaration took hold. Indeed, Abraham Lincoln's explanation eighty years after the drafting of the document that the "assertion that 'all men are created equal' was of no practical use in effecting our separation from Great Britain; and it was placed in the Declaration, not for that, but for future use" stands as a characteristic mid-nineteenth-century acknowledgment that the document meant something else as a bequest than it had to those who bequeathed it.[5] The nature of that inheritance was subject to contest, to be sure; even Lincoln reduced what had been held as a self-evident truth to an "assertion" and (most famously in the Gettysburg Address) a "proposition." For abolitionists in the antebellum period the hypocrisy of slavery in a land of liberty was overwhelmingly obvious, as was the irony that a text so associated with liberty had been principally authored by a slaveholder; apologists for slavery, on the other hand, claimed that black people, if they were men at all, were not included within the rights-bearing "all Men" of the Declaration and that the authors of the Declaration had not meant to include them.[6] But despite their interpretive divide, all parties agreed that the meaning of the Declaration was to be discovered in the second paragraph, and it is this fact that marks the difference between the text's meaning in its immediate moment and its meaning to subsequent generations.

But a careful reading of the contemporary reception suggests that we need to revise some parts of the story of how the new nation understood its Declaration. The general outline of the means by which an eighteenth-century assertion of sovereignty became a nineteenth-century proclamation of liberty is no doubt true, but the narrative does not account for a significant strain of thought or a particular kind of contemporary reader. Beginning in 1776, when a young Massachusetts man of mixed racial identity named Lemuel Haynes—he had a black father and a white mother, identified himself as a "Mulatto," and had been an indentured servant but never a slave—took the Declaration's self-evident truth of equality and rights as an epigraph for a manuscript essay entitled "Liberty Further Extended: Or Free thoughts on the illegality of Slave-keeping" (fig. 14), antislavery activists, both black and white, seized upon the first part of the Declaration's second paragraph and insisted it was the central fact of the text, the premise upon which everything else rests. Antislavery writers like Haynes no doubt constituted a minority of early readers. For most the Declaration was (like other contemporary state papers issued by Congress) an ephemeral and forgettable text. Haynes's citation of the self-evident truths of rights and equality for all men was likely an afterthought added to the head of an essay already substantially drafted by July 1776, but his use of the second paragraph was significant: for, following others who had taken the rhetoric of colonial rights as an opportunity for questioning the hollowness of commitments to individual liberty, Haynes hoped to extend the meaning of that paragraph and to identify unfree blacks as the potential subjects of the Declaration's political philosophy.[7] Haynes did not read the text the way someone might in the middle of the nineteenth century, but it is clear that we need to adjust our understanding of the contemporary meaning of the Declaration of Independence, paying more attention to the ways in which free and unfree blacks, in league with white activists, worked to place black slaves at the center of the language of rights. We also need to pay more attention to the way in which they may have been at the center of the language of rights all along.

This chapter argues that slaves were the animating but often buried referent for the language of rights; that antislavery activists, black and white, hoped to revivify that language, insisting that blacks were or should be included in the contemporary declarations about equality and freedom; and that claims about political equality were tangled up with a debate about mental equality, a debate that embraced concerns about imitation and originality. Though often taking in other locations and paying special attention to transatlantic dialogues, I focus on these issues particularly in Massachusetts and I do so for two reasons: it was there that the clash of rights resulted in the largest archive of black writing, an archive including petitions and poetry, newspaper essays and broadsides. Massachusetts also provides a salutary spot precisely because of the manner in which slavery came to an end during the Revolution: by a 1783 judicial interpretation of the Massachusetts Constitution of 1780. After the Rev-

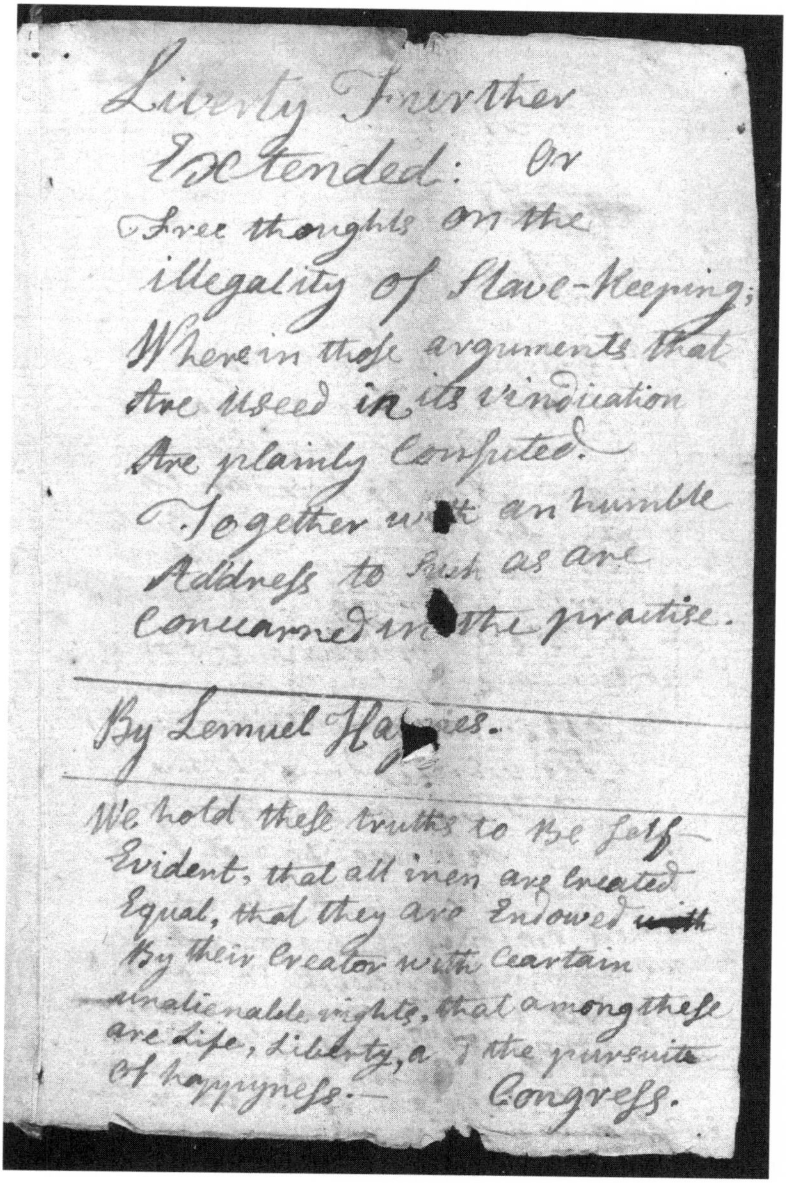
Liberty Further
Extended: Or
Free thoughts on the
illegality of Slave-keeping;
Wherein those arguments that
Are useed in its vindication
Are plainly Confuted.
Together with an humble
Address to such as are
Concearned in the practise.

By Lemuel Haynes.

We hold these truths to be self-
Evident, that all men are created
Equal, that they are Endowed ~~with~~
By their Creator with Ceartain
unalienable rights, that among these
are Life, Liberty, & the pursuit
of happyness. — Congress.

FIGURE 14. The manuscript title page of Lemuel Haynes's "Liberty Further Extended" (1776), with an epigraph from the second paragraph of the Declaration of Independence. Wendell Family papers, bMS Am 1907 (608). By permission of the Houghton Library, Harvard University.

olution, some believed that slavery had ended in Massachusetts because of popular opinion, an opinion moved along by blacks themselves, and one that had been encoded into the Constitution of 1780. In making such arguments, writers suggested that political change had to be organic— it had to conform to the will of the people. Such interpretations about the way in which the issue of slavery had been constitutionalized—that is, how slavery came to be seen as unconstitutional—may have been advanced because the state legislature had not enacted (as other states had and would) ordinary legislation to outlaw slavery, to compensate slave-holders, or to provide for the support of former slaves. Constitutionalizing the issue of slavery thus raised central problems for thinking about the relation between culture and constitutionalism.

The Revolution in Race and Rights

On the eve of the American Revolution, radicals on both sides of the Atlantic increasingly defined the constitutional relationship between Great Britain and the American colonies as a form of civil or political "slavery." While some pamphleteers may have employed this language in an abstract and technical sense, many speakers and writers derived additional rhetorical force from a shrill and perverse conflation of the identities of white colonists and black slaves.[8] Indeed, in the late 1760s and early 1770s, white colonists in Massachusetts criticized British policy by explicitly comparing the political relationship between the American colonies and Great Britain to the condition of black slaves under a tyrannical master. Almost immediately, free and unfree black writers appropriated the rhetoric of political slavery for their own purposes, comparing the real condition of blacks in slavery to the metaphorical condition of the colonies in a way that both reproduced and critiqued the language of the imperial debate. In a series of documents that began to circulate in 1773, the year in which a young enslaved black poet named Phillis Wheatley traveled from Boston to London to oversee the publication of her *Poems on Various Subjects*, groups of black slaves in Massachusetts petitioned the colonial legislature for freedom by modulating their grievances through the dominant vocabularies of natural rights and evangelical religion, claiming an analogy between their physical condition and the political situation of the colonies. When black slaves applied the metaphor of political slavery to themselves—that is, when they claimed to be the obvious but buried referent for that metaphor—they forced white readers to confront normative meanings inherent in the rhetoric of political slavery.

In ways we are only beginning to appreciate, the Age of Revolutions gave rise simultaneously to a modern language of rights and to modern forms of racism. Lynn Hunt has recently argued that the articulation of new forms of racism during the French Revolution demonstrates that "the systematic denigration of what you are not requires a doctrine, and such doctrines only appeared once inequality had to be justified."[9] Racism, as George Fredrickson and others have persuasively shown, was certainly not new. White colonial Americans and Europeans had developed a number of doctrines—some rooted in the Christian religion, others in African culture—to help explain racial slavery in the century and a half before the American Revolution.[10] The Revolution helped chip away at the legitimacy of such doctrinal justifications, but it also invented new ones. In the case of the slave petitions in Massachusetts in the early 1770s, some white readers clearly found the analogy between the black slave petitioners and the American colonies compelling, but others responded by narrowing the seemingly universalizing language of political liberty and by explaining why the case of black slaves in Massachusetts did not and could not resemble the case of Massachusetts itself. Like some modern historians of politics, a few contemporary theorists and writers argued that the connection between racial slavery and political slavery was merely a linguistic coincidence. In a way that would be unthinkable for modern historians, however, some radical white writers went on to claim that political slavery, a slavery of the mind, was far worse than racial slavery, a slavery of the body. Still others went further. When pressed to justify the uneven application of the language of liberty, to discriminate between the cases of white colonists and black slaves, whites also offered some of the first systematic accounts of the mental faculties of black people as naturally (rather than culturally) inferior to the mental faculties of white people and explained the enslavement of blacks as an effect rather than a cause of African intellectual and cultural inferiority.

The conflations of mental and political equality at work in debates about race and rights during the American Revolution become more legible and meaningful when seen in the context of aesthetic disputes over neoclassicism. The concerns of neoclassical aesthetics may seem far afield from issues of race and politics, but contemporary cultural discussions around the topic of neoclassicism shared with the political debates of the American Revolution a common metaphorical language of slavery. In the face of mounting criticism, neoclassical theorists in the third quarter of the eighteenth century offered advice to young artists and poets encouraging them to see imitation of the "old masters" not as a form of servility but as a step toward future originality. Opponents of neoclassicism, on the other hand, devalued the copying of prior aesthetic models and described imitation as a form of "slavery" and imitators as "slavish," a word that had come specifically to signify a lack of mental originality only in the 1750s. Wheatley's work emerged amid both a political and a cultural revolution, a moment when the imitative model of neoclassical aesthetics began to give way to new conceptions of creativity we commonly associate with romanticism. While some celebrated the example of Wheatley as evidence of the mental equality of blacks and whites, others cited the writings themselves as proof of the natural inability of black people to rise above the level of imitation. Wheatley and the black petitioners wrote at a moment when the fact of writing served but did not in itself support the claims for mental equality that were becoming so important in debates about political rights and personal liberty. The emerging cultural revolution against neoclassicism transformed the meaning of mental activity at precisely the moment that the political revolution against British rule placed mental activity at the center of what it meant to be a rights-bearing individual.

By examining the place of black people as referents for the metaphors of slavery in these contemporaneous revolutions, I argue that we can advance our understanding of how racial slavery informed two crucial debates and can draw some conclusions about the relationship between political and cultural ideas in the period, but the byproduct of such an investigation necessarily complicates traditional explanations of the spread of ideology and rights in the late eighteenth century. Because these revolutions have traditionally been treated by different disciplines, it has been easy to underestimate the influence of the cultural revolution on political ideologies. While scholars have argued that the vocabulary of political slavery was extended to black slaves during and after the American Revolution as a "'spill-over' effect" of the imperial debates, such interpretations can sometimes minimize eighteenth-century efforts to foreclose the expansion of rights and to exclude blacks from civil society by excluding them first from the category of humanity.[11] These efforts depended as much on emerging ideas about cultural production and imitation as on long-standing notions of race and slavery. By mapping the cultural revolution against neoclassicism onto the political revolt against civil slavery, we can begin to generate explanations for why white colonial writers (who so frequently compared themselves to slaves) were reluctant to expand the rhetoric of political slavery to include the real condition of black slaves.

Neo-roman political theorists in Europe and America were interested in understanding how people found themselves subject to tyrannical and despotic governments and why such people stayed subjected, so they described political slavery as a mental rather than a physical phenomenon, the effect not of chains and violence but of an irreversible intellectual debasement. Mental slavery made liberty impossible, radical writers argued, producing civilizations incapable of "culture" and cultures incapable of "civilization." The preoccupation with political slavery as a mental condition coupled with new cultural prejudices that depicted imitation as a subhuman activity (the province of parrots and apes) strongly influenced conceptions of race, slavery, and rights during and after the American Revolution. The issues raised by the appropriation and reappropriation of racial identities speak to the critical concerns of theorists of colonial discourse about the status and limits of subaltern agency, but the conclusions drawn from these cases of cultural and political mimesis should also interest historians of political and social thought.[12] Instead of drawing a direct (if deferred) line of causality from the rhetoric of political slavery to black emancipation, as some analysts have, we should look to that rhetoric to help us explain why justifications of black slavery based on the supposed mental and cultural inferiority of black people began to emerge precisely in this period, and why black writers in turn worked to shift rights discourse away from its new groundings in ideas about mental equality.[13]

The Problem of Political Slavery in the Age of Wheatley

When American colonists in the 1760s and 1770s claimed that they were enslaved to the British Parliament, they made an analogy between political bodies and natural bodies. Quentin Skinner, who has delineated what he conceives to be a "neo-roman theory of free states" in seventeenth-century England, explains that neo-roman theorists "assume that what it means to speak of a loss of liberty in the case of the body politic must be the same as in the case of an individual person. And they go on to argue—in the clearest proclamation of their classical allegiances—that what it means for an individual person to suffer a loss of liberty is for that person to be made a slave."[14] As the British radical Richard Price put it in 1778, any country "that is subject to the legislature of another country in which it has no voice, and over which it has no controul, cannot be said to be governed by its own will. Such a country, therefore, is in a state of slavery."[15] Or as the "Pennsylvania Farmer" John Dickinson argued in 1768, sliding from colonies to colonists, "those who are taxed without their own consent expressed by themselves are slaves. We are taxed without our consent expressed by ourselves or our representatives. We are therefore—SLAVES."[16] The presence of black slaves in the American colonies must have given the neo-roman analogy between political slavery and individual slavery a perverse meaning. But how exactly did race slavery inform political slavery, and how did these political metaphors in turn influence thoughts about race?

Accounts of political slavery frequently overlook the place of race in the making of the metaphor. This is particularly true of interpretations focusing on the republicanism of the period, interpretations that explain reaction against black slavery as an extension of the reaction against political slavery.[17] Scholars who have made a "linguistic turn" have devoted almost no attention to the relationship between the social reality and political rhetoric of slavery. Indeed, even historians who examine the "language of liberty" routinely treat the metaphor of political slavery in isolation from larger social or cultural meanings.[18] These interpretations stem in part from the explanations of the eighteenth-century political theorists themselves, who were often at pains to detail the differences between political and individual slavery. New World chattel slavery based on race was in fact a metaphoric referent for the "neo-roman theory of free states" at least as early as the seventeenth century, but for the writers who employed the language of political slavery the comparison between political slaves and black slaves was only of limited utility. As often as political writers compared political with racial slavery, they tended to qualify the comparison. The difference between political slavery and race slavery was that whites had a Lockean responsibility to overthrow an arbitrary government while blacks were to be pitied for their situation. As one writer in New York remarked in the middle of the century, "he that is obliged to act or not to act according to the arbitrary will and pleasure of a governor, or his director, is as much a *slave* as he who is obliged to act or not according to the arbitrary will and pleasure of a master or his overseer. And indeed, I never see anything of the kind but it gives me a lively idea of an overseer directing a plantation of Negroes in the West Indies; the only difference I know is that the slaves of the latter deserve highly to be pitied, the slaves of the former to be held in the utmost contempt."[19]

Black slaves deserved pity rather than contempt because, as Richard Price argued in a pamphlet popular on both sides of the Atlantic, political slavery was actually worse than individual slavery: "such a slavery [between states] is worse, on several accounts, than any slavery of private men to one another, or of kingdoms to despots within themselves.— Between one state and another, there is none of that fellow-feeling that takes place between persons in private life. Being detached bodies that never see one another . . . the state that governs cannot be a witness to the sufferings occasioned by its oppressions."[20] Price's rhetoric may have derived from older opposition thinking about civil slavery, or it may have been influenced more immediately by his friends in Boston, correspondents like Charles Chauncy who wrote to Price in 1772 of "those who are endeavouring to fasten on us chains of Slavery."[21] Price himself was less inclined than his American correspondents to write about political slavery as a physical condition involving chains; instead, he almost always represented it as a condition that resulted from a lack of mental fortitude, a lack that he noted in a 1775 letter to Chauncy would cause a people to "deserve to be slaves."[22] But from the beginning of the constitutional debate between Britain and the American colonies, colonial writers who used the metaphor were often trapped by their own rhetoric, comparing their situation to black slaves even as they justified black slavery because of its inherent dissimilarity to political slavery.[23]

What effect, then, could the concept of political slavery have on racial slavery? Traditional accounts of political slavery in the revolutionary vocabulary stress that the inconsistency between rhetoric and reality eventually made whites receptive to abolition and led northern black slaves to apply this emancipatory rhetoric to their own condition.[24] In such interpretations, causality has sometimes been a question of the "contagion" of liberty, an analytical metaphor that suggests ideas about freedom spread like a disease during the pre-revolutionary years. As a causal explanation, the metaphor can be sociologically restrictive, giving too little weight to the influence of new cultural attitudes about blackness that helped contain the contagion. Such explanations for the aftereffects of the Revolution have a long tradition, however, and were invoked as early as the late eighteenth century. Responding in 1795 to Virginia jurist St. George Tucker's request for information on the abolition of slavery in Massachusetts, Jeremy Belknap, the president of the Massachusetts Historical Society, remembered that it was the "inconsistency of contending for our own liberty, and at the same time depriving other people of theirs" that changed "publick opinion" in the decade before the Revolution. Most of the correspondents to whom Belknap circulated Tucker's letter agreed.[25]

These explanations retain interpretive power because of a lingering conception of the relationship between slavery and freedom as a "problem" or "paradox."[26] Our historical understanding of the social, economic, and cultural conditions of life under American slavery has widened in recent decades. But historians who have advanced our knowledge and who highlight the failure of the revolutionary generation to solve the problem of slavery still routinely invoke this explanatory framework.[27] And even recent historians who have developed new metaphors for understanding slavery (as a dance, a counterpoint, or a negotiation) and have significantly broadened our ideas about black agency under slavery occasionally still treat slavery as an ideological paradox or problem.[28] A counter-historiography has attempted to make sense of what it takes as only apparent problems or paradoxes, but what Edmund S. Morgan once described as the American paradox of liberty and slavery has recently been generalized by David Eltis as an "Atlantic paradox": How was it that the early modern peoples seemingly most committed to individual freedom were also the biggest players in the slave trade?[29] The language we use to frame this phenomenon necessarily shapes our understanding of race slavery during the American Revolution. It is the language of formal logic, and as such resonates with the word contemporaries themselves used most frequently: "inconsistency." If only society could be shown to be logically inconsistent, some early abolitionist writers implied, the problem and the paradox would resolve themselves. But, of course, recognizing the problem did not solve it. Even worse, such conceptions can cast whites as actors and blacks as merely reactors.[30]

We can throw the issues of civil and individual slavery into relief by considering the reception of *Poems on Various Subjects, Religious and Moral. By Phillis Wheatley, Negro Servant to Mr. John Wheatley, of Boston, in New England* (1773), a book that appeared in London on the eve of the American Revolution against colonial dependence and in the middle of a cultural revolution against the status of classical imitation. In the earliest British reviews of her volume, Wheatley's intellect functioned as the leading example of the way in which the capacity to write was not in itself an argument for mental equality. At the same time, the enslaved status of Wheatley's body exemplified the emptiness of colonial American Whig rhetoric, the failure of the language of liberty and political "slavery" to live up to the reality of its referents. The longest and most sustained review, published in the London *Monthly Review* a few months after her book appeared, developed both these points and was the only instance of what we might call—with obvious qualifications—a "peer" review.

The unsigned article, written by a white poet named John Langhorne, had remarkably little to say about Wheatley's poetry. Langhorne did not judge Wheatley's poems with anything like the critical rigor a reviewer had brought to bear on Langhorne's own poetry earlier in the year.[31] Like many who wrote about Wheatley in the 1770s, Dr. John Langhorne considered his review an occasion to speculate about the mental abilities of black people in general. But unlike those antislavery writers who seized on Wheatley's work as evidence of the mental equality of blacks, Langhorne saw the poems as positive proof that "genius" was not a product of the sun, a favorite cliché of those who equated poetry with solar inspiration. The central question for Langhorne was the relationship between Wheatley's putative "enlightenment" and the environment of Africa, for (despite the fact that by 1773 Wheatley had spent the majority of her short life in Boston) he considered her more African than American. The way he settled this question can be seen in how, when it came time to index his article, the editors of the *Monthly Review* chose to place it not under Wheatley's name or the title of her book (the typical practice for reviews) but as "MIND, the powers of, not enlightened in those climates that are most exposed to the action of the sun." When Langhorne turned from his theories about environment to the poems themselves, he condescended to praise the book as a limited achievement, especially for a young African woman, but the praise hardly constituted a challenge to advanced art practice in the metropolitan capital. In the end he criticized Wheatley's poems as "merely imitative" of poetic conventions and conjectured that "most of those people"—again presumably he meant Africans—"have a turn for imitation, though they have little or none for invention."[32]

But if the British reviewer classified Wheatley's poems as artifacts of African nature, he read her status as a product of American culture. Langhorne was the sole British reviewer to cite an instance of Wheatley's patriotic verse, the kind of poetry that Wheatley had all but excised from the 1773 volume in what seems to have been a conscious attempt to disconnect the fate of her poetry from the fate of the Whig campaign for political liberty. Langhorne specifically reproduced lines from her poem addressed to the secretary of state for North America, the Earl of Dartmouth. Wheatley had muted the poem slightly for publication in London, deleting a passage on the "injur'd Rights" of American colonists that had been included in an early version of the poem written in October 1772 and published by a New York newspaper in June 1773. But, even in the edited version available to British readers, the poem still accused the British administration of having lawlessly fashioned an "iron chain" with the intention to "enslave" America. The irony that an enslaved person could embrace the metaphorical Whig rhetoric of political slavery was not lost on Langhorne. After consigning the minds of black people to a secondary cultural status, Langhorne turned his critical eye to the political pretensions of Boston, the town where Wheatley had lived as a slave since the early 1760s. Writing in December 1773, at a moment when Boston had become the premier site of colonial resistance to Great Britain, Langhorne capitalized on what he saw as Boston's inconsistent and hypocritical love of liberty. "The people of Boston boast themselves chiefly on their principles of liberty," and yet Phillis Wheatley, a Bostonian, was still a slave. "One such act as the purchase of her freedom," Langhorne suggested, "would have done more honour than hanging a thousand trees with ribbons and emblems."

The critic's connection of Wheatley's slavery with the rhetoric and rituals of Boston's campaign for political liberty helps us situate Wheatley not only with respect to the contemporary attitudes toward imitation but, more significantly, within the context of a larger and still ongoing debate about the problem of slavery in the age of the American Revolution. How, after all, could the colonists begin to speak of liberty while holding slaves? British writers like Samuel Johnson considered the very question an argument-stopper, and even some colonists thought the presence of black slaves in the colonies compromised the political integrity of the metaphor.[33] And, of course, white writers were not the only ones to recognize the gap between rhetorical appeals to liberty and the social reality of chattel slavery. In Wheatley's Boston, the invocation of political slavery had unintended consequences, precipitating a discussion about rights between black and white writers. The discussion was uneven and asymmetrical, but it was also more urgent and more public than in any other British colony. I turn to this discussion later in this chapter, but for now it is important to note that the contemporary critiques of the mental faculties of black people as "imitative" rather than "inventive" helped support those British and American thinkers who saw political slavery and black slavery as radically different forms of bondage.

The reception of Langhorne's article on Phillis Wheatley in one of the largest Virginia slaveholding households reminds us that the circulation of British periodicals often provided the first and only knowledge literate colonial Americans had of Wheatley, and that tastes of an Anglicizing Virginia elite were often set by metropolitan reviewers; but it also testifies to the strange way in which white readers in a slave society like Virginia may have expressed their anxiety about mastering slaves like Wheatley by competing with and copying them. Reading this issue of the *Monthly Review* aloud to a circle of privileged white children in the slave society of Virginia three months later, Philip Vickers Fithian, a New Jersey tutor fresh from studies at Princeton, recorded the "astonishment" and disbelief of Bob, the decidedly unbookish sixteen-year-old son of the plantation owner Robert Carter III. Listening to the review, Bob was "sometimes wanting to see her, then to know if she knew grammer, Latin, &c. at last he expressed himself in a manner very unusual for a Boy of his Turn & suddenly exclaimed, Good God! I wish I was in Heaven." A plantation full of Phillis Wheatleys was no doubt a horrific challenge to the barely literate Bob, who grew up amid whispers of slave revolts in the household of one the largest slaveholders in Virginia. Within a week of inquiring whether Wheatley "knew grammer, Latin, &c.," and having almost certainly heard Fithian repeat the attestation from "her Master" John Wheatley that she had "a great inclination to learn the Latin tongue, and has made some progress in it" (an attestation reproduced in the *Universal Magazine*, where Fithian also read Wheatley's poem "On Being Brought from Africa to America"), Bob curiously announced that he too must learn Latin.[34] If Fithian discussed the question of the hypocrisy of the colonial rhetoric of liberty with the Carter children, he did not record it. Evidence from this group of real colonial readers suggests the ways in which Langhorne's critique of both African intelligence and the emptiness of the rhetoric of political liberty could be overwhelmed by the announcement of the very fact of a black poet. The prospect of Wheatley challenged assumptions of what might be accomplished under conditions of slavery; nevertheless, the idea that blacks would hit an aesthetic ceiling, being able to imitate but not invent, provided comforting assurance that the order of things would not change much.

Race, Slavery, and Cultural Imitation

Like Wheatley's British reviewer, critics in the second half of the eighteenth century increasingly described the mental faculties of black people as imitative. In his 1748 essay "Of National Characters," the Scottish philosopher David Hume wrote of blacks that "none ever discovered any symptoms of ingenuity." "In JAMAICA," he conceded, "they talk of one negro as a man of parts and learning; but 'tis likely he is admired for very slender accomplishments like a parrot, who speaks a few words plainly."[35] Since blacks were judged by different standards, Hume suggested, it took very little for a black person to pretend to culture. Even still, it was important to remember that such anomalies were the product of white example rather than natural "ingenuity." Left on their own, parrots would never talk, and blacks could never become cultured. Despite his being more interested in the relation of nation to culture than color to culture and despite relegating his opinion to a footnote, Hume's equation of blacks with bestial or subhuman imitation reached the German philosopher Immanuel Kant, who repeated it with approval in his 1764 aesthetic treatise *Observations on the Feeling of the Beautiful and Sublime*.[36] The footnote also reached a number of lesser thinkers, who echoed Hume's words with a slavishness that the Scottish philosopher himself associated with parrots.

But while Hume and Kant characterized black people as imitative, other writers questioned whether blacks were really capable of successful cultural imitation. Edward Long, a white Jamaican colonist who invoked Hume's footnote in his *History of Jamaica* (1774), criticized the "failure" of blacks there to reproduce European cultural practices. "It is astonishing," Long wrote, "that although they have been acquainted with Europeans, and their manufactures, for so many hundred years, they have, in all this series of time, manifested so little taste for arts, or a genius either inventive or imitative." Long observed that the examples of blacks who had pretended to culture were really no different than *"learned horses"* and *"talking dogs,"* creatures "who, by dint of much pain and tuition, were brought to exhibit the signs of a capacity far exceeding what is ordinarily allowed to be possessed by those animals." Long even translated out of Latin a poem by Francis Williams, a free black from Jamaica who had been educated in England (the "man of parts and learning" of Hume's footnote), with the hope that it would show once and for all that blacks were culturally inferior.[37] Thomas Jefferson echoed Long when he faulted blacks for failing to capitalize on the opportunity of imitating the whites in their proximity. "Many have been so situated," he bemoaned in his *Notes on the State of Virginia* (1782–85), "that they might have availed themselves of the conversation of their masters." Some blacks, he continued, "have been liberally educated, and have lived in countries where the arts and sciences are cultivated to a considerable degree, and have had before their eyes samples of the best works from abroad[;] . . . But never yet could I find that a black had uttered a thought above the level of plain narration; never see even an elementary trait of painting or sculpture."[38] Wheatley's poems could, at best, have represented for Jefferson an example of the absorption of white cultural models by one black person. Embracing a proto-romantic idea that equated personal suffering with artistic creation, Jefferson believed that the suffering of slaves should have given them a comparative advantage as poets. But Jefferson found Wheatley to be lacking in "imagination." Refusing even to grant her verses the status of "poetry," Jefferson dismissed her work as "below the dignity of criticism" while simultaneously questioning whether "the compositions published under her name" were really hers.[39]

For writers like Long and Jefferson, the capacity for civilization among nonwhites depended upon the replication and reproduction of white culture. As one colonial naturalist argued in 1775, hoping to displace Rousseau's romantic image of American Indians as "Noble Savages," American Indians lacked true "nobility" since they revealed no desire to embrace the colonizing culture. The Indians of Florida were "a people not only rude and uncultivated, but incapable of civilization: a people who would think themselves degraded to the lowest degree, were they to imitate us in any respect whatsoever, and they look down on us and all our manners with the highest contempt."[40] Clearly, colonial white writers were anxious about the disinterest of a nonwhite other in recognizing and reproducing the white self as the true peak of civilization. But at least one recent study has suggested that black appropriation and imitation of white culture produced as much anxiety as black disinterest. As Shane White and Graham White have argued, eighteenth-century black slaves sometimes "tested the boundaries of the system not only by appropriating items of elite apparel, but by combining elements of white clothing in ways which whites often considered inappropriate."[41] Colonial whites worried when blacks failed to reproduce white culture, and they worried when blacks did reproduce it. This white ambivalence and anxiety (in which blacks might become "almost but not quite" white by appropriating in inappropriate ways) suggests the unease that attended the blending of cultures in late eighteenth-century America.[42]

Perhaps the anxiety these white writers expressed was prompted as much by the fear that colonial whites were themselves an imitative people as by the "failure" of blacks to reproduce white models. The presence of black slaves was a source of special tension in a society imbued with Lockean notions of pedagogy.[43] What, exactly, did children learn from their slaveholding fathers? As Jefferson observed in the section of *Notes on the State of Virginia* devoted to "Manners," the "whole commerce between master and slave is a perpetual exercise of the most boisterous passions, the most unremitting despotism on the one part, and degrading submissions on the other. Our children see this, and learn to imitate it; for man is an imitative animal."[44] Comments like Jefferson's were most often found in the mouths of those enlightened slave owners who despised slavery for its effect on the "manners" of white masters rather than the bodies and minds of black slaves.[45] Jefferson did not say whether children would identify with and imitate the unremitting despot or the degraded slave, but some contemporaries explicitly worried that white children exposed to slavery would learn to imitate black slaves. In 1773, the year Wheatley traveled to London to publish her *Poems*, Josiah Quincy of Boston visited South Carolina and recorded his impressions of the influence of black slaves on white women and children. "By reason of this slavery," he wrote in his diary, "the children are early impressed with infamous and destructive ideas, and become extremely vitiated in their manners, they contract a negroish kind of accent, pronunciation and dialect, as well as [a] ridiculous kind of behaviour: even many of the grown people, and especially the women, are vastly infected with the same disorder. Parents instead of talking to their children in the unmeaning way with us, converse to them as though they were speak[ing] to a new imported African."[46] Quincy's moral was the opposite of Jefferson's. Slavery was a disease that infected women and children, making them more submissive than they should be; slavery also caused male masters to become so indiscriminate in their use of authority that they could not distinguish between their slaves and their children.[47] Inadvertently, Quincy's impressions provided one pessimistic answer to Hume's question about why blacks did not follow white models. The result of the mixture of black and white cultures, Quincy suggested, was not the elevation of blacks but the pronounced descent of whites.

It was probably the same sense of white vulnerability to black culture that led some white writers to worry as much about a black slave's "artfulness" as about the supposed inartistic character of the minds of black people. When the London edition of Phillis Wheatley's *Poems* appeared in Boston in late 1773 or early 1774, a Boston bookseller accused Wheatley of withholding some of her poems for future publication. "These don't seem to be near all her productions," he noted, but "she's an *artful* jade, I believe, & intends to have ye benefit of another volume."[48] Perhaps this Boston merchant recognized Wheatley as an astute business person, controlling the market for her poems (especially the patriotic poems she was known for in Boston) by gradual release, but he also tapped into a language that described blacks as "artful" in a pejorative sense, a language nowhere more evident than in advertisements for runaway slaves. Jefferson himself had posted one such notice in the *Virginia Gazette* in 1769. "RUN away from the subscriber in Abermarle," Jefferson's notice read, "a Mulatto slave called Sandy, about 35 years of age . . . he is greatly addicted to drink, and when drunk is insolent and disorderly, in his conversation he swears much, and in his behaviour is artful and knavish."[49] Within the genre of the runaway advertisement, Jefferson's language was completely conventional. In the 1760s and early 1770s, runaway black slaves—from New England to Georgia, and generally men—were described as "artful fellow[s]" who would, if allowed by gullible whites, "impose on [them] by [their] artfulness."[50] And while notices of runaway white slaves and servants shared with these advertisements a common anxiety about the ability of the runaway to "pass" for or "pretend" to be free, a survey of white runaway notices suggests that "artfulness" seems to have been a description assigned almost exclusively to blacks.[51]

Writers who felt compelled to defend the intelligence of black people often accepted the idea that blacks were imitative but grounded their arguments in a new language of cultural relativism. For them, imitation was a positive good. In his *Essay on the Causes of the Variety of Complexion and Figure in the Human Species* (1787), Samuel Stanhope Smith of New Jersey argued that blacks improved in both beauty and intelligence according to their proximity to whites. Blacks in America were more "ingenious and susceptible of instruction" than blacks in Africa. That this was largely because of the proximity of whites rather than sim-

ply because of climate could be demonstrated by the difference between
field workers and domestic workers. "The domestic servants," Smith argued, "who are kept near the persons, or employed in the families of
their masters, . . . see their manners, adopt their habits, and insensibly
receive the same ideas of elegance and beauty," but field workers "preserve, in a great degree, the African lips, and nose, and hair. Their genius
is dull, and their countenance sleepy and stupid."[52] Smith's theories drew
on the work of the Scottish philosopher and poet James Beattie, who
had countered Hume's criticism of black intelligence by an appeal to sta-
dialism, the notion that society develops in stages. "The inhabitants of
Great Britain and France were as savage two thousand years ago," Beattie wrote, "as those of Africa and America are at this day."[53]

Philadelphia physician Benjamin Rush took up Hume's footnote
at the very start of his own *Address on Slavery* (1773). Unlike Beattie,
who saw Africans as primitive versions of the European ideal, Rush focused on the effects of climate, asserting that it would not take two thousand years for Africans to equal Europeans, especially those Africans
now living in North America. "The accounts which travelers give us of
their ingenuity," Rush argued, "show us they are equal to the Europeans, when we allow for the diversity of temper and genius which is occasioned by climate."[54] Rush even invoked Phillis Wheatley as an example
of "singular genius and accomplishment" in a footnote to this passage
in the first edition of his *Address on Slavery*. But when a proslavery re-
spondent attacked Rush (in yet another footnote) for providing "only a
single example of a negro girl writing a few silly poems, to prove that the
blacks are not deficient in understanding," Rush silently removed his allusion to Wheatley in the second edition of his pamphlet.[55] Rush's decision to expunge his reference to Wheatley suggests the somewhat ambivalent place imaginative writing could have in the debate over mental
equality. As much as Wheatley's writings might be used as evidence of
mental equality, as poems they were open to aesthetic acceptance ("singular genius") or rejection ("a few silly poems") based on the vagaries of
individual taste.[56]

The Slavery of Neoclassicism

Tastes were always changing, and Wheatley's book appeared at a particular moment of cultural transition: the beginning of the romantic move-

ment against neoclassicism. While Wheatley's critics debated the imitative quality of black intelligence, high neoclassical aesthetic theory celebrated imitation as the foundation for artistic mastery. As the influential German art historian Johann Joachim Winckelmann put it in his 1755 pamphlet *On the Imitation of the Painting and Sculpture of the Greeks*, a text imported to Boston in 1772 by Wheatley's future publishers, Cox and Berry, and available at their bookshop down the street from the Wheatley household, "there is but one way for the moderns to become great, and perhaps unequaled [inimitable]; I mean, by imitating the ancients."[57] For Winckelmann and his British followers, "originality" meant a return to origins.[58] The imitation of nature, the supreme goal of early eighteenth-century aesthetics, neoclassicists argued, depended first upon the imitation of the ancients. But by the 1770s neoclassicism seemed to be threatened by a newer theory celebrating the relationship between artistic "genius" and nature unmediated by classical imitation.[59]

In 1774, a year after Wheatley's book appeared, Sir Joshua Reynolds presented a discourse on imitation in painting to his students at the Royal Academy in London. Despite (or perhaps because of) the growing tendency to see imitation of ancient models and old masters as "slavish" antiquarianism (the word "slavish" itself had only recently, in the 1750s, come to signify a lack of originality; by the early 1780s "servility" would mean following a model too closely), Reynolds felt the need to reiterate the Winckelmannian dogma of imitation as a positive good. Young Raphael had become an old master by imitating the old masters. Although Wheatley's reviewer Langhorne suggested that black people had a turn for "imitation" but not for "invention," these terms as Reynolds used them (only shortly after the reviewer had) were not necessarily in opposition. Within Reynolds's neoclassical aesthetic, "servility" did not mean the slavish imitation of old masters but rather following one master to the exclusion of others, a kind of mimetic monogamy. Those artists who chose to follow one artist only were to Reynolds the worst "narrow, confined, illiberal, unscientific, and servile kind of imitators" and were "justly to be censured for barrenness and servility."[60] Dr. Johnson, Reynolds's friend, agreed. Under the heading "IMITATION," American readers of a book of Johnson's maxims published in 1787 could learn that "no man was ever great by imitation," but they would also discover that "not every imitation ought to be stigmatised as a plagiarism.—The adoption of a noble sentiment, or . . . a borrowed ornament, may sometimes display so much judgment as will almost compensate for invention; and an inferior genius may, without any imputations of servility, pursue the path of the antients, provided he declines to tread in their footsteps."[61] While romantics regularly opposed "imitation" and "invention," neoclassical theory stressed imitation as a foundation for future invention rather than a separate aesthetic mode, just as neoclassical politics, as practiced in America in the decade following the publication of Wheatley's *Poems*, stressed the imitation of ancient republican models (models that both incorporated and legitimized slavery) as foundational for virtuous self-mastery.[62] Even still, proponents of the U.S. Constitution in 1787 like Noah Webster felt compelled to note that the document was not "a servile imitation of foreign constitutions of government."[63] And when it was admitted that some aspects of American politics had been copied from the British Constitution, American political writers often argued that "the copy is brought to a degree of perfection infinitely beyond the original."[64] The specter of plagiarism haunted politics as much as poetry.

The neoclassical idea that artists should follow examples of art rather than nature directly could be found even in cultural provinces like New England. In 1766 the Boston portrait painter John Singleton Copley wrote to Benjamin West in London that he was "sensable of the necessity of attending to Nature as the fountain head of all perfection, and the works of the great Masters as so many guides that lead to the more perfect imitation of her." But alas, Copley bemoaned, even "if I should have the good fortune to imitate nature with some degree of merit, yet it cannot please as an Eligent form equelly well imitated would do." West, who would later succeed Reynolds as president of the neoclassically dominated Royal Academy, completely agreed. West himself had left his native Pennsylvania in 1760 for the opportunity to see the great masterpieces of art in Italy and had found in Reynolds a sympathetic mentor and master.

In 1765 Copley had shipped a portrait of his half-brother Henry Pelham to London, where it was exhibited in 1766 as *Boy with a Flying Squirrel*. Like the portrait of Wheatley that served as a frontispiece to her *Poems*, Copley's portrait of his half-brother is a profile, the only one done during Copley's American period. But this was also an allegory of dependence—it was a political painting. Produced amid the controversy over the Stamp Act, and exhibited in London in 1766, Copley's portrait gave London viewers a way of figuring the dependent relationship be-

tween the British colonies (here figured as the squirrel) and Britain itself (the boy). The painting argued that the best colonial policy resembled a turned head (what Burke would call "salutary neglect" a few years
later); that the colonists labored hard and for themselves (evidenced by
the patience of the squirrel with the nut); and that the colonists did not
pretend to a species equality with the parent country, and could be managed with a loose chain. Such a relationship of careless care could hardly
be called (as the Stamp Act had been) a form of "slavery" since it was in
the service of the development of the colonies themselves.

Copley's correspondents in London were more interested in tech-
nique. Upon receiving a painting from Copley, West wrote that both he
and Reynolds believed that "if you are capable of producing such a Piece
by the mere Efforts of your own Genius, with the advantages of the Example and Instruction which you could have in Europe, You would be . . .
one of the finest Painters in the World, provided you could receive
these Aids before it was too late in Life, and before your Manner and
Taste were corrupted or fixed by working in your little way in Boston."[65]
Copley's independence—that he was not working under a master or in
sight of masterpieces—was in fact his chief problem: he left Boston for
London in July 1774. By the time Reynolds gave his lecture on the importance of imitation ("Discourse VI") in December of that year, Copley
was already copying the old masters in Rome.[66]

But Copley arrived in Europe at a transitional moment in the cultural status of imitation. In the 1760s the German painter Anton Mengs
claimed that "he who effectively studies and observes the productions
of great men with the true desire to imitate them, makes himself capable of producing such works which resemble them, because he considers the reasons with which they are done . . . and this makes him an im-
itator without being a plagiarist."[67] Reynolds's *Discourses* incorporated
and disseminated such ideas. But for those who rebelled against Reynolds, like the British artist and poet William Blake, imitation of any kind
was considered theft. A disgruntled former student at the Royal Academy, Blake noted in the margins of his copy of Reynolds's *Discourses*
(ca. 1808) that Reynolds's 1774 lecture on imitation would be "particularly interesting to Block heads, as it endeavours to prove That there
is no such thing as Inspiration & that any Man of a plain Understanding may by Thieving from Others become a Mich. Angelo."[68] Such
romantic pronouncements attempted to erase the prevalent Lockean
sensationalism and to render useless decades' worth of treatises that

promised to help readers of plain understanding cultivate both taste and genius.

When Wheatley's first critic, John Langhorne, claimed that all black people were imitative, he spoke in the new language of cultural racism; when he dismissed Wheatley's neoclassical poetry as "imitative," he spoke in the new language of romanticism.[69] Formally, Wheatley's poetry showed allegiances to neoclassical models, especially Alexander Pope. But the publication of Wheatley's *Poems* in London in 1773 coincided with a British vogue for uneducated poets and "natural geniuses." It also appeared at a moment when abolitionists wished to demonstrate both the innate mental equality of Africans as well as their educability.[70] These two movements—the vogue for natural geniuses and the abolitionist desire to prove equality—were in tension. We can register this tension in the marketing of Wheatley by her British publisher, Archibald Bell, who advertised Wheatley as "one of the greatest instances of pure, unassisted Genius, that the world ever produced," but who also included in his advertisement a letter from Wheatley's owner that mentioned the instrumental role the white Wheatley family had played in her education and poetic development.[71] Yet how could you identify a "genius" except by reference to prior models? Like many of her twentieth-century critics, Wheatley's contemporary supporters insisted that she was a genius "by her own application, unassisted by others" but measured her capacity for civilization by the conformity of her unassisted genius to Alexander Pope's neoclassical model.[72]

The clash between neoclassicism and romanticism produced a discourse about cultural "slavery" and the dangers of mental dependency. Charles-Louis Clérisseau, Jefferson's assistant in designing the classically inspired state capitol at Richmond, Virginia, called on French architects in 1778 to "wipe out that mark of servitude and mimicry which disfigures our works."[73] Such statements were hardly left to the Parisian avant garde. In 1760 in his *Rudiments of Latin Prosody* the Boston lawyer James Otis revealed the growing tensions between the two theories of cultural production. Otis used the word "slavery" as an example of a dactyl, a poetic foot consisting of one long syllable followed by two short ones (or an accent followed by two unaccented syllables). While dactyls were the basis of classical Latin poetry, Otis felt they represented an aberration from the natural iambic cadence of English speech, as his comparison between the English dactyl "slavery" and the Latin dactyl "*ludere*" (to play) made apparent. Otis's philology paralleled his politics, especially his 1764 pamphlet *The Rights of the British Colonies Asserted and Proved*. Both began with a desire to reduce things to first principles, rules, and laws. But Otis used "slavery" in another way that signaled part of the cultural transition to romanticism. Orators, Otis held, should "follow nature" in order to become the "masters" of their subject; they should not succumb to a "perpetual slavery to rule and example." And they should avoid "imitating the voice of another" at all costs.[74] Even as Otis compiled his list of rules and examples, he seemed to worry about their potential to limit the intellectual liberty of his readers.

The question Otis begged was whether art could really be taught. "Taste & Genius are Not Teachable or Acquirable, but are born with us," Blake wrote in the margins of his copy of Reynolds's neoclassical textbook. While we tend to associate neoclassicism with constraining rules and restrictions (the heroic couplet) and romanticism with the liberty of an unfettered mind (free verse), we should remember that romantic statements like Blake's about innate genius were above all essentialist, merely the brighter side of contemporaneous conceptions about the minds of black persons as naturally inferior. As the British writer Edward Young argued in his watershed *Conjectures on Original Composition* (1759), "modern writers have a *Choice* to make. They may soar in the Regions of *Liberty*, or move in the soft Fetters of easy *Imitation*."[75] Young prefigured Rousseau's famous statement in *On the Social Contract* (1762) that man was born free but was everywhere in chains, casting the political idea in cultural terms: "Born *Originals*, how comes it to pass that we die *Copies*? That medling Ape *Imitation*, as soon as we come to years of *Indiscretion* (so let me speak), snatches the Pen, and . . . destroys all mental Individuality." Imitation was for Young a subhuman activity: "Why are Monkies such masters of mimickry? Why receive they such a talent at imitation? Is it not as the *Spartan* slaves received a license for ebriety; that their Betters might be ashamed of it?"[76] Monkies and slaves had no choice, but their cultural "betters" did. Young's connection between imitation and apes was typical of the emerging reaction against neoclassicism. And while the analogy between blacks and apes was a popular early eighteenth-century innuendo, Young's slide from monkies to slaves represented a relatively new cultural prejudice,[77] one that informed the particular character of political slavery as Europeans and colonial British Americans described it on the eve of the American Revolution.

Wheatley's Petition

Wheatley's black and white contemporaries routinely recognized the "inconsistency" of black slavery and revolutionary political rhetoric. Sometimes this charge seemed to carry no moral judgment, as when Arthur Lee argued in 1764 that "the bondage we have imposed on the Africans . . . is highly inconsistent with civil policy."[78] Often this rhetoric acknowledged that the presence of slavery significantly compromised the imperial metaphorics. "For this People to be *talking* of *Liberty*, and, at the same Time to continue importing and making *Slaves* of whole Cargoes of their Fellow Creatures," one anonymous Boston author noted in 1773, "must be judged by those, who allow themselves to think freely, a Solaecism in Language."[79] Answering the question, "*Whether the slavery, to which Africans are in this province, by the permission of the law, subjected, be agreeable to the law of nature*?" at the Harvard commencement in 1773, one disputant remarked upon "the strangely inconsistent conduct of mankind, respecting this matter . . . that those, who are so readily disposed to urge the principles of natural equality in defence of their own Liberties, should, with so little reluctance, continue to exert a power, by the operation of which they are so flagrantly contradicted."[80] In arguing against the Sugar Act in 1764, James Otis paused to consider the faulty logic underwriting chattel slavery: "Does it follow that 'tis right to enslave a man because he is black? Will short curled hair like wool instead of Christian hair . . . help the argument? Can any logical inference in favor of slavery be drawn from a flat nose, a long or short face?"[81]

More often, "inconsistency" carried a strong moral and religious valence. Pennsylvania Quaker Anthony Benezet observed in 1767 that "the barbarous Treatment of the Negroes . . . is inconsistent with the plainest Precepts of the Gospel, the Dictates of Reason, and every common Sentiment of Humanity."[82] By 1787 Quakers in London maintained that even non-Quakers were beginning "to see the utter inconsistency of upholding [slavery] by the authority of any nation whatever."[83] When colonists invoked the word "slavery" to describe their imperial relationship to Britain but ignored chattel slavery, abstracting the signifier from its material referent, one minister exclaimed, "What inconsistence and self-contradiction is this! . . . When, O when shall the happy day come, that Americans shall be Consistently engaged in the cause of liberty?"[84] By the time Wheatley's *Poems* appeared in 1773, the rhetoric of slavery's inconsistency was so conventional that even some slaveholders conceded it. Patrick Henry found slavery "inconsistent with the Bible, and destructive of liberty," which "every thinking, honest Man rejects . . . in speculation"; nevertheless, in practice Henry owned slaves, pleading in 1773 that "the general inconveniency of living without them" overcame his recognition of the inconsistency of living with them.[85]

Some white writers feared that slaves themselves recognized this inconsistency, and the mental image of black slaves passing judgment over inconsistent whites became a frequent trope in antislavery writing. "Oh, the shocking, the intolerable inconsistence . . . [the] gross, barefaced, practiced inconsistence," the Rev. Samuel Hopkins of Connecticut exclaimed in 1776. The political "slavery" colonists complained of was "lighter than a feather" compared to the "heavy doom" of real slaves. Indeed, Hopkins argued, the colonists themselves had hypocritically oppressed black slaves "who have as good a claim to liberty as themselves, [and] are shocked with the glaring inconsistence."[86] Nathaniel Appleton in Boston in 1767 had made the same rhetorical move, silently shifting from the imagined judgment of black slaves to the judgment of Parliament: "Oh! ye sons of liberty, pause a moment, give me your ear," he begged. "Is your conduct consistent? can you review our late struggles for liberty, and think of the slave trade at the same time, and not blush? Methinks were you an African, I could see you blush. How should we have been confounded and struck dumb, had Great Britain thrown this inconsistency in our faces?"[87] Or, as James Swan put it in Boston in 1772, "It is for those, who are in a state of bondage to discribe [sic] the dread horrors, the tearing anguish, and the direful pains that alternately seize them when thinking, of their being among people who boast of their liberties, and at the same time act repugnant to the spirit of their constitution in keeping in slavery thousands of blacks, when they know it is also derogatory to the principles of christianity, and society."[88] Like Wheatley's reviewer Langhorne, writers in Great Britain did cite colonial slaveholding as evidence of ambivalence about liberty, but more significantly, black slaves also used the inconsistence between colonial rhetoric and reality to create a space to argue for their own independence and emancipation. Significantly, creating this space explicitly depended on a successful citation and critique of the natural rights language of the imperial debate.

When groups of black slaves submitted petitions for freedom to the Massachusetts House of Representatives in 1773 and 1774, they both

mimicked and mocked the imperial rhetoric of political slavery.[89] "Sir,"
one petition signed "on behalf of our fellow slaves" by Peter Bestes,
Sambo Freeman, Felix Holbrook, and Chester Joie began, "The efforts made by the legislative of this province in their last sessions to
free themselves from slavery, gave us, who are in that deplorable state, a
high degree of satisfaction. We expect great things from men who have
made such a noble stand against the designs of their fellow-men to enslave them." And, "as the people of this province seem to be actuated
by the principles of equity and justice, we cannot but expect your house
will again take our deplorable case into serious consideration, and give
us that ample relief which, as men, we have a natural right to."[90] Or, as
another petition from Boston argued, "your Petitioners apprehind we
have in common with all other men a naturel right to our freedoms without Being depriv'd of them by our fellow men as we are a freeborn Pe-
pel and have never forfeited this Blessing by aney compact or agreement
whatever."[91] In neighboring Connecticut in 1774, an African American
named Bristol Lambee reminded the Sons of Liberty that "LIBERTY,
being founded upon the law of *nature*, is as necessary to the happiness
of an African, as it is to the happiness of an Englishman."[92] In the years
immediately preceding 1773, white juries in Massachusetts increasingly
granted freedom to individual black slaves who sued their masters.[93] The
petitions to the Massachusetts legislature went unanswered; nevertheless, they entered the public sphere when newspapers and pamphlets reprinted the documents, often citing the implicit hypocrisy of maintaining slavery in a land of liberty.[94]

   Spoken in the revolutionary political vocabulary of religion and natural rights, these petitions from black contemporaries of Phillis Wheatley inform her most famous and pronounced public statement on slavery, a letter to the American Indian minister Samson Occom in which
she drew a parallel between the imperial debate and the biblical slavery
of Israelites in Egypt and then immediately reversed the analogy to figure white slaveholders as "our modern Egyptians" and black slaves as Israelites suffering the invasion of their "natural Rights."[95] For Wheatley,
as for the Boston slaves who petitioned for freedom, imitating and performing the language of political liberty inherently entailed a critique of
its limitations and exclusions. The early 1773 petitions also inform "Niobe in Distress for her Children," a poem about competing rights claims
that was Wheatley's only "imitation" (or translation) of a classical author as well as the longest poem in her collection. Situating this neo-

classical text within the context of this revolutionary circuit of analogies helps us better understand the play of metaphors that structured Anglo-American society at the moment of revolution, a society in which slaves were regularly seen as mentally imitative and aesthetic imitation was increasingly seen as "slavish."

Published the same year as the earliest petitions from Massachusetts slaves, Wheatley's "Niobe in Distress for her Children slain by Apollo, from *Ovid's* Metamorphoses, Book VI. and from a view of the Painting of Mr. *Richard Wilson*" opens with a poetic petition of its own:

> APOLLO's wrath to man the dreadful spring
> Of ills innum'rous, tunefull goddess, sing! . . .
> Inspire with glowing energy of thought,
> What *Wilson* painted, and what *Ovid* wrote.
> Muse! lend thy aid, nor let me sue in vain,
> Tho' last and meanest of the rhyming train!
>
> (lines 1–2, 5–8)

Wheatley's petition replicates standard neoclassical invocations to the muses, but in a poem that explicitly calls prayers "petitions" (line 66) and that thematizes the fall of a presumptuous "rebel" (line 104) from a "royal race" (line 53) who initiated a contest of "rights" (Wheatley's spelling of religious "rites," line 88), we should take the issue of "suing" seriously as a point where neoclassicism and contemporary slavery intersect. A 1768 legal gloss for the word "distress" in Wheatley's title indicates that the term meant not only personal grief, but "the taking of a personal chattel out of the possession of the wrongdoer into the custody of the party injured, to procure a satisfaction for the wrong committed," and could also refer to the chattel seized by this process.[96] Formally, Wheatley imitates Pope and Milton; thematically, her imitation resonates with the contemporary petitions that argued for freedom based on the emancipatory rhetoric of colonial rebellion.

The sources named in the title of Wheatley's poem, Richard Wilson's painting and Ovid's poetry, presented conservative, even reactionary, social messages about the transgression of rightful authority. Ovid's poem depicted the punishment of an individual who aspired to a status she did not deserve. Similarly, contemporary comments on Wilson's painting emphasize its conservative moral and its attractiveness to its original purchasers (Wilson made four Niobe oil paintings beginning in 1760).

As the *Royal Magazine* in London saw it, invoking religion to justify social hierarchy, Wilson's 1760 *Niobe* reminded viewers that the "necessity
of being contented with our condition, and not to exalt ourselves above
the station in which Providence has thought fit to place us, is a moral
that should be written, in indelible characters, on the hearts of children,
of men, of princes, and of the whole human race."[97] Paradoxically, this
message of social immobility had resonance for those aspiring members
of the middle class who, perhaps unaware of Wilson's direct quotation
of a Niobe statue from classical antiquity (a must-see on the European
Grand Tour), sympathized with the grieving mother and made William
Woollett's 1761 engraving of Wilson's painting the best-selling landscape
print in Britain up to that time.[98] It was most likely this engraving (this
"view of the Painting"), rather than the painting itself, that Wheatley
saw in London in 1773. She may even have seen the print in Boston.

But what precisely made Niobe an attractive subject for Wheatley's
only Latin "imitation"? Wheatley's great subject was not slavery but
death. On the one hand, a story involving a proud but grieving parent
whose pride led directly to the death of all fourteen of her children before she herself was turned into a petrified perpetual fountain of tears
allowed Wheatley to explore the power of divine retribution and to compose an extended elegy, raising the number of poems about mourning to
eighteen out of thirty-eight in her 1773 collection. Literary scholars have
ignored the relationship between "Niobe" and the elegies, but it should
not be discounted, since in the elegies we often find Wheatley at her
most forceful, especially when she is shaming mournful white parents
into dry-eyed silence. In "On the Death of a young Lady of Five Years
of Age," Wheatley insists that parents "Restrain . . . tears" (line 24)
and celebrate the death of a child as freedom from bondage: "Let then
no tears for her henceforward flow, / No more distress'd in our dark vale
below" (lines 9–10). The message was clear, and she quoted it back to
the society that had instilled it in her but seemed always to forget it:
"Freed from a world of sin, and snares, and pain. / Why would you wish
your daughter back again?" (lines 25–26). Again and again, Wheatley
tells mourners "Weep not" ("To a Lady," line 18); "let hope thy tears
restrain" ("To a Lady," line 24); "dry thy tears" ("To a Clergyman,"
line 43); "No more in briny show'rs, ye friends abound" ("To a Lady and
her Children," line 23). "Restrain the sorrow streaming from thine eye,"
she instructs the lieutenant governor of Massachusetts ("To His Honour," line 39).

Over and over, Wheatley insisted on God's providential logic and chastised parents for petitioning heaven with tears when they should "haste to join [the dead] on the hev'nly shore" ("To a Lady and her Children," lines 25–28). To say the least, such petitions were pointless: "let the fountains of your tears be dry'd / . . . Your sighs are wasted to the skies in vain" ("To a Gentleman and a Lady," lines 14–16). In Wheatley's poem, Niobe's pride derives from a misplaced and excessive love for her own children, something Wheatley warned against in her elegies. "But thou had'st far the happier mother prov'd, / If this fair offspring had been less belov'd," she explains ("Niobe," lines 31–32). Indeed, Niobe's explicit overfondness is the indirect cause of the loss of her children: "Thy love too vehement hastens to destroy / Each blooming maid, and each celestial boy" (lines 35–36). When Niobe finds her own subjects worshipping Latona, the mother of two gods, rather than herself (the mother of fourteen children), she not only orders them to stop but proudly and skeptically questions the effect of such prayer. "Why vainly fancy your petitions heard?" (line 66), she asks, sounding much like the Wheatley of the elegies. Indeed, the punishment ultimately visited upon Niobe for interrupting these "rights" (line 88) was to be metamorphosed into a (white) marble statue that never stopped crying, to become in effect the vain and misdirected white parent of the elegies who needed constantly to be reminded of the basic tenants of Calvinism and who, paradoxically, needed to be policed by Wheatley's position as a black Christian.[99]

As tempting as it might be to class "Niobe" with the religious elegies, we should also situate the poem within the political and legal context of the imperial debate between the colonies and Great Britain and the debate over the inconsistency of slavery in a revolutionary age. The poem, in which a proud and misdirected but ultimately loving parent inadvertently causes the death of her fourteen children, can be read as an allegory of the imperial crisis itself. The poem is framed by two "suits," Wheatley's invocation to the muses (line 7) and Niobe's "suit" to Apollo to spare her last living child. In between these petitions, the poem describes a competition of "rights" claims. Wheatley characterizes Niobe as holding a "potent reign" (line 12) and a "regal sceptre" (line 13), the heir of her father's kingdom after he was punished for excessive haughtiness to the gods. In the poem, a prophetess appears in Thebes and urges the women to worship Latona, mother of the gods Apollo and Artemis: "With rights divine, the goddess [Latona] be implor'd, / Nor be her sa-

cred offspring unador'd" (lines 45–46). Niobe's female Theban subjects pay "pious tribute to the goddess" (line 48). Significantly, Wheatley calls these Theban worshipers the "fair assembly" (line 51), a phrase
that could simply mean a group of women but that is also resonant with
whiteness (fair) and politics (as in the Massachusetts Assembly). Offended by the invasion of new objects of worship into her territory, Niobe and her "royal race" appear and interrupt the "rights," mocking the
worship of a new goddess. Explicitly jealous of the attention devoted to
the goddess over herself, Niobe orders the ceremonies to end. The maids
obey, "Their brows unbound, and left the rights unpaid" (line 88). Juno,
angered that Niobe has inspired "[e]ach Theban bosom with rebellious
fires" (line 96), sends her son Apollo to "punish pride, and scourge the
rebel mind" (line 104). Apollo first finds and slays Niobe's seven sons. At
this point Niobe again questions the authority of the gods and boasts of
her remaining seven daughters, whom Apollo subsequently slays as well,
saving the youngest one for last. Niobe clings to her remaining daughter and begs Apollo to spare her, but "In vain she begs, the Fates her suit
deny" (line 211), and her daughter dies in her arms. In a coda, noted as
"the Work of another Hand," Niobe metamorphoses into a statue forever spouting tears.

Who, exactly, were the "subjects" addressed and invoked by Wheatley's *Poems on Various Subjects*, and especially by her neoclassical imitation of "Niobe"? Within the context of a revolutionary rhetoric that
drew equally on politics and religion for its conception of "liberty," we
should see Wheatley's "Niobe" as a response to the contemporary petitions by Massachusetts slaves, as a consciously crafted attempt to imitate
the language of both neoclassicism and natural rights and to question
the status of these languages as the exclusive province of white colonists
and white poets. In the indeterminacy of Wheatley's poetics, white colonists could be the "fair assembly" of Theban women, prohibited from
exercising their natural "rights" by the arbitrary will of a haughty monarch. And they could simultaneously be the monarch herself, invoking her "royal [white] race" as a trump to her (black) subjects' natural
rights. By sympathizing with both Niobe and her subjects, Wheatley's
imitation of Ovid's conservative poem ultimately allowed white colonial
readers to see themselves within the context of their own rhetoric—as
slaves to British tyranny—but it may also have prompted them to reflect
on their status as tyrants themselves. For a few readers, perhaps, Wheatley's "Niobe" deepened the uncomfortable comparison between black

chattel slaves and white colonists by presenting a grieving mother figure who could represent both Great Britain and a prototypical slave mother, someone whose ability to protect her children was nullified by systemic and institutionalized forces beyond her control. "Niobe" is a complex work of allegorical art, a site where white readers might make multiple identifications; we should not expect the clarity of a political pamphlet or a petition, but we should not discount the political topicality of Wheatley's "imitation."

The Culturing of Natural Rights

In 1787 Jupiter Hammon, a black slave held in New York who had refused to align himself with a group of slave petitioners in Connecticut in the 1770s, noted the ideological inconsistency of slaveholding after the American Revolution. In his *Address to the Negroes In the State of New-York*, Hammon wrote: "That liberty is a great thing we may know from our own feelings, and we may likewise judge so from the conduct of the white-people, in the late war. How much money has been spent, and how many lives have been lost, to defend their liberty. I must say that I have hoped that God would open their eyes, when they were so much engaged for liberty, to think of the state of the poor blacks, and to pity us."[100] If black writers like Wheatley and Hammon were able to see a structural relationship between the position of black slaves to white colonists and the position of white colonists to Britain, then why did so many white writers argue that the relationship between the two forms of slavery was unclear? We can begin to understand by remembering that many theorists believed that the invocation of racial slavery failed to do justice to the horrors of political slavery, and that black slaves deserved "pity" (a word used by both Hammon and apologists for chattel slavery) instead of contempt. The suffering of the bodies of black slaves, some theorists argued, was insignificant compared with the mental and cultural debasement associated with political slavery.

For those writers who thought the metaphor through, political slavery was intimately connected with mental debasement. The connection they described was, however, a confusing and circular one between mind and body. Mental debasement was simultaneously the end result and the starting point of political slavery: slavery debased the mind, but subjects must be mentally debased to become slaves in the first place. Some writers regarded slavery as a mental phenomenon because they associated liberty with mental tranquillity. As one Boston writer noted in 1763, Montesquieu had defined political liberty as "a tranquillity of mind arising from the opinion each man has of his own safety."[101] Or, as Richard Price described it in one of the best-selling pamphlets in Britain and America, "the excellency of a free government" is "its tendency to exalt the nature of man.—Every member of a free state, having his property secure, and knowing himself his own governor, possesses a consciousness of dignity in himself, and feels incitements to emulation and improvement, to which the miserable slaves of arbitrary power must be utter strangers. In such a state . . . the mind is stimulated to the noblest exertions."[102]

Since political slavery debased further those who had a mental propensity or predisposition for slavery, slavery and cultural inferiority were mutually reinforcing. As a letter from the town meeting in Boston informed other Massachusetts towns in 1772, the "Sweeds were once a free, martial and valient people." But their "minds are now so debaced, that they rejoice at being subject to the caprice and arbitrary power of a Tyrant & kiss their Chains. It makes us shudder to think, [that] the late measures of Administration may be productive of the like Catastrophe."[103] Or as an anonymous Boston writer put it in 1765, "human nature is the same every where, and unlimited power is as much to be dreaded among us, as it is in the most barbarous nations upon earth: It is slavery that hath made them barbarous, and the same cause will have the same effect upon us. The inhabitants of Greece, Rome, and Constantinople, were once free and happy, and the liberal arts and sciences flourished among them; but slavery has spread ignorance, barbarism and misery over those once delightful regions, where the people are sunk into a stupid insensibility of their condition, and the spirit of liberty, after being depressed for a thousand years, seems now to be lost irrevocably."[104] The Virginian Arthur Lee argued that slavery was an "enemy" to the arts, but conceded (citing Hume) that "we now see both arts and sciences attain the highest perfection under arbitrary governments." Even still, Lee held that the "understandings [of Africans] are generally shallow," but (like Jefferson in *Notes on the State of Virginia*) he refused to wager whether this shallowness was the result of "native baseness" or the effect of slavery.[105] Many others were less reserved, and viewed the submission of blacks in slavery as de facto evidence of mental inferiority.

The recourse to ideas about art and culture could be seen most clearly in the debate over the compatibility of slavery and natural law at the Harvard commencement in 1773, the year Wheatley published her *Poems* in London and the year of the first petitions by blacks to the Massachusetts Assembly. The disputant who took the position that the slavery of Africans in America was not against the law of nature appealed specifically to a concept of culture as a humanizing force. He argued that it was far better for black people to reside in Massachusetts than in Africa, and painted a glowing picture of the culture they would be exposed to in America. In Africa they were "destitute of every means of improvement in social virtue, of every advantage for the cultivation of those principles of humanity, in which alone consists the dignity of the rational nature, and from which only source springs all that pleasure, that happiness of life, by which the human species is distinguished from the other parts of the animal creation." He asked his audience to imagine a black person in Africa: "Behold him actually clothed in all that brutal stupidity, that savage barbarity which naturally springs from such a source . . . Reflect, I say, a moment upon the condition of a creature in human shape (for in such a state of degradation one can hardly call him a man) . . . and compare it with the condition of a slave in this country." That this person may not consent to removal was immaterial, for "what can avail his consent, who through ignorance of the means necessary to promote his happiness, is rendered altogether incapable of choosing for himself?"

His opponent was put in the awkward position of conceding the cultural superiority of America without completely denigrating the mental faculties of black persons in Africa. There was no question for him that Africans "are extremely unacquainted with the politer arts, and almost wholly ignorant of every thing belonging to science, and consequently strangers to all the pleasures of a scholar and a philosopher." But, this second disputant argued, "they are still some degrees above brutes," and it is "not to be wondered that those who have been disposed to make a gain by this iniquitous practice of enslaving their fellow men, should be careful, for their justification, to represent them as nearly upon a level with the brute creation as possible"[106] It was the peculiar rhetoric of proslavery arguments, this disputant astutely observed, that dehumanized blacks at the same time it held out the absurd promise of humanity through the culture of slavery.

It was the same sort of ambiguity—the slave as a being who might be "humanized"—that was, fourteen years later, encoded in the U.S. Constitution. The text of the document itself famously avoids the word "slav-

ery" altogether, referring to slaves as "all other persons" (Art. I, sec. 2),
as "such Persons" (Art. I, sec. 9), and as "Person[s] held to Service or Labour" (Art. IV, sec. 2). For some southern politicians this language—with
its explicit acknowledgment of slaves as "persons" rather than property—
was a real political victory, since it augmented the national political representation of states with slaves. It was white northerners, not white
southerners, who wished black slaves to be considered as property rather
than as persons, and who suggested the compromise encoded in Article
I, section 2: that slaves would be counted the equivalent of three-fifths
of free persons.[107] Northern periodicals in 1787 fantasized about a South
without slavery and an America without blacks at all.[108] And many who
supported the Constitution found it difficult to use the word "slavery" to
describe the condition of real slaves. In arguing for the augmentation of
national power in *The Federalist*, James Madison referred to black slaves
as "an unhappy species of population" who in calm times were "sunk below the level of men" but who could "emerge into the human character"
during moments of civil violence and add strength to insurgent factions.
Addressing himself to both northern and southern readers, Madison argued that only a strong central government like the one outlined in the
Constitution could keep the "unhappy species" of blacks from becoming
fully human.[109]

Concepts of rights circulated in all directions in the aftermath of the
American Revolution. The slave petitioners of the 1770s spoke the language of political slavery and natural rights; but similar petitions of the
1780s would favor the languages of sentimentalism and sensibility, making appeals based not on the tortured logic of the imperial debate but
upon white readers' sense of their own humanity.[110] By the late 1780s the
sort of natural rights arguments about slavery that we celebrate in modern anthologies of African-American writing no longer had the kind of
strategic purchase they had a decade earlier. All of a sudden, petitions
by slaves that would have been made in a natural rights rhetoric in the
1770s were made in a sentimental language of feeling. The history of
rights discourse in the United States is a history of the severing of rights
from claims about mental equality, and a history of the recurring return
of such claims. Jefferson's admission in the early nineteenth century that
the "degree of talent" of individual black people was "no measure of
their rights" hardly represented the demise of such thinking, even perhaps for Jefferson.[111] Indeed, the question attributed to Sojourner Truth
in the mid-nineteenth century by one of her white admirers—"What's [in-

tellect] got to do with women's rights or Negroes' rights?"—testifies both to the extent to which reason remained a compelling site for some rights-bearing individuals to police the grounds of rights against trespass by those persons believed to be mentally incapable of bearing their own rights and the extent to which the voice of black persons themselves remained the best refutation of that position.[112] But the postrevolutionary shift from reason to feeling, and the slow, uneven removal of reason from rights discourse could have its own costs, costs we can measure in the disconnection of equal rights from actual equality and in the preservation of the very hierarchies that the language of rights was designed to help eradicate.

Black slaves animated the language of rights that found its most lasting expression in the claims of the second paragraph of the Declaration of Independence that all men are created equal and endowed with the inalienable rights to life, liberty, and the pursuit of happiness. Though the standard narrative of the evolving meaning of the Declaration stresses that the claims of the second paragraph were rarely commented upon by contemporaries and only came to be seen as the core of the document in the middle of the nineteenth century, it is clear that some contemporaries of the Revolution embraced the utility and radical potential for social change of the second paragraph. Beginning with Lemuel Haynes in Massachusetts, whose 1776 tract "Liberty Further Extended" was not published in his lifetime but may have served as the basis of a speech, abolitionists in the new nation pointed specifically to the second paragraph of the Declaration. "If liberty is one of the natural and unalienable rights of all men," said Jacob Green of New Jersey in a gloss on the second paragraph in a 1778 sermon, "if 'tis self-evident, i.e. so clear that it needs not proof, how unjust, how inhuman, for Britons, or Americans, not only to attempt, but actually to violate this right?" In an essay published in Pennsylvania that same year, the Quaker Anthony Benezet invoked the second paragraph of the Declaration as well as the first article of the Virginia Declaration of Rights and predicted that a people who could make such public declarations of equality and rights and still maintain slavery deserved whatever punishment they received during wartime. Three years later, Benezet again singled out the second paragraph of the Declaration, this time along with the Congressional Declaration of the Causes of Taking Up Arms (penned in part by Jefferson in 1775); Benezet felt that Americans should "consider how far they can justify a conduct so abhorrent from these sacred truths as that of drag-

ging these oppressed Strangers from their native land, and all those ten-
der connections we hold dear." In 1783 David Cooper offered an address
on the inconsistency of slavery in a land committed to liberty; on the
pages of his text he placed the words of American state papers on the
left with his comments on the right. Across from the second paragraph
of the Declaration, Cooper wrote: "If these solemn *truths* uttered at such
an awful crisis, are *self-evident*: unless we can shew that the African
race are not *men*, words can hardly express the amazement which naturally arises on reflecting, that the very people who make these pompous
declarations are slave-holders, and, by their legislative conduct, tell us,
that these blessings were only meant to be the *rights* of *whitemen* not of
all men."[113]

And slowly, as war gave way to peace, writers and activists made sure
that their audiences understood that the Declaration was not simply the
statement of slaveholders and others in Congress, but was in fact "the
voice of all America, through her representatives in solemn Congress uttered." In 1785 a Philadelphia writer who signed himself "Justice" cited
the second paragraph and noted that slavery "makes us as a nation condemn ourselves by our own declarations." Abolitionists cited the text of
the second paragraph and used it in speeches and writings, often appropriating it for an epigraph to their publications. Though the U.S. Constitution made no claims about the equality of men, the constitution of
the Pennsylvania Society for Promoting the Abolition of Slavery, drafted
in 1788, invoked the language of the second paragraph of the Declaration; so did abolitionists in Maryland in 1791. A similar society in New
Jersey placed the sentence on the title page of their 1793 constitution.
Ten years earlier, in 1783, the Rhode Island legislature passed an Act
for the Abolition of Slavery that mentioned in its preamble that "all men
are created equal, and endowed with the unalienable rights of life, liberty, and the pursuit for happiness."[114] "Our late warfare was expressly
founded on such principles" as the idea that "all men are created equal,"
James Dana explained to an antislavery audience in New Haven in 1790.
Had thousands really died during the Revolution in order to preserve
the thing that that so many claimed to be fighting against?[115]

By 1792, when African-American almanac maker Benjamin Banneker quoted the "true and invaluable doctrine . . . 'that all men are created equal'" back to Secretary of State Thomas Jefferson in an exchange
of letters that appeared in papers across the new nation, antislavery activists had worked for a decade and a half to make their audiences iden-

tify the Declaration of Independence specifically with the cause of African Americans.[116] This effort would intensify in the next decade and a half, even as the Declaration was coming to look like the property of the Democratic Republican political party. When, in the middle of Jefferson's second term as president, a convention of abolitionists in 1806 reminded its affiliates that "nearly one fifth of the nation drag the galling chain of slavery," it also told them not to abandon the cause "until the rulers of the land shall practice what they teach, that they 'hold these truths to be self-evident, that all men are created equal; that they are endowed by their Creator with certain unalienable rights: that among these are life, liberty, and the pursuit of happiness.'" At the next meeting of the same group, after the passage of an 1807 law prohibiting Americans from participating in the international slave trade, the abolitionists hoped that "our hearts will still be enlarged, and our hands still strengthened in the work, till the rulers, and the ruled, shall practice what the sacred charter of our liberty declares": "that all men are created equal" with "certain unalienable rights."[117] Though historians are no doubt correct that for most readers the Declaration had not taken on its modern meaning as a charter of rights, it is clear that the abolitionists had seized upon the idea that it was, and in doing so helped to make that charter more sacred than it had been to its authors, or at the very least sacralized the text in a different way. When Frederick Douglass famously asked a paying audience in Rochester, New York, on July 5, 1852, "What, to the American slave, is your 4th of July?" the question was not a new one based on a wholesale revision of the meaning of the text but was as old as the Declaration itself.[118]

Constitutionalizing Slavery

In 1795 a Virginia judge and law professor, St. George Tucker, wrote to Reverend Jeremy Belknap for information about the abolition of the slave trade and the emancipation and condition of former slaves in Massachusetts. Tucker hoped the information might help legislators in Virginia enact laws dealing with the slave trade and manumission, but Belknap, then president of the Massachusetts Historical Society, treated the matter as an historical rather than a legal inquiry. Belknap circulated Tucker's questions to forty correspondents, a group that included prominent white politicians and a black civic leader as well as some of the "oldest merchants now living" in the state; he then prepared a summary synthesizing the answers. Tucker asked for practical details about legislation, but Belknap's account stressed that radical social changes like the end of slavery had to be organic—that is, they had to come from the public rather than from politicians—in order to be legitimate.

The historian told the jurist that slavery and the slave trade had been abolished in Massachusetts as a result of changes in *"publick opinion"* brought about during the imperial debates preceding the American Revolution. Free and unfree blacks had played a part, petitioning the colonial and then state legislatures, but it had mostly been the "inconsistency of contending for our own liberty, and at the same time depriving other people of theirs" that caused whites to make the possibility of ending slavery a subject of political discussion in the decade before the Revolution. The Constitution of 1780 had declared all men to be born free and equal, and Belknap argued that this clause had been inserted "not merely as a moral or political truth, but with a particular view to establish the liberation of the negroes on a general principle, and so it was understood by the people at large." A court case in 1783 upheld this popular understanding, effectively ending slavery in Massachusetts, and five years later public outcry over the case of three free black men who had been kidnapped in Boston and shipped for sale to the West Indies prompted the Massachusetts state legislature to prohibit the slave trade.

Belknap offered Tucker the contours of an emerging story about the end of slavery in Massachusetts, one that placed rights and public opinion at the center of historical change, but Belknap's explanation for the organic end of slavery and the slave trade in Massachusetts significantly departed from the responses he received from some of his correspondents. It is clear that in preparing his summary Belknap relied on an older generation of merchants, men in their late sixties and early seventies, for the thrust of his interpretation; these men told Belknap that the slave trade had never flourished in the colony, that slavery itself had never had the endorsement of "popular opinion," and that the Revolution had effectively converted private doubts about the licitness of the slave trade into public action.

Of all Belknap's correspondents, only Prince Hall and John Adams advanced different rationales for changes in public opinion. Prince Hall, a prominent African-American leader who had petitioned the state to abolish slavery in 1777 and whose efforts in the wake of the abduction of the three free blacks in 1788 helped bring about the act to prohibit the slave trade, focused on the efforts of free and unfree blacks to influence public opinion in favor of their rights. For Adams, then vice president of the United States, the "real cause" was not arguments about the rights of man but the resentment of "common white people" who competed with slaves for employment. If slavery had continued, Adams speculated, whites "would have put the negroes to death, and their masters too, perhaps." As it was, the "scoffs and insults" of laboring whites "filled the negroes with discontent, made them lazy, idle, proud, vicious, and at length wholly useless to their masters." For Adams, libertarian rhetoric masked the true economic and social causes of antislavery sentiment.

Prince Hall and John Adams offered different explanations for the changes in public opinion than the one Belknap ultimately favored, but the response of James Winthrop, who argued that slavery had not legitimately ended in Massachusetts, was far more difficult to square with Belknap's interpretation. At the time he received the circular letter, Winthrop was chief justice of the Court of Common Pleas of Middlesex County. When asked how slavery had ended in Massachusetts, he answered that "by a misconstruction of our State Constitution, which declares all men by nature free and equal, a number of citizens have been deprived of property formerly acquired under the protection of law." In the end Belknap muted Adams's explanation of the class-based sources of the change in public opinion and made only passing nods to the efforts of black people described by Hall, but he found it impossible even to acknowledge Winthrop's denunciation of the legitimacy of the end of slavery. Perhaps as a response to such allegations, Belknap pointed to the federal census of 1790, which he took to be a barometer of public opinion, and to the absence of any slaves listed there: "This return, made by the marshall of the district," rather than any piece of legislation, "may be considered as the formal evidence of the *abolition of slavery* in Massachusetts, especially as no person has appeared to contest the legality of the return."

The idea that slavery was abolished in Massachusetts either simply by "publick opinion" (that mysterious force of the Enlightenment) or by judicial interpretation of the Constitution of 1780 resulted from the legislature's having never—unlike other northern states that had or would in the coming years—passed statutory enactments concerning manumission. Legislative silence meant that the state could avoid either compensating former slaveholders or explicitly providing for the newly free. Shortly after the judicial decision in 1783, state legislators debated a bill that seems—the actual text has never been located—to have focused on three things: first, it would have declared retrospectively that "there never were legal slaves in this Government"; second, it would indemnify "all Masters who have held slaves in fact"; and last, it would "make such provisions for the support of Negroes and Molattoes as the Committee may find most expedient." The bill passed through the House and was read once in the Senate, but never had a second reading. What exactly happened is a mystery, but candidates in the next election sometimes tarred their opponents by exposing them as supporters of the "execrable retrospective bill," and the legislature never took the matter up again. Why exactly the "retrospective bill" was "execrable" can only be a matter of speculation, but it most likely concerned the expense that might have fallen to the state of Massachusetts had legislation passed to compensate "masters" for forfeited property or to support the emancipated and compensate them for time served in slavery. These questions were even more on the surface in legislative and public debates about the state's prohibition of the slave trade—indeed, the relation between the international slave trade and domestic social welfare was evident in 1788, when the state legislature passed an "Act to Prevent the Slave Trade" on the same day as an "Act for suppressing and punishing of Rogues, Vagabonds, common Beggars, and other idle, disorderly and lewd Persons," a law that made clear that Massachusetts would not offer support to any "African or negroe" who was not a citizen and would deport them from the state after two months.

The explanation of public opinion as the cause of the overthrow of domestic slavery in Massachusetts obscured the question of reparations that must have animated discussions on the ground if not in the government. The state and even former slaveholders (because they did not have to post bonds for the support of former slaves) stood to gain by legislative silence in Massachusetts; former slaves did not. Belknap noted that, "unless *liberty* be reckoned as a compensation" for past slavery—and he suggested it was not—free blacks in Massachusetts in 1795 were worse off than they had been under slavery. Belknap described for Tucker a new controversy just emerging as he wrote: the state wasn't sure how to support black paupers or who should pay for their support. Some believed that former masters should be found and made to post bonds for the relief of their former slaves; others believed that (since they had been made free by public opinion) the public should aid the poor blacks. But what about former slaves who had migrated from other states? Or slaves in Massachusetts who had "stolen themselves" before 1783—who should pay to support them? Belknap reported that the state had asked the counties to pay, counties had asked the towns, and in some cases the towns simply refused. The American Revolution produced a civil war in rights talk, a contest between a heightened awareness of the rights of man and a heightened respect for the rights of property. As scholars and the public investigate the ways in which individual corporations and the U.S. government might make reparations for slavery, it is certainly not heartening to remember how and why, barely a decade out of slavery and in a state still in formation, the obstacles to formulating a coherent policy of support, compensation, or reparation for former slaves seemed almost insurmountable. Given the legislative obstacles, it was no wonder that Belknap looked to the evolution of "publick opinion" and to the judicial interpretation of the Massachusetts Constitution. For him, a document that declared equality had come to embody, perhaps strategically and after the fact, the will of the people to end an institution nowhere mentioned in the text itself.

CHAPTER FIVE

Being Alone in the Age of
the Social Contract

The most widely circulating, and most imitated, declaration of rights published during the American Revolution was not the Declaration of Independence but a Committee Draft of a Declaration of Rights, prepared principally by George Mason and framed for the Virginia Provincial Convention in late May 1776. The first article declared:

> That all men are born equally free and independent, and have certain inherent natural rights, of which they cannot, by any compact, deprive or divest their posterity; among which are, the enjoyment of life and liberty, with the means of acquiring and possessing property, and pursuing and obtaining happiness and safety.

It was a bold statement, but the Virginia Convention had not endorsed it. Nevertheless, it was not uncommon for bold but unendorsed statements from Virginia to circulate in colonial newspapers and to become enacted in other areas on the assumption that they had been adopted in Virginia. A decade earlier, in the spring of 1765, a divided Virginia House of Burgesses rejected several draft resolves against the Stamp Act, but newspapers outside of Virginia printed the rejected resolves in such a way as to suggest that they had been adopted. Believing that they were simply following Virginia's lead, other colonial legislatures enacted those rejected resolutions, asserting in particular that their inhabitants could ig-

nore parliamentary laws. The mechanisms of communication in late colonial America produced a confidence game by which, through the sheer
fact of printing and circulation, unenacted resolutions could sometimes
assume the appearance of authenticity and legitimacy and extreme positions could come to look acceptable.¹ This was the case with the draft of
the Virginia Declaration of Rights, a document that seemed by its very
language to overturn slavery.

Though the draft of the Virginia Declaration circulated in newspapers across the colonies and though its proposed first article was adopted
by other states (and in the case of the Vermont Constitution of 1777, was
followed by an explicit article abolishing slavery for males over twenty-
one years of age and females over eighteen), the expansive language of
the first article did not ultimately survive the editing process. The Virginia Convention modified the language of the final text, rendering the
first line as follows:

> That all men are *by nature* equally free and independent, and have certain
> inherent natural rights, of which, *when they enter into a state of society*, they
> cannot, by any compact, deprive or divest their posterity.

The culture of slavery made a mess of the talk of natural rights, even
when (as in the case of this revision) lawmakers tried to find a constitutional accommodation between the practice of slavery in Virginia and
the expressed commitment to universal equality. According to the logic
of the revised text, African-American slaves, though perhaps "by nature equally free and independent," had not entered into "a state of society" with white Virginians and thus could "deprive or divest their posterity" of "inherent natural rights" even without "any compact." But if
the Virginia Convention could settle on language that allowed for both
cultural practice and natural rights, the revision still highlighted a series
of problems: Were slaves best thought of as "by nature equally free and
independent"—that is, as having once possessed the rights to life, liberty,
property, and happiness that the Virginia Convention endorsed—or had
they never truly been individuals? Was it better to imagine slaves as a
class or group of people outside of society, or to think of each individual slave as a distinct and isolated case of lawful capture? And if slaves
were truly independent of society, if they were in a sense presocial beings, then why did that condition cancel out rather than guarantee their
natural rights? Natural rights were not, after all, the products of society

or of government; they were holdovers from a presocial and prepolitical state. That is what made rights natural.

Being alone presented special problems for an age obsessed by the social contract, by the public sphere, and by sociability itself. Consider, for instance, the way in which publicity and privacy confronted each other on the pages of Josiah Meigs's *New-Haven Gazette.* On October 4, 1787, an essayist writing under the pseudonym "Social Compact" offered readers wholehearted endorsement of the proposed Federal Constitution. "Social Compact" may have been an unusually abstract pseudonym for an individual, but the choice of the name and the theme of the essay exemplified the ways in which readers and writers in the age of the American Revolution routinely conflated written constitutions and social compacts, as if society was not itself a distinct mediator between government and the mythical "state of nature" described by political philosophers.[2] Ten months later, Meigs's paper reported the narrow ratification of the Constitution by the New York Convention, the crucial cementing vote in the document's adoption as a national "social compact." In the same issue Meigs printed a short literary sketch entitled "The Hermit's Soliloquy," a text contemporary readers might have regarded as an "unsocial" or (employing a word emerging at this moment) an "antisocial" compact. Here is the pledge the hermit made to himself:

> Under the brow of this little hill I have built my little hut: Here I live in lonely silence, secluded from every human eye. The awful stillness of the wilderness gives me opportunity to ruminate upon the follies and vices of my fellow mortals, with whom I formerly lived—To-day I will contemplate the human heart in the hermitage and in the social circle; I will draw up a judgment concerning its operations in those two different situations. To-day I will live justly; to-day virtue shall be my theme—And though I have nothing but roots and bark to eat, yet I will not complain; for what is vicious man, that he should be supported by infinite benevolence! I intend to spend one hour every day in correcting my faults, in regulating my passions and desires. I have no person with whom I can converse, yet I receive pleasure from speaking loud. Sociability is far from me, but truth I will embrace; gratitude to the Source of all existence shall fill my heart.[3]

Taking readers inside the hermit's hut, this short text showcased the public penetration of private space, modeling for its audience the conflict between the hermit's fantasies of privacy on the one hand and corresponding fantasies of the violation and public appropriation of that privacy on the other.[4] Original readers, in groups or individually, perhaps discovered an extreme example of moral reform embedded in the hermit's joy in exchanging sociability for postsocial privation. This was, after all, a voluntary analogue to the Philadelphia physician Benjamin Rush's prescription of forced solitude as a "mechanical means of promoting virtue" for the chronically vicious in 1786 and as a substitute for capital punishment in 1787: "the life of a hermit," as Rush described it, was "a life of passive virtue."[5] On the other hand, readers may have simply laughed at the hermit's Franklinian hour-a-day scheme for self-improvement, confident that virtue was meaningless outside of its active exercise in a social context. But whatever they made of the hermit, readers would almost certainly have recognized the hermit's retreat as the antithesis of the social compact itself.

Privacy, as recent accounts of the term in eighteenth-century Britain make clear, underwent a shift in this period from a classical conception of seclusion and withdrawal to a more recognizably modern notion of independence and intimacy.[6] We do not, of course, lack accounts of privacy in early America. Since the mid-1960s, legal scholars have engaged Supreme Court rulings on the right to privacy through historical meditations on legal protections for privacy in early America, but such studies often figure privacy as a transhistorical category, something that is either protected or ignored but is everywhere the same.[7] More persuasively, since the 1970s early Americanists have charted categorical revaluations of privacy by describing new ideas about gender and sexuality that emerged by the end of the eighteenth century. Historians and literary scholars have crucially dissected and deconstructed a "private/public dichotomy," especially but by no means exclusively as it was embedded in early republican notions that white married women should find a public role within a private sphere.[8] The stunning analysis of the public sphere that has followed Jurgen Habermas constitutes some of the strongest work in early American cultural and intellectual history in the last two decades; it is certainly worth noting, however, that those historians and literary scholars who have found Habermas useful have not taken up his claims for the categorical construction of privacy in conjunction with the rise of publicity to the same extent as those scholars of eighteenth-century France who, following the French translation of Habermas's book in 1978, made analysis of the history of "private life" a major component of their studies of the public sphere.[9] We still lack a larger conceptual and cultural history of privacy in early America to place beside and in dialogue with our new appreciation of publicity.

A larger cultural history of privacy in the "constitutional era" would consider the politics of the cultural preoccupation with solitude. Renunciations of the "social circle" and the appeal of being alone in such texts as "The Hermit's Soliloquy" constitute cultural reflections of and on revolutionary-era political issues: the compatibility of individual liberty and collective authority, the conflict between independence and union, the location of rights in a prepolitical state of nature or as products of a social compact, the relationship between private life and public sphere. While I try to remain true to fluctuating tensions between "self" and "society," two terms radically revised in the late eighteenth century, and to the period's simultaneous widening and constricting understanding of the word "politics," I also want to elucidate connections between two strands of historiography not often braided: the history of popular culture and the history of political thought.[10] Placing the problems of solitude at the center of public discussions of state formation forces us to reexamine central tensions of the revolutionary decades. What emerges, at least in my discussion here, is less a unified account of the "age of the social contract" (or the "constitutional era") than an argument against the possibility of such synthesis for a period marked by a fascination with both sociability and solitude, by narratives of entering into and exiting from civil society, by an excitement about written constitutions and an anxiety about textualizing rights, by competing concepts of the state as the product of individuals and of individuals as products of the state, and by a celebration of public deliberation tempered by a suspicion that individuals made better decisions when they did so alone and in private. Cultural historians have recently come to appreciate the force of what one Boston novelist in 1789 called "the power of sympathy," but we have not yet come to terms with what Joseph Story, later Associate Justice on the Supreme Court but at the time law student and would-be poet, referred to in 1799 as "the power of solitude."[11]

The Power of Solitude

What exactly was powerful about solitude? Discussions of solitude and retirement in the revolutionary period represented fantasy narratives of self-liberation from the public sphere, even as they addressed that public sphere and even as the public sphere enabled a meaningful distinction to arise between solitude and privacy. Texts that claim to catch postsocial individuals talking to themselves are of course by nature audience-oriented, directed toward a reading public (increasingly made up of solitary readers) curious and anxious about privacy. The print culture of late eighteenth-century America was populated by countless overheard hermits, romantic figures at the edge of the American Enlightenment variously imagined as communicating with themselves, with nature, and—far less often—with God.[12] Some overheard hermits addressed members of this public directly. "The Hermitess; Or, Fair Secluder," a short piece of fiction that shared a page of the *Massachusetts Magazine* with a misogynist account of the "Isle of Matrimony" and appearing just months after Judith Sargent Murray's seminal essay "On the Equality of the Sexes," described how one woman's meditative communion with the silence of nature was broken by overhearing another woman's soliloquy: "May the volatile and young, who dance in giddy circles of gaiety, learn from hence," the hermitess counseled, "that happiness is not the lot of mortals."[13] Postrevolutionary hermits tell stories of the failures of sociability, of societies so overdetermined by social distinctions that (if we adopt economic historian Albert O. Hirschman's terms) only "exit" could enable "voice."[14] The pleasures of solitude announced by such texts tested prevailing pieties about the natural sociability of human beings; successful accounts of seclusion in a "state of nature" seemed to trump claims for the necessity of the social compact itself. For "true liberty," as the most popular contemporary theorist put it, "was discovered only in solitude," where "man . . . enters into the state of nature."[15] Indeed, these texts that show individuals voluntarily exiting from society stand as counterpoints for the social contract's narrative of individuals voluntarily leaving the "state of nature" for the protections of civil governments. Accounts of seclusion and withdrawal from public life may have represented classical articulations of "privacy," but stories of individuals who became individuals by privatizing themselves were also pointed meditations on contemporary politics.[16]

In one sense, private withdrawal made thought about public things possible. Narratives about individuals who choose to leave society had a social function, of course, and one way to account for the prevalence of hermits in the print culture of late eighteenth-century America is to consider them as exemplary figures of the public sphere. In a series of monthly essays written by "The Hermit" and published in Philadelphia in the *American Magazine and Monthly Chronicle for the British Colonies* in 1758 and 1759, the editor Rev. William Smith suggested that the character of the solitary recluse offered the perfect analogue for the anonymous proprietors of the magazine.[17] The authority of "The Hermit" and of the magazine proprietors (a word that in the proprietary government of Pennsylvania carried political overtones; Smith was a loyal supporter of the Proprietary party over the democratic assembly) rested in their ability to offer advice to the public that could not be traced directly back to any particular source. It also suggested that the model for socially critical writing should not be someone engaged in the busy world like "The Spectator" (or any of the other essayists in the *American Magazine* based loosely on that character: "The Planter," "The Watchman," "The Prattler," and—in the midst of the French and Indian War— "The Antigallican") but someone removed from society, someone who had engaged in a "*Secession* from this world of vanity and strife."[18] Like the eponymous character of John Dickinson's *Letters from a Farmer in Pennsylvania to the Inhabitants of the British Colonies* (1767), who announced that he had been formerly "engaged in the busy scenes of life" but was "now convinced, that a man may be as happy without bustle, as with it," and who directed his remarks to those readers "whose employments in life may have prevented . . . attending to the consideration of some points that are of great and public importance," Smith's "Hermit" in his romantic solitude could reflect on society (and even at times stand in for society) from the vantage point of someone who stood apart from it.[19] For that reason, the title page of a poem entitled *Liberty* (1769) similarly claimed that the text, which itself praised "social ties," had been "Lately Found in a Bundle of Papers, said to be Written by a Hermit in New-Jersey." And readers of *A Pretty Story Written in the Year of Our Lord 2774* (1774), a patriot satire penned by one of Smith's former students, were encouraged to imagine (if not to believe) that the text had been "discovered in a Hermit's Cave."[20]

Retirees differed from hermits in obvious and crucial ways. Retirement, a specific kind of social privacy, was the pose of so many who, imitating the classical retreat suggested by the British poet John Pomfret's *The Choice* (1700), proposed to remove themselves to a rural "private Seat" populated by classic books, a few friends, and an occasional female companion. For the speaker in Pomfret's poem, retirement did not constitute a total renunciation of "society" (a word that appears favorably in describing the limited company of male friends) but a refinement of it, one that would isolate him from "Intrigues of State."[21] The trope of retirement from public life and especially state intrigue held special appeal for American politicians and their constituents in the period. For those whose wealth ensured a certain form of privacy already and who could afford to mimic the trappings of poverty, eighteenth-century landscape gardeners could outfit estates with rustic hermit huts. Jefferson hoped to have one constructed at Monticello, the name he adopted for his own estate after flirting with but ultimately rejecting "The Hermitage," a name that would imply a single occupant and further erase the slave labor that rendered a particular kind of solitude possible.[22] The cultural valorization of Washington's multiple retirements from and returns to public life fastened to a long-standing deferential ethic of elite private leisure and public service; it also reinforced the radical critique of professional politics that made rotation in office, amateur legislators, and term limits so appealing. Retirement even fascinated persons who had barely engaged in public life. In *Philosophic Solitude; or the Choice of a Rural Life* (1747), twenty-three-year-old William Livingston (who forty years later would be governor of New Jersey and a delegate to the Constitutional Convention) followed Pomfret, producing an eclogue in which the speaker wishes to "live retir'd, contented, and serene, / Forgot, unknown, unenvied, and unseen." But he is quick to point out that he is not a hermit: "Yet not I'd chuse, / Nor wish to live from all the world recluse." Instead, "social converse" would distinguish this from "a real hermitage."[23] A self-styled necessity may have governed such retreats, but the focus on explicit consent—on "choice" as a key word for both Pomfret and Livingston—united these forms of isolation.

In contrast, Philip Freneau's writings expressed the pleasures of the self-governing individual separated from all society, and suggested the cultural revaluation of hermitage, isolation, and privacy. His poem "Retirement," written in 1772 and first published in 1786, described the possession of a "hermit's house"—a "cottage I could call my own" occupied only by the speaker and separated from "domes of care" by a "wall with ivy overgrown"—as the site of more "real happiness" than being "a monarch crown'd," though clearly being a monarch and being alone were compatible rather than contradictory pleasures.[24] Growing out of the same equation of solitude with self-government, Freneau's short closet drama "The Hermit of Saba" staged the fatal encounter between the Hermit, the shipwrecked sole occupant of the Dutch West Indian island of Saba who treasures the island for the commodity of "contemplation" it affords, and a group of three mercenary mariners who see the island in terms of more concrete commodities—lemons, oranges, coconuts, cedar, lambs, goats, and gold. Freneau's text emptied the island of its inhabitants (which in 1775 had a population of 300 free whites and 130 black slaves) as part of an attempt to critique mercenary forms of colonization. Finding it impossible to "be happy in so dull a scene" without some material payoff, the colonizing European mariners murder the Hermit (who, though himself a European immigrant, comes to think of himself as a natural or naturalized inhabitant of Saba) because they mistake his boast that the island has made him rich as a claim of material wealth. Written in 1776 and published in 1788, Freneau's text grafted an appreciation of solitude and privacy onto the larger political and anticolonial meanings of American independence.[25]

And yet, for all its seeming blessings, political writers in the era of the American Revolution frequently described solitude as unnatural, an insupportable condition that rendered governments necessary and emptied the choice between solitude and state of any real meaning. American writers who self-consciously couched their arguments in a Lockean mold described the social compact as a double bind, one that rendered government a conscious product of the conglomeration of individual acts of consent but one that was ultimately less of a real choice than it might at first appear. "In solitude men would perish," the lawyer James Otis argued in *The Rights of the British Colonies Asserted and Proved* (1764), a pamphlet directed against Parliament's attempts to raise revenue from the colonies by taxing sugar, "and yet they cannot live [in society] without contests." These contests—jealousies and petty fights over life, liberty, and property—constituted the occasion for government. Indeed, Otis argued, "if life, liberty and property could be enjoyed in as great perfection in *solitude*, as in *society*, there would be no need of government." But the men Otis described did not really have a choice: man was "a weak, imperfect being," and "the valuable ends of life cannot be obtained without the union and assistance of many. Hence 'tis clear that men cannot live apart or independent of each other." Human beings are born into society, and God "has not left it to men in general to choose, whether they will be members of society or not, but at the hazard of their senses if not of their lives." What Otis seemed to offer was a paradox at the heart of his contractualism: individuals in society could choose to live alone, but individuals outside of society had no real choice but to be social.

[I]t is left to every man as he comes of age to chuse *what society* he will continue to belong to. Nay if one has a mind to turn *Hermit*, and after he has been born, nursed, and brought up in the arms of society, and acquired the habits and passions of social life, is willing to run the risque of starving alone, which is generally most unavoidable in a state of hermitage, who shall hinder him? I know of no human law, founded on the law of *nature*, to restrain him from separating himself from the species, if he can find it in his heart to leave them; unless it should be said, it is against the great law of *self-preservation*.

"The few *Hermits* and *Misanthropes* that have ever existed," Otis concluded, "show that those states are *unnatural*."[26] The link Otis made between solitude and suicide—that solitude constituted a form of suicide, and that suicide was unnatural—served to make the social contract all the more natural and inevitable. Hermits, the simultaneous embodiment of pre- and postsociality, presented special problems then for the narrative of civil government.[27]

Similar attacks on the putative independence of individuals only intensified in the 1770s. Revolutionaries who argued for independence from Britain frequently denied that independence was a natural state for individuals. The opening pages of Thomas Paine's *Common Sense*, published in Philadelphia in 1776, described the origin of government in the mental incapacity for solitude and the insufficiency of the self, an account of prepolitical life that resonated with Adam Smith's discussion of the division of labor published the same year. Paine argued that "the strength of one man is so unequal to his wants, and his mind so unfitted for perpetual solitude, that he is soon obliged to seek assistance and relief of another, who in his turn requires the same." While "four or five united would be able to raise a tolerable dwelling in the midst of a wilderness, . . . *one* man might labour out the common period of life without accomplishing any thing; when he had felled his timber he could not remove it, nor erect it after it was removed; hunger in the mean time would urge him from his work, and every different want call him a different way." This would ultimately "reduce him to a state in which he might rather be said to perish than to die."[28] In a world in which it was impossible for a solitary individual to regulate or even prioritize his desires (and these narratives, even when seemingly gender-neutral, treat exclusively of men), choosing to be alone was the same thing as choosing death. Such a view of the prepolitical life of individuals helps us understand why, despite the heavy use of familial rhetoric in *Common Sense*,

Paine contended that individuals provided bad models for and meta-phors of government, but it also helps explain why a term like "union" almost always had positive valences while a term like "independence" (for individuals and for states) could often seem equivalent to anarchy.

The attack on personal independence continued well after political independence. In a lecture on the social contract delivered at the Uni-versity of Pennsylvania in 1790 and again in 1791, the Federalist lawyer and framer James Wilson claimed that "the most exquisite punishment, which human nature could suffer, would be, in total solitude, to languish out a lengthened life," a comment that helps make sense of the calls for solitary confinement of prisoners as a substitute for capital punishment that were beginning to be made, by Benjamin Rush among others, in the period. Wilson proposed a series of thought experiments: Could some-one "reduced suddenly to solitude" procure even the simple necessi-ties of life? Daniel Defoe's widely read *Robinson Crusoe* (1719) might be cited as proof that a lone individual could survive, but Wilson was quick to remind his listeners that the foundation of Crusoe's subsistence were "the productions of society" he saved from his shipwreck. Besides, Crusoe's story was pure romance, one that failed to fully acknowledge that "sour discontentment, sullen melancholy, listless langour" rather than productivity are the natural outcome of being alone. A "solitary life must be continually harassed by dangers and fears," Wilson con-cluded. [29] The most obvious problem with these narratives of the social contract was that they confused presocial beings with postsocial beings, deriving their arguments about the state of nature from those individu-als who left rather than those who entered society, but there were other problems as well: Otis, Paine, and Wilson found it hard to imagine inde-pendence as a "natural" state for human beings, a failure of imagination that seemed to deny that consent was a precondition for governments or that private rights were as natural for individuals as the natural rights theorists maintained.

Individualisms

How can we reconcile such accounts of the terrors of solitude and the impossibility of independence with the declarations of rights that self-consciously reminded their readers that (in the words of the Pennsyl-vania Declaration of Rights of August 1776) "all men are born equally free and independent, and have certain natural inherent and inalienable rights, amongst which are the enjoying and defending life and liberty, acquiring, possessing and protecting property, and pursuing and obtaining happiness and safety"?[30] In a 1774 pamphlet James Wilson had argued, citing Jean Jacques Burlamaqui, that governments are founded in the consent of the governed, and that such consent was given "with a view to ensure and to increase the happiness of the governed, above what they could enjoy in an independent and unconnected state of nature."[31] But the solitary figures that Otis, Paine, and Wilson described in their accounts of the origin of government could hardly be thought of as enjoying anything close to "happiness," as that inalienable presocial right was discovered and articulated throughout the late 1770s. Given the way in which the condition of independence was understood ("sour discontentment, sullen melancholy, listless langour"), such declarations obviously walked a narrow line between construing such rights as importations from a solitary state or as creations of a social one. This was what Wilson himself feared when he faulted William Blackstone for referring to "natural rights" as "civil liberties": "If this view of things be just, then, under civil society, man is not only made *for*, but made *by* the government."[32] Like the more familiar debate between Burke and Paine, Wilson's engagement with Blackstone indicates the degree to which the naturalness of "natural rights" could remain an open question and a source of anxiety.

But slavery presented a still larger problem, one that fundamentally altered the way in which the social contract and natural rights could be understood. The 1777 Vermont Constitution stood alone among revolutionary rights declarations in following out the logic of the claim that "all men are born equally free and independent" by outlawing slavery for males over age twenty-one and females over eighteen.[33] Other states, such as Virginia, dealt with the reality of slavery by tempering the radical nature of such claims and by insisting that slaves existed outside of society. This was perhaps one reason why early nineteenth-century black autobiographies sometimes explicitly described fugitive slaves as hermits, figures whose hidden presence upset the social claims of presocial equality.[34] Slaves functioned in the 1770s as perverted markers of social independence, persons whose existence outside of society canceled out rather than guaranteed their natural rights. But in another sense, slaves were exemplary of the way in which (despite Wilson's warnings) rights in practice might have come to be understood less as natural holdovers from a presocial state than as artificial products created by (rather than merely confirmed by) governments.

Perhaps for this very reason—the anxiety that rights were products of government rather than of nature—the age of the written constitution and the printed enumeration of rights was also an age deeply divided about textualizing rights. Rights did not derive from texts, a young Alexander Hamilton observed in February 1775, and were "not to be rummaged for, among old parchments, or musty records," but they were nonetheless textual: they had been "written, as with a sun beam, in the whole *volume* of human nature, by the hand of the divinity itself."[35] Ten years earlier, Otis complained that political writers too often described rights as "rising out" of textual foundations like the Magna Charta rather than stemming from human nature or from God.[36] In *The Rights of Man* (1791), Paine simultaneously celebrated the writtenness of the American constitutions while chiding Burke for caring so much about "musty records and mouldy parchments."[37] The Mohawk Joseph Brant, in an article published in the *American Museum* in 1789, noted "among us, we have no law but that written on the heart of every rational creature by the immediate finger of the great Spirit of the universe himself."[38] The paucity and simplicity of law was one of the chief attributes of Thomas More's early sixteenth-century *Utopia*, and the fantasy of a citizenry that governed itself with few or even no written laws remained a popular theme in utopian writing.[39] In "Equality—A Political Romance," a utopian narrative serialized in a Philadelphia Deist newspaper in 1802, a native informant of "Lithconia" observed that the "laws are not contained in huge volumes—they are written in the hearts of the Lithconians."[40] Practical legislators may have laughed at such ideas, but the didacticism of the earliest state declarations of rights registered the dilemma between the claim that the rights being enumerated were transparent and derived from nature—that they were, in a sense, written on the heart— and the acknowledgment that the people needed to be taught to read them.[41] And the desire to keep written law to a minimum haunted them as well. Madison himself worried about "a luxuriancy of legislation." The "short period of independency has filled as many pages as the century which preceded it," he bemoaned in 1787: "Every year, almost every session adds a new volume." [42] In 1787 and 1788, Anti-Federalists treated with skepticism the Federalist claim that the enumeration of rights in a national constitution might actually increase governmental power; nevertheless, such claims reflected not simply the exigencies of

ratification or novel theories about sovereignty but a deeper dialectic between declaration and silence that structured political practice in the
revolutionary period.[43]

Close examination of a small drawing made by John Trumbull suggests the ways in which nature functioned as a site of refuge for those
burdened by the sheer volume and artifice of declared law. In Lebanon,
Connecticut, on April 19, 1782, Trumbull made a small pen and wash
sketch for a now unlocated painting he executed in London two years
later (fig. 15). The drawing, a rare single-figure nonportrait subject by
an artist who would become known for grand-style multifigure contemporary history paintings, depicts a barefoot, bearded man in flowing
robes seated on a cliff; the man looks off toward a source of illuminating light in the top left-hand corner of the image while he crushes un-
derfoot a book labeled "HOBBES." Inscribed with the title *And look
thro' Nature, up to Nature's God*, a line from Pope's popular *Essay on
Man* (1733), the drawing seemingly stages the rejection of the materi-
alism of Hobbes for the recognition in nature of the mediated presence
of God. But the language of "Nature" and "Nature's God" in the title
also linked the 1782 drawing to the language of the Declaration of Independence. As he recounted in his 1841 *Autobiography*, Trumbull had re-
nounced a career in the law for a career as a painter at approximately the
same time he produced the drawing. Whereas art elevated its beholders
and appealed to what was good in human beings, the law—as Trumbull
explained to his father in a recollected dialogue—"was rendered necessary by the vices of mankind." ("You appear to forget, sir, that *Connecticut is not Athens*" was the reply of Trumbull's father, then governor of
Connecticut.)[44] We can read the drawing in terms of Trumbull's own life
choice, but given the date of composition (the seventh anniversary of the
battles of Lexington and Concord) and the cultural status of Hobbes in
the Revolution, the image's thematization of a shift from one source of
authority to another and the explicit rejection of writing in favor of nature deserve closer scrutiny.

There is indeed something almost ridiculous about representing a
lone individual in a natural setting reading and rejecting Hobbes, whose
own depiction of the lives of lone individuals had led the Third Earl of
Shaftesbury in 1711 to describe the Hobbesian state of nature as the best
advertisement for society. In one of the most widely circulated treatises
combining aesthetics and politics in pre- and postrevolutionary America,
Shaftesbury's character "Theocles" joked that the only reason to adopt

FIGURE 15. John Trumbull, *And Look Thro' Nature, up to Nature's God,* 1782. Courtesy of the Charles Munn Collection, Fordham University Library, Bronx, New York.

the claim that "this imaginary *State of Nature*" is "*a State of WAR*" was to discourage individuals from preferring the practices of extreme solitude to the institutions of sociability: "To speak well of it, is to render it inviting, and tempt Men to turn Hermites."[45] If "HOBBES" signified any single book for Trumbull's contemporaries, it was without doubt *Leviathan*. If his philosophy could be summed up in a single line (as the phrase "solitary, poore, nasty, bruitish, and short" might for us), it was the contention that the state of nature was a state of war, a commonplace cited with disapproval in sermons, moral tracts, and political pamphlets of all stripes.[46] Alexander Hamilton's *Farmer Refuted* (1775) tarred its opponent by exposing him as a disciple of Hobbes's politics; of the principles of government laid down in Paine's *Common Sense*, a Loyalist opponent noted, "Even Hobbes would blush to own the author for a disciple."[47] A copy of *Leviathan* occupied a prominent and symbolic place as a Tory prop in a description of "a small cabinet of books, for the use of the studious and contemplative" in Mercy Otis Warren's closet satire *The Group* (1775).[48] Produced on a day marked for the commemoration of the beginning of the military phase of the American Revolution, Trumbull's drawing almost certainly would have carried political meanings for early viewers.

Trumbull's trampled book, whichever work of Hobbes it referenced, might also be thought of as an emblem of the dissatisfaction with the elevation of writing itself in the period, and here we might turn to Trumbull's best-known painting: his image of the founding of the United States as a legal and textual act in *The Declaration of Independence* (1787–1820) (fig. 16). This composition is an afterthought to the visual record of the Revolution as a series of military acts that Trumbull began to paint in 1786 and hoped to market as engravings in both the United States and Great Britain. The painting presents the legality of the Declaration in a particularly curious way: it depicts the Committee of Five (John Adams, Benjamin Franklin, Thomas Jefferson, Robert R. Livingston, and Roger Sherman) submitting the Declaration for review and signatures as a scene of treaty-making between that committee and the president of the Continental Congress, the foregrounded figures replicating the formal groupings in Benjamin West's famous *Penn's Treaty with the Indians* (1771–72), a painting Trumbull knew from his time in London as a studio assistant for West.

In general, and even in *The Declaration of Independence* in particular, Trumbull seems to reject the interpretation of state papers as sources

FIGURE 16. Asher B. Durand, 1823 engraving of John Trumbull's *The Declaration of Independence*. Prints and Photographs Division, Library of Congress (LC-USZ62-41413).

of or safeguards for rights—the manuscript papers Jefferson holds are just a few of the many papers on Hancock's messy desk, a desk dominated by the presence of revealed religion in the form of a large folio Bible. The Bible counterbalances and legitimates the as yet undeclared Declaration, but notably even in this civil setting the flags, drums, and banners (military trophies captured from the British) that figure in other paintings in the series occupy the center of the painting. If the painting succeeds in representing a source of and a protection for rights, it does not do so by elevating the status of the paper Declaration but by placing the committee in charge of drafting the Declaration and the document itself between the religious and military symbols, in between the materialized source of natural rights in the revealed word of God and the "Appeal to Heaven" through warfare that constituted the Lockean final court of appeal for subjects of tyranny.[49] Trumbull's solution to a problem of representing ideology (the question of how to represent natural rights pictorially) would not suit everyone: paintings derived from Trumbull's *Declaration* by Quaker artist Edward Hicks in the 1840s shifted the locus of authority by dramatically enlarging the size of the Bible and removing the military symbols altogether.

But how should or could rights be represented visually? Popular revolutionary iconography often differed radically from revolutionary ide-

ology when it concerned the source and basis of rights. John Dickinson
never appealed to or even mentioned Magna Charta in his citation-heavy
Letters from a Farmer in Pennsylvania (1768), one of the most important and widely read pre-revolutionary pamphlets, but a contemporary
engraving underwritten by one of Dickinson's publishers and designed
as a supplement to a Philadelphia newspaper depicts the Pennsylvania
Farmer in a book-lined study resting his right elbow on a folio-size book
labeled "MAGNA CHARTA" (fig. 17).[50] In contrast to an abstract concept of natural or inalienable rights, documents or other textual authorities were easy to render graphically and hence to canonize in popular
understandings of the meaning of the Revolution. The fact that no late
eighteenth-century American artist chose to depict the framing of the
Constitution of the United States in the Federal Convention, as Trumbull and others had done for the Declaration, testifies to the postratifica-
tion insistence that the document was a national social compact and did
not derive any special meaning from the individuals who framed it or the
conditions under which it was framed.[51] It may also speak to a lack of
clarity about just what happened in a social compact.

The cornerstone of the social compact theory of state formation as it
was elaborated on both sides of the ratification debates centered on ex-
ternalized justice and the centralization of sovereignty brought about by
the voluntary surrender of a portion of an individual's natural rights, but
partisans of the document and their opponents described the terms of
that surrender in radically different ways. Federalists, following the lead
of the official letter from George Washington (as president of the Federal Convention) to the president of the Continental Congress that was
appended to almost every printing of the proposed Constitution in 1787
and 1788, and that may have functioned as a constitutional supplement
of sorts for early readers and ratifiers, tended to draw analogies between
the proposed voluntary "sacrifice" of rights by states (routinely gendered
as female entities) under the Federal Constitution and by individuals exiting a state of nature: "It is obviously impracticable in the foederal government of these States, to secure all rights of independent sovereignty
to each, and yet provide for the interest and safety of all—Individuals entering into society, must give up a share of liberty to preserve the rest.
The magnitude of the sacrifice must depend as well on situation and circumstance, as on the object to be obtained."[52] Washington's letter, with
its call for forms of unequal state "sacrifice," departed from those accounts of the social compact that stressed that everyone surrender the

FIGURE 17. James Smither, "The Patriotic American Farmer" (John Dickinson), 1768. Courtesy of The Library Company of Philadelphia.

same amount of natural liberty in order to obtain security. Federalists like David Ramsay of South Carolina held that "relinquishments of natural rights, are not real sacrifices: each person, county or state, gains more than it loses, for it only gives up a right of injuring others, and obtains in return aid and strength to secure itself in the peaceable enjoyment of all remaining rights."[53] Anti-Federalists rarely employed the language of "sacrifice," choosing instead to think of the social compact as a moment when men (and always, even when seemingly gender-neutral, the language suggests only men) reserve more than they "contribute," "part with," or "yield up a part of their natural liberty," and that such reservations should be the focus of a Federal Bill of Rights.[54]

The dialectic between private and public liberty as well as the period-wide anxiety about independence and solitude that characterizes the political thought of the American Revolution made "the closet"—the imaginary space of private theoretical speculation on the one hand and the real domestic space of private religious devotion on the other—a site of special attention. In general, the essays of *The Federalist* are typical in their distaste for decisions made behind closed doors, even as they evade the Anti-Federalist charge that the Constitution was itself produced in this way. In *Federalist* no. 69, Hamilton compared the "publicity" of the mode of appointment of the president, by an electoral college that had been described as secretive by Anti-Federalists, with the "privacy in the mode of appointment [of office holders] by the Governor of New-York, closeted in a secret apartment with at most four, and frequently with only two persons." Such closeting reeked of the same charges of conspiracy often leveled at the Federal Convention, and in defending the product of the Convention's deliberations, Madison asked, "Would it be wonderful if under the pressure of all these difficulties, the Convention should [not] have been forced into some deviations from that artificial structure and regular symmetry, which an abstract view of the subject might lead an ingenious theorist to bestow on a Constitution planned in his closet or in his imagination?" Practical politicians like Madison, Jefferson, and Gouverneur Morris ridiculed so-called "closet politicians" because the hermetic quality of constitutional schemes drawn up "in the closet" failed to embody collective decision-making and because "closet politicians" believed that governments created people more than people created governments.[55]

But it was also hard to square the disparaging view of the lone individual legislating for others from his closet with an emerging sense in Madison's own political thought that individuals sometimes made better and more socially motivated decisions about minority rights when they did so alone and in the privacy of their closets. In his "Vices of the Political System" memorandum of spring 1787 and again to Jefferson in a letter of October 24, 1787, Madison remarked that character-based mechanisms for protecting minority rights rarely worked: "The conduct of every popular Assembly, acting on oath, the strongest of religious ties, shews that individuals join without remorse in acts agst. which their consciences would revolt, if proposed separately in their closets." The problem then was to get people to act in public the way they would act if alone, dissociated from and unaware of their political group identities. In his letter to Jefferson, Madison expressed doubts about the ability of the Constitution to protect minority rights because the proposed text specifically excluded the institutional mechanism he most desired: the power of the national government to "negative" or veto state laws. The argument of *Federalist* no. 10, a text in which "Publius" sought to locate the very protection for minority rights in space and in the multiplicity of interests that Madison himself believed to be institutionally absent from the document, might be thought of as the extension of the logic of such a closeting strategy—the sheer scale of a republic can keep majorities from recognizing their size, forcing groups to behave more like private individuals in their closets than public actors infatuated with and aware of their own collective strength.[56] Rights carried into society by solitary individuals, in other words, might paradoxically best be protected by solitary individuals exiting from society.

Popular Hermits

In 1786 and 1787 advocates for revised and expanded federal powers loudly proclaimed that the people of the United States had been thrown into a "state of nature" by the weaknesses of the Articles of Confederation. In those same years, a pair of popular texts about an old hermit began to circulate in New England. Passing from Madisonian political thought to the still largely under-studied world of late eighteenth-century American popular literature allows us to consider the ways in which the culture of solitude and privacy reflected on and participated in larger political discussions.

Short of noting the frequency and kind of editions, it is impossible to say how popular these texts were or how or by whom they were read. The first text, most often entitled *A Wonderful Discovery of a Hermit*, emerged in a number of locations and appeared in formats that spoke to different kinds of readers: single-sheet broadsides with accompanying woodcuts printed in Boston and vended by rural peddlers brought the story to areas beyond the centers of print capital; small, badly printed chapbooks emerging from Springfield and Worcester, Massachusetts, from Hartford and Norwich, Connecticut, from Portsmouth, New Hampshire, and Providence, Rhode Island, most likely found ready readers among children; printings in Massachusetts almanacs put the text in the hands of provincial adults for at least a year.

Reflecting new interests in the western frontier and published in the aftermath of the Land Ordinance of 1785, the story these New England readers encountered concerns two gentlemen adventurers from Virginia who "agreed to travel into the western parts of this vast country to explore the regions which belong to these United States, which are yet unknown to us." Accompanied by two slaves, this state-sanctioned exploratory company travels westward for over two months "without seeing the least appearance, or even track of any human being." They eventually stumble over a lone inhabitant of the American interior, not exactly the typical unauthorized squatter imagined by Congress but an "Old Hermit" who enjoys a simple but happy life in a cave.[57] It doesn't take much to convince the Hermit to tell his story. He is quite old: by his own estimates he was born in 1558 in London, 227 years before the Virginians "discovered" him. His father was a lowly mechanic who valued learning and provided that his son should be educated, but soon after his education, the young boy fell in love with a nobleman's daughter. The results were predictable: the nobleman refused the match and confined his daughter; the daughter died of lovesickness; and the dejected young boy set sail for Italy. There was a storm, he was blown off course, and (Crusoe-like) he landed on the shore of North America and migrated inland to the cave in which he was found 210 years later. The Hermit doesn't eat meat (and consequently all animals are friendly to him), and he attributes his long life and "good constitution" to the blessing of heaven and simple food. The Virginia gentlemen inform the Old Hermit about the "present state of the nation," which in 1785 is called "America." They urge the Hermit to leave the cave and return to civilization, but the Hermit politely declines. He believes he could not live in society again.[58]

The sequel, *An Account of the Wonderful Old Hermit's Death and Burial*, was partly a satire on the popularity of the first story and partly a commentary on the fatal effects of publicity on privacy (fig. 18). It

An Account of the Wonderful *Old Hermit's Death*, and Burial.

SOMETIME in June, 1786, Doctor SAMUEL BRAKE, a gentleman eminent both for Phyfic and Surgery, and a man indefatigable in the fearch of Curiofities, hearing of the wonderful Account of the HERMIT, fet out with a full determination to go and find him. The Doctor furnifhed himfelf with the beft intelligence Capt. *Buckland* could poffibly give him, and took with him two Attendants well armed, and as much Provifions as was neceffary for fuch a Journey, and being favoured with good weather they foon came to the Allegany Mountains.——Here the Doctor difcovered a certain Root never known nor heard of before, which proves a remedy for all difeafes.——After a great deal of trouble they found the Hermit, but it was entirely by accident that they happened at laft to difcover him; for the Country was very wild, covered with fhrubs as thick as poffible, and the trees grew large beyond defcription.——One day the Doctor difcovered with his Spy-Glafs, a very high Hill, at a confiderable diftance; and thought he would go and take an Obfervation from the top of that Hill;—when he arrived there he foon found the Old Hermits path, juft as Capt Buckland had directed.—They followed the path down the valley, and foon came to the Hermit's Cave;—nothing was feen of the Hermit for fome time, and they fuppofed that he was afleep in his Cave, and not one foul durft venture into his old Habitation, at length, whilft they were liftening at the mouth of the Cave, they difcovered the Hermit at a little diftance, coming with a handful of Roots which he had been gathering for food;—he walked in a flow and grave manner, and when he faw them he came and embraced them;—but did not feem to be fo much furprifed to fee them as when he was firft difcovered by Capt. Buckland, &c.—He invited them in a very friendly manner into his Cave, and was overjoyed to fee them. The Cave was very curious, which appeared to be dug out of a folid white flint rock; but as particular defcription has been given of it before, it will be needlefs to fay any thing farther concerning it.—The Hermit made

particular enquiry after Capt. *Buckland* and Mr. *Fielding*, and faid that he received great fatisfaction from a vifit which they had made him, and added, that they were the firft human beings that he had feen from the time he firft landed on this fhore, which was about 200 years.—Doctor Brake tarried there feveral days, and in that time became very intimate with the Hermit, and found feveral things which were not difcovered before :—Two Books in particular, which he brought with him from England, one in Poetry the other in Profe—The Hermit appeared to have had a good education, when he was young, and difcovered a furprifing greatnefs of mind.—His eyes were good, but his teeth were very poor, he had but little hair on his head, but his beard was very long.—He could not articulate his words very diftinctly, but his language was better than any fpoken in England at the time he left it, which makes it appear evident that he was an extraordinary genius when he was young ;—He fhewed Doctor Brake his Books, Writings, &c. he had a large Pile of em in one corner of his Cave, fome were done on barks of trees, and fome on fkins made into a kind of Parchment.—The Doctor obtained liberty to take a copy of the Hermit's Compofition.—One contained principally Moral Sentiments, and the following Sentences were found written in one of them "*Young Men and young Women beware of feducing appearances which may furround you, and recollect what others have fuffered from the power of headftrong defire.—This world is but a wildernefs.—Eager paffions and violent defires were not made for Man—Pitch upon that courfe of life which is beft, and habit will render it the moft delightful.*" —

After a while the Doctor determined to try the old fellow with a little rum, and fee what the effect would be; but it was with great difficulty that he could perfuade him to drink : The Doctor told him that it was an excellent cordial that tended to ftrengthen the conftitution, 'till at laft the poor innocent Hermit was perfuaded to drink a little of that horrid bane, which hath fent thoufands out of the world.—He

drank about three quarters of a gill of that poifon liquour, and in a quarter of an hour there was a fenfible alteration in his looks and conduct ;—and in half an hour he appeared wild and almoft mad, and attempted to tell a kind of a love ftory;—and in about an hour he was entirely fenfelefs, and remained in that fhocking fituation until twelve o'clock at night, and then died.

Poor Old Man ! he lived about 200 years in his Cave, enjoying all the happinefs of a retired life ! and might have lived 200 years more, had he not drank that horrid draught! Curfed liquor ! Thoufands have fell a facrifice to its bewitching power !

Among the Hermit's writings was found his WILL, which appeared to have been made foon after he was firft difcovered.—He had given his Cave to Capt. Buckland and Mr. Fielding, as alfo all his Writings: His curious Cane he willed to one of Capt. Buckland's Servants, which was all the Hermit was poffeffed of, excepting a few old Skins which had ferved to cloath him, thofe he gave to the other Servant, as a reward for his kindnefs in finging a lovefong to him before they departed.

Doctor Brake was much affected at the fudden death of the Hermit, more efpecially the manner in which he was brought to his untimely death ;—but the Doctor faid that he felt no remorfe of confcience, as he really fuppofed that a little of that cordial would ferve to raife his fpirits and make him more cheerful with his new vifitors.

The next day the Doctor and his Attendants employed themfelves about burying the Old Gentleman in as decent a manner as poffible in his Cave, which was done with great folemnity and good order.——The Doctor ordered one of his Attendants to fhave the Hermit, and his Beard is carefully preferved as a very great curiofity, it being at leaft twelve inches long.

N. B. Doctor Brake mentions that this good Old Man made it his conftant cuftom to devote himfelf to Prayer every Day, and there is no doubt of his final and everlafting happinefs.

☞ Thofe who do not credit the above may apply to Dr. Brake for better information.

FIGURE 18. *An Account of the Wonderful Old Hermit's Death and Burial*, 1787. Courtesy of the American Antiquarian Society, Worcester, Massachusetts.

circulated far less widely than the first, and seems to have been printed only as a broadside and only in Boston and Worcester in 1787 and 1788. It concerns a Dr. Samuel Brake, a physician whose curiosity is piqued by the narrative of the Virginia gentlemen and who decides in June 1786 to retrace their path. Dr. Brake quickly rediscovers the Hermit, and we learn new details: the Hermit has written a book of moral philosophy that warns young men and women about the dangers of seducing appearances. Dr. Brake does not try to get the Old Hermit to return to civilization, but he does try to convince the Hermit to break his simple diet with a glass of rum, "an excellent cordial that tended to strengthen the constitution." Under pressure from the doctor, the Hermit accepts the drink, but the rum proves poisonous rather than preservative and the Hermit dies. Brake turns from executioner to executor after he discovers a will written by the Old Hermit, in which the Hermit gives most of his goods—his books and his cave—to the Virginia gentlemen who discovered him a year earlier, reserving his cane and a few old skins for the slaves.[59] While the narrator of the sequel goes out of his way to attribute the Hermit's death to "cursed liquor" ("Thousands have fell a sacrifice to its bewitching power!"), one thing seems obvious: the Old Hermit was doomed by his own publicity.

It might be easy, probably too easy, to read these texts in the context of the contemporary ratification debates, stressing for instance a word like "constitution." The first text confirms that constitutions are preserved through republican simplicity and self-denial; the second demonstrates the dire consequences for healthy constitutions of tampering by even well-meaning experts. The rhetoric of the framers as physicians, working to preserve the body politic, was embraced by Federalists and mocked by Anti-Federalists. One Philadelphia Anti-Federalist sarcastically referred to the framers as "a number of skilled physicians" who "met together in Philadelphia last summer for the purpose of exploring and, if possible, removing the cause of this direful disease" (an excess of democracy) and who relied on the textbook of John Adams to prescribe "king, lords, and commons, or in the American language, President, Senate, and Representatives." It was a real shame, he joked, that Anti-Federalists "had the horrid audacity to think for themselves in regard to this new system of government" and "wickedly began to doubt concerning the perfection of this evangelical Constitution, which our political doctors have declared to be a panacea, which (by inspiration) they know will infallibly heal every distemper in the Confederation and finally ter-

minate in the salvation of America."[60] These popular texts, then, perhaps served as illustrative allegories of popular Anti-Federal slogans in
New England about austerity and a constitutional cure worse than the
disease. But even if this was the case, and there is little to support such
a reading, the Old Hermit was also easily co-opted for Federalism: an
image of "The venerable Hermit of the Western Country" appeared in
a 1790 pictorial broadside printed in Albany for children that also celebrated the recent ratification of the Constitution by North Carolina.[61]
Such readings inevitably sound flat, forced, and unidirectional: the relationship between culture and ideology is rarely one to one.

A more nuanced, multidirectional reading suggests that these texts
mitigated fears about social contraction by offering radically alternative
narratives about society and about individualism—that society was morally corrupting rather than morally enabling, that it was unjust and created artificial class and social distinctions that kept the sons of mechanics from marrying the daughters of noblemen and made slaves of some
and gentlemen of others, that it led humans to eat animals instead of
befriending them, that public interest could have fatal consequences for
individual privacy. These popular texts were stories of individual rights
on the one hand and "stories of peoplehood" on the other.[62] They give
us glimpses of what a larger cultural understanding of the origins and
meanings of government might look like, but they tell us too about popular understandings of succession, legitimacy, and private property. It is
hard to think of a hermit drafting a will, and it would have been impossible in the period to think of the Hermit as the sole occupant and owner
of the American West. These narratives provide, in some respects, for
comfortable conquests of that land based on the fiction of prior English occupancy and legal title. And perhaps for this very reason, for the
way in which he privatized the West, the Old Hermit achieved a certain
celebrity in the popular culture of the early republic. An exhibition of
wax statues in New York, the temporary home of the new government,
in September 1789 featured a life-sized figure of "An Old Hermit" in the
company of the president of the United States, members of the British
royal family, and an "Indian Chief . . . holding a real scalp."[63] The history of successive western occupation narrated in the popular Old Hermit texts found political reinforcement and material form in such amusements, and it must have been tempting for visitors to read this fictive
character with and against real political actors in a line of symbolic succession for the West, a constant presence that papered over the ruptures

of possession materialized in the bodies of the unsocial Indian, of the British monarchy, and finally of Washington.[64]

To read history or politics into, rather than out of, popular literature will inevitably produce unsatisfying results.[65] The cultural materials assembled here should be considered not simply as in dialogue with but as part of the history of political thought, fragments of a tense and never fully resolved divide in American culture between self and society, natural right and positive law, privacy and publicity. Cultural history, and especially the study of popular culture, can help us reshape our understandings of the "constitutional era," but it requires us to see popular texts as contexts for the period as well as to see the period as the context for them: that is, to accommodate our own ingrained understanding of the figure-ground relations of literature and history to the multidirectional realities of historical experience.

CHAPTER SIX

The Godless Constitution
and the Sacred Rights of Man

Revolutionary politicians, always careful to mark the proper scope of constituted power, often described God as a being with unlimited legislative, executive, or judicial authority. The preamble to the Massachusetts Constitution of 1780, drafted by John Adams, acknowledged the goodness of "the great Legislator of the Universe" in allowing people to make a social compact. In one of the most important statements on the separation of church and state, his "Memorial and Remonstrance" of 1785, James Madison argued that all men were subjects first to "the Governour of the Universe" and only then members of civil society. And in the Declaration of Independence Thomas Jefferson had the representatives in Congress appeal to "the Supreme Judge of the World" for the rectitude of their intentions.[1] Of course, many others would have described God as holding all of these offices simultaneously. In an age committed to the separation of powers, God was one of two conspicuous examples of the legitimate unification of power. The other was an individual in the state of nature—or, more properly speaking, "the people" in whom all power had originally inhered and whose voice was so often equated with the voice of God. These two entities were the authorizing poles of politics in the early United States, the direct and indirect sources of the powers of government and of the rights government was instituted to protect. It could be said (and often was) that both of these figures stood outside of normal politics.

The Constitution of the United States does not mention God, a fact recognized as soon as the text began to circulate. After a first reading, and sensing a conspiracy, a young law student in Virginia lectured his teacher that "the Constitution is de[i]stical in principle, and in all probability the composers had no thought of God in all their consultations." The student was shocked that the word "God" had not appeared in the most obvious and conventional place, for "eaven the oath that binds the Precedent [President] does not meantion his name."[2] It was indeed a striking omission, for every state constitution written during and since 1776 had mentioned God in a preamble, in a scripted oath of office, in a religious test for office-holding, or in a declaration of the sacred rights of conscience. In fact, of the thirteen constitutions or declarations of rights drafted during the Revolutionary War, only Virginia's had failed to use the actual word "God": in May 1776 the Virginia Convention had preferred to invoke "our Creator," as Jefferson would in drafting the congressional Declaration of Independence a few weeks later.[3]

The absence of the word "God" was an obstacle, even for supporters of the Constitution. In February 1788, having just attended the Connecticut ratifying convention, William Williams explained to readers of a Hartford newspaper that he was uneasy that officeholders under the Constitution would not have to meet a religious qualification and that the text made no "explicit acknowledgement of the being of a God, his perfections and his providence." Though few transcripts from the Connecticut ratifying convention exist, and his claim cannot be verified, Williams told his readers that he had proposed a new preamble to his colleagues:

> *We the people of the United States*, in a firm belief of the being and perfections of the one living and true God, the creator and supreme Governour of the world, in his universal providence and the authority of his laws: that he will require of all moral agents an account of their conduct, that all rightful powers among men are ordained of, and mediately derived from God, therefore in a dependence on his blessing and acknowledgment of his efficient protection in establishing our Independence, whereby it is become necessary to agree upon and settle a Constitution of federal government for ourselves, and *in order to form a more perfect union* &c.

To Williams, who had been a member of Congress and had belatedly signed the Declaration of Independence in August 1776 (though he had not been present to vote for it in July), the absence of God in the Constitution went beyond the omission of a particular word or of an acknowl-edgment of God's hand in the American Revolution. Williams was dis-turbed by what it meant for "We the people" to claim the power and the right to erect a government without acknowledging that the power had come from somewhere, that it derived from someone or something other than themselves. He was uneasy at the implication in the actual Pre-amble that the people were independent and accountable only to each other and not to God. Williams was generally localist rather than na-tionalist in his political sentiments, and he was lampooned (as "William Wimble") by the group of nationalist poets known as the Connecticut Wits. He looked like an Anti-Federalist; and for that reason his town se-lected him to represent them at the ratifying convention and instructed him to vote against ratification, but economic reasons led him to ignore those instructions and to support the text. His case was unusual, to be sure, but he was not alone in his apprehensions about the absence of the word "God."[4]

Of course, careful readers might have teased out some latent acknowl-edgment of God from the text, which had a small residue of religious lan-guage. It is probable that certain late eighteenth-century readers, having attended or encountered ordination sermons in which older Christian ministers invested younger men with ministerial power through the lay-ing on of hands, heard something mildly ecclesiastical in one of the main verbs of the Preamble—that the people "do ordain and establish this Constitution." William Williams may have been such a reader, for in his new preamble he had declared that "all rightful powers among men are ordained of, and mediately derived from God." (Others would of course have recognized "ordain" as a standard term of statutory enactment meaning simply to institute; it was a dead metaphor.) And some perhaps heard religious overtones in the idea in the Preamble that the Constitu-tion was designed "to secure the Blessings of Liberty." This was a phrase laden with ambiguity. Were these to be understood as the blessings of the goddess Liberty or was liberty itself the blessing? (And if the latter, who exactly had conferred or was to confer the blessing of liberty?) The oath for the president, which was the only oath specifically scripted in the text of the Constitution, did not mention God and allowed for the of-ficeholder to affirm rather than swear; even still, the president was asked to "solemnly swear (or affirm)," and to most contemporaries this would imply the gravity of a religious ritual. The most explicit reference to reli-gion came in the second paragraph of Article VII: "Done in Convention

by the Unanimous Consent of the States present the Seventeenth Day
of September in the Year of our Lord one thousand seven hundred and
Eighty seven and of the Independence of the United States of America the Twelfth." The American revolutionaries had not made a serious
attempt, as French revolutionaries later would, to change the calendar.
The twin time schemes here, the religious and the political, were probably meant to mimic standard British practice, whereby legislation was
identified both by the year since the birth of Christ and by the reign of
a particular monarch. But in any event, such implicit references would
have provided little comfort. The Constitution had been silent on religion. Numerous supporters and opponents of the text wondered what it
could mean that the Constitutional Convention had failed to acknowledge God, to include religious tests, or to make a positive declaration
about religious liberty.

And even after ratification was a fact, some supporters still hoped
that the word could be inserted into the text. Benjamin Rush in the middle of June 1789 wrote to Vice President John Adams that "many pious
people wish the name of the Supreme Being had been introduced somewhere in the new Constitution," and he suggested that "perhaps an acknowledgement may be made of his goodness or of his providence in the
proposed amendments."[5] Since the majority of state constitutions (including Rush's own in Pennsylvania) had made explicit reference to "Almighty God" in the articles of their declarations of rights devoted to religious freedom, and since eight states during ratification had specifically
proposed a declaration of religious freedom, Rush would have had good
reason to suspect that such an acknowledgment might find its way into
the text of the Constitution. But of the three states that had proposed
specific wording for the protection of religious freedom during ratification, only Virginia had explicitly mentioned "our Creator," lifting the
language directly from the state's own Declaration of Rights from 1776.
It was not to be. A week before Rush sent his note to Adams, James
Madison had offered a slate of amendments to the House of Representatives, and the wording of what would (after debate and revision in Congress) become part of the First Amendment had not mentioned God:
"The civil rights of none shall be abridged on account of religious belief or worship, nor shall any national religion be established, nor shall
the full and equal rights of conscience be in any manner, or on any pre-
text infringed."[6] Although the wording changed several times before the
final version—"Congress shall make no law respecting an establishment

of religion, or prohibiting the free exercise thereof"—passed through both chambers of Congress in late September, at no time did any of the proposed amendments mention God.

Commentators since the eighteenth century have described the Constitution as a "godless" document, by which they have meant not only that the text omits the word "God" but also that the document represents (for some better, for others worse) a moment of political desacralization or even secularization. Political secularization generally means a separation of state and church. Though this was the effect of the Constitution, it would be hard to claim that it was the intent. The text as it emerged from the Philadelphia Convention was, after all, largely agnostic on questions of religion: it did not empower Congress to establish a national religion (and, in the First Amendment, expressly prevented it from doing so), but it also did not empower Congress to dismantle the religions established in particular states (and again in the First Amendment, expressly prevented it from doing so). In proposing amendments, Madison had first suggested an injunction to the effect that "No state shall violate the equal rights of conscience" should be placed alongside the other express limitations on the powers of states in Article I, section 10. This would have empowered the federal government to enforce religious liberty within the states, a very nationalist power indeed, but his colleagues in the House of Representatives dropped it from the second draft of proposals. In the end, of course, the handful of states that had singular or plural establishments of religion abandoned them by legislative enactments, but before that happened (and before the Fourteenth Amendment made states as accountable as Congress for the First Amendment) violations of the rights of conscience could not have been alleviated by the federal government.

If political secularization is generally easy to see, a matter of telling whether church and state are separate, social and cultural secularization is a more difficult concept—and it is notoriously hard to measure. Tracking the career of the word "God," on the other hand, is relatively easy, and doing so makes certain relations between religion and politics visible in ways that standard accounts of established state churches or struggles for religious freedom do not. The Federal Constitution was unique among the American constitutions because it did not use the word "God," but the word itself had a curious career over the eighteenth century and had experienced a sharp decline in use during the revolutionary period overall. Indeed, an examination of the rises and falls of the word suggests that the word's presence in the state constitutions may be more curious than its absence in the Constitution of the United States. But despite dramatic changes in religious vocabulary and a marked drop in the use of the word "God" in the period of the Revolution, it was next to impossible for Americans who employed arguments rooted in natural rights to dispense with God (both the word and the concept) as a foundation for rights. The forces at work in political secularization were complex and contradictory, and the sacralization of rights as God-given in the revolutionary age was intimately related to the understanding of government as a work of human art.

The Godless 1780s

In the last decade religion has come to occupy a key place in the study of the European Enlightenment, but it has never been easy to think about the American Enlightenment without emphasizing religion.[7] Though it remains a convenient shorthand for narrating transitions of authority in American history, few current scholars of the American Enlightenment are comfortable with the idea (made manifest in early twentieth-century intellectual history) that theology yielded precedence to law and politics in the late eighteenth century or with the characterization of the revolutionary era as a moment of exclusively enlightened thought sandwiched between the Puritanism of the seventeenth century and the evangelicalism of the nineteenth century. Indeed, in one of the most nuanced accounts of the relation of religion and law in the late eighteenth century, Robert A. Ferguson has recently shown how a dialectic of liberty fundamentally shaped political discourse; religion gave way to law, but by no means was it a simple or even inevitable transition. Most historians of the early republic accept and acknowledge the continuing and sometimes increasing vitality of religion in the age of the American Enlightenment, even if they have not followed intellectual historians like Alan Heimert or social historians like Patricia Bonomi in drawing lines of causality directly from the Great Awakening of the 1730s and 1740s to the American Revolution.[8] Scholars may differ in their interpretations of the nature of the "Nature's God" invoked in the Declaration of Independence or over the question of the "godlessness" of the U.S. Constitution, but they have learned to see how putatively secular events like the Revolution were both open for sacralization and (as Jon Butler has observed) "good" for religion.[9]

But even as religion was on the rise, the word "God" declined dramatically over the course of the eighteenth century. The word is famously absent from the Constitution, but it was also relatively absent from the printed texts of the decade in which the Constitution was drafted and adopted, and more broadly from the revolutionary period overall. What some scholars have termed "quantitative intellectual history" and others have simply called the history of the book can shed light on the career of individual words across time, though of course any word can often mask deep disagreements about meaning.[10] Quantifying the appearance or absence of the word "God" cannot answer the largest questions—about the relationship between religion and the origins of the American Revolution; about the rise of secularism; about the sacralization of states and nations—but the quantitative evidence affirms, amplifies, and complicates some of what we already know from other sources, and it invites us to consider particular uses of the word "God" against larger synchronic and diachronic horizons.[11]

The titles of books, broadsides, and other imprints published in colonial British America and the early United States reveal that the word "God" experienced a decline in both absolute and relative terms in the 1780s. In part, the decline followed a midcentury surge. The word had appeared on more and more title pages since the publishing activities surrounding the Great Awakening in the late 1730s and early 1740s but had declined somewhat in absolute terms in the 1770s. It appeared in far fewer titles in the 1780s than in either the 1770s or the 1790s; a graphic representation of this data (chart 1a) can suggest something like a post-revolutionary depression in the use of the word "God."[12] The word, however, did not entirely disappear. Indeed, "God" appears in the titles of approximately the same number of imprints in the 1780s (110 titles) as in the 1710s (106 titles), but printing output as well as population had risen significantly between 1710 and 1790; and so a graph of the relative percentage of imprints with the word "God" in their titles offers a more dramatic picture (chart 1b). Taking the overall output from colonial and early national presses into account, we can see that the word held moderately steady between the 1710s and a century high-point in the 1750s, with "God" appearing on the title pages of between 11 and 13 percent of all imprints during those five decades. Graphically rendered, the effect of the Great Awakening now looks far less like a surge than simply an effort to maintain standing in a growing market. Given the slightly lower percentages for the 1720s, the real effect of the Great Awakening for the word "God" was to postpone the decline by decades. The word began a

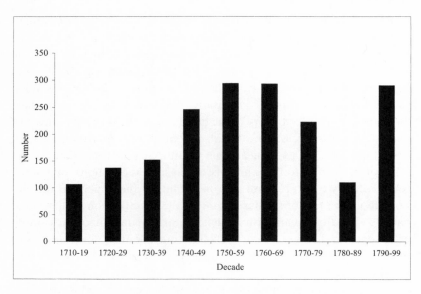

CHART IA. Number of American imprints with "God" on the title page, 1710–1799

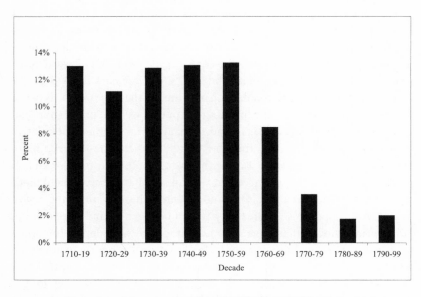

CHART IB. Percentage of American imprints with "God" on the title page, 1710–1799

sharp drop in the 1760s (to just over 8 percent), fell lower in the 1770s (to under 4 percent), and reached a century low-point of under 2 percent of all imprints in the 1780s before showing some very small indications of revival in the 1790s, due in part to the beginnings of the Second Great Awakening late in that decade.

Concepts of agency changed over the long eighteenth century, and occasionally printers repackaged seventeenth-century texts with more putatively "secular" titles. This happened, for instance, in a revolutionary-era Boston reprinting of Mary Rowlandson's famous captivity narrative from 1682, *The Soveraignty and Goodness of God* (fig. 19), which appeared in 1773 under the title *A Narrative of the Captivity, Sufferings and Removes of Mrs. Mary Rowlandson* (fig. 20). The new title was in fact just as old as the 1682 title: a version of it had been used to market the text in London in the late seventeenth century. Nevertheless, the shift in titles and the layout of the title page in the late eighteenth-century printing made Rowlandson rather than God the chief agent of the text. Such cases of repackaged texts with dramatically different titles were rare, and titles fluctuated in length over the eighteenth century. Titles may provide only a rough barometer of the fate of the word "God"; nevertheless, the appearance of the word within the imprints generally corresponds to information compiled from title pages.[13]

The word "God" was not alone: the careers of a cluster of other key words (chart 2) suggests a significant shift in the way in which late colonial readers and writers ascribed agency to themselves and to powers beyond themselves. By two measures, both in titles and in the texts themselves, the word "God" declined. An analysis of six other words— "religion," "Christ," "Jesus," "creator," "providence," and "deity"— suggests roughly parallel overall declines from the 1750s through the 1770s and 1780s, with some intriguing small gains. Like the word "God," the words "Christ" and "Jesus" reach eighteenth-century lows in the 1780s, and "religion" is at its lowest point in half a century; but the terms "creator" and "deity" (which both decline in the 1770s) show small recoveries in the 1780s. The word "providence," the only one of these terms to decline when all the others went up in the 1740s—in other words, the only term on the list that didn't enjoy a boost from the Great Awakening—appears in imprints of the 1780s with almost the same frequency as "God." By the 1790s the word "religion" would top this list of terms, all of which appeared in less than a quarter of all imprints. The analysis suggests that other words we might expect to stand in for or possibly replace the word "God" shared that word's overall decline.[14]

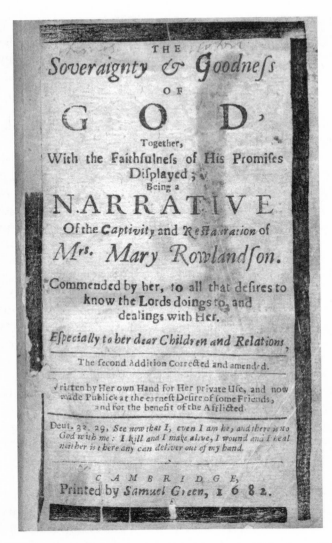

FIGURE 19. Title page of Mary Rowlandson, *The Soveraignty and Goodness of God,* 1682. Courtesy of the Trustees of the Boston Public Library, Boston.

Nonreligious publishing expanded dramatically in the late eighteenth century, and so one must be very careful with these rough numbers. On the one hand, what the charts measuring percentages (for example, chart 1b) show is the growth of nonreligious titles in the second half of the century. Data published by G. Thomas Tanselle in 1981 and by Mark Noll in

2002 indicate that publications in "theology" (to use the term employed by Tanselle, taken directly from Charles Evans's *American Bibliography*) and "religion" (Noll's term) declined throughout the second half of the century and fluctuated greatly in the period between 1765 and 1785. Tanselle calculates that "theology" accounted for 29 percent of all publications between 1765 and 1773, but dropped to 10 percent between 1774 and 1778, and rose to 18 percent between 1779 and 1785. Noll finds that "religious titles" constituted almost 40 percent of the market in 1760 and only 22 percent in 1790, dropping to a low of 16 percent in 1775.[15]

On the other hand, in thinking about percentages, we should observe that American publishing output did not experience dynamic growth in the 1780s, as it had in the 1770s and would again in the 1790s. Indeed,

A

NARRATIVE

OF THE

CAPTIVITY, SUFFERINGS AND REMOVES

OF

Mrs. *Mary Rowlandson,*

Who was taken Prisoner by the INDIANS with several others, and treated in the most barbarous and cruel Manner by those vile Savages : With many other remarkable Events during her TRAVELS.

Written by her own Hand, for her private Use, and now made public at the earnest Desire of some Friends, and for the Benefit of the afflicted.

BOSTON :

Printed and Sold at JOHN BOYLE's Printing-Office, next Door to the *Three Doves* in Marlborough-Street. 1773.

1773

FIGURE 20. Title page of *A Narrative of the Captivity . . . of Mrs. Mary Rowlandson*, 1773. Courtesy of the American Antiquarian Society, Worcester, Massachusetts.

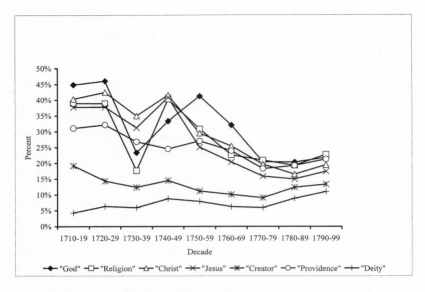

CHART 2. The careers of seven words in American imprints over the eighteenth century, 1710–1799

the 1780s were the only decade in the second half of the eighteenth century in which total print output did not rise dramatically: based on the increasing output from the 1740s (1,880 imprints) to the 1750s (2,217) to the 1760s (3,453) to the 1770s (6,272), and the dramatic output of the 1790s (14,425), we might expect that the total for the 1780s would have been in the range of 10,000 imprints; but it was in fact only 6,300, a mere 28 more than the previous decade. Perhaps, had the overall output grown steadily, instead of in spurts, we might see more references to God in the 1780s imprints. But when we break the imprints into smaller segments by considering typical genres we find the same general pattern within genres that we see overall.[16]

The dramatic decline in the word "God" was not the effect of the growth of "nonreligious" imprints: it was a phenomenon within all imprints, including "religious" ones.[17] Perhaps the most telling change can be seen in published sermons.[18] Nearly 90 percent of the 291 published sermons of the 1750s mention God, but less than 50 percent of the 447 sermons of the 1770s do so, and the percentage for the 1780s is only slightly higher. Fewer sermons were published in the 1780s than in the 1770s, but even if we were partially to attribute the low numbers for the word "God" in the 1780s to the failure of ministers to get their sermons into print, we would still face an astounding fact: ministers in the 1780s were more likely than other writers to mention God, to be sure, but they did so in only half of their published sermons, a drop from nearly 90 percent thirty years earlier. Ministers should not be understood as holdouts to the larger trend but as one of the best indexes for the decline of the word "God."

Two categories of writers, white women and African-American men, deserve special notice. Female-authored imprints of the 1780s were more likely than most male-authored imprints to mention God; the number of these imprints is small but the trend is the same. The highest percentage (58 percent) is in the 1750s, when seven of twelve female-authored publications mention God, and lowest (37 percent) in the 1780s, when twenty-six of seventy-one female-authored imprints mention God. The small numbers of imprints by women from the 1750s to the 1780s certainly invite scrutiny, but when the number of imprints by women almost tripled in the 1790s (from 71 imprints in the 1780s to 245 imprints in the 1790s), and when the kinds of printed works by women diversified, the percentage of imprints mentioning God also grew (from 37 percent in the 1780s to 47 percent in the 1790s) when we might have expected it to decline.

The numbers of imprints by African, African-American, and Afro-British authors are also small, but they suggest a curious reversal of the general trend. While only five of the eleven black-authored imprints of the 1770s (or 45 percent) mention God—and twelve of the thirty-three black-authored imprints of the 1790s (or 36 percent) mention God—fully two-thirds (67 percent) of the black-authored imprints of the 1780s mention God. Aside from noting that the percentages are higher for all black writers than for white male writers, and that the publications of Phillis Wheatley (the only black female author) constitute over a quarter of the very small sample and skew the results for the 1780s, we should probably avoid generalizing from this data. It is worth noting, however, that when compared with the general pattern, the data from black and female authors help illustrate the ways in which traditional accounts of providence lost their conceptual purchase for many white male writers in the late eighteenth century, just as those same traditional accounts continued to have real religious and political meaning in the lives of white women and began to have meaning for free and unfree black writers (who might claim both their enslavement and their subsequent escape from enslavement as points in the unfolding of God's providence).[19]

By any number of measurements, then, the use of the word "God" declined in the revolutionary decades, but would people in the 1780s have experienced the decade as relatively "Godless"? Perhaps not: for the quantitative evidence relates to production rather than consumption. Readers purchased and read imprints from different years, they read imported books, and no doubt individual regions or towns did not necessarily follow the overall trends. On the other hand, if the published sermons are a fair indication of oral delivery, sensitive older listeners may have heard the word less frequently in the mouths of their ministers, and sensitive readers who had come of age in the 1750s may have felt a long-term qualitative change, if they could not have registered a quantitative one. And even younger readers who reached maturity in the 1770s and 1780s may have sensed shorter-term fluctuations.

An annual breakdown between the beginning of the French and Indian War in 1754 and the end of the century (chart 3) shows that the high point for "God" in titles is 1757 (with 21 percent or forty-eight titles mentioning God, significantly higher than the decade average of 13 percent), and for "God" in all text is 1756 (63 percent or 142 imprints, significantly higher than the decade average of 40 percent). The absolute and relative high points, then, are associated with years during the French and Indian War. The low point for "God" in titles is 1788 (0.86 percent or five titles) and for "God" in all text is 1779 (4.64 percent, or twenty-four imprints), and the second lowest for the latter is 1787 (4.78 percent or thirty imprints; the numbers for 1779 and for 1787 are both significantly lower than the decade averages for the 1770s and 1780s of around 20 percent). The absolute and relative low points fall during the Revolutionary War and during the framing and ratification of the Constitution. And, of course, percentages can hide moderately large absolute numbers, especially given the rise in total print output. What the annual percentages suggest is the way in which a word like "God" functioned beyond the realm of theology or religion. Theological titles may have only constituted 10 percent of the print market in 1774, as Tanselle has noted, but fully half of all imprints that year mentioned God. And, in absolute terms, the 361 imprints mentioning God in 1774 represents the high point for the eighteenth century (the next highest absolute number is 346 imprints mentioning God in 1790, which represents just over 40 percent of all imprints).

Despite some highs, we can still see the general pattern of decline, but we need to come to a better understanding of the varying function and fluctuating use of the word "God." We can begin by comparing two

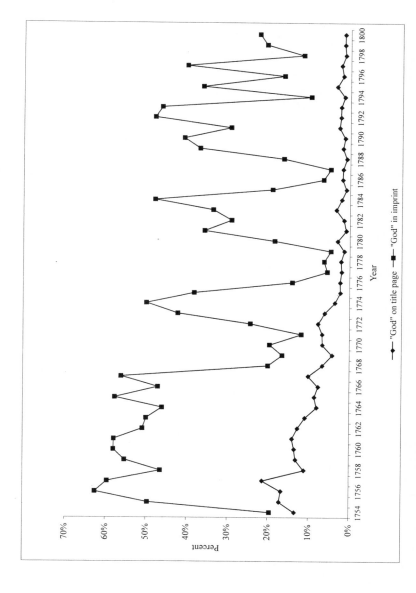

CHART 3. Mentions of "God" in American imprints, 1754–1800

wars. The percentages for the French and Indian War (1754–63) begin at over 60 percent and mostly hover between 50 and 60 percent, falling below 50 percent only once (in 1758). And the percentages remain in this range (50 to 60 percent) until 1768, at which point they drop to about 20 percent. The percentages for the American Revolution look very different, with fluctuations from highs of 50 percent to lows of 5 percent. Indeed, the annual numbers can be startling—exactly 50 percent of the 722 imprints include the word "God" in 1774, while less than 5 percent of the 517 imprints of 1779 or the 627 imprints of 1787 do so—yet what becomes apparent from the annual counts are shorter-term rises and falls, not simply fluctuations from year to year but what look like waves of "depressions" and "peaks" in the use of the word "God." Three such waves are readable in both relative and absolute terms in the "constitutional era," the period between 1765 and 1791: first, a decline in the late 1760s leading to a low in 1771, followed by a rise peaking in 1774 (when 50 percent of imprints mention God); second, a decline beginning in 1775 and reaching a low in 1779, followed by a rise with a small peak in 1781, then a shorter fall, and a rise to a peak in 1784 (when again nearly 50 percent of imprints mention God); and, third, a decline beginning in 1785 and reaching a low in 1787, followed by a rise resulting in a smaller peak in 1790 (when over 40 percent of imprints mention God).[20] It is tempting to speculate that the increases are attributable to claims about the providential nature of the American Revolution—that God was, in effect, on the patriot side. Such statements did occur, to be sure, but hardly with the frequency we might imagine.

Instead, one thing becomes visible from multivariate analysis: the word "God" benefited appreciably in the revolutionary period from the increased employment of the language of natural rights (chart 4). Arguments based in natural rights enjoyed some frequency between 1766 and 1769, but declined from 1770 to 1772. In 1773 natural rights rhetoric fully eclipsed arguments rooted in precedent and civil rights. The number of imprints using the phrase shot up in 1774, peaked in 1775, fell slightly in 1776, and dropped just as dramatically in 1777. Even still, throughout the war they remained at the heightened levels seen in the period of 1766–69; and in the year following the Treaty of Peace of 1783, the numbers again rose, almost doubling. The language of natural rights, unlike the language of charter rights or the rights of Englishmen, was a deliberately sacralizing rhetoric (the "sacred rights of mankind"). It drew its source and its strength from appeals to God, and it is no coincidence

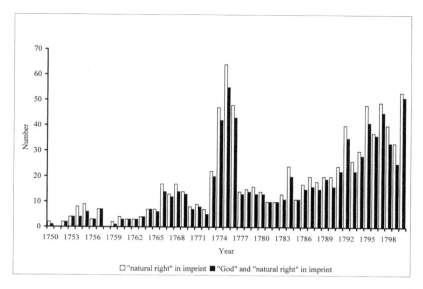

CHART 4. "God" and "natural rights" in American imprints, 1750–1800

that the word "God" appeared in almost every imprint using the phrase "natural rights," not only in the "constitutional era" but in the second half of the century.

The steady association between God and natural rights, and the growing popularity of claims based in natural rights, meant that God increased in political utility at precisely the point at which the word itself seemed to disappear. We should certainly not mistake the relative absence of the word "God" in the 1770s and 1780s for "secularization."[21] Religion itself—the thing and, to a small extent, the word—was on the rise in the same period. And it might be tempting to associate the general overall decline in the use of the word "God" in the 1770s and 1780s with the advent of American nationalism. David A. Bell, a historian of French nationalism, for instance recently argued that declining references to providence beginning in the late seventeenth century and the production of an image of a noninterfering God were the preconditions in the invention of a modern, specifically "terrestrial" nationalism in France.[22] The numbers are far too rough to make any claims about secularism or the rise of the nation, but the short-term charts do tell an intriguing story, one in which appeals to God should be tied more closely to particular political events and to the growth of new languages of rights.

The God of Rights

On July 4, 1776, John Adams, Benjamin Franklin, and Thomas Jefferson, having served together on the committee to draft the Declaration, were appointed to a committee of the Continental Congress to design a seal for the United States. It was perhaps not the most pressing affair in the summer of 1776, but Congress intended to affix the seal to major documents, and on July 9 John Adams suggested to Maryland congressman Samuel Chase that the Declaration itself would not be signed by all the representatives until the seal was ready.[23] Congress may have desired a symbolic surrogate for the coat of arms of the king, which had been ceremoniously removed from public places in Philadelphia and burned on July 8, for when the committee made its report about the seal on August 20 it described one side as the "Arms of the United States of America."[24] The seal committee consulted with a local painter, Pierre Eugene DuSimitiere, who suggested a heraldic device: a central shield of six parts representing emblems of "the Six principal nations of Europe from whom the Americans originated" surrounded by the initials of the thirteen states and flanked by an armor-clad Goddess of Liberty on one side and "an American Soldier" armed with a rifle and a tomahawk on the other; above the genealogical shield would appear the "Eye of Providence in a radiant Triangle whose Glory extends over the Shield and beyond the Figures."[25]

John Adams had a different idea. He proposed (as he told his spouse Abigail while the committee was preparing its report in mid-August) a classical subject: "the Choice of Hercules." He had a particular engraving in mind, one that appeared (Adams explained) "in some Editions of Lord Shaftsbury's Works." In 1712 Shaftesbury had commissioned Paolo de Mattaeis to paint the *Judgment of Hercules*; an engraving of this image by Simon Gribelin appeared in the third volume of the second edition of Shaftesbury's *Characteristicks* two years later and in subsequent editions throughout the eighteenth century (fig. 21). For Adams, the device should show, as the engraving had, the "Hero resting on his Clubb. Virtue pointing to her rugged Mountain, on one Hand, and perswading him to ascend. Sloth, glancing at her flowery Paths of Pleasure, wantonly reclining on the Ground, displaying the Charms both of her Eloquence and Person, to seduce him into Vice." Shaftesbury had written a fifty-page essay on how best to depict this particular topic. John Adams owned a copy of the 1773 edition of Shaftesbury's text, but cru-

Paulo de Mattheis Pinx: *Sim: Gribelin ſculps:*

FIGURE 21. Simon Gribelin after Paolo de Mattheis, *The Judgment of Hercules,* from Shaftesbury's *Characteristicks,* 5th ed., 1773. Courtesy of the University of Chicago Library.

cially Shaftesbury regularly described the topic as the "Judgment" (not the "Choice") of Hercules, a judgment between Virtue and Pleasure (not Sloth). It is easy to see why the image, an important early eighteenth-century moral emblem, would have appealed to Adams, why he wished to emphasize "Choice," and why he changed Pleasure to Sloth: it emblematized for him the drama of republican citizenship, a drama in which human agents are constantly tempted away from virtue.[26] The viewer was supposed to know, of course, that Hercules had made the right choice, but for Shaftesbury it was important that any depiction of this scene represent a moment when Hercules, as an attentive auditor, listened to Virtue make her case. The resolution had not yet been made. It was a moment of "Anticipation" and "pondering," of "Suspense and Doubt."[27] For whatever reason, Adams's proposal did not seem compelling to the committee, perhaps because (as he told Abigail) it was "too complicated" for a seal or because "it is not original."[28] It seems likely though that this parable of suspense and doubt, of uncertainty and anticipation, was sim-

ply too unresolved. In any event, no trace of his idea made it into the report the committee presented Congress in late August, which endorsed
DuSimitiere's design for one side of the seal, replacing the soldier with
the Goddess Justice.[29]

For the other side of the seal, Franklin recommended a reference to
a different path than the one described by Adams—the parting of the
Red Sea in the biblical account of Exodus. A scrap of paper in his hand
describes the seal as he seems to have first imagined it: "Moses standing on the shore, and extending his Hand over the Sea, thereby caus-
ing the same to overwhelm Pharoah [sic] who is sitting in an open Chariot a Crown on his Head & Sword in his Hand. Rays from a Pillar of
Fire in the Clouds reaching to Moses to express that he acts by Command of the Deity. Motto, *Rebellion to Tyrants is Obedience to God.*"[30]
At some point on this scrap of paper, Franklin inserted a caret after the
word "Moses" to insert "in the Dress of High Priest," but this amendment was blotted out.[31] Unlike Adams's focus on a moment of individual
choice, a constantly replayed morality tale emblematizing human agency
under republican governments, Franklin's design had a clear antimonar-
chical bent: it was as much a lesson for tyrants as for citizens.

Jefferson had yet another idea. John Adams told Abigail that Franklin had wanted "Moses lifting up his Wand, and dividing the Red Sea,
and Pharaoh, in his Chariot overwhelmed with the Waters," but that Jefferson had countered with "The Children of Israel in the Wilderness, led
by a Cloud by day, and a Pillar of Fire by night, and on the other Side
Hengist and Horsa, the Saxon Chiefs, from whom We claim the Honour
of being descended and whose Political Principles and Form of Government We have assumed."[32] Though we have only John Adams's description, it would seem that Jefferson wished for the heraldic side primarily
to represent what he took to be not simply ethnic but political genealogy,
a much more exclusive representation of the Saxon constitution of the
people than the six contributory nations (England, Scotland, Ireland,
France, Germany, and Holland) proposed by DuSimitiere. For the remaining side, Jefferson (like Adams) may have had a specific image in
mind: the title page of the Geneva Bible with its depiction of a scene
from the book of Exodus. And like Adams's "Choice of Hercules," the
image Jefferson described for this side was a moment of suspense (Exodus 13) rather than resolution (Exodus 14), a time before the overwhelm-
ing of the Pharaoh or the institution of Mosaic Law.

In the end the committee opted to present Franklin's proposal, with its depiction of a clear victory over oppression, rather than Jefferson's or Adams's emblems of suspense. A manuscript in Jefferson's hand suggests that Jefferson revised Franklin's proposal only slightly so that it would depict the Israelites (this was Jefferson's main graphic contribution) as well as Moses: "Pharaoh sitting in an open chariot a crown on his head passing thro' the divided waters of the Red sea in pursuit of the Israelites: rays from a pillar of fire in the cloud, expressive of the divine presence, & command, reaching to Moses who stands on the Shore & extending his hand over the sea, causes it to overwhelm Pharaoh. Motto. Rebellion to tyrants is obed[ience] to god." This is what the seal committee recommended to Congress on August 20, almost three weeks after the Declaration had been engrossed and signed by available representatives. Congress did not approve the design, but tabled it and charged another committee three years later with the same task.

Though a religious subject, the approved language describing the seal conspicuously highlighted human agency. Congress did not approve of the design, and so it is probably wrong to read too much into its description. But it may also be wrong to suggest that what attracted Franklin and Jefferson was the miraculous element in Exodus, the intervention of God.[33] The biblical text of Exodus emphasizes that God had overthrown the Egyptians, but both Franklin and Jefferson emphasize Moses's agency. In Franklin's original words, Moses "acts by Command of the Deity," but it is his act that causes the waves to overwhelm Pharaoh. Jefferson's revision of Franklin's proposal, the one forwarded to Congress, mentions "divine presence, & command," but the cause of Pharaoh's defeat is entirely Moses, "who stands on the Shore & extending his hand over the sea, causes it to overwhelm Pharaoh." Franklin and Jefferson's political philosophy fundamentally required God as an authorizing agent with some distance from worldly politics. For both Franklin and Jefferson, the motto "Rebellion to Tyrants is Obedience to God" (as was his usual practice, Jefferson did not capitalize the word "God" in the motto) found meaning within a philosophy of godless politics and sacred rights, one in which God served a crucial role outside of and before politics. It was meaningful not because politics was mingled with religion, but precisely because it should not be.

God was the author of rights. Alexander Hamilton argued in 1775 that the "sacred rights of mankind are not to be rummaged for, among old parchments, or musty records," and that they are "written as with a sun beam, in the whole *volume* of human nature, by the hand of divin-

ity itself; and can never be erased or obscured by mortal power."[34] Ten
years earlier, John Adams described rights as "antecedent to all earthly
government": they "cannot be repealed or restrained by human laws"
because they are "derived from the great legislator of the universe."[35]
In 1776, John Dickinson explained to a Committee of Correspondence that:

> Kings or parliaments could not give the rights essential to happiness—we
> claim them from a higher source—from THE KING OF KINGS and the
> LORD OF ALL THE EARTH. They are not annexed to us by parchments
> or seals. They are created in us by the decrees of Providence, which establish
> the laws of our nature. They are born with us; and cannot be taken away from
> us by any human power. In short, they are founded on the immutable max-
> ims of reason and justice. It would be an insult on the DIVINE MAJESTY
> to say, that HE has given or allowed any man or body of men a right to make
> me miserable.[36]

Though Dickinson differed from Adams and Jefferson on the issue
of declaring independence in 1776, he was in perfect accord about the
source of rights.

The document Congress drafted to announce political separation
from Britain included four explicit references to God, and would have
included one more had Congress not excised Jefferson's indictment of
the king for the slave trade. The rights Jefferson described in the deleted
passage on colonial slavery in the Declaration of Independence were
"sacred," an adjective he had also employed in his original rough draft
of the second paragraph. The final version of the Declaration made four
explicit references to divinity—"Nature's God" in the first paragraph;
"Creator" in the second; and "the Supreme Judge of the World" and "the
Protection of divine Providence" in the final paragraph. Though the appeals to religious language have sometimes made later commentators
uncomfortable, they were foundational rather than fleeting. The references in the final paragraph effectively equated God as an audience with
the "Mankind" mentioned in the first paragraph and the "candid World"
of the second: as Adams explained to his spouse, the Declaration was
meant to justify the United States of America "in the Sight of God and
Man." And if the first paragraph announced a secular time (the "Course
of human Events"), it also appealed to "the Laws of Nature and of Nature's God." But it was in the second paragraph that religious vocabu-

lary did the most work, and it is there that the rights claims of the Declaration differ most noticeably from those that would enter contemporary
state constitutions. George Mason had not referenced God in drafting a
similar statement for the Virginia Declaration of Rights a few weeks earlier. The Virginia Declaration, as it circulated in draft, had stated "That
all men are born equally free and independent, and have certain inherent natural rights, of which they cannot, by any compact, deprive or divest their posterity; among which are, the enjoyment of life and liberty,
with the means of acquiring and possessing property, and pursuing and
obtaining happiness and safety." The Virginia Convention, of course,
later revised the draft statement so that readers would not think it included slaves: it was only when men "entered into society," which slaves
had not done, that their rights had any meaning.[37] But in both the original and revised version of the statement Mason had not felt obliged to
name the source of the natural rights he enumerated; the Virginia Convention separated the declaration of equality and natural rights in the
first article from the mention of a Creator in the sixteenth article. And
in the coming years the draftsmen of most state constitutions simply adopted Mason's draft language and failed to name an author of rights.

Like Mason's Virginia Declaration of Rights, Jefferson's original
draft of the Declaration of Independence had avoided an explicit reference to the author of rights; and the final version suggests that Jefferson had come to the explicit references to God in a circuitous way.
According to a version of the draft in John Adams's handwriting, Jefferson had originally written "that all Men are created equal and independent; that from that equal Creation they derive Rights inherent and unalienable." At some point before Adams made his transcription of the
text, and perhaps at the urging of a fellow committee member, Jefferson
had changed "We hold these truths to be sacred & undeniable" to "We
hold these truths to be self-evident."[38] Jefferson's original draft, then,
described the truths held as "sacred" and the rights enumerated as derived from "equal Creation" and inhering in "all men"; but Jefferson had
not explicitly named an agent, except insofar as a "Creation" implied a
creator. The shift in phrasing from Mason's "all men" as "born equally
free and independent" to Jefferson's "all men" as "created equal" had
perhaps begged the question of agency to other members of the Committee of Five or even to Jefferson himself, for at some point after discussions with Franklin and Adams Jefferson replaced the phrase about
derivation of rights from "equal Creation" in favor of the sense that "all

men . . . are endowed by their creator with certain [inherent &] inalienable rights."[39] By choosing "created" rather than Mason's "born," Jefferson had perhaps painted himself into a verbal corner, but in reality the
Declaration as eventually published simply made explicit what was implicit in the other declarations of rights—the sense that appeals to the
rights of men were (or should be) ultimately guaranteed by pointing to
God as the author of rights.[40]

Separating States and Churches

God was the author of natural rights, but were the rights of conscience
(as many states described them) truly natural rights? This was a tricky
question, and one that the states settled in different ways. While some
said religious liberty was a natural right, others said it was a privilege—
and still others said it was a duty. In its final article, the Virginia Declaration of Rights had stipulated that "Religion, or the duty which we owe
to our Creator, and the manner of discharging it, can be directed only by
reason and conviction, not by force or violence; and, therefore, all men
are equally entitled to the free exercise of religion, according to the dictates of conscience; and that it is the mutual duty of all to practise Christian forbearance, love, and charity towards each other." Virginia had an
established church in 1776, and fourteen articles separated the statement
about religion from the opening (revised) declaration "That all men are by
nature equally free and independent, and have certain inherent rights . . .
namely, the enjoyment of life and liberty, with the means of acquiring
and possessing property, and pursuing and obtaining happiness and
safety." The Virginia Declaration stopped short of naming religion as a
right—instead it was a duty of citizens (first to the Creator; then to "each
other") and an entitlement. The passive construction left ambiguous who
was authorizing the entitlement, God or the state of Virginia? And if religious liberty did derive from the state, then how could it be said (as Virginia did in the full title of its Declaration of Rights) that this was one of
the rights that constituted "the basis and foundation of government"?

Other states were less ambiguous, and they placed declarations about
religion closer to the top of their enumerations of rights. Though in certain respects deriving from the Virginia Declaration, the constitutions of
Pennsylvania and Delaware placed declarations about religion immediately after declarations that all men were born equally free and independent and that they had "certain natural inherent and inalienable rights."

Those states declared that "all men have a natural and unalienable right to worship Almighty God according to the dictates of their own consciences." North Carolina adopted this precise language, but placed this right much further down its list.[41] The third and fourth articles of the New Hampshire Bill of Rights, produced in 1783 (and thus with the advantage of the others' example), offered a helpful narrative about the social contract:

III. When men enter into a state of society, they surrender up some of their natural rights to that society, in order to insure the protection of others; and, without such an equivalent, the surrender is void.

IV. Among the natural rights, some are in their very nature unalienable, because no equivalent can be given or received for them. Of this kind are the rights of conscience.

The fifth article of the New Hampshire Bill of Rights went on to explain that "[e]very individual has a natural and unalienable right to worship God according to the dictates of his own conscience, and reason." And the sixth declared that since "morality and piety, rightly grounded on evangelical principles, will give the best and greatest security to government," and since morality and piety were most likely to be propagated "by the institution of the public worship of the Deity," the "people of this state have a right to impower, and do hereby fully impower the legislature" to authorize individual towns, parishes, and churches, to tax inhabitants for the support of that public worship.[42] Like several other states, New Hampshire provided against the establishment of a single church or religious sect, allowing taxpayers to designate where their money would go. The natural right to worship God according to one's own conscience could not be alienated, but it could become the civil right of states (for their own "security") to compel citizens to support religion.

The states with establishment schemes often seemed to conceive of religion more as a civic duty than as a natural right. When it enumerated "natural, civil, or religious rights," the Maryland Constitution described the right to free exercise in terms of "the duty of every man to worship God in such manner as he thinks most acceptable to him," and declared that the legislature did have the right to "lay a general and equal tax for the support of the Christian religion" so long as each individual could direct the funds collected to the denomination of his choice or to the poor in his own county.[43] Vermont in 1777 held that "no authority" could "interfere with, or in any manner controul, the rights of conscience, in the

free exercise of religious worship: nevertheless, every sect or denomination of people ought to observe the Sabbath, or the Lord's day, and keep
up, and support, some sort of religious worship, which to them seem most
agreeable to the revealed will of God."[44] And Massachusetts in 1780 declared that "it is the right as well as the duty of all men in society, publicly, and at stated seasons, to worship the Supreme Being, the great creator and preserver of the universe."[45]

The length of the articles relating to religion in establishment-state
declarations of rights and constitutions testified that religious liberty was
sometimes a difficult right to declare. The committee draft of the Massachusetts Constitution of 1780 had phrased Article 3 of the Declaration
of Rights this way: "Good morals being necessary to the preservation of
civil society: and the knowledge and belief of the being of God, His providential government of the world, and of a future state of rewards and
punishment, being the only true foundation of morality, the legislature
hath therefore a right, and ought, to provide at the expense of the subject, if necessary, a suitable support for the public worship of God."[46] But
in revising this article, the committee eventually produced the longest
one in the Declaration of Rights: it now stated that civil government depended on morality, that morality "cannot be generally diffused through
a community, but by the institution of the public worship of God," that
the state could compel municipal authorities to support "the public worship of God, and . . . the support and maintenance of public protestant
teachers of piety, religion and morality, in all cases where such provision
shall not be made voluntarily," and that it could compel the "subjects"
to attend religious instruction. It was by far the most controversial plank
in the proposed bill of rights when the constitution was debated in the
towns in 1780.[47] In a similar vein, the longest article in South Carolina's
Constitution of 1778 treated religion, providing for the establishment of
"the Christian Protestant religion" and setting forth the way in which religious societies were to be incorporated. Whenever fifteen or more men
above the age of twenty-one professing "the Christian Protestant religion" desired, they might form a church and seek representation as part
of the established religion of the state by subscribing in a book to the following articles:

1st. That there is one eternal God, and a future state of rewards and
     punishments.
2d. That God is publicly to be worshipped.
3d. That the Christian religion is the true religion.

4th. That the holy scriptures of the Old and New Testaments are of divine inspiration, and are the rule of faith and practice.

5th. That it is lawful and the duty of every man being thereunto called by those that govern, to bear witness to the truth.[48]

Religion was not a simple right like the others but needed to be explained, protected, and encouraged in special ways. It was not even clear that it was a right.

If some states described religion in terms of rights, and others in terms of duties, a few seemed to follow the ambiguous example of Virginia: they suggested that it was best to think of liberty of conscience as a grant of liberty from the state, not as a natural right. New Jersey described "the inestimable privilege of worshiping Almighty God in a manner agreeable to the dictates of [one's] own conscience."[49] And New York's Constitution of 1777 put it this way: "this convention doth . . . in the name and by the authority of the good people of this State, ordain, determine, and declare, that the free exercise and enjoyment of religious profession and worship, without discrimination or preference, shall hereafter be allowed, within this State, to all mankind. Provided, That the liberty of conscience, hereby granted, shall not be so construed as to excuse acts of licentiousness, or justify practices inconsistent with the peace or safety of this State."[50] That religious liberty was "allowed" and "hereby granted" suggested that it was not a natural right, though John Jay, who had drafted the article, described the New York Constitution's protection of liberty of conscience in this way: "the rights of conscience and private judgment . . . are by nature subject to no control but that of the Deity and in that free situation they are now left. Every man is permitted to consider, to adore, to worship his Creator in the manner most agreeable to his conscience. No opinions are dictated, nor rules of faith prescribed, no preference given to one sect to the prejudices of others."[51] As the New York Constitution illustrates, the distinction between right and privilege derived from the state's declaring religious liberty even as it simultaneously declared that it had the right to limit religious freedom out of concern for the safety of the state.

While several states provided for public support of religion as a way of bringing "security" to the state, a number of states reserved the right to interfere in religion whenever religion threatened that security. In the original draft of the Virginia Declaration of Rights, Mason held that "all men should enjoy the fullest toleration in the exercise of religion, according to the dictates of conscience, unpunished and unrestrained by the magistrate, unless, under color of religion, any man disturb the peace, the happiness, or the safety of society." The Virginia Convention changed "toleration" to "free exercise," a suggestion from James Madison, and eliminated the clause about disturbing the peace, but the clause made its way into other state declarations and constitutions. In Delaware, "all persons professing the Christian religion ought forever to enjoy equal rights and privileges in this state, unless"—and here Delaware adopted the rejected draft language of Virginia—"under colour of religion, any man disturb the peace, the happiness or safety of society."[52] And Maryland also adopted the rejected phrasing, extending it by adding that any individual under the color of religion shall not "infringe the laws of morality, or injure others, in their natural, civil, or religious rights."[53] Georgia strengthened it by insisting that the free exercise of religion "be not repugnant to the peace and safety of the State."[54] It is probable that in all these cases, the drafters were thinking about the effect that religion might have on the institution of slavery. Though such clauses receive far less attention in modern discussions of church and state than do contemporaneous declarations of religious freedom or the schemes for the public support of religion, it is clear that the notion of religion as a threat to the social and political order constituted an important corollary to the idea that religion operated as a security to the state.

The Constitutionalization of Religious Rights

The Vermont Constitution of 1777 stated that "no man ought, or of right can be compelled to attend any religious worship, or erect, or support any place of worship, or maintain any minister, contrary to the dictates of his conscience." A Council of Censors had revised the constitution in 1785, and they did not alter this phrasing. But in 1783 the legislature had passed a bill allowing majorities in every town to designate one particular denomination for public support, and this was a problem for a man named Joseph Thomson. Thomson had been one of the founders of the town of Windsor, but he had left the Congregational Church to "build with the Baptists" in 1779, and this decision was the trigger that would involve him firsthand in debates about the establishment of religion in Vermont. Thomson served as a selectman for Windsor, warning vagrants out of the town in 1779.[55] In early 1783 he was a town lister, which means that he was involved in assessing property values for purposes of taxation, and a petition he signed as part of his job was favorably handled by the state legislature in February 1783. He clearly knew some of the legislators, for he had received a government contract to supply coal and candles to the state legislature in 1781.[56]

In October 1783 the Vermont legislature passed "An Act to enable Towns and Parishes, to erect proper Houses for public Worship, and support Ministers of the Gospel." This act stipulated that public support would go only to the church that the majority of the town used (majority here defined as two-thirds of eligible voters), and that "every person or person, being of adult age, shall be considered as being of opinion with the major part of the inhabitants" unless they obtained a signed certificate from "some minister of the gospel, deacon, or elder" that they were of "a different persuasion" and this certificate was recorded by the town clerk. To later commentators the bill seemed like a good accommodation, and much better than Article 3 of the Massachusetts Constitution, since it allowed majorities in individual towns to establish whichever church they wished.[57] But Baptists like Isaac Backus (and, when he came to New England in the early 1790s, John Leland) disapproved of such certificate laws, since they placed dissenters in the position of affirming (by obtaining a certificate) the right of the legislature to pass such acts.[58]

It is not clear what happened in Thomson's case. He may have refused to obtain a certificate or the town of Windsor may have refused to honor the exemption for members of minority religions. In either event, shortly after the 1783 act went into effect, the town decided to establish the Congregationalists and tried to collect money from Thomson, even though (as his minister Elisha Ransom put it in 1785) "they knew said Thomson to be of another sentiment." In July 1784 an anonymous essayist who sided with Thomson in the fight for disestablishment described his case in the pages of the *Vermont Journal*, pleading for towns to instruct their representatives to repeal the "unconstitutional act" of 1783. It seems that the "major part" of the town had confiscated some of Thomson's cows and sold them to collect the tax to pay the Congregationalist minister, the very same man that Thomson had left in 1779.

It wasn't that Thomson was averse to supporting religion, for Thomson's defender believed that Thomson had "perhaps paid more to his minister than any man according to his interest." But Thomson clearly believed that he should not pay to support a religion he had left, and he sued for justice. His supporters worried "that almost, if not quite all the court, are of opinion with the majority," and that Thomson would surely lose.[59] In the end Thomson won, but "the cost of each side was considerable," and the town was able to tax Thomson for the cost, "with his brethren and other denominations among them." When dissenters protested that they should not be obliged to help the town recover its legal expenses since they had "recorded certificates," they were told that they were not exempt, for "if it was a religious matter once, it is a civil matter now."[60] By late 1785 Thomson became one of the three founding members of the Baptist Church in Windsor.[61] And three years later Joseph Thomson did something unusual: he paid a local printer to bring out an edition of John Locke's *Letter Concerning Toleration,* and he sold the copies himself.[62]

Locke's *Letter,* first published in Latin in 1685 and translated into several European languages (including English) that same year, was the only one of Locke's works to enjoy several eighteenth-century American editions. It had been reprinted in Boston in 1743 and in Wilmington, Delaware, in 1764 before Thomson caused it to be printed in Windsor in late 1788. But Thomson was not just the publisher. He was almost certainly the editor of the text as well.[63] For the 1788 Windsor edition was not simply a reprint; it was an edited text whose editor was attempting to negotiate the difference between Locke's late seventeenth-century defense of toleration under an established church and late eighteenth-century dissenters' conceptions of free exercise without establishment.

The title page (fig. 22) featured an epigraph from the English dissenter Richard Price's laudatory *Observations on the Importance of the American Revolution*: "Civil Governours go miserably out of their Province, whenever they take upon them the Care of Truth. If it wants such aid, it cannot be of GOD." Price's *Observations* had been published in London in 1784, reprinted in pamphlet form throughout the United States, and even serialized in a Windsor newspaper in 1785. Though it made internal sense, the epigraph had in fact been cobbled together from two different chapters of Price's work. In the first sentence Price had meant to censure politicians who argued that states needed the support of established churches; in the second he had meant to chide the Anglican Church itself for believing it needed the support of the state. This reworking probably didn't matter to the intended audience. The presence of Price on the title page was meant to signal to readers in the know that the desired outcome wasn't mere toleration but the noninterference of the state. Unlike Locke, Price was a dissenting minister who argued against the idea of toleration itself, for much the same reason that Madison had moved

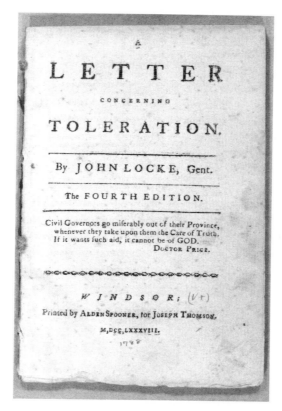

FIGURE 22. Joseph Thomson's 1788 Vermont edition of Locke's *Letter Concerning Toleration*. Courtesy of the American Antiquarian Society, Worcester, Massachusetts.

the Virginia Convention to change the wording of its protection of religious liberty from toleration to free exercise: toleration suggested the inherent superiority of one denomination over others. In a dedicatory letter addressed to the governor of Vermont, Thomas Chittenden, and signed simply by "The Editor," Price was again cited, for this very reason: "It is a presumption in any to claim a right to any superiority over their brethren; such a *claim is implied* whenever any of them *pretend* to tolerate the rest."[64] "The Editor" was of Price's opinion, but he nevertheless hoped that the "real utility" of Locke's *Letter* would be apparent to candid readers who could see past the author's own limited claims and find in them justification for more than toleration.

It was clear that Locke's text was a product of English culture a century ago, and it would thus take some tweaking to make it speak to modern readers in Vermont. Locke's *Letter* was full of what the Vermont editor termed "peculiarities belonging to the age, country and genius of that people." Some of these were "Arminian strokes" common to the period in which it was written, and the editor made no attempt to remove them though he hoped they would not disgust his readers. (Arminians were intellectual followers of the Dutch Protestant Jacobus Arminius [1560–1609], who had opposed Calvin on predestination, among other matters.) "But in this edition," the editor told the governor of Vermont, speaking of those cultural peculiarities, "I have corrected some few of them, and some of the obsolete terms—retrenching some of his negative sentences—suppressing some redundanc[i]es that carried the essence of tautology—explaining some things that appeared unintelligible, perhaps by the fault of the Translator; yet endeavoring by none of these small amendments to confront the ideas of the author." Despite his claims, most of the editing was in fact quite minor. The editor italicized some passages for emphasis where other eighteenth-century editions had not, and on one occasion he capitalized a word (perhaps predictably, it was "oppression"). He substituted one word for another and sometimes added a word here and there. When Locke had written that a state's embrace of religion frequently "serves for a cloak to covetousness, rapine, and ambition," the Vermont editor replaced "ambition" with "slaughter." And when Locke had said that this statement applied "both in America and Europe" (Locke may have been thinking of the infamous intolerance of the Massachusetts Bay colony), the editor emphasized that it applied "both in Turkey, America, and Europe."[65]

The Vermont editor trimmed a few words, a sentence here and there, and sometimes an extended example, but the most significant editorial change was the deletion of an entire paragraph concerning atheists. Locke had argued that there were four cases under which states should not exercise toleration: when religions expressed opinions "contrary to human society," when the religion teaches something that undermines the commonwealth (the idea that kings "may be dethroned by those that differ from them in religion"), or when the price of entry into the religion involves swearing allegiance to another prince (for Locke, this referred to Muslims). And "lastly," Locke wrote:

> Those are not at all to be tolerated who deny the being of a God. Promises, covenants, and oaths, which are the bonds of human society, can have no hold upon an atheist. The taking away of God, though but even in thought, dis-

solves all. Besides also, those that by their atheism undermine and destroy all religion can have no pretence of religion whereupon to challenge the privilege of a toleration. As for other practical opinions, though not absolutely free from all error, yet if they do not tend to establish domination over others, or civil impunity to the Church in which they are taught, there can be no reason why they should not be tolerated.[66]

It is possible that the editor took the first part of the excised paragraph as an unnecessary tautology (atheists are not a religion, and should not be tolerated as if they belonged to one). Or it may be that the editor disliked the close conjunction of atheists with "other practical opinions." But it is more likely that the editor simply disliked the sentiment and wished to render Locke more liberal than he was. It was a move that would have resonated with readers. The Vermont Constitution of 1777 had stipulated that no "man who professes the protestant religion" could "be justly deprived or abridged of any civil right, on account of his religious sentiment"; when the Council of Censors came to revise this in 1785, they removed the requirement of Protestantism, breaking one link between religion and civil rights. But if this passage was not useful, the rest of the book had what the editor called "real utility."

Locke's Vermont editor and publisher wished to challenge the state's scheme for establishing religion. In his dedication letter, the editor told the governor that he was pleased "that infringements on our natural rights in matters of religion, are ceased, in comparison to what they were centuries ago; and that the constitution of Vermont affords us a mirror to behold the virtue of the compilers, as well as safety to all the subjects of your domain, while its parts remain inviolate, and the governed cease from the *spirit* of innovation and faction; which is the hearty prayer of one of your subjects, that the laws may go forth from the Legislature, and be executed according to the true intent of the constitution; and that perfect uninterrupted liberty in matters of religion, may take place, so that all struggles and scribbles may in this respect be useless."[67] The problem, the reason for struggles and scribbles as he saw it, was that the "spirit of innovation" was all too apparent and that the legislature had enacted a law that was at odds with "the true intent of the constitution." It was this charge that Thomson most wanted to make. It was not simply that his natural rights had been compromised, but his civil rights had been violated. And so had the constitution of the state: to Thomson, the law was unconstitutional.

The claim that a particular piece of legislation concerning religion was unconstitutional connected this obscure Vermont man whose confiscated cows ultimately led him to edit John Locke to one of the most famous statements of religious liberty produced in the period, James Madison's "Memorial and Remonstrance" addressed to the legislature of Virginia (and sometimes seen as intellectually indebted to Locke's *Letter*).[68] Madison and his subscribers wrote in June 1785 to urge legislators not to enact "A Bill establishing a provision for Teachers of the Christian Religion," a bill they described as "a dangerous abuse of power." Madison raised fifteen reasons why he and others felt the way they did, and in three cases referred to inconsistencies between the proposed bill and the state's Declaration of Rights. The Declaration of Rights and the constitution of Virginia of which it was a part had not been framed by a special convention or ratified by the people of the state: it was thus difficult to say that the constitution was more than a legislative enactment itself. A year earlier, Madison himself had prepared notes for a speech in favor of revising the state constitution, and his first argument was that the body that framed the document operated "without due power from the people" and that "power from the people [was] no where pretended" in the text; in essence, he noted, the "Constitution rests on acquiescence," a "dangerous basis."[69]

Perhaps for this reason Madison had not explicitly called the proposed bill unconstitutional. Nevertheless, the printed broadside of the text (issued in Alexandria under the direction of George Mason) used to solicit subscribers included four explicit references to the Declaration of Rights. Madison began (invoking the sixteenth article of the Declaration of Rights in quotation marks, and identifying it with a note on the right-hand margin of the page) that "We hold it for a fundamental and undeniable truth, 'that religion or the duty which we owe to our Creator and the manner of discharging it, can be directed only by reason and conviction, not by force or violence.'" As we have seen, the Virginia Declaration had not exactly called religion a natural right. Madison nevertheless glossed this clause by observing that "this right is in its nature an unalienable right. It is unalienable, because the opinions of men"—and here he cribbed from the language of Jefferson's draft Bill for Establishing Religious Freedom in Virginia—"depending only on the evidence contemplated by their own minds cannot follow the dictates of other men: It is unalienable also, because what is here a right towards men, is a duty towards the Creator." But the proposed bill Madison remonstrated against was unconstitutional for a second reason: it "violates the equality which ought to be the basis of every law." For (citing the first article of the Declaration of Rights) "if 'all men are by nature equally free and independent,' all men are to be considered as entering into Society on equal conditions." That is, all those who had entered society (and, again, slaves had not) should be considered (citing the sixteenth article again) as "retaining an 'equal title to the free exercise of Religion according to the dictates of Conscience.'" Madison misquoted the language of the sixteenth article of the Virginia Declaration, which had actually said that "all men are equally entitled to the free exercise of religion" rather than that they had an "equal title" to it. It was perhaps a minor slip, but it clarified in Madison's favor some of the ambiguity of the understanding of the rights of religion in the sixteenth article by emphasizing that men held this title from God rather than that the state had granted the title.

In the final argument of the "Remonstrance" Madison went even further in altering the original wording of Article 16, inserting the word "right" into a gloss or paraphrase and placing it within quotation marks: finally, he said, "'the equal right of every citizen to the free exercise of his Religion according to the dictates of conscience' is held by the same tenure with all our other rights." Madison had rendered the obscurities of Article 16 clear: religious liberty was to be understood as a natural right. For if we look for its origins, Madison argued, "it is equally the gift of nature." And (citing a fuller, but not precise, title for the Declaration of Rights) Madison noted that "if we consult the 'Declaration of those rights which pertain to the good people of Virginia, as the basis and foundation of Government,' it is enumerated with equal solemnity, or rather studied emphasis." (It was wrong, in other words, to think that religion was not a right, even though the word "right" had not appeared in the particular article.) The legislature had a choice: it could pass the bill, and claim that their will alone could allow them to "sweep away all our fundamental rights"; or they could decide that they lacked the authority and "that they are bound to leave this particular right untouched and sacred."

Though he had silently changed the wording of part of the constitutional text in an attempt to demonstrate that the bill violated the constitution, Madison stopped short of calling the bill unconstitutional; but he did not shy away from saying explicitly that the bill was an affront to the "holy prerogative" of "the Supreme Lawgiver of the Universe."[70] It was this latter sentiment, rather than the constitutional questions, that connected Madison and the men who signed his "Memorial and Remonstrance" with more popular elements in the state. Madison's statement attracted over fifteen hundred signatures on thirteen copies of the text, but it was eclipsed at the time by another remonstrance that received almost five thousand names on twenty-nine petitions. While Madison focused on the ways in which the proposed bill was at odds with the title and the first and sixteenth articles of the Virginia Declaration of Rights, this more popular petition (produced by a still-unknown author and known as the Westmoreland County Petition) argued that the proposed bill violated "the Spirit of the Gospel."[71] The coalition that fought together for liberty of conscience in Virginia thus expressed very different conceptions of which text would be violated, the state constitution or the Bible, even as they agreed that the proposed bill went against God's will.

The Unfree Conscience

The original phrase from the Virginia Declaration of Rights that Madison had misquoted twice in the "Memorial and Remonstrance" of 1785—that "all men are equally entitled to the free exercise of religion, according to the dictates of conscience"—was a curious one and one that Madison had played a crucial role in drafting a decade earlier. The original committee draft of May 1776 of the Declaration of Rights, the draft that subsequently circulated and whose language influenced many other state constitutions, had stipulated that all men should "enjoy the fullest toleration in the exercise of religion, according to the dictates of conscience," but Madison had suggested substituting "free exercise" for "toleration." It was a change that would have a momentous effect and would later enter the First Amendment, though not because Madison originally urged it; his draft for what became the First Amendment had not included the phrase. It is telling that even though the Virginia draft Declaration circulated with the word "toleration," five other states (Pennsylvania, Delaware, Georgia, New York, and Vermont) followed the language of the actual Virginia Declaration and claimed "free exercise" of religion or of religious worship as a right. Only South Carolina used the word "toleration," and did so because its constitution established "the Christian Protestant religion" as "the established religion of this state."[72] Most states, in other words, did not embrace toleration as a concept for the simple reason that the concept only truly made sense if the state had an established church. "Free exercise" was the phrase of the hour. And though Madison is most often associated with the change from "toleration" to "free exercise," the phrase itself was not his but Thomas Paine's, who argued in *Common Sense* four months before Madison's proposed rewording, that a "Continental Charter" (equivalent to the Magna Charta) should secure "freedom and property to all men, and above all things, the free exercise of religion, according to the dictates of conscience."[73] It was almost certainly the appearance of the phrase in Paine's pamphlet, rather than in the revised draft of the Virginia Declaration, that led so many state constitution writers to adopt it.

In declaring that "all men are equally entitled to the free exercise of religion, according to the dictates of conscience," the Virginia Declaration had curiously yoked an assertion of liberty and an admission of its opposite: essentially it said that the state should not infringe religious freedom because at the level of conscience men were not, strictly speaking, free. While six states invoked Madison's "free exercise," eight states adopted the other half of the article he cited twice in his "Memorial and Remonstrance": "the dictates of conscience." These states included Virginia, Pennsylvania, Delaware, and Vermont, all of which had verbally endorsed "free exercise," but it also included Massachusetts and New Hampshire, states with constitutional schemes for the state support of religion.

Conscience was a tricky concept. In the early settlement of New England, Roger Williams and John Cotton famously disagreed about what "liberty of conscience" might mean. For Williams, as for some much later in the eighteenth century, liberty of conscience meant the noninterference of the state in the individual's choice to practice any religion that did not threaten the security of the state; to Cotton it meant a more restricted grant from the state—a freedom from persecution for those who practiced the true Christian religion.[74] In 1659, in a defense of Massachusetts Bay's right to execute Quakers, the minister John Norton noted that "conscience, properly so called, denoteth . . . two distinct knowers of the same thing, viz. God & conscience." For Norton, conscience was "God's vice-[regent] in the soul"; God was the "primary judge" and conscience was the "secondary & subordinate judge." Above all, conscience was not (as Williams and later dissenters argued) a faculty that could receive error: it was, Norton pointed out, "a meer creature of God." What the dissenters called "conscience," their opponents claimed, was really "will."[75]

But if conscience was a term laden with ambiguity, the phrase "dictates of conscience" that eight states placed into their constitutions did not settle the matter either way. Those who employed it might mean that conscience was not under the control of individuals (God dictated to the conscience) or they might mean that conscience was itself a dictator (it told individuals what to believe). In either case, whether the conscience was understood as agent or principal, the state was said to have no right to interfere. The phrase "dictates of conscience" could be found in many places: in popular periodical texts like *The Independent Whig* and *The Spectator*; in sermons and commentaries by the likes of Samuel Clarke and Pierre Bayle. And it had many meanings. An Anglican minister in 1709, performing a funeral sermon for the deceased governor of New York and New Jersey, noted that a "Perfect and Upright Man" always regulates "his Thoughts, Words and Actions, according to the dictates of Conscience, the Rules of right Reason, and the declared Will of God."[76] Preaching in Boston in 1743, Reverend Nathaniel Appleton wished to distinguish between a "free and voluntary Obedience to Conscience, and a servile slavish Subjection to it," for "Men may follow the Dictates of Conscience" not out of love or delight, but out of fear of future "Trouble and Distress of Mind." This was like obeying civil law out of fear of bodily punishment—it was behaving backwards.[77] In a series of *Letters on the Improvement of the Human Mind*, written for "a Young Lady," published in London in 1773 and printed in Worcester, Massachusetts, a decade later, Hester Chapone noted that God's "chosen people," the ancient Israelites, had been prepared for the reception or rather "restitution of those primitive laws, which probably he had revealed to Adam, and his immediate descendents, or which, at least, he had made known by the dictates of conscience, but which time and degeneracy of mankind, had much obscured."[78] Playing on the same theme in a 1784 dialogue published in Newburyport, Massachusetts, two theologians disputed the meaning of Romans 2:14–15: "For, when the Gentiles which have not the law, do by nature the things contained in the law, these having not the law are a law unto themselves; which shew the work of the law written in their hearts." One disputant (who represented the author's position) argued that Paul had meant that the "Gentiles had not the law by nature, as the Jews had.—For it was publicly given to the Jews: and was therefore their privilege. It was originally a Jewish Book, in a sense, which others would not claim. In this view therefore, the Gentiles remained in a state of nature." But it was wrong to think that the

Gentiles "were not unregenerate." They were "the real friends of God, who obeyed him from the heart, according to the dictates of conscience, which was their native law."[79]

Still others spoke of conscience in terms of the philosophy of moral sense. A Fourth of July orator in Portsmouth, New Hampshire, in 1788 observed that "every individual, possessed, in any degree, with rational faculties, is bound by the law of his nature, to act according to the light of REASON, in matters *within the province of Reason*, and agreeably to the dictates of Conscience, in every concern of a *moral*, or *religious* nature." The problem was that "Reason and the moral sense may deliver their mandates—but our unruly passions often prompt us to disobey them."[80] In a three-paragraph sermon published in Philadelphia in 1789 on Jacob's first-born son Reuben (see Genesis 49:3–4), who "signifies man in his first birth, or in a state of nature" in which he can "exercise his reason and all the faculties of understanding" but (without a new birth) is not "master of his passions," an unnamed preacher argued that only a man who governed his own passions could govern a state. He quoted Paul to say "Let us be obedient and subject to the dictates of God's Spirit in our consciences."[81] The chief correspondent in a 1793 epistolary novel "by an American Lady" counseled that "self-approbation . . . greatly contributes to our enjoyment; nor can we be deprived of a tranquil and happy mind, while we reverence the dictates of conscience."[82] What it meant to follow conscience was an open matter.

When the dictates of conscience could mean such different things, it was no wonder that the text often taken as the single greatest defense of liberty of conscience in the age of the American Revolution, the Virginia Act for Establishing Religious Freedom, avoided the word "conscience" altogether.[83] The most conspicuous word in its text was "opinions": it appeared eleven times in the draft bill that Jefferson prepared in 1777 and that was privately "printed for the consideration of the PEOPLE" in 1779; in the act as guided through the Virginia legislature by Madison in late 1785, and slightly revised and passed into law in early 1786, the word "opinions" appears nine times. Jefferson's very long preamble began by stating that the legislature was "Well aware that the opinions and belief of men depend not on their own will, but follow involuntarily the evidence proposed to their minds." The legislators were to hold that it had been a presumption on the part of legislators and rulers to set up "their own opinions and modes of thinking as the only true and infallible"; that it was wrong to compel someone to pay for the "propagation of opinions which he disbelieves"; that it was clear that "our civil rights have no dependence on our religious opinions, any more than our opinions in physics or geometry"; that it was a violation of natural rights to deprive anyone of a public office "unless he profess or renounce this or that religious opinion"; that "the opinions of men are not the object of civil government, nor under its jurisdiction"; and that it was dangerous to allow a magistrate to "intrude his powers into the field of opinion." And so, in the enacting clause, the legislature would declare that no person should suffer "on account of his religious opinions and beliefs" and that "all men shall be free to profess . . . their opinions in matters of religion" without decreasing or enlarging their civil rights. The focus on opinion rather than on conscience was no doubt a deliberate strategy that reconceived (as J. G. A. Pocock has put it) of matters of belief as "now only matters of opinion," which could be seen as trivializing religious faith and opening the question of truth or falsehood.[84] But just as central, the priority given to opinion (and at the very top, to epistemology) in this famous text concerning religious freedom expressed a strong sense that individuals did not have a choice about what they believed. This was the main reason that the state should not interfere with those beliefs and opinions.

As the bill worked its way through the Virginia legislature in December 1785, the senate proposed replacing the long preamble with a simple citation to Article 16 of the Virginia Declaration of Rights. Such a move would have meant that the text, currently free of the word "conscience," would now include the phrase "dictates of conscience," but the change was not accepted.[85] Some in the legislature, Jefferson later reported, wished to clarify that "the holy author of our religion" mentioned in Jefferson's draft was "Jesus Christ."[86] This change was also not made, but ultimately some of the statements that struck members of the senate as deistical were removed. Indeed, the legislative history of the Virginia statute reveals that some legislators opposed the preamble rather than the enactment—that is, they opposed the partly deistical rationale claimed as the intention for the law rather than the law itself.

Once the bill became law, Madison reported to Jefferson, then in Paris, that the changes "did not affect the substance though they somewhat defaced the composition," but at least one change did alter the intent of the bill. The first sentence of the draft bill had emphasized that the Virginia legislature was "Well aware that the opinions and belief of men depend not on their own will, but follow involuntarily the evidence proposed to their own minds" and "that Almighty God hath created the mind free," but the final version began "Whereas, Almighty God hath created the mind free" and eliminated Jefferson's opening statement. The senate thus changed Jefferson's emphasis on an unfree will acted upon by external evidence to a factual statement of a free mind created by God. This gave God priority to the mind, and since the subject of Jefferson's opening was the legislature that was "well aware" that men's opinions were involuntary, the change also placed God prior to the legislature. It was no wonder that Jefferson, when he came to print copies of the act in Paris in 1786, silently changed the legislature's "Whereas" back to "Well aware," for (though he did not try to smuggle back the claim that opinions were involuntary) he wished to convey that what the legislature was expressing were opinions and beliefs. It was this hybrid text—neither his original bill nor that legislative act—that he appended to printings of his *Notes on the State of Virginia*, and which many readers would have known.[87] A French translation produced under Jefferson's supervision, and published alongside the English text began with the word "*Convaincus*"—the legislators were convinced of what they said; to say "whereas" was to convert their convictions into facts.[88] Perhaps sensing the provisional nature of what was stated in the preamble, Richard Price both celebrated the text and made a few edits of his own when he reprinted it in London in 1786.[89]

Madison also told Jefferson that the new law had "extinguished for ever the ambitious hope of making laws for the human mind," but the final paragraph of the act itself acknowledged that the protection it offered was not a constitutional provision but an ordinary law that, like all others, was subject to revision or repeal by future legislators.[90] To insist that any assembly, "elected by the people for the ordinary purposes of legislation only," had the power to restrain succeeding assemblies went against the central Jeffersonian ethos that the earth belongs to the living. The legislators in 1786 (as Jefferson drafted it in 1777) were to say that they knew that a declaration that this act was irrevocable would be "of no effect in law." "Yet," they were to say (and did), that they were "free to declare, and do declare, that the rights hereby asserted are of the natural rights of mankind, and that if any act shall be hereafter passed to repeal the present, or to narrow its operation, such act will be an infringement of natural right." In effect, Jefferson wished to raise an acknowledged act of ordinary legislation to the level of a constitutional protection. Though he went out of his way to stress that what was being

protected was the right to hold opinions, and though his original opening and even his postenactment toying with the text confirmed his sense
that what was being stated in the preamble was itself opinion, it was not
opinion to assert a right to opinion. To make such an assertion was simply to transcribe a natural right into a positive right.

In Religion as in Politics

By the time of its enactment, Jefferson's bill had been circulating in public for seven years. It had been printed (most likely privately) "for the
consideration of the PEOPLE" of Virginia in 1779. By April 1780, newspapers in Massachusetts reprinted the Jefferson draft and at least one
town, reviewing the proposed Massachusetts Constitution of 1780, offered the text of Jefferson's bill in lieu of the controversial third article of
that text (which provided for state establishment, compulsory church at-
tendance, and public tax support for churches).[91] And when the act became law in 1786, the text circulated even more widely. Describing the
Act for Establishing Religious Freedom as "novel in its kind," the editor
of the *Pennsylvania Evening Herald* reprinted the text on February 4,
1786.[92] Isaiah Thomas printed Madison's "Memorial and Remonstrance"
in his *Massachusetts Spy* that year, and even issued a separate pamphlet
that included Jefferson's act. A prefatory letter explained that it probably would not "please, or even be read," but that "the rights of conscience and religious privileges are so clearly stated, and with so much
ingenuity and ability contended for" that it deserved "the deliberate pe-
rusal of every sober man" for the question it addressed was "seriously
interesting to the Christian, the Citizen, and the Politician." Massachusetts supported religious establishments: "Truth is uniformly the same in
all places and all times, in Virginia and . . . Massachusetts," the preface
author noted, "but may not meet the same favourable reception."[93] *The
American Recorder and Charleston Advertiser* noted that Virginia had
passed "no less than one hundred and twelve acts" and chose to reprint
only "An Act for establishing Religious Freedom." Two weeks later, a
reader requested the Charleston paper to reprint the Memorial and Remonstrance "of many respectable citizens . . . which is said to have been
very instrumental in producing the Act."[94] But another paper in South
Carolina, the *Columbian Herald*, serialized an attack over five issues
during May and June 1786.[95] That attack, written by John Swanwick of

Philadelphia in the spring of 1786, was the only extended critical reading of the text outside of Virginia and the longest rebuttal to Jefferson's bill.

John Swanwick, who a year later would sponsor Charles Willson Peale's exhibition of Italian paintings and offer a rebuttal of sorts to Benjamin Rush's *Thoughts on Female Education*, was certainly a curious figure: a merchant in his mid-twenties, he was a partner in a successful import-export firm (with markets in the East Indies), an investor in the Bank of the United States (and former protégé of Robert Morris, one of its founders), and held a government position as a treasurer of the superintendent of finance for the collection of continental taxes in Pennsylvania. In 1786 and throughout ratification, he supported a stronger central government, a fact he alluded to a number of times in his charges against the Virginia statute. Jefferson knew Swanwick and described him as "a learned and respectable merchant in Philadelphia"; Jefferson had even sought Swanwick's advice and approval on his 1784 pamphlet "On Finance." And Swanwick would later find himself in Jefferson's party. Despite supporting the Constitution and Federalist candidates (including Morris) in the late 1780s and early 1790s, Swanwick would later serve as a Democratic Republican member of the Federal Congress during the period in which Jefferson was vice president.[96]

Swanwick's *Considerations on an Act of the Legislature of Virginia, Entitled, An Act for the Establishment of Religious Freedom*, published in early 1786, was addressed to ministers in Philadelphia. Swanwick was a religious man and knew several ministers personally. He belonged to St. Peter's Church, and was close with Samuel Magaw, professor of moral philosophy and vice provost of the University of Pennsylvania and the rector of St. Paul's Episcopal Church in Philadelphia, who was a fellow visitor and speaker at the October 1787 examinations at the Young Ladies' Academy. (When Magaw's second wife Lucia died in 1790, Swanwick wrote a poem on her death.) A few months after the passing of the Virginia act, and after Swanwick's pamphlet against it, Magaw's Fourth of July sermon for 1786 introduced a "Form of prayer and thanksgiving to Almighty God, for the inestimable blessings of religious and civil liberty."[97] Magaw was surely part of Swanwick's intended audience.

Swanwick, contemplating "the tolerating spirit prevailing all over America," first wondered if the Virginia act was even necessary. Given that people generally supported what Swanwick understood by "religious freedom," did it really need to be a law? When he thought more about it, he decided that if religious liberty did require "to be fixed by a

permanent law," then this particular law was certainly a bad one "on account of the erroneous reasoning it contains, and its being more a general declamation against all religion, than an attempt to fix the freedom
on a liberal and just foundation." The problem for Swanwick was that by
virtue of this law "a door is opened wide for the introduction of any te-
nets in religion, however degrading to Christianity, or however tending
to its destruction," and that it seemed "to open the gates of skepticism
and immorality to the people of that state." He reminded readers that
in the Pennsylvania Constitution "a pledge of security to the Christian
faith hath been interwoven with its political sanctions," but he feared the
spread of similar acts in neighboring states. The act, he thought, would
"hazard the morals and manners of the people under its care to the guid-
ance of reason only." The Virginia Act Establishing Religious Freedom
was in reality "calculated to destroy all religion."[98]

The bulk of Swanwick's pamphlet was devoted to a close reading and
refutation of Jefferson's long preamble to the act. Of the claim that God
had "created the mind free," he wrote, "I know of no situation in which
the mind can be said to be free, in the sense of this bill, unless it be said
that of a state of nature with the savages of the wilderness." Like Jefferson, Swanwick emphasized a certain kind of mental unfreedom, but this
was not the involuntary epistemology that Jefferson had wished to lead
with in the act; it was the obligation to follow the truth, which for Swanwick meant the truth of Christianity. And Swanwick wondered if the legislators even acknowledged that truth. He said he could not determine
what the legislators meant when they spoke of "the Holy Author of our
religion." Were they talking about Christianity or natural religion? In
other words, was the "Author of our religion" Christ or God? And the
Philadelphia writer despaired that the Virginians had suggested that the
world had been exclusively governed by "false religions." Hadn't nations
also embraced a true religion?

For the sentence that came to embody for later generations the real
heart of the act, Swanwick reserved special scorn:

"That our civil rights have no dependence on our religious opinions, any
more than our opinions in physic or geometry," is an assertion contradicted
by the experience of mankind. Since nothing is more evident, than that in
proportion as the minds of men have become enlightened by the influences
of a pure and free system of religion, their civil rights have become more perfectly enlarged and ascertained. So that the genius of government in all na-

tions has ever borne great affinity to the state of religion therein; being either arbitrary, liberal, or free, in proportion as their spiritual systems were so; and what duration or form the civil rights of any country will assume, where no religion whatever is professed, remains yet to be discovered.

Swanwick citied numerous enlightened authorities, from Montesquieu to Franklin to Hugh Blair, all of whom could be shown, by lengthy quotations, to be against the sense of parts of the preamble at the very least, and even in some cases against the supposed effect of the act. The idea that religion didn't help people augment their civil rights was absurd to Swanwick: after all, it was religious-minded people like the Quaker Anthony Benezet in Philadelphia who were most concerned about the rights of enslaved black people. It was obvious to Swanwick from all of the sources he cited that "religion has a very powerful influence on our civil rights." And it wasn't just that the great minds of the enlightenments in France, Scotland, and America could be mustered to prove that the assertions of Jefferson's preamble were ambiguous, false, or worse: a comparative examination of the sense of the other states in the union embodied in their constitutions strongly suggested to Swanwick that the collective understanding of the people of the United States was that government and religion needed each other to survive. [99]

And what, Swanwick asked, would be the effect of the act on either religion or government? "Under the specious appearance of establishing religious freedom," Swanwick argued, the act "in fact tends to remove the necessity of any religion whatever among the people." The legislators in Virginia had invoked "our religion," to be sure, but it was a "strange religion which operated like a suicide on itself." Could any person think something was important if his state "neither requires him in any manner whatever to contribute, nor encourages him in any shape to engage in"? It was obvious that the keeping of the Sabbath would discontinue, that churches would sink into decay, and that every ordinance of religion, "no longer under the protection of government," would be "speedily abolished." What then would happen to the state? Without the restraints of religion, the people would propagate all those vices that verged on, but did not yet overstep, the boundaries of "human laws." And when that happened, it was only a matter of time before the people elected legislators who didn't have to pass religious tests. (And Swanwick held that such tests were a "natural right" of the people.) These men would be unchecked by fears of future damnation and were sure to "repeal those

laws which stand in the way of their favourite crimes." And all of this followed from the false declaration of the opening sentence of the Virginia
act, under the sanction of "an idea that God, having created the mind of
man free, he thence has a right to do in all things as may seem good in
his own eyes—an extension of freedom at which the humane mind must
shudder."[100]

This dismal prospect, the twin deaths of the state and the churches,
was the direct result of the failure of the state to support religion by taxing its citizens—and taxation was a subject Swanwick knew intimately.
He was, after all, the superintendent of finance for the collection of continental taxes in Pennsylvania, and it was perhaps only natural that he
would embed within his close reading of the Virginia statute a critique
of the current state of the federal government under the Articles of Confederation. And so, when Jefferson wrote (and Virginia endorsed) the
claim that "to compel a man to furnish contributions of money for the
propagation of opinions which he disbelieves, is sinful and tyrannical,"
Swanwick saw in this banal generalization the end of all political order.
It was neither sinful nor tyrannical to ask people to support something
they didn't believe in—during the war, would it have been sinful or tyrannical to compel a man "to pay for the establishment of the independency of America, because he should alledge that he did not in his conscience believe that measure would be salutary or useful"? This should
have been a sensitive subject for Swanwick, whose family had arrived
in America from Liverpool only in 1770 and whose father had been a
collector at the Royal Customs House and a zealous loyalist (Swanwick
himself had sworn allegiance to the patriots). But the answer to that
question was "surely not," "for where a society of people adopt a belief that certain principles of action will be salutary or useful to them,
the good order of it requires that any small part of it who may differ
from the rest, should acquiesce in the measures adopted for the general
good." And if the smaller part did not wish to follow the larger part, they
had it in their power to leave the state. For Swanwick, this was the heart
of political legitimacy, the basic majoritarian premise upon which both
society and government should operate.

The problem Swanwick had with this small piece of the Virginia statute was that the sentiment it expressed seemed to be ever-present in the
politics of the 1780s, and especially in the document that loosely knit the
states together. If one wanted to see a good example of why individuals
should be compelled to support measures that the majority believed in,

even when those individuals did not, one needed to look no further than to the Articles of Confederation, "where the consent of all the states to any one measure being requisite, is almost ever the cause of inaction and injurious delays"; the latter clearly "shews the disadvantages under which that community must labour, where the sentiments of one or of a few can impede the operations of the general system." "Anarchy and confusion" was the natural result of such thinking, which allowed individuals in a minority position the right to interfere with the will of the majority: for "if every man were to be his own lawgiver the community must become dissolved." "And what applies to the civil," Swanwick concluded, also applies to "the religious situation of any country."[101] James Madison, who had worked so hard to defeat precisely the kind of tax Swanwick favored and to pass Jefferson's statute so that similar taxes would not be proposed, would have surely agreed that anarchy and confusion reigned in the politics promoted by the Articles of Confederation. Swanwick and Madison would also have been in sympathy about the lack of power of the national government in Congress to compel states to pay their share of the burden, whether they believed in congressional measures or not. But Madison obviously differed in his understanding of the relationship between religion and politics, and he differed in his understanding of majoritarian rule. He had admitted in his "Memorial and Remonstrance" that the will of the majority was the only rule "by which any question which may divide a Society, can be ultimately determined." But he had quickly pointed out that there was a corresponding truth that trumped that one: "it is also true," he wrote, "that the majority may trespass on the rights of the minority."[102] And while Swanwick argued about religion by analogy to politics, Madison argued in the other direction. He held that what was true about the relation of minorities to majorities in religion was also true about the relation of minorities to majorities in politics. It is his central political insight.

In Politics as in Religion

During ratification some Federalists claimed in a self-serving and strategic way that divine agency had been at work in the production of the text of the Constitution. In December 1787, Benjamin Rush suggested to members of the Pennsylvania ratifying convention that the Constitution was of divine origin, but an opponent named Robert Whitehill quipped that he was sorry that "so imperfect a work should have been ascribed to God."[103] Later that month, Joseph Barrell of Boston suggested to his brother Nathaniel, an Anti-Federalist on his way to the Massachusetts Convention, that the Constitution "appears to be dictated by Heaven itself." Nevertheless, Nathaniel voted against ratification.[104] In January 1788, in *Federalist* no. 37, Madison remarked of the unanimity of the Constitutional Convention that it was "impossible for the man of pious reflection not to perceive in it, a finger of that Almighty hand which has so frequently and signally extended to our relief in the critical stages of the revolution," a typical Madisonian ventriloquism that stopped short of claiming that the writer was actually advancing this view; and of course Madison was speaking of the Convention itself rather than directly about its product.[105] That same week, Massachusetts Anti-Federalist James Winthrop, writing as "Agrippa," agreed that the "happy form" of a federal republic "seems to mark us out as a people chosen of God," but he didn't think the Constitution was a work of God.[106]

In a comparison of the Anti-Federalists with the ancient Jews published in a Philadelphia paper in April 1788 (and often reprinted in early editions of his *Autobiography*), Benjamin Franklin claimed that the negative reception of the Constitution had been anticipated by the negative reception of the Israelites to the "Constitution fram'd for them by the Deity himself." He cautiously pulled back at the end of his essay, begging not to be misunderstood: he did not mean to say "that our General Convention was divinely inspired, when it form'd the Constitution," merely because it had been opposed, but he claimed to have "so much Faith in the general Government of the world by *Providence*, that I can hardly conceive a Transaction of such momentous Importance to the Welfare of Millions now existing, and to exist in the Posterity of a great Nation, should be suffered to pass without being in some degree influenc'd, guided, and governed by that omnipotent, omnipresent, and beneficent Ruler, in whom all inferior Spirits live, and move, and have their Being."[107] Madison and Franklin stopped short of claiming divine authorship, but the implication was there for the taking and many did not hesitate to take it. Yet the obvious problem with such a sacralizing strategy— and the reason wise Federalists stopped short—was that it made the problems of the text seem to be the fault of divine wisdom: If the Constitution truly was handed down from on high, why would it need amendments? If God's agency was legible in the text, then why hadn't the framers made an explicit mention of religious freedom?

From Paris in late December 1787, Jefferson told Madison that he did not like "the omission of a bill of rights providing clearly & without the aid of sophism" for freedom of religion and other rights. The "aid of sophism" Jefferson was particularly referring to was James Wilson's claim (in a speech of October 6, 1787) that all powers not expressly given to Congress were reserved to the states, and thus to even mention certain rights was to augment congressional power.[108] It was a hard-sell argument, one adopted by many Federalists and one that Anti-Federalists could not tolerate. At the Virginia ratifying convention in June of 1788, Patrick Henry urged that it was ludicrous to expect people who worried that their rights of conscience could be invaded by the Constitution to settle for "syllogistic argumentative deductions." "The sacred right ought not to depend on constructive logical reasoning," Henry argued. Besides, while syllogism might do for lawyerly Federalists like Wilson, a bill of rights was the simplest way to build the trust of the "not so well informed" and "our common citizens."[109] Indeed, rights needed to be declared to help inform common citizens; this was why the early state bills of rights were fashioned with didactic language about what government "ought not" to do.

Henry's call at the Virginia Convention for an amendment securing religious freedom led Madison and others to argue that the best security for religious freedom was not a bill of rights; it was denominational competition. Madison worried that a declared right would amount to little if a state or a nation had "a majority of one sect." But "happily for the States, they enjoy the utmost freedom of religion," and "this freedom arises from that multiplicity of sects, which pervades America, and which is the best and only security for religious liberty in any society. For where there is such a variety of sects, there cannot be a majority of any one sect to oppress and persecute the rest."[110] And, though he was the first to voice the sentiment at the convention, Madison was clearly not alone in this view of denominational diversity as an extraconstitutional protection for religious freedom. Five days later, Governor Edmund Randolph agreed that "the variety of sects which abounds in the United States is the best security for the freedom of religion."[111] Or as Zachariah Johnston argued a week later, the "diversity of opinions and variety of sects in the United States, have justly been reckoned a great security with respect to religious liberty. The difficulty of establishing an uniformity of religion in this country is immense.—The extent of the country is very great. The multiplicity of sects is very great likewise."[112]

Here was the central argument of Madison's famous *Federalist* no. 10 applied to the circumstances of religion.

It is telling that the claims for religious liberty advanced in Virginia so closely matched Madison's argument for civil liberty in *The Federalist*: it was his best example. There was no reason to believe, as Madison put it to his colleagues at the Virginia Convention, that "uniformity of Government will produce that of religion."[113] This was obviously the case in a large state like Virginia, with its singular government and multiple faiths. Indeed, it seems that this view was so accepted that Madison was able to transfer the argument from religious competition to civil competition, and from religious liberty to civil liberty in *Federalist* no. 51. In that paper, when he came to restate the argument of *Federalist* no. 10, he observed that "in a free government, the security for civil rights must be the same as that for religious rights. It consists in the one case in the multiplicity of interests, and in the other, in the multiplicity of sects."[114]

The legal separation of church and state, when and where it did happen, was not exclusively a product of statements like Madison's "Remonstrance" or Jefferson's draft "Bill for Establishing Religious Freedom"; it was a collaboration between those kinds of rational statements and the statements of religious leaders—and many embraced the ideal of denominational diversity. This was a coalition with very different intentions that had come together for the same end. Religious proponents of religious liberty suggested that diversity was good: it meant a competition that would lead to truth. As the Baptist John Leland put it in 1791, having left Virginia to join a battle over established religions in New England, the state should encourage a man to "bring forth his arguments and maintain his points with all boldness: then, if his doctrine is false, it will be confuted, and if it is true (tho' ever so novel) let others credit it." What Leland and others imagined (avant la lettre) was a marketplace of ideas, but he would have been as happy as the Massachusetts Baptist Isaac Backus if the United States ended up ultimately as a Baptist nation.[115] On the other hand, Madison and other political proponents of diversity in religion bracketed the concept of religious truth as politically irrelevant, and they hoped that no idea would capture the minds of the majority of a population. If it did, minorities were sure to suffer. To Crèvecoeur's "American Farmer" in 1782, the pluralism of American religious life was a problem: for in a society in which "all sects are mixed" a kind of "religious indifference is imperceptibly disseminated from one end of the continent to the other."[116] To Madison in 1788, this was the saving grace. Cultural diversity, he thought, was a better safeguard for liberty than law or religion would ever be.

The First First Amendment

On June 8, 1789, Madison proposed a new preamble as the first amendment to the Constitution. Madison envisioned that the Constitution should be amended internally, that protections against a national religion or the infringement of the rights of conscience should be enumerated immediately after the enumerations of the powers of Congress in Article I. His new preamble was the one amendment that would in a sense be external. He suggested to colleagues in the House of Representatives that "there be prefixed to the constitution a declaration" to this effect:

> That all power is originally vested in, and consequently derived from the people.

> That government is instituted, and ought to be exercised for the benefit of the people; which consists in the enjoyment of life and liberty, with the right of acquiring and using property, and generally of pursuing and obtaining happiness and safety.

> That the people have an indubitable, unalienable, and indefeasible right to reform or change their government, whenever it be found adverse or inadequate to the purposes of its institution.[117]

Madison's new preamble was a revision of several texts. He stitched together the wording of revolutionary state declarations of rights and of proposed amendments from state ratifying conventions, but perhaps most importantly he restated the rights of the second paragraph of the Declaration of Independence.

Here, in Madison's proposed amendment, was the central political philosophy of the American Revolution—the idea that government was an artificial institution designed for the benefit of the people and that it could be changed when it did not benefit them. Though it largely followed the narrative of the second paragraph of the Declaration of Independence, Madison's new preamble differed in important ways. Jef-

ferson had written that "Governments are instituted among Men" to
secure "certain unalienable Rights"; Madison, however, described those
rights primarily as benefits—or even as products of governments—and
he named only one unalienable right: the "indubitable, unalienable, and
indefeasible right to reform or change" a government "found adverse or
inadequate to the purposes of its institution." Like Jefferson, Madison
favored passive constructions—neither said explicitly who it was that instituted governments, though both would have agreed that civil governments were works of human art. But more significantly, the absent agent
in the opening declaration, the figure doing the investing in the statement "That all power is originally vested in, and consequently derived
from the people," revealed a foundational instability in the economy of
rights. Jefferson had found it difficult to state that "all Men are created
equal" without mentioning "their Creator," but Madison avoided claims
of equality altogether and he did not mention God. The missing agent of
the first sentence perhaps did not need to be named, since it was a central tenet that God was the author of rights.

Madison's proposal did not become the first amendment, of course,
and the Preamble was not altered. Madison's proposed amendments
were handed to a House select committee, and by the end of July 1789
they had shortened the first amendment simply to this: "In the introductory paragraph before the words, '*We the people*,' add, 'Government being intended for the benefit of the people, and the rightful establishment
thereof being derived from their authority alone.'"[118] Though still rendered in the passive voice, this abbreviation made a strong claim that the
people were not simply second-order mediators, the bearers of powers
that had been vested in them by divine origin, but the true origin of authority. When the House debated this amendment in August, Elbridge
Gerry of Massachusetts objected (as one newspaper reporter phrased it)
because the "phraseology of this clause . . . might seem to imply that all
Governments were instituted and intended for the benefit of the people,
which was not true." It was obvious to Gerry that most governments originated in fraud or force, and he didn't want Congress to produce maxims
that were false. He suggested that they should say instead that government "of right" was intended for the benefit of the people, a change that
his colleagues rejected.

Thomas Tudor Tucker of South Carolina objected to the very idea of
amending the Preamble—after all, the Preamble was not really part of
the Constitution, or at least no more than the letter signed by Washing-

ton that was often annexed to the text, and who would think of amending that letter? Still others (the reporter did not name them) thought that
this first amendment was unnecessary "since the words, 'We the people,'
contained in itself the principal of the amendment fully." Roger Sherman of Connecticut, who had served with Jefferson on the Committee of
Five that produced the draft of the Declaration of Independence, argued
(again, as the reporter put it) "that if the constitution had been a grant
from another power, it would be proper to express this principle; but as
the right expressed in the amendment was natural and inherent in the
people, it is unnecessary to give any reasons or any ground on which
they made their constitution." It was, Sherman remarked, "the act of
their own sovereign will." "It was also said," the reporter noted, that the
new language "would injure the beauty of the preamble." Madison was
a practical politician who had been elected after a congressional campaign in which he publicly repudiated the logic about the danger of a bill
of rights he and other Federalists had helped advance during ratification.
Madison published a letter in which he acknowledged the need for a bill
of rights; Jefferson took the repudiation so seriously that he even pasted
a clipping of Madison's letter to the press in his own copy of *The Federalist*.[119] In Congress in August 1789, Madison argued that it was prudent
to add this statement to the Preamble because it had been recommended
by three states, though he agreed the principle in the proposed amendment "was on all hands acknowledged" and therefore did not need to be
expressed. It could be done, he was heard to say by one reporter, "without injuring the beauty or sense of the preamble." Another heard him
challenge the House to find a better place for the proposed language.
And for the moment, the House narrowly endorsed his view and adopted
his first amendment by a vote of 27 to 23 on August 14, 1789.[120]

But then something happened and the original first amendment dis-
appeared. While we have three reports of the debates on August 14,
1789, only one—and that one very spare—exists for August 19. On that
day, Roger Sherman renewed a proposal he had made six days earlier.
The records of debate for August 13, the day Sherman made his original proposal, are fuller, and they reveal the degree to which conceptions
of amendment spoke to larger ideas about the form and legitimacy of the
Constitution and to the sacralization of the text. Sherman believed that
Madison's whole scheme for amending the Constitution was wrong. It
was wrong to incorporate amendments rather than to place them at the
end of the text as supplements. To Sherman, a congressional alteration or

suggestion of alteration was essentially a repeal of part of the Constitution, and Congress lacked the power to repeal the Constitution. As one reporter noted, Sherman had said that the "original form of the constitution ought to remain inviolate and all amendments which the Congress were authorized to make were only legislative acts which ought to be detached from the constitution and be supplementary to it." To Sherman, as he insisted during the debate, this was not merely a formal question; that is, it was not form but authorization that he wished to discuss. As other members joined the debate, the dialogue shifted. Sherman's supporters argued "that an alteration would be a destruction of the instrument; that the original constitution ordained and signed by its framers was lodged in the archives of Congress, and was the sacred constitution of the Union." To alter the Constitution would mean that later readers would imagine that the framers signed a document that they hadn't actually written. That text should, as George Clymer of Pennsylvania put it, "remain a monument to justify those who made it." And worse, it would mean that the amendments, which were to be approved by the state legislatures, would be indistinguishable from the text that had been ratified not by the legislatures but by special conventions of the people. The Constitution, Sherman's supporters argued, "was a sacred act which could never be annulled, but by the power which gave it birth."[121]

Those who sided with Madison, and who wished to see amendments made within the body of the Constitution, argued that the "simplicity" of the Constitution would be destroyed by placing amendments as supplements. Wouldn't there inevitably be supplements to the supplement, amendments to the amendments, which would render the text "complex and obscure" and could eventually run to a "long train of laws which might fill a volume"? One advocate for incorporating amendments joked that he had seen "an act entitled an act to amend a supplement to an act entitled an act for altering part of an act entitled an act for certain purposes therein mentioned"—was this really what the supplement advocates wanted? Madison argued that form was always of less importance than substance, but like Sherman, he believed that this formal matter was significant. There is, he was reported to have said, "a neatness and propriety" in incorporating the amendments, for then "the system will remain uniform and entire" and "more simple." As for the names of the signers, opponents of Sherman's plan said these were no longer relevant since the text had been ratified by the people. Certain states had ratified on the condition that amendments be "inserted," not appended. And the

Constitution itself, in Article V, stipulated that amendments were to be considered as "Part of this Constitution," not as supplements to it. Sherman's proposal for supplementary amendments would lead people to think that the amendments were not really part of the Constitution—the people would in effect have two constitutions. And if, as Sherman's supporters suggested, the "sacredness of the original" was favored over the amendments, then alterations would have no effect at all—amendments would be "considered in point of light inferior to the original." The reporter noted that the reasoning on both sides was "very ingenious and interesting," but in the end, on August 13, Sherman's proposal for supplementary amendments was defeated.[122]

After debating amendments for a week, Sherman raised his proposal to make amendments supplementary again on August 19, and this time it passed in the House by at least a two-thirds and perhaps by as much as a three-quarters vote. Presumably few had changed their minds and decided that the original constitutional text should be preserved because it was sacred or that amendments should be supplemental because insertions and deletions would mar the beauty of the document signed in 1787; instead, practical politics won out and the representatives who had opposed such claims joined those who had made them. As a necessary correlate of this decision, the representatives rejected Madison's proposed amendment to the Preamble. Additional amendments that would have replicated the sentiment of the proposed but now defeated preamble—and even the wording of Madison's draft of June 8—were suggested by the Senate in September, but these too were ultimately rejected. The idea that the people had been invested with power by another being was either too obvious or too controversial to incorporate into the Constitution. Though reasons of practical politics motivated Madison to propose the new preamble, Congress decided that the revolutionary conception of the state as a work of art derived from the power of the people and changeable by them was either a principle so basic that it did not need to be expressed or so dangerous that it threatened the stability of the new government.

Epilogue
The Age of Constitutions

Only a European artist could have imagined a scene like the one depicted in an anonymous print produced around 1800 to commemorate the death of George Washington (fig. 23). Given the state of the graphic arts in America at the turn of the nineteenth century, only a European engraver could have accomplished it. Perhaps only a European viewer could have understood it, though the artist may have intended to export the print to the United States. Wigless, draped in classical garb, and seated on a throne, a Moses-like George Washington cradles a tablet inscribed "The American Constitution." An engraver's tool in his right hand indicates that Washington has just finished writing the Constitution, perhaps taking dictation from the heavens. The artist has surrounded Washington with classical gods, muses, and allegorical figures. On the lower left, Britannia, with a tamed lion, looks up to the victorious general in peaceful submission. Representatives of the arts of poetry, warfare, and philosophy encircle the president, offering him advice; architecture, sculpture, and painting sit by themselves nearby. In the middle ground on the right stands the goddess Minerva, who had been described by one expatriate Philadelphia artist in 1790, in analogy to the newly created office held by Washington, as the "Presidentess of Learning."[1] Minerva gestures to Mercury, who himself points to the temple of fame, the place where Washington will now retire. Floating above it all, an angel bearing the arms of the United States trumpets the event named in the title of the engraving: "Washington giving the Laws to America."

"America," the figure of nature to be cultured by Washington's classical advisers and by the Constitution itself, appears in the lower right-hand corner. "America" is the largest figure but also the least distinct

Washington giving the Laws to America

FIGURE 23. "Washington Giving the Laws to America," ca. 1800. Courtesy of the Print Collection, Miriam and Ira D. Wallach Division of Arts, Prints and Photographs, The New York Public Library, Astor, Lenox and Tilden Foundations.

and most obscure. Ambiguously gendered with a wreathed head and a barely covered body, this figure reclines on a cornucopia and turns its gaze away from Washington. If Washington is the lawgiver, then this figure is, for want of a better term, the law-taker. Though typical for European representations of legislators, the image presented an inversion of the American revolutionary commonplace about the origins of legitimate constitutions.

Few in the United States in 1800 who remembered the deep divisions over ratification or who saw themselves surrounded by bitter partisan battles could have understood the Constitution as a work of either Washington or as a product of divine origin. As I have argued in this book, revolutionary Americans embraced the idea that the state was a work of human art, one framed with a specific population in mind and one that could be taken to be an expression of the genius of the people. In revolutionary America, and especially in the debates surrounding the framing and ratification of the Constitution of the United States, talk of law-taking, of accepting or receiving laws, loomed large. To be sure, revolutionaries often spoke of solitary legislators. They celebrated the names of Moses, Solon, Lycurgus, and Numa among the ancients; from the colonial past they held up William Penn, who even Montesquieu had called a "real Lycurgus."[2] Reflecting on these figures, revolutionary Americans wondered whether their own politicians were equal to the task of erecting new governments in a moment of insurgency. But the legislators of revolutionary America differed from the figure of the legislator so celebrated in contemporary Europe or the one so fancifully depicted in this European print, the solitary sage who could reform a people by creating a new code of laws.

Legislators in the early United States derived their authority, or at the very least claimed their authority, from the people for whom they legislated. They were "delegates" or "representatives" who had been commissioned by the people to frame laws. In some cases these legislators were directly chosen by the electorate; in other cases they were selected by other elected representatives. In a sense, and in the ideal, the legitimacy of law in revolutionary America was premised on the idea that lawgivers were law-receivers as well: no legislator could live above or outside the law. But the revolutionary ideal of legislation was also premised on a notion that all law-receivers were, by the mechanisms of representation, essentially lawgivers. This was why the Constitution began with the phrase "We the People." Revolutionary politicians drafted constitutions behind closed doors, but they spoke frequently of the people "out of doors" who would have to accept the laws. And what they said was that no abstract theorist, no individual legislator locked away in a closet, could frame a workable constitution. Instead, constitutions had to come from or grow out of the manners, customs, tastes, and genius of people themselves. To succeed, constitutions had to have cultural origins, had to seem by virtue of a reality or a fiction of consent to come from the people themselves.

Late eighteenth- and early nineteenth-century Americans participated in and witnessed an age of democratic revolutions that was also, as John Adams observed, an age of constitutions. "The last twenty-five years of the last century, and the first fifteen years of this," Adams wrote in a private letter in March 1815, "may be called the age of revolutions and constitutions." The United States, Adams fancifully noted, "began the dance, and have produced eighteen or twenty models of constitutions." Though these constitutions were by no means perfect, Adams believed they were "the best for us that we could contrive and agree to adopt." Constitutions framed by wise legislators and based on abstract principles had not proven durable in his lifetime. "Since we began the career of constitutions," Adams noted, "the wisest, most learned, and scientific heads in France, Holland, Geneva, Switzerland, Spain, and Sicily, have been busily employed in devising constitutions for their several nations. And brilliant compositions they have produced, adorned with noble sentiments in morals, wise maxims in politics, if not sound doctrines in religion and salutary precepts in private life. But has there been one that has satisfied the people? One that has been observed and obeyed, even for one year or one month?" Adams concluded that the problem was that the people of Europe were incapable "of understanding any constitution whatsoever." [3]

Though Adams devoted his attention in his March 1815 letter to the dire possibilities of constitutionalism in Europe, the immediate context for his remarks was the prospect of constitutionalism for the emerging independent states of Latin America. Adams thought the prospect was dim, for he believed that the population was not prepared for self-government. In a more sanguine, but more imperial, mood that same month the architect of the Capitol, William Thornton, published in Washington his *Outlines of a Constitution for United North & South Columbia*, a "general plan of a grand government" for the Americas. If constitution-makers could imagine themselves as architects, then who better than an architect to frame a constitution for the hemisphere? As Thornton developed his blueprint, he fantasized that the age of the revolutions might become the age of a single constitution for the united states of the Americas.

Between 1776 and 1826 the new states of the Americas drafted almost sixty constitutions, twenty of them in Latin America. In 1811 Manuel García de Sena, a native of Venezuela, translated Thomas Paine's *Common Sense*, the Declaration of Independence, and the Constitution into Spanish and had these works published in Philadelphia. A decade later, also in Philadelphia, Vincente Rocafuerte published a similar anthology of constitutional documents from the United States. But while some Latin Americans dreamed of exporting the language and concepts of U.S. constitutionalism to Latin America, Simón Bolívar objected in 1819 to the very idea that one nation's constitution could serve as a model for any other's, and he did so in the name of the Enlightenment's major constitutional thinker. Does not Montesquieu state, he asked his colleagues in Venezuela, citing the very passage that had been so often invoked by American revolutionaries, "that laws should be suited to the people for whom they are made; that it would be a major coincidence if those of one nation could be adapted to another; that laws must . . . be in keeping with . . . the religion of the inhabitants, their inclinations, resources, number, commerce, habits, and customs?" "This is the code we must consult," Bolívar exclaimed, "not the code of Washington!"[4] Many of the newly independent states of the Americas did look to the U.S. Constitution for inspiration and even for particular language. It was an age of revolutionary and constitutional mimesis, but Bolívar's remark is a powerful reminder of the commitment to local customs in the age of revolutions and constitutions.

We live in a second age of constitutions. In the last twenty years, since the celebrations of the bicentennial of the Constitution of the United States in 1987, sixty-nine countries—from the nations of post-Communist Central and Eastern Europe, to South Africa, to Afghanistan and Iraq—have drafted constitutions. Many other nations have revised their constitutions, and only a handful of states now lack written constitutions. At the time of the bicentennial of the Constitution, the major public question about written constitutions concerned hermeneutics or intentionality. Now the question is about how well constitutions travel. Over the past decade and a half, as constitutional consultants have traveled the circuit from law schools in the United States to capitals in the former "Eastern Bloc" to Kabul and Baghdad, it has become difficult to think of modern written constitutions as fundamental expressions of a particular people. It has also become harder to distinguish between culturally conditioned constitutional practices and putatively culture-free constitutional norms. Everywhere constitutions are framed or revised people debate the relation of culture and politics. Are manners, morals, customs, and tastes the foundations upon which governments must be erected or are they the products of political form, to be molded and remolded at will? It is this lingering and unresolved question, endlessly debated in the eighteenth century, that connects our age of constitutions with theirs.

Notes

Abbreviations used in citations

CAF: The Complete Anti-Federalist, ed. Herbert J. Storing, 7 vols. (Chicago, 1981).

DHRC: The Documentary History of the Ratification of the Constitution, ed. Merrill Jensen et al., 19 vols. to date (Madison, 1976–).

FFC: The Documentary History of the First Federal Congress, 1789–1791, ed. Linda Grant DePauw et al., 17 vols. to date (Baltimore, 1972–).

LDC: Letters of Delegates to Congress, 1774–1789, ed. Paul H. Smith, 24 vols. (Washington, 1976–93).

PJA: Papers of John Adams, ed. Robert J. Taylor et al., 14 vols. to date (Cambridge, Mass., 1977–).

PJM: The Papers of James Madison, ed. William T. Hutchinson et al., 17 vols. (Chicago and Charlottesville, 1962–91).

PTJ: The Papers of Thomas Jefferson, ed. Julian Boyd et al., 33 vols. to date (Princeton, 1950–).

RFC: The Records of the Federal Convention of 1787, ed. Max Farrand, 3 vols. (New Haven, 1911–1937).

Introduction

1. Madison, Notes, September 17, 1787, in *RFC,* 2:648. Max Farrand's transcript ignores minor revisions ("tell" for "judge" here). Five newspapers reported a version of Franklin's remarks, beginning with the *Salem Mercury,* December 21, 1787; see *DHRC,* 13:215 n. 4.

2. *Journals of the House of Representatives of Pennsylvania, 1776–1781* (Philadelphia, 1782), 478, 636.

3. "An Act for the gradual abolition of Slavery" (March 1, 1780), in *A Neces-*

sary Evil? Slavery and the Debate over the Constitution, ed. John P. Kaminski (Madison, 1995), 13. Kaminski ascribes the preamble to Paine, but Gary B. Nash and Jean R. Soderlund attribute it to George Bryan. See *Freedom by Degrees: Emancipation in Pennsylvania and Its Aftermath* (New York, 1991), 99–113.

4. In 1775 Folwell published a proposal to print an American edition of Thomas Chippendale's *Gentleman's and Cabinet-Maker's Assistant*; the war intervened.

5. William Macpherson Hornor, Jr., *Blue-Book of Philadelphia Furniture: William Penn to George Washington* (Alexandria, Va., 1988), 176, 186, 216. On furnishing the Pennsylvania State House during the Revolution, see Edward M. Riley, "The Independence Hall Group," *Transactions of the American Philosophical Society*, n.s., 43, no. 1 (1953): 7–42; and on Folwell, see Charles F. Montgomery, "Furniture," *American Art Journal* 7, no. 1 (May 1975): 52–67.

6. Jennifer Anderson, "Nature's Currency: The Atlantic Mahogany Trade and the Commodification of Nature in the Eighteenth Century," *Early American Studies* 2, no. 1 (Spring 2004): 57–61.

7. Washington, Diary, September 17, 1787, in *RFC*, 3:81.

8. Madison, Notes, September 17, 1787, in *RFC*, 2:643. For the debate summarized in the next paragraph, see *RFC*, 2:643–47.

9. See Robert A. Dahl, *How Democratic Is the American Constitution?* (New Haven, 2001); Sanford Levinson, *Our Undemocratic Constitution* (New York, 2006); and Terry Bouton, *Taming Democracy: "The People," the Founders, and the Troubled Ending of the American Revolution* (New York, 2007).

10. Charles Pinckney of South Carolina argued that a constitution "must be suited to the habits & genius of the People it is to govern, and must grow out of them." Madison, Notes, June 25, 1787, in *RFC*, 1:402.

11. Burckhardt wrote "Kuntstwerk"; see *The Civilization of the Renaissance in Italy: An Essay*, trans. S. G. C. Middlemore (1860; New York, 1954), 3–99.

12. Lionel Gossman, *Basel in the Age of Burckhardt* (Chicago, 2000), 284, 533 n. 126.

13. Rousseau wrote "l'ouvrage de l'art"; *Du contrat social* (1762), III.xi; see also *A Dissertation on Political Economy: to which is added, A Treatise on the Social Compact* (Albany, 1797), 134.

14. On government as artifact in the Declaration of Independence, see Michael P. Zuckert, *Natural Rights and the New Republicanism* (Princeton, 1994), 9–10; and on the preoccupation with the artifice of political contracts a century earlier, see Victoria Kahn, *Wayward Contracts: The Crisis of Political Obligation in England, 1640–1674* (Princeton, 2004).

15. On "nature" in American politics, see the essays by Jack N. Rakove, Nancy L. Rosenblum, and Rogers M. Smith in James W. Ceaser, *Nature and History in American Political Development: A Debate* (Cambridge, Mass., 2006).

16. Montesquieu, *The Spirit of the Laws*, trans. Thomas Nugent (1750; New York, 1949), 6.

17. Samuel Stanhope Smith, *Lectures . . . on the Subjects of Moral and Political Philosophy* (Trenton, 1812), 277.

18. Montesquieu, *Spirit of the Laws*, 305.

19. For constitutional histories responding to originalism, see Alfred F. Young, "Conservatives, the Constitution, and the 'Genius of the People'"(1987), in *Liberty Tree: Ordinary People and the American Revolution* (New York, 2006), 183–214; Michael Warner, "Textuality and Legitimacy in the Printed Constitution" (1987), in *The Letters of the Republic: Publication and the Public Sphere in Eighteenth-Century America* (Cambridge, Mass., 1990), 97–117; Jack N. Rakove, *Original Meanings: Politics and Ideas in the Making of the Constitution* (New York, 1996); Akhil Reed Amar, *The Bill of Rights: Creation and Reconstruction* (New Haven, 1998); Larry D. Kramer, *The People Themselves: Popular Constitutionalism and Judicial Review* (New York, 2004); and Woody Holton, *Unruly Americans and the Origins of the Constitution* (New York, 2007).

20. On legal originalism, see Akhil Reed Amar, *The American Constitution: A Biography* (New York, 2005); Dennis J. Goldford, *The American Constitution and the Debate over Originalism* (Cambridge, England, 2005); John C. Yoo, *The Powers of War and Peace: Foreign Affairs and the Constitution after 9/11* (Chicago, 2005); and Daniel A. Farber and Suzanna Sherry, *Desperately Seeking Certainty: The Misguided Quest for Constitutional Foundations* (Chicago, 2002). On eighteenth-century originalism, see H. Jefferson Powell ("The Original Understanding of Original Intent") and Charles A. Lofgren ("The Original Understanding of Original Intent?") in *Interpreting the Constitution: The Debate over Original Intent*, ed. Jack N. Rakove (Boston, 1990), 53–150; Joseph M. Lynch, *Negotiating the Constitution: The Earliest Debates over Original Intent* (Ithaca, 1999); and Jonathan O'Neill, *Originalism in American Law and Politics: A Constitutional History* (Baltimore, 2005).

21. See William H. Riker, *The Strategy of Rhetoric: Campaigning for the American Constitution*, ed. Randall L. Calvert, John Mueller, and Rick K. Wilson (New Haven, 1996), and David J. Siemers, *Ratifying the Republic: Antifederalists and Federalists in Constitutional Time* (Stanford, 2002).

22. See James H. Hutson, "The Creation of the Constitution: The Integrity of the Documentary Record," in *Interpreting the Constitution*, ed. Rakove, 151–78.

23. On persistent localism during the ratification debates, see Trish Loughran, *The Republic in Print: Print Culture in the Age of U.S. Nation Building, 1770–1870* (New York, 2007), 105–52.

24. On "parchment barriers," see *The Federalist*, ed. Jacob E. Cooke (Middletown, Conn., 1961), 333, 338, 343; and Madison to Jefferson, October 17, 1788, in *PJM*, 11:298.

25. See *Legal Studies as Cultural Studies: A Reader in (Post)Modern Critical*

Theory, ed. Jerry Leonard (Albany, 1995), 155–74; *Law and the Domains of Culture*, ed. Austin Sarat and Thomas R. Kearns (Ann Arbor, 1998), 1–20; Paul W. Kahn, *The Cultural Study of Law: Reconstructing Legal Scholarship* (Chicago, 1999); and *Constitutionalism and American Culture: Writing the New Constitutional History*, ed. Sandra F. VanBurkleo, Kermit L. Hall, and Robert J. Kaczorowski (Lawrence, Kans., 2002). For defenses of textualism, see Antonin Scalia, *A Matter of Interpretation: Federal Courts and the Law*, ed. Amy Gutmann (Princeton, 1997), 3–48; and Amar, "A Note on Text and Textualism," in *The Bill of Rights*, 295–301.

Prologue

1. Alexander Pope, *Essay on Man*, Epistle 3, lines 303–4.

2. For the best account of Pope's *Essay on Man* in colonial British America, see Nicole Eustace, *Passion Is the Gale: Emotion, Power, and the Coming of the Revolution* (Chapel Hill, 2008), 19–57; for the general reception of Pope, see Agnes Marie Sibley, *Alexander Pope's Prestige in America, 1725–1835* (New York, 1949). For individual associations with the poem, see *A Catalogue of Choice and Valuable books . . . to be sold . . . by Benj. Franklin* (Philadelphia, 1744), 13; "List of Books at Mount Vernon" [ca. 1764], in *Papers of George Washington*, Colonial Series, 10 vols. (Charlottesville, 1983–95), 7:345; Abigail Adams to John Quincy Adams, June 10, 1778, in *The Letters of John and Abigail Adams*, ed. Frank Shuffelton (New York, 2004), 335; Edmund Berkeley and Dorothy Smith Berkeley, *The Life and Travels of John Bartram* (Tallahassee, 1982), 193; Ernest Earnest, *John and William Bartram* (Philadelphia, 1940), 147; N. Bryllion Fagin, *William Bartram: Interpreter of the American Landscape* (Baltimore, 1933), 21; *Jefferson's Literary Commonplace Book*, ed. Douglas L. Wilson (Princeton, 1989), 89–93, 178; *An Autobiographical Sketch by John Marshall*, ed. John Stokes Adams (Ann Arbor, 1937), 4; William G. Soler, "Some Important Influences upon John Dickinson's Thought" (Ed. D. thesis, Temple University, 1953), 283–85; "Commonplace Book" [1759–72], in *PJM*, 1:19, 29 n. 71; Julian D. Mason, Jr., ed., *The Poems of Phillis Wheatley*, rev. ed. (Chapel Hill, 1989), 197 n. 13; *My Dearest Julia: The Love Letters of Dr. Benjamin Rush to Julia Stockton*, ed. Whitfield J. Bell, Jr. and L. H. Butterfield (New York, 1979), 39, 43; *Only for the Eye of a Friend: The Poems of Annis Boudinot Stockton*, ed. Carla Mulford (Charlottesville, 1995); Michael A. Bellesiles, *Revolutionary Outlaws: Ethan Allen and the Struggle for Independence on the Early American Frontier* (Charlottesville, 1993), 182; *Ethan Allen and His Kin: Correspondence, 1772–1819*, ed. John J. Duffy et al. (Hanover, N.H., 1998), 120; *The Works of James Wilson*, ed. Robert Green McCloskey, 2 vols. (Cambridge, Mass., 1967), 1:141, 207, 227, 233–34, 237, 241, 260; *The Papers of George Mason*, ed. Robert A. Rutland,

3 vols. (Chapel Hill, 1970), 3:1257; David Lee Clark, *Charles Brockden Brown* (Durham, N.C., 1952), 208–9; and "Conversations with Charles Lanman," *The Writings and Speeches of Daniel Webster*, 18 vols. (Boston, 1903), 13:578.

3. Twelve printings produced in America between 1776 and 1790 survive: Providence, 1776; Philadelphia, 1778; Newburyport, Mass., 1780; Bennington, Vt., 1785; New York, 1786; Hartford, 1787; Boston, 1787; Philadelphia, 1788; Philadelphia, 1789; Lansingburg, N.Y., 1790; Concord, N.H., 1790; and Worcester, Mass., 1790.

4. William Warburton, *A Vindication of Mr. Pope's Essay on Man* (London, 1739); Brean S. Hammon, *Pope and Bolingbroke: A Study in Friendship and Influence* (Columbia, Mo., 1984), 87.

5. David Hume, "That Politics May Be Reduced to a Science" and "Of Liberty and Despotism," in *Essays: Moral, Political, and Literary,* ed. Eugene F. Miller, rev. ed. (1777; Indianapolis, 1987), 14–15 and 94.

6. Immanuel Kant, "Eternal Peace," *Essays and Treatises on Moral, Political, and Various Philosophical Subjects*, 2 vols. (London [i.e., Hamburg?], 1798–99), 1:260–61 n. [2].

7. Donald S. Lutz ranked Pope number 21 in a list of the thirty-six most-cited political writers published between 1760 and 1805; see Lutz, "The Relative Influence of European Writers on Late Eighteenth-Century American Political Thought," *American Political Science Review* 78, no. 1 (March 1984): 194 (table 3). The maxim was so well known that in 1779 the London owner of a copy of Jean Louis de Lolme's widely read book on the English Constitution, now held by the University of Chicago, inscribed it on a blank page in the front of his book; see de Lolme, *The Constitution of England* (London, 1777), Regenstein Library, University of Chicago (JN 117.L67).

8. John Adams, *Thoughts on Government* (Philadelphia, 1776), 4–8.

9. John Adams to William Cooper, [ante March 27, 1776], in *PJA*, 4:73.

10. *Constitution of Massachusetts* (1780), part I, art. XXX.

11. Sidney [Benjamin Rush?], "Maxims for Republics," *United States Magazine* 1 (Jan. 1779): 13–14, reprinted in *American Museum* 2 (July 1787): 80–82; see also Willi Paul Adams, *The First American Constitutions: Republican Ideology and the Making of the State Constitutions in the Revolutionary Era*, trans. Rita and Robert Kimber, expanded ed. (1980; Lanham, Md., 2001), 114, 117 n. 5.

12. Abigail Adams to John Thaxter, Jr., October 26, 1782, *Adams Family Correspondence*, ed. L. H. Butterfield et al., 8 vols. to date (Cambridge, Mass., 1963–), 5:27.

13. Arthur Lee to the Earl of Shelburne, July 23, 1783, in *LDC*, 20:443.

14. *Diary of John Quincy Adams*, ed. David Grayson Allen, 2 vols. (Cambridge, Mass., 1981), 2:67 (July 19, 1786). A newspaper gave a different phrasing: "Whether the happiness of a people most depends upon the excellency of

the constitution, or the administration of civil government?" (*Independent Ledger*, July 24, 1786).

15. James Madison, Notes, September 17, 1787, in *RFC*, 2:642–43. Franklin's speech was reprinted fifty times during the ratification debates; see *DHRC*, 13:215, 592. On Pope's couplet during ratification, see *DHRC*, 4:379 n. 8, and 5:507.

16. "Z.," *Independent Chronicle* (Boston), December 6, 1787, in *DHRC*, 4:373.

17. "To the Printer," *Massachusetts Gazette*, December 14, 1787, in *DHRC*, 4:376.

18. *Pennsylvania Herald*, December 1, 1787, in *DHRC*, 2:422 (and see 5:508).

19. "Federal Farmer," *Observations Leading to a Fair Examination of the System of Government Proposed by the Late Convention* ([New York], 1787), 2.

20. "Poplicola," *Boston Gazette*, December 24, 1787, in *DHRC*, 5:507–11.

21. [Alexander Hamilton], *Federalist* no. 68, March 12, 1788, in *DHRC*, 16:378.

22. "Cornelius," *Hampshire Chronicle*, December 18, 1787, in *DHRC*, 4:417.

Chapter One

1. *Four Letters on Interesting Subjects* (Philadelphia, 1776), 15, 18. A. Owen Aldridge attributed *Four Letters* to Paine; see *Thomas Paine's American Ideology* (Newark, Del., 1984), 219–39.

2. Paine, "To George Washington," *The Rights of Man: Part First*, in *Complete Writings of Thomas Paine*, ed. Philip S. Foner, 2 vols. (New York, 1969), 1:244.

3. On impersonal states, see Quentin Skinner, "The State," in *Political Innovation and Conceptual Change*, ed. Terence Ball, James Farr, and Russell L. Hanson (Cambridge, England, 1989), 102.

4. Joseph Huntington, *A Discourse . . . on the Health and Happiness, or Misery and Ruin of the Body Politic* (Hartford, 1781), 10, 23–24. The transition from priestly rule to monarchy (1 Sam. 8) preoccupied revolutionary-era New England ministers; see Gad Hitchcock, *An Election Sermon* (Boston, 1774), 7–11.

5. Huntington, *Discourse,* 23. Huntington's 1784 election sermon further compared ancient Israel and the Confederation; see *God Ruling the Nations for the Most Glorious End* (Hartford, 1784), 24. For Israel and the new Constitution, see Samuel Langdon, *The Republic of the Israelites an Example to the American States* (Exeter, N.H., 1788).

6. Huntington, *Discourse,* 13–21, 26–27.

7. See Adams, *Defence of the Constitutions,* 3 vols. (London, 1787–88), 1:362; Jefferson to Adams, February 23, 1787, and Adams to Jefferson, March 1, 1787,

in Lester J. Cappon, ed., *The Adams-Jefferson Letters* (1959; Chapel Hill, 1987), 174–75, 176–77.

8. Huntington, *Discourse*, 6.

9. Ibid., 5–6, 7, 8, 16, 19, 23.

10. Ibid., 20–23.

11. See Ernst Barker, *The Political Thought of Plato and Aristotle* (New York, 1959), and Leonard Barkan, *Nature's Work of Art: The Human Body as the Image of the World* (New Haven, 1975), 61–115.

12. See Cary J. Nederman and Kate Langdon Forham, *Medieval Political Theory—A Reader: The Quest for the Body Politic, 1100–1400* (London, 1993), and Forham's introduction to Christine de Pizan, *The Book of the Body Politic*, ed. and trans. Kate Langdon Forham (Cambridge, England, 1994), esp. xx–xxi.

13. See Niccolo Machiavelli, *The Discourses*, ed. Bernard Crick, trans. Leslie J. Walker and Brian Richardson (Middlesex, England, 1970), 385ff. (III.i).

14. Skinner, "The State," 102; and Skinner, *Liberty before Liberalism* (Cambridge, England, 1998), 1–57.

15. Thomas Hobbes, *Leviathan*, ed. Richard Tuck (Cambridge, 1996), 9, 86. The phrase "state of nature" is not in *Leviathan*; see A. P. Martinich, *A Hobbes Dictionary* (Oxford, 1995), 293. On the background to metaphors of circulation, see Joyce E. Chaplin, *The First Scientific American: Benjamin Franklin and the Pursuit of Genius* (New York, 2006), 78.

16. Christopher Pye, "The Sovereign, The Theatre, and the Kingdom of Darknesse: Hobbes and the Spectacle of Power," *Representations* 8 (Autumn 1984): 101; Norman Jacobson, "The Strange Case of the Hobbesian Man," *Representations* 63 (Summer 1998): 1–12; Danielle S. Allen, *Talking to Strangers: Anxieties of Citizenship since Brown v. Board of Education* (Chicago, 2004), 81–83; Martin Brückner, *The Geographic Revolution in Early America: Maps, Literacy, and National Identity* (Chapel Hill, 2006), 93–95.

17. On the body politic in New England, see Jim Egan, *Authorizing Experience: Refigurations of the Body Politic in Seventeenth-Century New England Writing* (Princeton, 1999); on ideas of the body in early America, see Joyce E. Chaplin, *Subject Matter: Technology, the Body, and Science on the Anglo-American Frontier, 1500–1676* (Cambridge, Mass., 2001), and *A Centre of Wonders: The Body in Early America*, ed. Janet Moore Lindman and Michele Lise Tarter (Ithaca, 2001).

18. William Perkins, "A Treatise on the Vocations or Callings of Men," in Edmund S. Morgan, *Puritan Political Ideas, 1558–1794* (Indianapolis, 1965), 39.

19. John Winthrop, "A Model of Christian Charity," in Morgan, *Puritan Political Ideas*, 84, 88–89, 92.

20. William Hubbard, *The Happiness of a People In the Wisdome of their Rulers Directing And in the Obedience of their Brethren Attending* (Boston,

1676), in *The Puritans*, ed. Perry Miller and Thomas H. Johnson, 2 vols. (New York, 1963), 1:247.

21. Abraham Williams, *An Election Sermon* (Boston, 1762), 1–2.

22. John Higginson, *The Cause of God and His People in New-England* (Cambridge, Mass., 1663), 19. For the use of 1 Peter 2:13, see Williams, *Election Sermon*, 6.

23. John Barnard, *The Throne Established by Righteousness*, in *The Puritans*, 1:274.

24. Williams, *Election Sermon*, 27, 6.

25. John Wise, *A Vindication of the Government of New-England Churches* (Boston, 1717), 32ff.

26. Charles Chauncy, *Civil Magistrates must be Just* (Boston, 1747), 9–11, 22–23.

27. John Barnard, *The Throne Established by Righteousness* (Boston, 1734), in *The Puritans*, 1:274.

28. Higginson, *The Cause of God and His People in New-England*, 22.

29. Wise, *A Vindication of the Government of New-England Churches*, 45–46.

30. Pufendorf, *Of the Law of Nature and Nations*, trans. Basil Kennett (1672; Oxford, 1703), 151 (bk. 7, chap. 2, sec. 13).

31. Skinner, "The State." Hobbes claimed that "a city . . . is one person whose will, by the compact of many men, is to be received for the will of them all." See *De cive: The English Version*, ed. H. Warrender (Oxford, 1983), 89.

32. The only organ of Hobbesian anatomy Wise omitted was the "Nerves," or "*Reward* and *Punishment*." See Hobbes, *Leviathan*, 9.

33. "Agreement between the Settlers at New Plymouth—1620," in Francis N. Thorpe, ed., *Federal and State Constitutions*, 7 vols. (Washington, D.C., 1909), 3:1841. This document became the "Mayflower Compact" in the 1790s, when it was read through the lens of contractualism.

34. *Fleets Pocket Almanack For . . . 1788* (Boston, [1787]), 1. Connecticut's revolutionary "constitution" (the 1662 charter) included the phrase, but it did not remain in the Constitution of 1818. See Thorpe, ed., *Federal and State Constitutions*, 1:530.

35. Constitution or Form of Government for the Commonwealth of Massachusetts—1780, Preamble, in Thorpe, ed., *Federal and State Constitutions*, 3:1888.

36. *Oxford English Dictionary (OED)*, 2nd ed., s.v. "congress" (citing examples from 1737 and 1765).

37. John Dickinson, Edward Biddle, and Charles Thompson were the committee; see *Journal of the Proceedings of the Congress, Held at Philadelphia, September 5, 1774* (Philadelphia, 1774), 114.

38. The publishers consigned 350 copies to Samuel Adams to sell and dis-

tribute; see Adams to William and Thomas Bradford, January 7, 1775, in *LDC*, 1:292, and *Pennsylvania Journal*, November 30, 1774.

39. Edwin Wolf called it an "unesthetic seal" in the preface to a facsimile edition. See "Introduction," *Journal of the Proceedings of the Congress . . . : A Facsimile* (Philadelphia, 1974), n.p.; see also Lester C. Olson, *Emblems of American Community in the Revolutionary Era: A Study in Rhetorical Iconology* (Washington, D.C., 1991), 42–43, and David Hackett Fischer, *Liberty and Freedom: A Visual History of America's Founding Ideas* (New York, 2005), 131.

40. On declining providentialism, see Gordon S. Wood, "Conspiracy and the Paranoid Style: Causality and Deceit in the Eighteenth Century," *William and Mary Quarterly*, 3rd ser., vol. 39, no. 3 (July 1982): 401–41.

41. "Few people," Otis wrote, "have extended their enquiries after the foundation of any of their rights, beyond a charter from the crown. There are others who think when they have got back to old *Magna Charta*, that they are at the beginning of all things. They imagine themselves on the borders of Chaos (and so indeed in some respects they are), and see creation rising out of the unformed mass, or from nothing. Hence, say they, spring all the rights of men and of citizens." See *The Rights of the British Colonies Asserted and Proved* (Boston, 1764), 31. On appeals to the Magna Charta during the American Revolution, see Peter Linebaugh, *The Magna Carta Manifesto: Liberties and Commons for All* (Berkeley, 2008), 119–27.

42. See John Trenchard, "Liberty proved to be the unalienable Right of all Mankind," in *Cato's Letters*, ed. Ronald Hamowy, 2 vols. (Indianapolis, 1995), 1:405 (no. 59, December 30, 1721).

43. Alexander Hamilton, *The Farmer Refuted* (New York, 1775), in *The Papers of Alexander Hamilton*, ed. Harold C. Syrett and Jacob E. Cooke (New York, 1961–85), 1:122.

44. Letter to Gen. Gage, October 11, 1774, in Congress, *Journal* (1774), 54.

45. Michael Kammen, *Spheres of Liberty: Changing Perceptions of Liberty in American Culture* (Madison, 1986), and Elise Marienstras, "Liberty," in *The Blackwell Encyclopedia of the American Revolution*, ed. Jack P. Greene and J. R. Pole (Oxford, 1991), 609-15, emphasize liberty as female. For contemporary French illustrations, see Antoine de Baecque, *The Body Politic: Corporeal Metaphor in Revolutionary France, 1770–1800*, trans. Charlotte Mandell (Stanford, 1997); and Lynn Hunt, "Pornography and the French Revolution," in *The Invention of Pornography: Obscenity and the Origins of Modernity, 1500–1800*, ed. Hunt (New York, 1993), 301–39.

46. Joel Barlow, "Genealogy of the Tree of Liberty," Notebook [ca. 1796–97?], Barlow Papers, Houghton Library, Harvard University, bMS Am 1448 (13); Neil Hertz, "Medusa's Head: Male Hysteria under Political Pressure," *Representations* 4 (Fall 1983): 54 n. 36; and Henri Grégoire, *Essai historique et patriotique sur les arbres de la liberté* (Paris, [1794]). On liberty trees in revolution-

ary America, see Fischer, *Liberty and Freedom*, 19–49, and Alfred F. Young, *Liberty Tree: Ordinary People and the American Revolution* (New York, 2006), 325–94.

47. Peter Prejudice, "The New Breeches," *Federal Gazette* (Philadelphia), April 15, 1788, in *DHRC*, 17:128.

48. See "The ANATOMY of Man's Body," in Andrew Beers, *The Columbian Almanack . . . For . . . 1788* (New York, [1787]), 2.

49. Francis Hopkinson, "Ode," July 4, 1788, in *DHRC*, 18:247 (lines 29–32).

50. See Perry Miller, "The Puritan State and Puritan Society," *Errand into the Wilderness* (1956; New York, 1964), 142.

51. Thomas Paine, *Common Sense*, in *Complete Writings*, ed. Foner, 1:4.

52. [Benjamin Thurston], *An Address to the Public, Containing Some Remarks on the Present Political State of the American Republicks* (Exeter, N.H., [1786?]), 8.

53. [Madison], *Federalist 51*, in *The Federalist*, ed. Jacob E. Cooke (Middletown, Conn., 1961), 349.

54. See Michel Foucault, "Governmentality," in *The Foucault Effect: Studies in Governmentality*, ed. Graham Burchell, Colin Gordon, and Peter Miller (Chicago, 1991), 87–104.

55. Noah Webster, *A Compendious Dictionary of the English Language* (Hartford, 1806), s.v. "Libertinism" and "Licentiousness."

56. See Robert Bell's *Observations relative to the Manufactures of Paper and Printed Books in the Province of Pennsylvania* (Philadelphia, 1773) and *Illuminations for Legislators, and for Sentimentalists* ([Philadelphia], 1784). On Bell as publisher, see Richard B. Sher, *The Enlightenment and the Book: Scottish Authors and Their Publishers in Eighteenth-Century Britain, Ireland, and America* (Chicago, 2006), 511–31; for the sensibility Bell sought to cultivate, see Sarah Knott, "Sensibility and the American War for Independence," *American Historical Review* 109, no. 1 (January 2004): 19–40.

57. John Norman (engraver), *A Collection of Designs in Architecture* (Philadelphia, 1775), 3.

58. For quips about "longstanding members," see Dr. Alexander Hamilton, *The History of the Ancient and Honorable Tuesday Club*, ed. Robert Micklus, 3 vols. (Chapel Hill, 1990), 1:xix, 2:84.

59. See Alessandra Ponte, "Architecture and Phallocentrism in Richard Payne Knight's Theory," in *Sexuality and Space*, ed. Beatriz Colomina (Princeton, 1992), 273–305.

60. Massachusetts Constitution of 1780, part I, art. XXX, in Thorpe, ed., *Federal and State Constitutions*, 3:1893.

61. Paine, *Common Sense*, in *Complete Writings*, ed. Foner, 1:29. Paine may have derived his coronation image from an illustration by Henry Fuseli in the sole eighteenth-century English-language edition of the authority Paine cited in

the immediately preceding paragraph, "Dragonetti on Virtues and Rewards"; see Giacinto Dragonetti, *A Treatise on Virtues and Rewards* (London, 1769), 182.

62. Adams, *A Defence of the Constitutions of Government of the United States of America* (Philadelphia, 1787), xii.

63. Alexander Hamilton, *Federalist* 82 (Cooke, ed., 553).

64. See Gerard Stourzh, "Constitution: Changing Meanings of the Term from the Early Seventeenth Century to the Late Eighteenth Century," in *Conceptual Change and the Constitution*, ed. Terrence Ball and J. G. A. Pocock (Lawrence, Kans., 1988), 35–54; and Michael Warner, *The Letters of the Republic: Publication and the Public Sphere in Eighteenth-Century America* (Cambridge, Mass., 1990), 97–117.

65. The sentence "His penis was in a state of erection" appeared in a British medical journal available in New York. See H. Watson, in *Medical Communications by a Society for Promoting Medical Knowledge* 2 (1787): 158; and *Samuel Campbell's Sale Catalogue for 1787* (New York, 1787), 16. For other 1787 references, see John Hunter, *A Treatise on the Venereal Disease* (Philadelphia, 1787), 11; and *A Treatise on the Gonorrhoea* (Norfolk, Va., 1787), 14–15. For "political architects," see "FEDERAL SENTIMENTS," *Massachusetts Centinel,* September 19, 1787.

66. Hobbes, *Leviathan*, 96, 101.

67. John Locke, Second Treatise, in *Two Treatises of Government*, ed. Peter Laslett, rev. ed. (Cambridge, England, 1988), secs. 175, 211, 220, 225.

68. David Hume, "Idea of a Perfect Commonwealth," *Essays Moral, Political, and Literary*, ed. Eugene F. Miller, rev. ed. (Indianapolis, 1987), 528.

69. [Agreement of the Settlers at Exeter in New Hampshire], July 5, 1639, in Donald S. Lutz, ed., *Colonial Origins of the American Constitution* (Indianapolis, 1998), 3–4.

70. *Letters of John and Abigail Adams*, ed. Frank Shuffelton (New York, 2004), 59.

71. John Adams to Richard Henry Lee, November 15, 1775, in *PJA*, 3:307.

72. *OED*, s.v. "Fabric," def. in I and III.

73. John Adams to Abigail Adams, March 19, 1776, in *Letters*, ed. Shuffelton, 145.

74. [Paine], *Four Letters on Interesting Subjects*, 19.

75. Hunter, *Treatise on the Venereal Disease*, 11.

76. *Treatise on the Gonorrhoea*, 14.

77. Benjamin Colman, *Government the Pillar of the Earth* (Boston, 1730), 12–17, reprinted in *Political Sermons of the American Founding Era, 1730–1805*, ed. Ellis Sandoz (Indianapolis, 1991), 11–24.

78. Joseph Buckminster, *A Sermon, Preached before His Excellency the President, the Honorable Council, and the Honorable the House of Representatives* (Portsmouth, 1787), 6, 26–27, 28.

79. Dudley Atkins Tyng, *An Address to the Ancient and Honorable Society of Free and Accepted Masons* (Newburyport, 1787), 9.

80. Joseph Pilmore, *A Sermon, Preached in St. Pauls's Church Philadelphia* ([Philadelphia, 1787]), 17.

81. Isaac Backus, *An Address to the Inhabitants of New-England* (Boston, 1787), 3.

82. Joel Barlow, *An Oration . . . in Commemoration of the Independence of the United States* (Hartford, 1787), 15.

83. Huson Langstroth, *A Watch-word in Love to Friends in this Land* (Philadelphia, 1787), broadside.

84. *Order of Procession and Public Worship to be observed in the Dedication of Franklin College* (Philadelphia, 1787), n.p.

85. Elizur Goodrich, *The Principles of Civil Union and Happiness considered and recommended* (Hartford, 1787), 5, 8–9, 27, 37–38, 8.

86. George Washington, *A Circular Letter* (1783; Philadelphia, [1787]), 17–18, 16.

87. *A Concert of Prayer Propounded to the Citizens of the United States* (Exeter, N.H., 1787), 8, 9–10.

88. See, for instance, Charles Pinckney, *Observations on the Plan of Government submitted to the Federal Convention* (New York, [1787]), 16.

89. *Fragments on the Confederation of the American States* (Philadelphia, 1787), 5, 16.

90. *Anecdote for Great Men* (Hartford, 1787), 19, 14. On the relation of bodies to buildings, see Robert Blair St. George, *Conversing by Signs: Poetics of Implication in Colonial New England Culture* (Chapel Hill, 1998), 116–203.

91. *Rules of the Society of St. George* (New York, 1787), v, iv, 7.

92. Noah Webster, *An American Selection of Lessons in Reading and Speaking*, 3rd ed. (Philadelphia, 1787), 214.

93. Thomas Dawes, *An Oration . . . in Celebration of the Anniversary of American Independence* (Boston, 1787), 7–8.

94. [John Stevens], *Observations on Government* (New York, 1787), 40.

95. [John Quincy Adams], *Observations on Paine's Rights of Man* (Edinburgh, 1792), 16–17. Adams's reply to Paine was first published in newspaper form in 1791.

96. William Blackstone, *Commentaries on the Laws of England*, 4 vols. (1765–69; Philadelphia, 1771–72), 1:161, in Jack P. Greene, *Colonies to Nation, 1763–1789* (New York, 1967), 87–88.

97. [Paine], *Four Letters on Interesting Subjects*, 18–19.

98. [Stevens], *Observations on Government*, 8, 40.

99. In August 1787, Tench Coxe referred to the Federal Convention as "THE AUGUST BODY now sitting in our capital"; see *An Enquiry into the Principles on which a Commercial System For the United States of America should be Founded* (Philadelphia, 1787), 5.

100. *The Independent Citizen, Or, The Majesty of the People asserted against the Usurpations of the Legislature of North-Carolina, in several acts of Assembly* ([Newbern, 1787]), 8, 15, 4, 8.

101. Including a now lost broadside: [James Peller Malcom], *Liberty Leading America to her Temple* ([Philadelphia, 1787?]).

102. Robert R. Livingston, *An Oration . . . In Commemoration of the Fourth Day of July* (New York, 1787), 14–15.

103. *Observations on the Articles of Confederation* (New York, [1787]), 16.

104. Noah Webster, *An Examination into the Leading Principles of the Federal Constitution* (Philadelphia, 1787), 32.

105. Pinckney, *Observations*, 5.

106. Madison to Jefferson, April 25, 1784, in *PJM*, 8:21; Madison to James Monroe, April 9, 1786, in *PJM*, 9:25; Madison, "Vices of the Political System of the United States," April 1787, in *PJM*, 9:353–57. On the impotency of Congress, see Max M. Edling, *A Revolution in Favor of Government: Origins of the U.S. Constitution and the Making of the American State* (New York, 2003), 73–88.

107. James Madison, Notes, June 8, 1787, in *RFC*, 1:166.

108. David Daggett, *An Oration, Pronounced in the Brick Meeting-House, in the City of New-Haven, on the Fourth of July, A.D. 1787* (New Haven, [1787]), 8, 15, 22.

109. Edmund Randolph, *A Letter . . . on the Federal Constitution* ([Richmond, 1787]), 12. Randolph described Vice President John Adams in 1791 as "impotent" now that the "standard of republicanism has been erected"; Randolph to Madison, July 21, 1791, in *PJM*, 14:51.

110. [David Humphreys], "Undelivered First Inaugural Address: Fragments," *The Papers of George Washington*, Presidential Series, ed. W. W. Abbot and Dorothy Twohig et al., 13 vols. to date (Charlottesville, 1987–), 2:162. For the draft in Washington's handwriting, see Nathaniel E. Stein, "The Discarded Inaugural Address of George Washington," *Manuscripts* 10, no. 2 (Spring 1958): 12, 17.

111. My discussion benefits from work on revolutionary France, especially Antoine de Baecque, "Pamphlets: Libel and Political Mythology," in *Revolution in Print: The Press in France, 1775–1800*, ed. Robert Darnton and Daniel Roche (Berkeley, 1989), 165–76; Lynn Hunt, "Pornography and the French Revolution," in *The Invention of Pornography*, 301–39.

112. *Encyclopedia Britannica* (1771), 2:836.

113. See *The Case of Impotency, as Debated in England*, 3rd ed. (London, 1719), 103–27.

114. For the illegality of the Philadelphia Convention and ratification procedures, see Bruce Ackerman, *We The People: Foundations* (Cambridge, Mass., 1991), 41–42, 173–79, 328 n. 4; for the higher legality of conventions, see Gordon S. Wood, *The Creation of the American Republic, 1776–1787* (Chapel Hill, 1969), 306–43; and for seventeenth-century backgrounds, see Edmund S. Morgan, *In-*

venting the People: The Rise of Popular Sovereignty in England and Amer-ica (New York, 1988), 78–93. On the violation of compact, see *RFC*, 1:122–23, 126–27, 129, 314–16; and James Madison, *Federalist* 40 (Cooke, ed., 258–67).

115. Winthrop analogized marriage between political subject and magistrate with the equally metaphoric notion of the Christian as bride of Christ; see *The Journal of John Winthrop, 1630–1649*, ed. Richard S. Dunn, James Savage, and Laetitia Yeandle (Cambridge, Mass., 1996), 588. For competing theories of spir-itual marriage in the 1630s and 1640s, see Janice Knight, *Orthodoxies in Mas-sachusetts: Rereading American Puritanism* (Cambridge, Mass., 1994); and for tensions between marital theory and practice in Massachusetts and the Chesa-peake colonies, see Mary Beth Norton, *Founding Mothers & Fathers: Gendered Power and the Forming of American Society* (New York, 1996), 57–95, 317–22.

116. *The Diary of Colonel Landon Carter of Sabine Hall, 1752–1778*, ed. Jack P. Greene, 2 vols. (Charlottesville, 1965), 2:1009 (April 1, 1776). On the decline of patriarchal thought, see Jay Fliegelman, *Prodigals and Pilgrims: The American Revolution against Patriarchal Authority* (Cambridge, England, 1982).

117. William Stuart to Griffith Evans, July 11, 1788, in *DHRC*, 18:258–59. Stuart's literary references were no doubt ironic: Desdemona suffered more than simple divorce, and Abelard was emasculated.

118. Ibid.

119. Jeremiah Hill likened the United States to a "healthy promising boy ris-ing to maturity" and the Constitution to "her [*sic*] new *wedding Suit*"; see Hill to George Thatcher, February 26, 1788, in *DHRC*, 16:209.

120. Dana D. Nelson, *National Manhood: Capitalist Citizenship and the Imagined Fraternity of White Men* (Durham, N.C., 1998), 34.

121. Resolution of Congress, February 21, 1787, in *RFC*, 3:14.

122. Pinckney, *Observations*, 12.

123. Randolph, *Letter . . . on the Federal Constitution*, 16.

124. For firmness, see Alexander Hamilton, *Federalist* 71 (Cooke, ed., 481–86); for origins of the single executive, see Jack N. Rakove, *Original Meanings: Pol-itics and Ideas in the Making of the Constitution* (New York, 1996), 244–87.

125. *A Concert of Prayer*, 10.

126. Robert Davidson, *An Oration, on the Independence of the United States of America* (Carlisle, 1787), 14.

127. William Cowper, *The Task* (Philadelphia, 1787), [iii].

128. Thomas Coke and Francis Asbury, *An Address to the Annual Subscrib-ers for the Support of Cokesbury-College* (New York, 1787), 4.

129. John Tasker Howard and Eleanor S. Bowen, eds., *Music Associated with the Period of the Formation of the Constitution* (Washington, D.C., [1937]), 17; and *Broadsides Relating to the Ratification of the Constitution . . .* (Washington, D.C., [1937]), 7.

130. [David Humphreys], "Undelivered First Inaugural Address," *Papers of*

George Washington, 2:162. Madison drafted Washington's address, the House of Representatives' response, and Washington's rejoinder; see *PJM,* 12:120–23. On Washington's body, see Bruce Burgett, *Sentimental Bodies: Sex, Gender, and Citizenship in the Early Republic* (Princeton, 1998), 55–77.

131. "A Republican," *Fellow Citizens! The first concern of Freemen, calls you forth into action* . . . ([Philadelphia, 1796]), broadside, reprinted in Noble Cunningham, Jr., ed., *The Making of the American Party System, 1789–1809* (Englewood Cliffs, N.J., 1965), 150.

132. For venereal disease as a "constitutional" problem, see Hunter, *Treatise on the Venereal Disease,* 1, and *A Treatise on the Gonorrhoea,* 8.

133. Stein, "Discarded Inaugural," 13; James Madison's revised draft, *PJM,* 12:120–23. On sexual defamation in early American politics, see Annette Gordon-Reed, *Thomas Jefferson and Sally Hemings: An American Controversy* (Charlottesville, 1997), and Patricia U. Bonomi, *The Lord Cornbury Scandal: The Politics of Reputation in British America* (Chapel Hill, 1998).

134. David Daggett, *An Oration . . . on the Fourth of July,* 14–15.

135. James Campbell, *An Oration, in Commemoration of the Independence of the United States* (Philadelphia, 1787), 12, 24.

136. *Proceedings and Debates of the General Assembly of Pennsylvania,* 4 vols. (Philadelphia, 1787–88), 1:133, 134.

137. "The New Roof," *Pennsylvania Packet,* December 29, 1787; John Murrin, "A Roof without Walls: The Dilemma of American National Identity," in *Beyond Confederation: Origins of the Constitution and American National Identity,* ed. Richard Beeman, Stephen Botein, and Edward C. Carter II (Chapel Hill, 1987), 333–48.

138. *The Constitution of the United States* (New Haven, 1787) and *Constitution of the United-States* (Portsmouth, N.H., 1787) print the articles of the Constitution in six and seven columns of text beneath a larger-type Preamble portico.

139. "FEDERAL SENTIMENTS," *Massachusetts Centinel* (Boston), September 19, 1787.

140. Francis Hopkinson, "The Raising: A New Song for Federal Mechanics," *Pennsylvania Gazette,* February 6, 1788, in *DHRC,* 16:47–48.

141. "Cantata for the Fourth of July, 1788," *Pennsylvania Packet,* July 17, 1788, in Howard and Bowen, eds., *Music Associated with . . . the Constitution,* 6, 17. The "Cantata" also appeared as a broadside in New York.

142. Hamilton, *Federalist* 27 (Cooke, ed., 172).

143. [Francis Hopkinson], "Account of the grand federal procession," *American Museum* (Philadelphia) 4 (July 1788): 59–60; [Benjamin Rush], "Observations on the Federal Procession," *American Museum* 4 (July 1788): 75–76. For architecture as craft in 1788, see Laura Rigal, *The American Manufactory: Art, Labor, and the World of Things in the Early Republic* (Princeton, 1998),

21–54, and Dell Upton, *Architecture in the United States* (New York, 1998), 57–58.

144. "Explanation of the Frontispiece," *Columbian Magazine* 2 (1788): iii–iv. The print was probably produced in December 1788.

145. *A Form of Discipline, For . . . the Methodist Episcopal Church* (New York, 1787), 39.

146. "Helvidius Priscus II," *Independent Chronicle* (Boston), January 10, 1788, in *DHRC*, 15:332.

Chapter Two

1. See Leonard L. Richards, *Shays's Rebellion: The American Revolution's Final Battle* (Philadelphia, 2002), 52, 57, 61, 73; and *DHRC*, 6:1155–56.

2. "Commencement, Hanover, Aug. 31," *Courier of New Hampshire,* September 5, 1795; Leon Burr Richardson, *History of Dartmouth College,* 2 vols. (Hanover, N.H., 1932), 1:253.

3. *Proposals for Printing . . . A Philosophical History of the Advancement of Nations . . . by John Wheelock . . .* ([Boston, ca. 1796–1803]), iii–iv, vi. See also Wheelock's commencement address, *An Essay on the Beauties and Excellencies of Painting, Music and Poetry* (Hartford, [1774]).

4. Richardson dates this event to 1800; for publisher Joseph Nancrede's summary of the reports, see Richardson, *History of Dartmouth,* 1:260.

5. "Commencement," *Courier of New Hampshire,* September 4, 1794. Students at Yale debated the same question in 1813; see Anna Haddow, *Political Science in American Colleges and Universities, 1636–1900* (New York, 1939), 105.

6. Richardson, *History of Dartmouth,* 1:264; Daniel Webster, "The Influence of Opinion" (August 25, 1801), *Writings and Speeches,* 18 vols. (Boston, 1903), 1:494–504.

7. Montesquieu, *The Spirit of the Laws,* trans. Thomas Nugent, 2 vols. (London, 1750; New York, 1949), 1:300 (bk. XIX, chap. 16). On *manières* and *moeurs,* see Melvin Richter, *The Political Theory of Montesquieu* (Cambridge, England, 1977), 107–8; and Montesquieu, *The Spirit of the Laws,* trans. Anne M. Cohler, Basia C. Miller, and Harold S. Stone (Cambridge, England, 1989), 317.

8. Constitution of New Hampshire (1783), Bill of Rights, arts. 4–6; Richardson, *History of Dartmouth,* 1:261.

9. *Proposals for Printing . . . A Philosophical History,* ii.

10. Richards, *Shays's Rebellion,* 91.

11. [Benjamin Austin], *Observations on the Pernicious Practice of the Law* (Boston, 1786), 6.

12. On Samuel Fowler Dickinson (grandfather of Emily), see Richard B. Sewall, *The Life of Emily Dickinson,* 2 vols. (New York, 1974), 1:28–43.

13. "Commencement, Hanover, August 29," *Courier of New Hampshire*, September 6, 1796.

14. Samuel F. Dickinson, *An Oration, in Celebration of American Independence; Delivered at Belcherstown, July 4, 1797* (Northampton, Mass., 1797), 7. The actual title of the oration, as it appears on the half-title page, is "The Connection of Civil Government with Manners and Taste." For a similar statement by another writer born in 1775, see Paul Allen, *An Oration, on the Principles of Taste, Delivered before the Federal Adelphi* (Providence, 1800).

15. J. G. A. Pocock, "Virtue, Rights, and Manners: A Model for Historians of Political Thought," *Virtue, Commerce, and History* (Cambridge, England, 1985); Isaac Kramnick, "'The Great National Discussion': The Discourse of Politics in 1787," *Republicanism and Bourgeois Radicalism: Political Ideology in Late Eighteenth-Century England and America* (Ithaca, 1990), 260–88; Gordon S. Wood, *The Creation of the American Republic, 1776–1787* (Chapel Hill, 1969), 606–15; Ruth Bloch, "The Gendered Meanings of Virtue in Revolutionary America," *Signs* 13 (1987): 37–58; Richard L. Bushman, *The Refinement of America: Persons, Houses, Cities* (New York, 1992).

16. See Lawrence E. Klein, *Shaftsbury and the Culture of Politeness: Moral Discourse and Cultural Politics in Eighteenth-Century England* (Cambridge, England, 1994); David S. Shields, *Civil Tongues & Polite Letters in British America* (Chapel Hill, 1997); John Brewer, *The Pleasures of the Imagination: English Culture in the Eighteenth Century* (New York, 1997); and Roger Chartier, *On the Edge of the Cliff: History, Language, and Practices*, trans. Lydia G. Cochrane (Baltimore, 1997), 107–23.

17. Terry Eagleton, *The Ideology of the Aesthetic* (Oxford, 1990); Luc Ferry, *Homo Aestheticus: The Invention of Taste in the Democratic Age*, trans. Robert De Loaiza (1990; Chicago, 1993); Gilles Lipovetsky, *The Empire of Fashion: Dressing Modern Democracy*, trans. Catherine Porter (1987; Princeton, 1994); F. R. Ankersmit, *Aesthetic Politics: Political Philosophy beyond Fact and Value* (Stanford, 1996); Mary Poovey, *A History of the Modern Fact: Problems of Knowledge in the Sciences of Wealth and Society* (Chicago, 1998), 157–74.

18. Compare, for instance, Henry Home, Lord Kames's statement that bodily labor disqualified individuals from "voting" on taste with similar statements that labor should disqualify individuals from voting in politics. See Kames, "Standard of Taste," *Elements of Criticism*, 7th ed., 2 vols. (Edinburgh, 1788), 2:499; and Gordon S. Wood, *The Radicalism of the American Revolution* (New York, 1992), 56, 269–70.

19. On taste and politics in eighteenth-century Europe, see Howard Caygill, *Art of Judgment* (Oxford, 1989), 38–102; Josef Chytry, *The Aesthetic State: A Quest in Modern German Thought* (Berkeley, 1989); and Luc Ferry, *Homo Aestheticus*.

20. David Hume, "Of the First Principles of Government," in *Essays: Moral, Political, and Literary*, ed. Eugene F. Miller, rev. ed. (Indianapolis, 1987), 32;

and see Edmund S. Morgan, *Inventing the People: The Rise of Popular Sovereignty in England and America* (New York, 1988), 13–15.

21. David Hume, "Of the Standard of Taste," *Essays*, 226–29, 238–39. Andrew Cannon Smith describes "authoritarian" taste in *Theories of the Nature and Standard of Taste in England, 1700–1790* (Chicago, 1937), 122.

22. Poovey, *A History of the Modern Fact*, 170.

23. See Ferry, *Homo Aestheticus*, 53–62.

24. Oliver Goldsmith, review of *A Philosophical Enquiry*, by Edmund Burke, *Monthly Review* 16 (May 1757): 473.

25. Burke, *A Philosophical Enquiry into the Origin of Our Ideas of the Sublime and Beautiful*, ed. James T. Boulton (Notre Dame, 1968), 11–12, 38–52.

26. Alexander Gerard, *An Essay on Taste . . . With Three Dissertations On the Same Subject. By Mr. De Voltaire, Mr. D'Alembert, F.R.S., Mr. De Montesquieu* (London, 1759). For other English editions, see Montesquieu, "An Essay upon Taste," in *The Complete Works of M. De Montesquieu*, 4 vols. (London, 1777), 4:119–45.

27. Montesquieu, *Spirit of the Laws*, 1:34 (bk. IV, chap. 5).

28. Montesquieu, "Taste," in Diderot, d'Alembert, et al., *Encyclopedia: Selections*, trans. Nelly S. Hoyt and Thomas Cassirer (Indianapolis, 1965), 361.

29. Montesquieu, *Spirit of the Laws*, 1:6 (bk. I, chap. 3).

30. René Wellek, *A History of Modern Criticism, 1750–1950: The Later Eighteenth Century* (New Haven, 1955), 24, 107; Francis Hutcheson, *An Inquiry Into the Original of Our Ideas of Beauty and Virtue . . .* (London, 1725), 1.

31. Joseph Addison, *The Spectator*, 8 vols. (London, [1750]), 6:56–57 (no. 409, June 19, 1712); Benjamin Franklin, *The Autobiography*, in J. A. Leo Lemay, ed., *Benjamin Franklin: Writings* (New York, 1987), 1319–20.

32. See entries for May 9, 1756 and January 1759 in *Diary and Autobiography of John Adams*, ed. L. H. Butterfield, 4 vols. (Cambridge, Mass., 1961), 1:26, 72.

33. Douglass Adair, ed., "James Madison's Autobiography" (ca. 1831), *William and Mary Quarterly*, 3rd ser., 2 (1945): 197.

34. Webb, *An Inquiry into the Beauties of Painting* (London, 1760), 18, cited in Janice G. Schimmelman, "A Checklist of European Treatises on Art and Essays on Aesthetics Available in America through 1815," *Proceedings of the American Antiquarian Society* 93 (1983): 97, 165–68.

35. James Ralph, "Preface. Being an Essay on Taste," *A Critical Review of the Public Buildings, Statues and Ornaments in, and about London* (London, 1734), i–ii.

36. [James Ralph], "An Essay on Taste. Extracted from a late Author," *The American Magazine and Historical Chronicle* 1 (July 1744): 466–69.

37. Voltaire, "Taste," *Encyclopedia: Selections*, 337–38.

38. Montesquieu, "Taste," *Encyclopedia: Selections*, 341.

39. James Littlejohn, Esq., "The Friend, No. XI," *New-Haven Gazette and the Connecticut Magazine* 1 (June 22, 1786): 145–46.

40. James Littlejohn, Esq., "The Friend, No. XII," *New-Haven Gazette and the Connecticut Magazine* 1 (July 6, 1786): 161–63.

41. Gerard, *An Essay on Taste*, 1–2.

42. Wellek, *A History of Modern Criticism*, 1:109.

43. Hugh Blair, *Lectures on Rhetoric and Belles Lettres*, 4th ed., 3 vols. (1783; London, 1790), 1:39. For American printings, see "An Essay on Taste. From a new Work," *Boston Magazine* 1 (November 1783): 27–29, and *Boston Magazine* 1 (December 1783): 53–55; Hugh Blair, "Difference between Taste and Genius," *New-Haven Gazette and the Connecticut Magazine* 1 (May 18, 1786): 108. For Blair's place in early national culture, see Jay Fliegelman, *Declaring Independence: Jefferson, Natural Language, and the Culture of Performance* (Stanford, 1993).

44. "Observations on Taste, Modern Table-Talk, and Luxury in Eating," *American Magazine and Historical Chronicle* 2 (December 1745): 541–44.

45. "The Man of Taste," *New England Magazine of Knowledge and Pleasure* 1 (August 1758): 28.

46. Blair, *Lectures on Rhetoric*, 1:30.

47. On reactions to second-class imperial status, see T. H. Breen, "Ideology and Nationalism on the Eve of the American Revolution: Revisions *Once More* in Need of Revising," *Journal of American History* 84, no. 1 (June 1997): 13–39.

48. On provincial anxieties, see John Clive and Bernard Bailyn, "England's Cultural Provinces: Scotland and America," *William and Mary Quarterly*, 3rd ser., 11 (1954): 200–13.

49. Kames, *Elements of Criticism*, 2:496.

50. [James Ralph], *The Touch-Stone: or, Historical, Critical, Political, Philosophical, and Theological Essays on the reigning Diversions of the Town . . . By a Person of some Taste and some Quality* (London, 1728), xviii; reissued as *The Taste of the Town* (London, 1731). Ralph described taste as a unifying category for different classes in his "Essay on Taste" in *A Critical Review*, i–viii.

51. John Swanwick, "POEM, On the Prospect of seeing the fine ARTS flourish in AMERICA," in *Thoughts on Education* (Philadelphia, 1787), 33.

52. Dickinson, *Oration*, 15–16.

53. See the debates on June 12, 1787, over what the people will accept; *RFC*, 1:214–15.

54. *A Review of the Constitution . . . By a Federal Republican* (Philadelphia, 1787), 7–8.

55. Joel Barlow, *An Oration, Delivered . . . at the Meeting of the Connecticut Society of the Cincinnati, July 4, 1787* (Hartford, 1787), 4; Joel Barlow, "A Dissertation on the Genius and Institutions of Manco Capac," *The Vision of Columbus* (Hartford, 1787), 77–91.

56. Augustus Chatterton (pseud.), *The Buds of Beauty* (Baltimore, 1787), v.

57. John Adams, *A Defence of the Constitutions of Government of the United States* (Philadelphia, 1787), iii–iv.

58. Nathanael Emmons, *The Dignity of Man* (Providence, [1787]), 33.

59. The term "refinement" appears only in essays written by Alexander Hamilton. See *The Federalist*, nos. 9, 22, 26, 33, 61, 72.

60. [James Madison], *Federalist* 10, in *The Federalist*, ed. Jacob E. Cooke (Middletown, Conn., 1961), 62.

61. James Madison, "Fashion," *The National Gazette*, March 20, 1792, in *PJM*, 14:257–59. On fashion in the early United States, see Linzy A. Brekke, "The 'Scourge of Fashion': Political Economy and the Politics of Consumption in the Early Republic," *Early American Studies* 3, no. 1 (Spring 2005): 111–39, and Kate Haulman, "Fashion and the Culture Wars of Revolutionary Philadelphia," *William and Mary Quarterly*, 3rd ser., 62, no. 4 (October 2005): 625–62.

62. Noah Webster, "Remarks on the Manners, Guvernment [*sic*] and Debt of the United States" (1787), reprinted in Webster, *A Collection of Essays and Fugitiv [sic] Writings* (Boston, 1790), 87, 90.

63. David Daggett, *An Oration . . . on the Fourth of July* (New Haven, [1787]), 20.

64. Tench Coxe, *An Address to an Assembly of the Friends of American Manufactures* (Philadelphia, 1787), 30.

65. [Benjamin Thurston], *An Address to the Public, Containing Some Remarks on the Present Political State of the American Republicks* (Exeter, [1787]), 25.

66. Joseph Lyman, *A Sermon Preached Before His Excellency James Bowdoin, Esq.* (Boston, [1787]), 41–43.

67. [Peter Markoe], *The Algerine Spy in Pennsylvania* (Philadelphia, 1787), 74, 76.

68. Robert Andrews, *The Virginia Almanack, for . . . 1788* (Richmond, 1787), n.p. [17–18, 33, 34].

69. "The Picture of a Beau's Dressing Room," *Columbian Magazine* 1 (September 1787): 659–65.

70. John Fry, "To the Youth of the Female Sex. On Dress, &c.," in *Select Poems* (London; Philadelphia, 1787), 60.

71. "Dress," *The United States Almanac, For . . . 1788* (Elizabeth-Town, N.J., [1787]), 7.

72. Benjamin Rush, *Thoughts upon Female Education* (Philadelphia, 1787), 24.

73. "Sumptuary Laws formerly in England," in *The North-American Calendar: or, the Rhode-Island Almanack, For . . . 1788* (Providence, [1787]), 11.

74. Rush, *Thoughts upon Female Education*, 22.

75. Robert Davidson, *An Oration, on the Independence of the United States of America* (Carlisle, Pa., 1787), 4, 9.

76. Elizur Goodrich, *The Principles of Civil Union and Happiness Considered and Recommended* (Hartford, 1787), 56–57.

77. [Nicolas Collin], "Foreign Spectator," *Philadelphia Independent Gazetteer*, October 2, 1787; *DHRC*, 13:292–93; and see Jan Lewis, "'Of Every Age Sex & Condition': The Representation of Women in the Constitution," *Journal of the Early Republic* 15 (Fall 1995): 359–87.

78. Rush, *Thoughts upon Female Education*, 11–12, 15–16, 16–17.

79. Swanwick, *Thoughts on Education*, 4, 10, 11–22, 26.

80. "POEM, On the Prospect of seeing the fine ARTS flourish in AMERICA," in ibid., 35.

81. James Fordyce, *Sermons to Young Women* (Philadelphia, 1787), 20.

82. [James Forrester], *The Polite Philosopher* (Boston, 1787), 35.

83. James Mitchell Varnum, *The Case, Trevett against Weeden* (Providence, 1787), iv.

84. Rush, *Thoughts upon Female Education*, 20, 21.

85. [Markoe], *Algerine Spy*, 100, 107.

86. For Webster's efforts to nationalize copyright, see Webster to James Madison, July 5, 1784, in *PJM*, 8:96.

87. Noah Webster, *An Examination into the Leading Principles of the Federal Constitution* (Philadelphia, 1787), 51–52. Webster objected to Article 1, section 4.

88. Noah Webster, *A Grammatical Institute of the English Language... Part II*, 4th ed. (Hartford, [1787]), 23–24, 121–23; and Webster, *An American Selection of Lessons in Reading and Speaking*, 3rd ed. (Philadelphia, 1787).

89. *The Genuine Principles of the Ancient Saxon, or English Constitution* (Philadelphia, 1776), 34.

90. On the meanings of "frame" in Samuel Johnson's *Dictionary* (1755), see Robert Ferguson, "The American Enlightenment," in Sacvan Bercovitch, ed., *The Cambridge History of American Literature*, 8 vols. (Cambridge, 1994–), 1:484–85.

91. "MAXIMS and OBSERVATIONS—Moral and Miscellaneous," in *Stoddard's Diary: Or, The Columbia Almanack, For . . . 1788* (Hudson, N.Y., [1787]), 19.

92. See Douglass Adair, *Fame and the Founding Fathers*, ed. Trevor Colbourn (New York, 1974).

93. [Webster], *An Examination*, 10.

94. For an in-depth examination of one cultural venue in Philadelphia, see David R. Brigham, *Public Culture in the Early Republic: Peale's Museum and Its Audience* (Washington, D.C., 1995). For art criticism and aesthetic treatises

available in America, see Helen Park, "A List of Architectural Books Available in America before the Revolution," *Journal of the Society of Architectural Historians* 20 (October 1961): 115–30; David Lundberg and Henry F. May, "The Enlightened Reader in America," *American Quarterly* 28 (1976): 262–93; Janice G. Schimmelman, "Books on Drawing and Painting Techniques Available in Eighteenth-Century American Libraries and Bookstores," *Winterthur Portfolio* 19 (1984): 193–205; Schimmelman, "A Checklist of European Treatises on Art and Essays on Aesthetics"; and Schimmelman, *Architectural Books in Early America* (New Castle, Del., 1999).

95. On interpretive problems ratification poses, see Jack N. Rakove, *Original Meanings: Politics and Ideas in the Making of the Constitution* (New York, 1996), 94–130. For an account of perspectival thinking among painters and politicians, see Wendy Bellion, "'Extend the Sphere': Charles Willson Peale's Panorama of Annapolis," *Art Bulletin* 86, no. 3 (September 2004): 529–49.

96. *A Letter of His Excellency Edmund Randolph, Esquire, on the Federal Constitution* ([Richmond, 1787]), 13, 14.

97. Wellek, *History of Modern Criticism*, 1:234.

98. [Forrester], *Polite Philosopher*, 16.

99. *Encyclopedia Britannica* (1771), s.v. "Beauty," 1:536.

100. Rhys Isaac, "Ethnographic Method in History: An Action Approach," in Robert Blair St. George, ed., *Material Life in America* (Boston, 1988), 54–55; *The Four Books of Andrea Palladio's Architecture,* [trans. Isaac Ware] (London, 1738), 1; and Park, "A List of Architectural Books Available in America."

101. Hamilton, *Federalist* 82 (Cooke, ed., 553); and Madison, *Federalist* 37 (Cooke, ed., 236).

102. *A Review of the Constitution*, 7, 37.

103. "TRUTH and TASTE," *Columbian Magazine* 1 (October 1787): 682.

104. "The Fate of Beauty; or the Involuntary Prostitute," in Chatterton [pseud.], *Buds of Beauty*, 23–30.

105. Madison, *Federalist* 47 (Cooke, ed., 324–25).

106. Webster, *An Examination*, 52.

107. "Caeser II," *New York Daily Advertiser*, October 17, 1787, in *DHRC*, 13:396–97.

108. "Harrington" [Benjamin Rush], "To the Freemen of the United States," *Pennsylvania Gazette*, May 30, 1787, in *DHRC*, 13:116; on Rush's authorship, see *DHRC*, 13:116 n.

109. John Brooks, *An Oration, Delivered to the Society of the Cincinnati in the Commonwealth of Massachusetts, July 4th 1787* (Boston, 1787), 12.

110. Samuel Ellsworth, *There shall be Wars and Rumours of War before the Last Day cometh* ([Bennington, Vt.], 1787), 4–6.

111. [John Quincy Adams], *Observations on Paine's Rights of Man* (1791; Edinburgh, 1792), 11, 19–20.

112. [Hamilton], *Federalist* 1 (Cooke, ed., 3).

Chapter Three

1. State legislatures described their representatives in three ways: Virginia, Pennsylvania, North Carolina, Delaware, Georgia, South Carolina, and Maryland sent "deputies"; New Jersey and Massachusetts sent "commissioners"; and New York, Connecticut, and New Hampshire sent (and Rhode Island declined to send) "delegates." See *DHRC*, 1:192—229.

2. Rufus King, Notes, June 6, 1787, in *RFC*, 1:142.

3. Robert Yates, Notes, June 6, 1787, in *RFC*, 1:141. For problems with Yates's notes, see James H. Hutson, "The Creation of the Constitution: The Integrity of the Documentary Record," in Jack N. Rakove, ed., *Interpreting the Constitution* (Boston, 1990), 151–78.

4. James Madison, Notes, June 6, 1787, in *RFC*, 1:132–33.

5. William Pierce, Notes, June 6, 1787, in *RFC*, 1:147; Alexander Hamilton, Notes, June 6, 1787, in *RFC*, 1:145–46.

6. John Lansing, Notes, June 6, 1787, in James H. Hutson, ed., *Supplement to Max Farrand's Records of the Federal Convention of 1787* (New Haven, 1987), S:56.

7. Both spellings appear in *RFC*.

8. Early versions of *Federalist* no. 10 include Madison's April 1787 memorandum "Vices of the Political System of the United States," his June 6, 1787 notes, and letters to Washington (April 16, 1787) and Jefferson (October 24, 1787); see *PJM*, 9:348–57, 9:382–87, and 10:205–20.

9. Charles Pinckney to Rufus King, January 25, 1789; and Pinckney to Madison, March 28, 1789, in *RFC*, 3:355.

10. For "public voice," see James Madison, *Federalist* no. 10, November 22, 1787, in *DHRC*, 14:179; and Christopher Looby, *Voicing America: Language, Literary Form, and the Origins of the United States* (Chicago, 1996). For "public mind," see Alexander Hamilton, *Federalist* no. 26, December 22, 1787, in *DHRC*, 15:68; and Christopher Grasso, *A Speaking Aristocracy: Transforming Public Discourse in Eighteenth-Century Connecticut* (Chapel Hill, 1999), 327–85.

11. John Adams, *Thoughts on Government*, in *PJA*, 4:87; and Adams to William Hooper, and Adams to John Penn (both ante March 24, 1776), in *PJA*, 4:75, 80.

12. Hanna Fenichel Pitkin, *The Concept of Representation* (Berkeley, 1967), 60–61.

13. F. R. Ankersmit, *Aesthetic Politics: Political Philosophy beyond Fact and Value* (Stanford, 1996), 28. Ankersmit cites Adams from Pitkin (379 n. 15).

14. Thomas Whatley discusses "virtual" representation in *The Regulations Lately Made Concerning the Colonies and the Taxes Imposed upon Them* (London, 1765). On Adams's metaphor, see J. R. Pole, *Political Representation in England and the Origins of the American Republic* (1966; Berkeley, 1971), 339; Gordon Wood, *The Creation of the American Republic, 1776–1787* (Chapel Hill, 1969), 180; and Edmund S. Morgan, *Inventing the People: The Rise of Popular Sovereignty in England and America* (New York, 1988), 240.

15. Jack N. Rakove believes Adams's maxim best reflects American ideas of representation in the period; see *Original Meanings: Politics and Ideas in the Making of the Constitution* (New York, 1996), 203, 398 n. 2.

16. On the slipperiness of "representation," see Roger Chartier, "The Powers and Limits of Representation," *On the Edge of the Cliff: History, Language, and Practices*, trans. Lydia G. Cochrane (Baltimore, 1997), 90–103.

17. Adams to William Hooper, ante March 27, 1776, in *PJA*, 4:74.

18. Adams to John Penn, ante March 27, 1776, in *PJA*, 4:80.

19. Adams did not use the miniature metaphor in his November 1775 plan for "a total Revolution in the Government" in a "single Month," the earliest version of *Thoughts*; see Adams to Richard Henry Lee, November 15, 1775, in *PJA*, 3:307–8.

20. On the rise of "actual representation," see Bernard Bailyn, *The Origins of American Politics* (New York, 1968) and Wood, *Creation*, 183.

21. John Adams to James Warren, May 12, 1776, in *PJA*, 4:182.

22. Paine suggested a Congress with 390 members, with state delegations of 30 members; see *Common Sense*, in Philip S. Foner, ed., *Complete Writings of Thomas Paine*, 2 vols. (New York, 1969), 1:28.

23. Adams to James Warren, April 20, 1776, in *PJA*, 4:132, 131.

24. Francis Dana to John Adams, July 28, 1776, in *PJA*, 4:416.

25. Josiah Quincy outlined a process of "fermentation," "sublimation," and "political Refinement" that would allow the government to collect the wisdom of a "*few wise Men*" from the "*ignorant Multitude*" and to convert the "*many headed Monster*" of democracy into a representative republic; see Quincy to John Adams, June 13, 1776, in *PJA, *4:303–7.

26. John Adams, *A Defence of the Constitutions of Government of the United States* (Philadelphia, 1787), iv.

27. Melancton Smith, Speech at the New York Ratifying Convention (June 1788), in *CAF*, 6:157.

28. "John DeWitt," III, in *CAF*, 4:27.

29. "Brutus," III, in *CAF*, 2:383, 380.

30. Herbert J. Storing, "What the Anti-Federalists Were For," in *CAF*, 1:43; Wood, *Creation*, 164.

31. "The Federal Farmer," in *CAF*, 2:229. Though often ascribed to Virginian Richard Henry Lee, the Federal Farmer *Letters* may have been written by Melancton Smith of New York. See Rakove, *Original Meanings*, 228–29.

32. "John DeWitt," III, in *CAF*, 4:27. This fiction of assembling the whole may derive from James Burgh's *Political Disquisitions* (1774), which Adams believed "ought to be in the hands of every American who has learned to read"; see Wood, *Creation*, 165.

33. John Locke, *Two Treatises of Government,* ed. Peter Laslett (Cambridge, England, 1988), Second Treatise, sec. 212.

34. *Result of the Convention of Delegates holden at Ipswich in the County of Essex* (Newbury-Port, 1778), reprinted in J. R. Pole, ed., *The Revolution in America, 1754–1788* (Stanford, 1970), 459–60.

35. "Brutus," November 15, 1787, in *CAF*, 2:377.

36. "Brutus" may have drawn his terms from the most popular treatise on semiotics available in eighteenth-century America, Antoine Arnauld and Pierre Nicole's *Logic, or, The Art of Thinking* (1668), first translated into English in 1685. For a discussion of this text, see Louis Marin, *Portrait of the King,* trans. Martha M. Houle (Minneapolis, 1988). Among modern semioticians, "Brutus" is closest to Umberto Eco, who defines a sign simply as a thing that "on the grounds of previously established social convention, can be taken as something standing for something else"; see Eco, *A Theory of Semiotics* (Bloomington, 1976), 16.

37. Pitkin, *Concept of Representation,* 60–91, 112–43.

38. Noah Webster, *An Examination . . . of the Federal Constitution* (Philadelphia, 1787), 19–20.

39. "The Impartial Examiner," III, June 4, 1788, in *CAF*, 5:193.

40. James Madison, *Federalist* no. 10, November 22, 1787, in *DHRC*, 14:179.

41. Samuel Chase, Notes of Speeches Delivered to the Maryland Ratifying Convention, April 1788, in *CAF*, 5:89.

42. Hamilton, *Federalist* no. 35, January 5, 1788, in *DHRC*, 15:270.

43. [Moses Mather], *America's Appeal to the Impartial World* (Hartford, 1775), cited by Wood, *Creation*, 164.

44. For a study focusing on artists rather than patrons, see Wesley Craven, *Colonial American Portraiture* (Cambridge, England, 1986).

45. Timothy H. Breen, "The Meaning of 'Likeness': American Portrait Painting in an Eighteenth-Century Consumer Society," *Word and Image* 6 (1990): 35–50; Margaretta M. Lovell, "Painters and Their Customers: Aspects of Art and Money in Eighteenth-Century America," in *Of Consuming Interests: The Style of Life in the Eighteenth Century,* ed. Cary Carson, Ronald Hoffman, and Peter J. Albert (Charlottesville, 1994), 284–306; Paul Staiti, "Accounting for Copley," in Carrie Rebora, Paul Staiti, et al., eds., *John Singleton Copley in America* (New York, 1996), 25–50; Margaretta M. Lovell, "Mrs. Sargent,

Mr. Copley, and the Empirical Eye," *Winterthur Portfolio* 33 (1998): 1–40; Robert Blair St. George, *Conversing by Signs: Poetics of Implication in Colonial New England Culture* (Chapel Hill, 1998), 298–377.

46. Andrew Oliver, ed., *Portraits of John and Abigail Adams* (Cambridge, Mass., 1967), 47–49.

47. See the reports of his early efforts in *New York Gazetter*, December 3, 1784, and *New York Packet*, November 2, 1786.

48. Oliver, ed., *Portraits,* 25–30.

49. Abigail Adams to John Adams, July 24, 1780, in ibid., 209.

50. For a reading of the miniature as a fetish in narratives of the 1790s, see Julia Stern, *The Plight of Feeling: Sympathy and Dissent in the Early American Novel* (Chicago, 1998), 11, 188.

51. For miniatures in this period, see Dale T. Johnson, "An Introduction to the History of American Portrait Miniatures," in Johnson, ed., *American Portrait Miniatures in the Manney Collection* (New York, 1990), 13–26; Christopher Lloyd and Vanessa Remington, "Toward a Sociological Interpretation of Miniatures," *Masterpieces in Little: Portrait Miniatures from the Collection of Her Majesty Queen Elizabeth II* (London, 1996), 39–46; and Anne Sue Hirshorn, "Anna Claypoole, Margaretta, and Sarah Miriam Peale: Modes of Accomplishment and Fortune," in Lillian B. Miller, ed., *The Peale Family: Creation of a Legacy, 1770–1870* (New York, 1996), 221–47.

52. Carol Aiken, "Materials and Techniques of the American Portrait Miniaturist," in Johnson, ed., *American Portrait Miniatures*, 27–36.

53. Copley to [an English Mezzotinter], January 25, 1765, in *Letters and Papers of John Singleton Copley and Henry Pelham, 1739–1776* (Boston, 1914), 31.

54. John Wollaston, cited in Kenneth Silverman, *A Cultural History of the American Revolution* (New York, 1976), 18, 23.

55. *Daily Advertiser* (New York), September 24, 1787.

56. "From Philadelphia, Mrs. Benbridge (the wife of Mr. Benbridge, Portrait Painter) a very ingenious Miniature Paintress," *South Carolina Gazette*, April 5, 1773. See also the description of a female Scottish pastel artist in the *South Carolina Gazette*, December 31, 1772.

57. "A MINIATURE PAINTER Lately arrived from France, PETER HENRI," *Daily Advertiser* (New York), May 2 and June 4, 1788; "Mr. ALDWORTH, (late from London) paints miniature likenesses," *South Carolina and American General Gazette*, December 31, 1778; "Lewis Turtaz, Limner and miniature painter, from Lausanne in Switzerland," *South Carolina Gazette*, March 30, 1767; "William Rowland, Portrait-Painter, (Lately from Glasgow) Proposes . . . to begin painting in miniature," *Rivington's New York Royal Gazette*, December 6, 1777.

58. [Lawrence Kilburn], *New York Gazette*, July 8, 1754.

59. "Striking Likenesses in Miniature Profile, taken by John Colles," *Rivington's New York Royal Gazette*, May 10, 1780.

60. [John Grafton], *South Carolina Gazette*, November 4, 1774; [A. Delanoy,] *New York Gazette*, January 7, 1771.

61. [J. Stevenson], *South Carolina Gazette*, September 21, 1773.

62 "PETER HENRI," *Daily Advertiser* (New York), May 2, 1788.

63. "The Drawing and Painting Academy," *South Carolina Gazette*, December 31, 1772; "Mr. Quesnay begs leave to inform the Public," *New York Packet*, September 20, 1784; *New York Gazetter*, November 16, 1784; "PROPOSALS Of the Mode for effectuating the Institution of the Academy of Polite Arts, in New York, By Alexander Marie Quesnay," *New York Gazetter*, December 3, 1784.

64. *New York Gazette*, July 8, 1754.

65. *New York Gazetter*, December 3, 1784; see also *New York Packet*, November 2, 1786.

66. [Mr. Mack], *Carey's Pennsylvania Evening Herald*, February 12, 1785.

67. [Philip Parisen], *New York Daily Gazette*, September 20, 1791.

68. [John Colles], *Royal Gazette* (New York), May 10, 1780; [John Colles], *Pennsylvania Packet*, April 29, 1783; [Cooke & Co.], *Pennsylvania Packet*, July 22, 1784; [Cooke & Co.], *Maryland Gazette*, September 10, 1784; [Lewis Clephan], *Independent Journal* (New York), May 16, 1787; see also [Rembrandt Peale for Raphaelle Peale], *Mercantile Advertiser*, May 18, 1802.

69. *New York Gazette*, July 8, 1754.

70. *South Carolina Gazette*, September 20, 1770.

71. Ibid., November 4, 1774.

72. *New York Packet*, August 28, 1786.

73. *Pennsylvania Packet*, July 22, 1784; see also *Maryland Gazette*, September 10, 1784.

74. *Independent Gazetteer* (Philadelphia), November 20, 1784.

75. *South Carolina Gazette*, February 19, 1784.

76. *Carey's Pennsylvania Evening Herald*, February 12, 1785.

77. *Aurora* (Philadelphia), January 3, 1798; see also *Gazette of the United States*, April 23, 1796, and May 12, 1796.

78. *Federal Gazette* (Philadelphia), June 16, 1800; see also *Mercantile Advertiser*, May 18, 1802.

79. See Karin Calvert, "Children in American Family Portraiture, 1670–1810," *William and Mary Quarterly* 39 (1982): 87–113.

80. John Walters, "Portraits in Miniature, Large Pictures copied in ditto," *Pennsylvania Journal*, January 5, 1782, and July 31, 1782; *Independent Gazetteer* (Philadelphia), June 21, 1783; *Pennsylvania Packet*, July 20, 1784.

81. Cooke and Co., *Pennsylvania Packet*, July 22, 1784; see also *Maryland Gazette*, September 10, 1784.

82. "Miniature," *Encyclopedia Britannica* (Edinburgh, 1771), 3:249–50.

83. "Lewis Turtaz," *South Carolina Gazette*, March 30, 1767.

84. Harold E. Dickson, *Arts of the Young Republic: The Age of William Dunlap* (Chapel Hill, 1968), 40.

85. *Royal Gazette* (New York), May 10, 1780.

86. Charles Carroll to Charles Willson Peale, October 29, 1767, in *The Selected Papers of Charles Willson Peale and His Family*, ed. Lillian B. Miller, Sidney Hart, and David C. Ward, 5 vols. in 6 (New Haven, 1983–2000), 1:70.

87. [D.L.?], *The School of Wisdom* (New Brunswick, 1787); Titian Ramsay Peale, "Miniature Painting with Necessary Instructions," ca. 1798, Peale Papers, American Philosophical Society, Philadelphia.

88. Joshua C. Taylor, *The Fine Arts in America* (Chicago, 1979), 11–12.

89. William Dunlap, *History of . . . the Arts of Design in the United States*, 2 vols. (New York, 1834), 1:265.

90. Neil Harris, *The Artist in American Society: The Formative Years, 1790–1860* (1966; New York, 1970), 7.

91. *Rivington's New York Gazetteer*, August 4, 1774.

92. "LEWIS CLEPHAN Portrait Painter," *Independent Journal* (New York), May 16, 1787.

93. *Pennsylvania Packet*, July 22, 1784; see also *Maryland Gazette*, September 10, 1784.

94. Hirshorn, "Anna Claypoole," 229.

95. "On Miniature painting by Mrs. Stille" [ca. mid-1760s], cited in Silverman, *Cultural History of the American Revolution*, 18–19.

96. Stern, *The Plight of Feeling,* 11, 188.

97. "To the Ladies," *Pennsylvania Packet*, December 29, 1800. In 1803 Charles Willson Peale promoted the physiognotrace in similarly gendered terms, but nearly two-thirds of surviving silhouettes are of men; see David R. Brigham, *Public Culture in the Early Republic: Peale's Museum and Its Audience* (Washington, D.C., 1995), 71–72.

98. Ebenezer Pemberton, *The Divine Original and Dignity of Government Asserted* (Boston, 1710), 39.

99. *Pennsylvania Packet*, June 13, 1787.

100. For brief histories, see Peter T. Daniels, "Shorthand," in Daniels and William Bright, eds., *The World's Writing Systems* (New York, 1996), 807–20; and Karl Brown and Daniel C. Haskell, *The Shorthand Collection in the New York Public Library* (New York, 1934).

101. "Short-Hand Writing," *Encyclopedia Britannica* (1771), 3:586–99 (and Plates CL–CLII). The article described John Byrom's method.

102. William Holdsworth and William Aldridge, *Natural Short-Hand* (London, [1770?]), 2.

103. [Charles Brockden Brown], "Remarks on Short-hand Writing," *Monthly Magazine* 3 (August 1800): 92–96.

104. *New-York Daily Gazette*, April 2, 1789, cited in *FFC*, 10:xl.

105. Pennsylvania Constitution of 1776, sec. 14; New York Constitution of 1777, art. xv. For the publication of records, see Willi Paul Adams, *The First American Constitutions: Republican Ideology and the Making of the State Constitutions in the Revolutionary Era*, trans. Rita and Robert Kimber (Chapel Hill, 1980), 249–51.

106. *Charleston Evening Gazette*, September 29, 1785.

107. "Juvenis," *Charleston Evening Gazette*, September 27, 1785. This summary draws from the introduction to volume 10 of *FFC*.

108. And, like miniature portraits, the transcript could also serve devotional ends; see Charles E. Hambrick-Stowe, *The Practice of Piety: Puritan Devotional Disciplines in Seventeenth-Century New England* (Chapel Hill, 1982), 117, and David Hall, *Worlds of Wonder, Days of Judgment: Popular Religious Belief in Early New England* (New York, 1989), 265 n. 56.

109. *Scriptural Truths Demonstrated, in Thirty-Two Sermons, or Declarations of Stephen Crisp, . . . Carefully Taken in Characters or Short-Hand* (Philadelphia, 1787); *The Debates and Proceedings of the Convention of the State of New York . . . Taken in Short Hand* (New York, 1788), 2

110. [John Carey], *The System of Short-hand Practiced by Mr. Thomas Lloyd, in Taking Down the Debates of Congress* (Philadelphia, 1793).

111. *Lloyd's Stenography, Publicly practised by him for nearly half a century* (Philadelphia, 1819).

112. "Minute," *Encyclopedia Britannica* (1771), 3:251. For an example of minutes from 1787, see *Minutes of the Warren Association, at their Yearly Meeting* (Boston, 1787). John Trumbull's *M'Fingal, An Epic Poem in Four Cantos* (Hartford, 1782) mimicked the minutes of a town meeting in verse and was reprinted in Philadelphia by Mathew Carey in 1787.

113. John Carey to James Madison, February 8, 1792, in *PJM*, 14:225.

114. [Carey], *System of Short-hand*, 11.

115. *FFC*, 10:xxxiv.

116. The *Virginia Herald* (Fredericksburg) of January 28, 1790, cited a positive notice in the London *Analytical Review*; see Marion Tinling, "Thomas Lloyd's Reports of the First Federal Congress," *William & Mary Quarterly*, 3rd ser., 18 (1961): 535 n 48.

117. Jonathan Elliot, *The Debates in the Several State Conventions . . .* , 2nd ed., 4 vols. (1827–30; Washington, D.C., 1836), 1:iii.

118. [William Findley?], *Address from an Officer in the Late Continental Army* ([Philadelphia? Richmond?, 1787]), 5.

119. John Adams to Mercy Otis Warren, November 25, 1775, in *PJA*, 3:319.

120. John Adams to Mercy Otis Warren, January 8, 1776, in *PJA*, 3:397.

121. John Angell, *Stenography; or Shorthand Improved* (London: [1758]), Plate 6: "An Alphabet of Words."

122. "Short-Hand Writing," *Encyclopedia Brittanica,* 3:599; [Charles Brockden Brown], "Remarks on Short-hand Writing," 96.

123. "Short-Hand Writing," *Encyclopedia Brittanica,* 3:586.

124. [Carey], *System of Short-hand,* 13.

125. Ibid., 3-4, 12-13.

126. These rights belonged to Hall and Sellers, who won the contract to print documents for and of the Pennsylvania Convention and issued the bare *Minutes of the Convention* (Philadelphia, 1787) in German and English.

127. Samuel Vaughn, Jr. to James Bowdoin, November 30, 1787, in *DHRC,* 2:263.

128. *Independent Gazetter,* December 3, 1787.

129. Francis Hopkinson to Thomas Jefferson, December 14, 1787, in *PJM,* 12:423.

130. Printed in Philadelphia by Daniel Humpheys in 1787.

131. *Debates of the Convention, of the State of Pennsylvania, on the Constitution . . . Taken Accurately in Short-Hand, By Thomas Lloyd* (Philadelphia, 1787 [actually 1788]). An advertised second volume, containing Anti-Federalist speeches, was never published.

132. *Maryland Gazette,* May 15, 1788.

133. The habit of citing or presenting portions from the Convention debates without crediting the transcriber can be found in most modern discussions.

134. *Daily Advertiser,* June 22, 1789.

135. Tinling,"Thomas Lloyd's Reports," 530.

136. Charles Pinckney, *Observations on the Plan of Government submitted to the Federal Convention* (New York, [1787]), 3-4.

137. George Washington to James Madison, October 22, 1787, in *RFC,* 3:106-23.

138. On the "oratorical revolution," see Jay Fliegelman, *Declaring Independence: Jefferson, Natural Language, and the Culture of Performance* (Stanford, 1993).

139. James Mitchell Varnum, *The Case, Trevett against Weeden* (Providence, 1787), iii-iv.

140. Noah Webster, *An American Selection of Lessons in Reading and Speaking,* 3rd ed. (Philadelphia, 1787), 6.

141. Elliot, *Debates* 1:iv. On eloquence in the Massachusetts state convention, see Jeremy Belknap, January 25, 1788, in Massachusetts Historical Society, *Collections,* 5th ser., 3 (1877): 6, 16.

142. Samuel Lorenzo Knapp, *Lectures on American Literature, with Remarks on Some Passages of American History* (New York, 1829), 109-10.

143. Transcript of September 28, 1787, in *Proceedings and Debates of the General Assembly of Pennsylvania. Taken in Short-Hand by Thomas Lloyd. Volume the First* (Philadelphia, 1787), 7, 122.

144. *Gentleman's Magazine* 2 (July 1732): 864–66.

145. Ibid., 2 (August 1732): 883–84.

146. Ibid., 2 (October 1732): 989; and ibid., 2 (November 1732): 1035.

147. Ibid., 7 (Supplement 1737): 830, 792, 799.

148. Ibid., 8 (June 1738): 283–92.

149. [Carey], *System of Short-hand*, 3, 14.

150. Thomas Lloyd, subscription proposal for *The Congressional Register*, in *Daily Gazette* (New York), April 11, 1789.

151. Tinling, "Thomas Lloyd's Reports," 530.

152. [Calvin Willard?], "Preface" to William Hill Brown, *Ira and Isabella* (Boston, 1807), vi–viii.

153. Daniel Humphreys, "To the Subscribers," in *Proceedings and Debates of the General Assembly of Pennsylvania. Taken in Short-Hand by Thomas Lloyd*, 4 vols. (Philadelphia, 1787–88), 1:2.

154. *Scriptural Truths Demonstrated*, 2.

155. To Noah Webster, February 13, 1788, in *Letters of Benjamin Rush*, ed. L. H. Butterfield, 2 vols. (Princeton, 1951), 1:450.

156. Madison to Edmund Randolph, June 24, 1789, cited in *FFC*, 10:xx.

157. Madison to Jefferson, May 9, 1789, in *PJM*, 12:142.

158. Aedanus Burke, September 26, 1789, resolution; see *FFC*, 11:1502–3.

159. *Gazette of the United States*, September 30, 1789, in *FFC*, 10:xi.

160. [Carey], *System of Short-hand*, 15.

161. For a similar charge about Lloyd's omission of Pennsylvania Anti-Federalist speeches, see *Maryland Gazette*, May 22, 1788.

162. Madison, "Preface to Debates in the Convention of 1787," in *RFC*, 3:550–51.

163. A point often ignored in using Madison's notes. For an early understanding of the notes, see the long review of *The Madison Papers* in the *North American Review* 53 (1841): 41–79.

164. "Brutus," November 15, 1787, in *CAF*, 2:377; Madison, *Federalist* no. 10, November 22, 1787, in *DHRC*, 14:179.

165. *RFC*, 2:222 n. 12; Madison Papers, Library of Congress. The transcript of Madison's notes by Jefferson's nephew John Wayles Eppes, from the early 1790s, includes Morris's speech; see Edward Everett Papers, microfilm reel 45A, Massachusetts Historical Society, Boston.

Chapter Four

1. *Pennsylvania Evening Post*, July 2, 1776; and see Thomas's subsequent advertisements for a male slave for sale (*Pennsylvania Packet*, August 15, 1778) and for a female runaway named Sophia (*Pennsylvania Packet*, August 5, 1780).

On the injured bodies of slaves, see Simon P. Newman, *Embodied History: The Lives of the Poor in Early Philadelphia* (Philadelphia, 2002), 82–103; and on interracial sex, see Clare A. Lyons, *Sex among the Rabble: An Intimate History of Gender and Power in the Age of Revolution, Philadelphia, 1730–1830* (Chapel Hill, 2006).

2. References to the Declaration are to the first broadside printing by John Dunlap.

3. On runaway slaves and the Revolution in Philadelphia, see Gary B. Nash and Jean R. Soderlund, *Freedom by Degrees: Emancipation in Pennsylvania and Its Aftermath* (New York, 1991), 94–95, 138–39; Billy G. Smith and Richard Wojtowicz, *Blacks Who Stole Themselves: Advertisements for Runaways in the Pennsylvania Gazette, 1728–1790* (Philadelphia, 1989), 123–33; and David Waldstreicher, "Reading the Runaways: Self Fashioning, Print Culture, and Confidence in Slavery in the Eighteenth-Century Mid-Atlantic," *William and Mary Quarterly*, 3rd ser., 56 (1999): 243–72. On slaves who fought for the British, see Simon Schama, *Rough Crossings: Britain, the Slaves, and the American Revolution* (London, 2005), and Cassandra Pybus, *Epic Journeys of Freedom: Runaway Slaves of the American Revolution and Their Global Quest for Liberty* (Boston, 2006). On revolutionary abolitionism, see Richard S. Newman, *The Transformation of American Abolitionism: Fighting Slavery in the Early Republic* (Chapel Hill, 2002), 16.

4. See Merril D. Peterson, *The Jeffersonian Image in the American Mind* (New York, 1960); Philip F. Detweiler, "The Changing Reputation of the Declaration of Independence: The First Fifty Years," *William and Mary Quarterly*, 3rd ser., 19, no.4 (October 1962): 557–74; John Philip Reid, "The Irrelevance of the Declaration," in *Law in the American Revolution and the Revolution of the Law*, ed. Hendrick Hartog (New York, 1981), 46–89; Pauline Maier, *American Scripture: Making the Declaration of Independence* (New York, 1997); David Thelen, "Reception of the Declaration of Independence," in *The Declaration of Independence: Origins and Impact* (Washington, D.C., 2002), 191–212; and David Armitage, *The Declaration of Independence: A Global History* (Cambridge, Mass., 2007).

5. Robert M. S. McDonald, "Thomas Jefferson's Changing Reputation as Author of the Declaration of Independence: The First Fifty Years," *Journal of the Early Republic* 19, no.2 (Summer 1999): 169–95; Lincoln, "Speech at Springfield, Illinois," June 26, 1857, in Armitage, *Declaration*, 26; on facsimiles, see David Hackett Fischer, *Liberty and Freedom: A Visual History of America's Founding Ideas* (New York, 2005), 207–8.

6. See, for instance, "From Poulson's *Daily Advertiser*," *Pennsylvania Correspondent*, June 4, 1805.

7. Ruth Bogin, "'Liberty Further Extended': A 1776 Antislavery Manuscript by Lemuel Haynes," *William and Mary Quarterly*, 3rd ser., 40, no.1 (January 1983): 85–106.

8. Quentin Skinner, *Liberty before Liberalism* (Cambridge, England, 1998), 1–57, esp. 13.

9. Lynn Hunt, "The World We Have Gained: The Future of the French Revolution," *American Historical Review* 108, no.1 (February 2003): 19.

10. George Fredrickson, *The Comparative Imagination: On the History of Racism, Nationalism, and Social Movements* (Berkeley, 1997), and *Racism: A Short History* (Princeton, 2002).

11. The phrase "'spill-over' effect" is from Bernard Bailyn, *The Ideological Origins of the American Revolution* (Cambridge, Mass., 1967), x (and see 232–46); see also Orlando Patterson, "Freedom, Slavery, and the Modern Construction of Rights," in Olwen Hufton, ed., *Historical Change and Human Rights: The Oxford Amnesty Lectures, 1994* (New York, 1995), 131–78, esp. 156ff.; and Jack N. Rakove, *Declaring Rights* (Boston, 1997), 23.

12. For the most prominent account of mimicry, see Homi Bhabha, *The Location of Culture* (London, 1994), 85–122.

13. Ira Berlin, *Many Thousands Gone: The First Two Centuries of Slavery in North America* (Cambridge, Mass., 1998), 224. For scientific racism, see Winthrop Jordan, *White over Black: American Attitudes toward the Negro, 1550–1812* (Chapel Hill, 1968), esp. 269–311, 440–45, 482–541; George M. Fredrickson, *The Black Image in the White Mind* (New York, 1971); and Stephen Jay Gould, *The Mismeasure of Man* (New York, 1981), 30–72.

14. Skinner, *Liberty before Liberalism*, 36.

15. Richard Price, *Two Tracts on Civil Liberty* (1778), cited in Skinner, *Liberty before Liberalism*, 50.

16. Cited in Bailyn, *Ideological Origins*, 233.

17. Ibid.; Gordon S. Wood, *The Creation of the American Republic, 1776–1787* (Chapel Hill, 1969); J. G. A. Pocock, *The Machiavellian Moment: Florentine Political Thought and the Atlantic Republican Tradition* (Princeton, 1975). For critiques, see Alfred Young, "Afterword: How Radical Was the American Revolution?" in *Beyond the American Revolution*, ed. Young (DeKalb, Ill., 1993), and T. H. Breen, "Ideology and Nationalism on the Eve of the American Revolution: Revisions *Once More* in Need of Revising," *Journal of American History* 84, no. 1 (June 1997): 13–39.

18. J. C. D. Clark, *The Language of Liberty, 1660–1832: Political Discourse and Social Dynamics in the Anglo-American World* (Cambridge, England, 1994).

19. *New York Evening Post*, November 16, 1747, in Bailyn, *Ideological Origins*, 234.

20. Richard Price, *Observations on the Nature of Civil Liberty*, 5th ed. (London, 1776), 19.

21. Charles Chauncy to Richard Price, October 5, 1772, in *The Correspondence of Richard Price, Volume I: July 1748–March 1778*, ed. W. Bernard Peach and D. O. Thomas (Durham, N.C., 1983), 143.

22. Price to Chauncy, February 25, 1775, in ibid., 188.

23. For examples of the rhetoric of political slavery, see Thomas Gordon, "An Enquiry into the Nature and Extent of Liberty" (1721), in *Cato's Letters*, ed. Ronald Hamowy (Indianapolis, 1995), 430; "Philoleutherus," *The Constitutional Courant*, September 21, 1765, in Merrill Jensen, ed., *Tracts of the American Revolution* (Indianapolis, 1967), 83; [T. Parsons and E. Pearson], *A Forensic Dispute on the Legality of Enslaving the Africans* (Boston, 1773), 7; John Adams, "Novanglus," January 30, 1775, in Jensen, *Tracts*, 315; Richard Price, *Observations*, 2–7; and [Adam Ferguson], *Remarks on a Pamphlet Lately Published by Dr. Price* (London, 1776), 3. Of course, some writers found the rhetoric of political slavery overheated; see Martin Howard, *A Letter from a Gentleman at Halifax . . .* (Newport, 1765), 8–9.

24. Gordon S. Wood, *The Radicalism of the American Revolution* (New York, 1992), 179, 186–87; Bailyn, *Ideological Origins*, 232–46.

25. See "Queries Respecting the Slavery and Emancipation of Negroes in Massachusetts," Massachusetts Historical Society, *Collections*, 1st ser., 4 (1795): 201; "Belknap Papers," *Collections of the Massachusetts Historical Society*, 5th ser., 3 (1877): 384, 392, 401–2, 432–37.

26. Edmund S. Morgan, "Slavery and Freedom: The American Paradox," *Journal of American History* 59 (1972): 6, and Jordan, *White over Black*, xii; for an alternate explanation, see David Brion Davis, *The Problem of Slavery in the Age of Revolution, 1770–1823* (Ithaca, 1975), 11.

27. Gary B. Nash, *Race and Revolution* (Madison, 1990); James Oakes, *Slavery and Freedom: An Interpretation of the Old South* (New York, 1990), 3.

28. Berlin, *Many Thousands Gone*, 2, 4, 219–55.

29. See Robin Blackburn, *The Overthrow of Colonial Slavery, 1776–1848* (London, 1988), and *The Making of New World Slavery: From the Baroque to the Modern, 1493–1800* (London, 1997); Alexander Saxton, *The Rise and Fall of the White Republic: Class Politics and Mass Culture in Nineteenth-Century America* (London, 1990); David Roediger, *The Wages of Whiteness: Race and the Making of the American Working Class* (London, 1991); and Theodore Allen, *The Invention of the White Race*, 2 vols. (London, 1994–97). For the continuing pull of the "paradox," see David Eltis, *The Rise of African Slavery in the Americas* (Cambridge, England, 2000).

30. Benjamin Quarles, "The Revolutionary War as a Black Declaration of Independence," in Ira Berlin and Ronald Hoffman, eds., *Slavery and Freedom in the Age of the American Revolution* (Charlottesville, 1983), 290.

31. [Thomas Dawson?], review of *The Origin of the Veil*, by John Langhorne, *Monthly Review* 48 (January 1773): 69–70.

32. [John Langhorne], review of *Poems on Various Subjects, Religious and Moral*, by Phillis Wheatley, *Monthly Review* 49 (December 1773): 457–59, and Index to volume 49 (n.p.). Langhorne wrote the only extended review of Wheat-

ley's *Poems* in either England or America. Almost without exception, British reviewers in 1773 proclaimed that Wheatley's poems were "not remarkably beautiful" (*Critical Review*) and "display no astonishing power of genius" (*London Magazine*); see Mukhtar Ali Isani, "The British Reception of Phillis Wheatley's *Poems on Various Subjects*," *Journal of Negro History* 66 (1981): 144–49.

33. Johnson's question was "How is it that we hear the loudest *yelps* for liberty amongst the drivers of negroes?"; cited in Judith N. Shklar, *American Citizenship: The Quest for Inclusion* (Cambridge, Mass., 1991), 40.

34. Fithian also read the review in the *Universal Magazine* 53 (September 1773): 153; see *Journal and Letters of Philip Vickers Fithian, 1773–1774: A Plantation Tutor of the Old Dominion*, ed. Hunter Dickinson Farish (Williamsburg, Va., 1943), 96. On Fithian, see John Fea, *The Way of Improvement Leads Home: Philip Vickers Fithian and the Rural Enlightenment in Early America* (Philadelphia, 2008).

35. David Hume, "Of National Characters" (1748), in *Essays Moral, Political, and Literary*, ed. Eugene F. Miller (Indianapolis, 1987), 208 n. 10. For contexts, see Henry Louis Gates, Jr., "Editor's Introduction," *"Race," Writing, and Difference* (Chicago, 1986), 1–20; Richard Popkin, "The Philosophical Basis of Eighteenth-Century Racism," *Studies in Eighteenth-Century Culture* 3 (1973): 245–62; and Emmanuel Chukwudi Eze, ed., *Race and the Enlightenment: A Reader* (Oxford, 1997), 1–9.

36. Immanuel Kant, *Observations on the Feeling of the Beautiful and Sublime*, trans. John T. Goldthwait (Berkeley, 1960), 110–11.

37. Edward Long, *The History of Jamaica*, 3 vols. (London, 1774), 2:375, 478–83.

38. Thomas Jefferson, *Notes on the State of Virginia*, ed. William Peden (New York, 1972), 140.

39. Ibid. On Jefferson's ideas about aesthetics and race, see Dana D. Nelson, *The Word in Black and White: Reading "Race" in American Literature 1638–1867* (New York, 1992), 16–20.

40. Bernard Romans, *A Concise Natural History of East and West Florida* (New York, 1775), 39, in Roy Harvey Pearce, *Savagism and Civilization: A Study of the Indian and the American Mind* (1953; Baltimore, 1965), 48.

41. Shane White and Graham White, "Slave Clothing and African-American Culture in the Eighteenth Century," *Past & Present* (August 1995): 148.

42. Bhabha, *Location of Culture*, 85–92; see also Mechal Sobel, *The World They Made Together: Black and White Values in Eighteenth-Century Virginia* (Princeton, 1987).

43. See Jay Fliegelman, *Prodigals and Pilgrims: The American Revolution against Patriarchal Authority* (Cambridge, England, 1982).

44. Jefferson, *Notes*, 162; see also Daniel Blake Smith, *Inside the Great*

House: Planter Family Life in Eighteenth-Century Chesapeake Society (Ithaca, 1980), 83, 85, 286–87.

45. For another example, see Arthur Lee, *An Essay in Vindication of the Continental Colonies of America, from a Censure of Mr ADAM SMITH, in his Theory of Moral Sentiments. With Some Reflections on Slavery in General* (London, 1764), 41–42.

46. Josiah Quincy, Journal, March 1773, in Roger Bruns, ed., *Am I Not a Man and a Brother?: The Antislavery Crusade of Revolutionary America, 1688–1788* (New York, 1977), 223.

47. For a similar statement, see James Otis, *The Rights of the British Colonies Asserted and Proved* (Boston, 1764), 29.

48. Israel Andrews to William Burrell, January 28, 1774, in James Rawley, "The World of Phillis Wheatley," *New England Quarterly* 50 (1977): 676. Wheatley's 1773 volume omitted her most explicitly political poems.

49. *Virginia Gazette*, September 14, 1769, in Bruns, ed., *Am I Not a Man*, xxxvi.

50. See, for example, *Georgia Gazette* (Savannah), February 2, 1764, in *Runaway Slave Advertisements: A Documentary History from the 1730s to 1790*, ed. Lathan A. Windley, 4 vols. (Westport, Conn., 1983), 4:2. For notices in the North, see Graham Russell Hodges and Alan Edward Brown, eds., *"Pretends to be Free": Runaway Slave Advertisements from Colonial and Revolutionary New York and New Jersey* (New York, 1994).

51. A survey of Daniel Meaders' *Eighteenth-Century White Slaves: Fugitive Notices* (Westport, Conn., 1993) suggests "crafty" as an analogous term to describe lower-class and enslaved whites.

52. Samuel Stanhope Smith, *An Essay on the Causes of the Variety of Complexion and Figure in the Human Species* (Philadelphia, 1787), 77 n. [2], 58.

53. James Beattie, cited in Granville Sharp, *The Just Limitation of Slavery* (London, 1776), 29n.

54. Benjamin Rush, *An Address . . . on the Slavery of the Negroes in America*, 2nd ed. (Philadelphia, 1773), 2.

55. Richard Nisbet, *Slavery Not Forbidden by Scripture* (Philadelphia, 1773), 23n, in William H. Robinson, ed., *Critical Essays on Phillis Wheatley* (Boston, 1982), 32.

56. For Wheatley's place in the mental equality debate, see Henry Louis Gates, Jr., "Preface to Blackness: Text and Context" (1978), in Angelyn Mitchell, ed., *Within the Circle: An Anthology of African American Literary Criticism from the Harlem Renaissance to the Present* (Durham, N.C., 1994), 235–55; and Charles W. Akers, " 'Our Modern Egyptians': Phillis Wheatley and the Whig Campaign against Slavery in Revolutionary Massachusetts," in Robinson, ed., *Critical Essays*, 159–71.

57. Johann Joachim Winckelmann, *Reflections on the painting and sculpture*

of the Greeks with instructions for the connoisseur (1755), trans. Henry Fuseli (London, 1765), in David Irwin, ed., *Winckelmann: Writings on Art* (London, 1972), 61. For the presence of this text in the catalog of Boston booksellers Cox and Berry, see Janice G. Schimmelman, "A Checklist of European Treatises on Art and Essays on Aesthetics Available in America through 1815," *Proceedings of the American Antiquarian Society* 93, no. 1 (1983): 169.

58. See Jay Fliegelman, *Declaring Independence: Jefferson, Natural Language, and the Culture of Performance* (Stanford, 1993), 164–78.

59. David Solkin, *Richard Wilson: The Landscape of Reaction* (London, 1982), 61. On the idea of "genius" in eighteenth-century Europe, see Martha Woodmansee, *The Author, Art, and the Market* (New York, 1994), esp. 35–55.

60. Sir Joshua Reynolds, "Sixth Discourse" (December 10, 1774), in Henry William Beechy, ed., *The Literary Works of Joshua Reynolds*, 2 vols. (London, 1852), 1: 394–95, 396.

61. Samuel Johnson, *The Beauties of Johnson* (Philadelphia, 1787), 63.

62. See Caroline Winterer, *The Culture of Classicism: Ancient Greece and Rome in American Intellectual Life, 1780–1910* (Baltimore, 2002).

63. [Noah Webster], *An Examination into the Leading Principles of the Federal Constitution* (Philadelphia, 1787), 13.

64. [John Stevens], *Observations on Government* (New York, 1787), 52.

65. Copley to West, November 12, 1766; Copley to West, November 24, 1770; Captain R. G. Bruce to Copley, August 4, 1766 (reporting West and Reynolds), in *Letters and Papers of John Singleton Copley and Henry Pelham* (Boston, 1914), 51, 98, 41. British radical John Wilkes believed that Copley would be better off in America, "undebauch'd by the wickedness of European Courts, and Parliamentary Prostitution" (ibid., 95). On the transatlantic context for Copley's painting, see Jennifer Roberts, "Copley's Cargo: *Boy with a Squirrel* and the Dilemma of Transit," *American Art* 21, no. 2 (Summer 2007): 20–41.

66. Jules David Prown, *John Singleton Copley*, 2 vols. (Cambridge, Mass., 1966), 2:246.

67. Hugh Honour, *Neo-classicism*, rev. ed. (1968; New York, 1977), 107.

68. William Blake, "Annotations to Reynolds' *Discourses on Art*," in *Eighteenth-Century English Literature*, ed. Geoffrey Tillotson, Paul Fussell, Marshall Waingrow, and Brewster Rogerson (San Diego, Calif., 1969), 1510, 1511, 1513.

69. Wheatley's neoclassical verses have always been read against a partial romantic sensibility; see Henry Louis Gates, Jr., *Figures in Black: Words, Signs, and the "Racial" Self* (New York, 1987), 64.

70. See, for example, the glowing review of *Poems on several Occasions. By John Bennet, a Journeyman Shoemaker*, in *Monthly Review* 51 (December 1774): 483. For Wheatley's place in this cultural context, see Charles Scruggs, "Phillis Wheatley and the Poetical Legacy of Eighteenth-Century England," *Studies in Eighteenth-Century Culture* 10 (1981): 279–95.

71. Archibald Bell, advertisement, *Morning Post and Advertiser* (London), September 3, 1773, in Robinson, ed., *Critical Essays*, 28; John Wheatley, "A Copy of a LETTER sent by the Author's Master to the Publisher," in Wheatley, *Poems on Various Subjects, Religious and Moral* (London, 1773), vi.

72. [Susanna Wheatley?], *London Chronicle*, July 1–3, 1773, at 3, in Robinson, ed., *Critical Essays*, 25.

73. Honour, *Neo-classicism*, 109.

74. James Otis, *The Rudiments of Latin Prosody* (Boston, 1760), 26, 35n, 43, 72; Otis, *The Rights of the British Colonies Asserted and Proved* (Boston, 1764).

75. Edward Young, *Conjectures on Original Composition*, 2nd ed. (London, 1759), in Tillotson et al., eds., *Eighteenth-Century English Literature*, 874.

76. Ibid., 877–78.

77. See Jordan, *White over Black*, 29–32, 65, 235–39, 490–97, 510.

78. Lee, *Essay in Vindication of the Continental Colonies*, 43; James Swan, *A Dissuasion to Great-Britain and the Colonies from the Slave Trade to Africa* (Boston, 1772), in Bruns, ed., *Am I Not a Man*, 200; in contrast, see Thomas Thompson, *The African Trade for Negro Slaves, Shewn to be Consistent with Principles of Humanity, and with the Laws of Revealed Religion* (Canterbury, England, 1772), in Bruns, ed., *Am I Not a Man*, 217–20.

79. *The Appendix: or, some Observations on the Expediency of the PETITION of the AFRICANS, living in BOSTON* (Boston, [1773]), 4.

80. [Parsons and Pearson], *Forensic Dispute*, 4–5.

81. Otis, *Rights of the British Colonies*, 29.

82. Anthony Benezet, *A Caution and a Warning to Great Britain and Her Colonies* (Philadelphia, 1767), in Bruns, ed., *Am I Not a Man*, 113.

83. *The Epistle from the Yearly-Meeting, Held in London* ([Philadelphia], 1787), 1.

84. Levi Hart, *Liberty Described and Recommended* (Hartford, 1775), cited in Bailyn, *Ideological Origins*, 243.

85. Patrick Henry to Robert Pleasants, January 18, 1773, in Bruns, ed., *Am I Not a Man*, 221–22.

86. Samuel Hopkins, *A Dialogue Concerning the Slavery of Africans . . .* (Norwich, 1776), cited in Bailyn, *Ideological Origins*, 244.

87. Nathaniel Appleton, *Considerations on Slavery* (Boston, 1767), in Bruns, ed., *Am I Not a Man*, 136.

88. Swan, *A Dissuasion*, 12.

89. Petition of April 20, 1773, in Herbert Aptheker, ed., *A Documentary History of the Negro in the United States* (New York, 1969), 7–8. For readings of the Massachusetts petitions, see Benjamin Quarles, "The Revolutionary War as a Black Declaration of Independence," in Berlin and Hoffman, eds., *Slavery and Freedom in the Age of the American Revolution*, 290; Thomas J. Davis, "Emancipation Rhetoric, Natural Rights, and Revolutionary New England: A Note on Four Black Petitions in Massachusetts, 1773–1777," *New England Quar-*

terly 62 (1989): 248–63; James Oliver Horton and Lois E. Horton, *In Hope of Liberty: Culture, Community, and Protest among Northern Free Blacks, 1700–1860* (New York, 1997), 55–56; Joanne Pope Melish, *Disowning Slavery: Gradual Emancipation and "Race" in New England, 1780–1860* (Ithaca, 1998), 81.

90. Petition of April 20, 1773, in Aptheker, ed., *Documentary History,* 7–8.

91. Petition of May 25, 1774, in ibid., 8–9.

92. Bristol Lambee, "To the Sons of Liberty in Connecticut," *Providence Gazette,* October 22, 1774.

93. A. Leon Higginbotham, *In the Matter of Color: Race and the American Legal Process, The Colonial Period* (New York, 1978), 84–86; *Legal Papers of John Adams,* ed. L. Kinvin Wroth and Hiller B. Zobel, 3 vols. (Cambridge, Mass., 1965), 2:48–67.

94. The 1773 petitions appeared as a printed circular letter to individual state representatives in the *Massachusetts Spy,* January 26, 1773, and July 29, 1773; in [John Allen], *An Oration on the Beauties of Liberty,* 4th ed. (Boston, 1773), 73–80; and in *The Appendix.*

95. Wheatley to Occom, February 11, 1774, in *The Collected Works of Phillis Wheatley,* ed. John C. Shields (New York, 1988), 176–77. This letter appeared in eleven New England newspapers in 1774.

96. William Blackstone, *Commentary on the Laws of England* (London, 1768), 3:6.

97. *Royal Magazine* (London), 3 (September 1760): 119, in Solkin, *Richard Wilson,* 64.

98. For Sir Joshua Reynolds's critique of Wilson's *Niobe,* see "Fourteenth Discourse" (December 1788), in Beechy, ed., *Literary Works of Reynolds,* 2:90.

99. Significantly, the translation of Niobe's metamorphosis is described in the *Poems* as "the Work of another Hand" (p. 112).

100. Jupiter Hammon, *An Address to the Negroes In the State of New-York* (New York, 1787), 13.

101. T. Q., Letter, *Boston Gazette,* April 18, 1763.

102. Price, *Observations,* 17.

103. *The Votes and Proceedings of the Freeholders . . . of Boston . . .* (1772), in Jensen, ed., *Tracts,* 254–55.

104. "Philo Patriae," *The Constitutional Courant,* September 21, 1765, in Jensen, ed., *Tracts,* 89.

105. Lee, *Essay in Vindication of the Continental Colonies,* 37–38; Jefferson, *Notes,* 139.

106. [Parsons and Pearson], *Forensic Dispute,* 25–29, 36.

107. For the debate on the language of slavery at the Constitutional Convention, see *RFC,* 2:374, 415–17; for the northern origins of the three-fifths clause, see *RFC,* 1:201. And compare John Adams, Notes of Debates, July 30, 1776, in W. C. Ford et al., eds., *Journals of the Continental Congress, 1774–1789,* 34 vols. (Washington, D.C.: 1904–37), 6:1080.

108. See "Chronicle of the Year 1850," *Columbian Magazine* I (1787): 6.

109. [James Madison], "The Foederalist" no. 42, January 23, 1788, in *DHRC*, 15:443.

110. See, for example, the 1782 petition reprinted as [Belinda], "Petition from an African Slave to the Legislature of Massachusetts," *American Museum* I (June 1787), 538–40.

111. Thomas Jefferson to Henri Gregoire, February 25, 1809, in Merrill D. Peterson, ed., *Thomas Jefferson: Writings* (New York, 1984), 1202.

112. See Nell Irvin Painter, *Sojourner Truth: A Life, a Symbol* (New York, 1996), 164–78.

113. Bogin, "'Liberty Further Extended,'" 94; Jacob Green, *A Sermon Delivered at Hanover, (in New-Jersey) April 22d, 1778* (Chatham, N.J., 1779), 13; Anthony Benezet, *Serious Considerations on Several Important Subjects* (Philadelphia, 1778), 28–29; Benezet, *Short Observations on Slavery* ([Philadelphia, 1781?]), 1–2; [David Cooper], *A Serious Address to the Rulers of America on the Inconsistency of their Conduct respecting Slavery* (Trenton, 1783), 12–13.

114. [Cooper], *Serious Address*, 13; "Justice," "From the *Freeman's Journal* [Philadelphia]," *New-Hampshire Gazette*, July 22, 1785; *Constitution of the Pennsylvania Society for Promoting the Abolition of Slavery* (Philadelphia, 1788), 19, 21. For the Maryland Society, see a report in the *Providence Gazette*, May 7, 1791; see also *The Constitution of the New-Jersey Society, for Promoting the Abolition of Slavery* (Burlington, N.J., 1793). For the 1783 Rhode Island law, see *Providence Gazette*, September 20, 1783.

115. James Dana, *The African Slave Trade* (New Haven, 1790), 28.

116. *Copy of a Letter from Benjamin Banneker to the Secretary of State, With his Answer* (Philadelphia, 1792), 7–8; for other printings, see *Baltimore Evening Post*, October 13, 1792; *Virginia Gazette*, October 31, 1792; and (as an example of Jefferson's antislavery credentials) *Gazette of the United States*, November 17, 1796.

117. *Minutes . . . of the Eleventh American Convention for Promoting the Abolition of Slavery* (Philadelphia, 1806), 29; *Minutes . . . of the Twelfth American Convention for Promoting the Abolition of Slavery* (Philadelphia, 1809), 19.

118. Frederick Douglass, *Oration, Delivered . . . July 5th, 1852* (Rochester, 1852), in *The Frederick Douglass Papers, Series 1: Speeches, Debates, and Interviews, 1845–1891*, ed. John W. Blassingame (New Haven, 1979–), 2:359–88.

Chapter Five

1. See Jack N. Rakove, *Declaring Rights: A Brief History with Documents* (Boston, 1998), 77; John E. Selby, *The Revolution in Virginia, 1775–1783* (Charlottesville, 1983), 102–3; and Pauline Maier, *American Scripture* (New York,

1997). On the Stamp Act resolutions, see Gordon S. Wood, *The American Revolution* (New York, 2002), 29; and David D. Hall and Hugh Amory, "Afterword," *The Colonial Book in the Atlantic World*, ed. Hall and Amory (Cambridge, England, 2000), 483–84.

2. "Social Compact," "To the Printer," *New-Haven Gazette and Connecticut Magazine* 2, no. 33 (October 4, 1787): 262; Thad W. Tate, "The Social Contract in America, 1774–1787: Revolutionary Theory as a Conservative Instrument," *William and Mary Quarterly*, 3rd ser., 22, no. 3 (July 1965): 375–91; and see Christopher Grasso, *A Speaking Aristocracy: Transforming Public Discourse in Eighteenth-Century Connecticut* (Chapel Hill, 1999), and Christopher Collier, *All Politics Is Local: Family, Friends, and Provincial Interests in the Creation of the Constitution* (Hanover, N.H., 2003).

3. "The Hermit's Soliloquy," *New-Haven Gazette and Connecticut Magazine* 3, no. 31 (August 7, 1788): 7.

4. For "fantasies of publicity," see Michael Warner, *The Letters of the Republic: Publication and the Public Sphere in Eighteenth-Century America* (Cambridge, Mass., 1990), 151–76. On practices of newspaper circulation, see Thomas C. Leonard, *News for All: America's Coming of Age with the Press* (New York, 1995), 3–32.

5. Benjamin Rush, *An Oration . . . containing an Enquiry into the Influence of Physical Causes upon the Moral Faculty* (Philadelphia, 1786), 24; Rush, *An Enquiry into the Effects of Public Punishments* (Philadelphia, 1787), 12.

6. See Patricia Meyer Spacks, *Privacy: Concealing the Eighteenth-Century Self* (Chicago, 2003), and Thomas Laquer, *Solitary Sex: A Cultural History of Masturbation* (New York, 2003).

7. See David H. Flaherty, *Privacy in Colonial New England* (Charlottesville, 1972).

8. For gender and privacy (or privatization) in early America, see Nancy F. Cott, *The Bonds of Womanhood: "Women's Sphere" in New England, 1780–1835* (New Haven, 1977); Linda Kerber, *Women of the Republic: Intellect and Ideology in Revolutionary America* (Chapel Hill, 1980); Laurel Thatcher Ulrich, *Good Wives: Image and Reality in the Lives of Women in Northern New England, 1650–1750* (New York, 1982); Cathy N. Davidson, *Revolution and the Word: The Rise of the Novel in America* (New York, 1986); Ruth H. Bloch, "The Gendered Meanings of Virtue in Revolutionary America," *Signs: Journal of Women in Culture and Society* 11 (Fall 1987): 37–58; Jan Lewis, "The Republican Wife," *William and Mary Quarterly*, 3rd ser., 44, no. 3 (October 1987): 689–721; Rosemary Zagarri, "Morals, Manners, and the Republican Mother," *American Quarterly* 44 (June 1992): 192–215; and, in the wake of the reception of Habermas though not always formulated in his terms, see Cornelia Hughes Dayton, *Women before the Bar: Gender, Law, and Society in Connecticut, 1639–1789* (Chapel Hill, 1995); Mary Beth Norton, *Founding Mothers and Fathers:*

Gendered Power and the Forming of American Society (New York, 1996); David S. Shields, *Civil Tongues and Polite Letters in British America* (Chapel Hill, 1997); Bruce Burgett, *Sentimental Bodies: Sex, Gender, and Citizenship in the Early Republic* (Princeton, 1998); Julie Ellison, *Cato's Tears and the Making of Anglo-American Emotion* (Chicago, 1999); Richard Godbeer, *Sexual Revolution in Early America* (Baltimore, 2002); Ruth Bloch, *Gender and Morality in Anglo-American Culture, 1650–1800* (Berkeley, 2003); and Elizabeth Maddox Dillon, *The Gender of Freedom: Fictions of Liberalism and the Literary Public Sphere* (Stanford, 2004).

9. Roger Chartier, ed., *A History of Private Life: Passions of the Renaissance*, trans. Arthur Goldhammer (1985; Cambridge, Mass., 1989); Joan Landes, *Women and the Public Sphere in the Age of the French Revolution* (Ithaca, 1988); Chartier, *The Cultural Origins of the French Revolution*, trans. Lydia G. Cochrane (Durham, 1991); Dena Goodman, "Public Sphere and Private Life: Toward a Synthesis of Current Historiographical Approaches to the Old Regime," *History and Theory* 31 (1992): 1–20.

10. On transformations of "self" and "society" in the eighteenth century, see Dror Wahrman, *The Making of the Modern Self: Identity and Culture in Eighteenth-Century England* (London, 2004), and Mary Poovey, "The Liberal Civil Subject and the Social in Eighteenth-Century British Moral Philosophy," *Public Culture* 14, no. 1 (Winter 2002): 125–45.

11. Story mentioned the project of "a poem of about fifteen hundred lines, on 'The Power of Solitude'" in a letter to Thomas Welsh on October 9, 1799, published a first version in 1802, and revised and expanded the poem for a second edition in 1804. See William W. Story, ed., *Life and Letters of Joseph Story*, 2 vols. (Boston, 1851), 1:83; and Joseph Story, *The Power of Solitude: A Poem in Two Parts*, 2nd ed. (Salem, 1804). An important intertext is Sarah Wentworth Morton's *The Virtues of Society* (Boston, 1799), which Story praised in his letter to Welsh. On sympathy, see Elizabeth Barnes, *States of Sympathy: Seduction and Democracy in the American Novel* (New York, 1997), and Julia A. Stern, *The Plight of Feeling: Sympathy and Dissent in the Early American Novel* (Chicago, 1997). On fascination with narratives of the "individual isolated in the pursuit of self-satisfactions that could not easily be publicly justified," see Jonathan Lamb, *Preserving the Self in the South Seas 1680–1740* (Chicago, 2001; quote at p. 4). For French and British interest in the consequences of isolation and the issue of presociality, see Julia V. Douthwaite, *The Wild Girl, Natural Man, and the Monster: Dangerous Experiments in the Age of Enlightenment* (Chicago, 2002), esp. 93–133.

12. Magazine articles about hermits increased from the 1780s to the 1790s, but literary magazines may not be the best place to look for popular fascination. American almanacs provide a better indication of popular interest in hermits, and with over twenty almanacs mentioning hermits or featuring stories about

hermits, the 1780s represent the high point of interest (and almanacs printed in late 1787 for the year 1788 represent the decade's high point).

13. Lavinia, "The Hermitess; Or, Fair Secluder," *Massachusetts Magazine* 2 (November 1790): 689.

14. On preferences for "exit" over "voice" in early America, see Albert O. Hirschman, "Exit and Voice in American Ideology and Practice," *Exit, Voice, and Loyalty: Responses to Decline in Firms, Organizations, and States* (Cambridge, Mass., 1970), 106–19; and see Hirschman, *Crossing Boundaries: Selected Writings* (New York, 1998), 93–110.

15. Johann Georg Zimmerman, *Solitude Considered, with Respect to Its Influence upon the Mind and the Heart*, trans. J. B. Mercier (Leipzig, 1784–85; New London, Conn., 1806), 216–17, cited in Alexander Nemerov, *The Body of Raphaelle Peale: Still Life and Selfhood, 1812–1824* (Berkeley, 2001), 26.

16. For changing meanings, see Raymond Williams, "Private," *Keywords: A Vocabulary of Culture and Society*, rev. ed. (New York, 1985), 242.

17. "The Hermit, no. II," *American Magazine* (Philadelphia) 1 (December 1758): 123–25.

18. "Theodore, or the Hermit, no. VIII," *American Magazine* (Philadelphia) 2 (October 1759): 623.

19. John Dickinson, *Letters from a Farmer in Pennsylvania to the Inhabitants of the British Colonies* (Philadelphia, 1767), in *Empire and Nation*, ed. Forrest McDonald (Englewood Cliffs, N.J., 1962), 3 (Letter I), 38 (Letter VII).

20. [Thomas Hopkinson], *Liberty, A Poem . . . said to be Written by a Hermit in New-Jersey* (Philadelphia, 1769), 5; [Francis Hopkinson], *A Pretty Story Written in . . . 2774* (Philadelphia, 1774), 3; and [Israel Dewey], *A Letter to the Rev. Samuel Hopkins . . . By a Lunar Hermit,* ([Newport], 1774).

21. John Pomfret, "The Choice," in *Eighteenth-Century English Literature*, ed. Geoffrey Tillotson, Paul Fussell, and Marshall Waingrow (San Diego, 1969), 790–92 (lines 5, 91, and 96).

22. Dell Upton, *Architecture in the United States* (New York, 1998), 31, citing Edwin Morris Betts, ed., *Thomas Jefferson's Garden Book, 1766–1824* (Philadelphia, 1944), 25–26.

23. William Livingston, *Philosophic Solitude; or the Choice of a Rural Life* (1747; Trenton, 1782), lines 87–92.

24. Philip Freneau, "Retirement," *The Poems of Philip Freneau, Written Chiefly during the Late War* (Philadelphia, 1786), 59.

25. Philip Freneau, "The Hermit of Saba," *The Miscellaneous Works of Philip Freneau* (Philadelphia, 1788), 34. For the population of Saba in 1775, see Lester J. Cappon, Barbara Bartz Petchenik, and John Hamilton Long, eds., *Atlas of Early American History: The Revolutionary Era, 1760–1790* (Princeton, 1976), 98.

26. James Otis, *The Rights of the British Colonies Asserted and Proved* (Boston, 1764), 10–11.

NOTES TO PAGES 224–228346   NOTES TO PAGES 224–228

27. J. G. A. Pocock, *Barbarism and Religion*, vol. 2, *Narratives of Civil Government* (Cambridge, England, 1999).

28. Thomas Paine, *Common Sense*, ed. Isaac Kramnick (New York, 1988), 66; see also Jacob Duché, *The Duty of Standing Fast in our Spiritual and Temporal Liberties* (Philadelphia, 1775), 11–12.

29. James Wilson, "Lecture VII: Of Man, As a Member of Society," in *The Works of James Wilson*, ed. Robert Green McCloskey, 2 vols. (Cambridge, Mass., 1967), 1:235.

30. Pennsylvania Convention, Declaration of Rights, 1776, in Jack N. Rakove, ed., *Declaring Rights*, 85.

31. Wilson, *Consideration on the Nature and Extent of the Legislative Authority of the British Parliament* (1774), in *Works*, 2:723.

32. Wilson, "Lecture XII: On the Natural Rights of Individuals," in *Works*, 2:588–89.

33. Constitution of Vermont (1777), chap. 1, art. 1.

34. See, for example, [Robert Voorhis], *Life and Adventures of Robert, the Hermit of Massachusetts* (Providence, 1829).

35. Alexander Hamilton, *The Farmer Refuted* (New York, 1775), in *The Papers of Alexander Hamilton*, ed. Harold C. Syrett and Jacob E. Cooke, 27 vols. (New York, 1961–87), 1:122.

36. Otis, *Rights of the British Colonies*, 31.

37. Thomas Paine, *Rights of Man, Common Sense, and Other Political Writings*, ed. Mark Philp (New York, 1995), 95.

38. Joseph Brant, *American Museum* (Philadelphia) 6 (September 1789): 226–27, reprinted in Colin G. Calloway, ed., *The World Turned Upside Down: Indian Voices from Early America* (Boston, 1994), 179–80.

39. [Thomas More], *The Common-wealth of Utopia* (Philadelphia, 1753), 93–94 (bk. 2, chap. 7).

40. "Equality—A Political Romance" appeared in *The Temple of Reason* (Philadelphia) in 1802, and was republished in 1837. The Lithconians, the narrator noted, had "no less than ten infallible constitutions, all declared to be founded on the rights of man, in the short period of forty years" (n.p.).

41. For a similar tension in revolutionary France, see Lynn Hunt, *Politics, Culture, and Class in the French Revolution* (Berkeley, 1984), 72–73.

42. James Madison, "Vices of the Political System of the United States," April 1787, in *PJM*, 9:353.

43. In his earliest commonplace book, Madison transcribed the maxim "The King's and the People's rights never agree better than by not being spoken of" from the *Memoirs* of Jean Francois Paul de Gondi, Cardinal de Retz; see *PJM*, 1:8.

44. John Trumbull, *Autobiography, Reminiscences and Letters of John Trumbull, from 1756 to 1841* (New York, 1841), 89.

45. Anton Ashley Cooper, Third Earl of Shaftesbury, *Characteristicks of Men, Manners, Opinions, Times*, 3 vols. ([London], 1711), 1:162, 170, 158, 175; 2:319. For the latter's availability in America, see Janice G. Schimmelman, "A Checklist of European Treatises on Art and Essays on Aesthetics Available in America through 1815," *Proceedings of the American Antiquarian Society* 93 (1983): 154–61, 172. Among aesthetic treatises, only Edmund Burke's *Sublime and Beautiful* (London, 1757) circulated more widely before 1815.

46. *Letters between Theophilus and Eugenio, on the moral pravity of man* (Philadelphia, 1747) cited Hobbes to the effect that "every man is born in a state of war" between reason and appetite rather than a true struggle between individuals (p. 2).

47. Hamilton, *Farmer Refuted* (New York, 1775), in *Papers of Hamilton*, 1:86–87; Charles Inglis, *The True Interest Of America Impartially Stated*, 2nd ed. (Philadelphia, 1776), vi.

48. [Mercy Otis Warren], *The Group* (Boston, 1775), 11.

49. On an "Appeal to Heaven," see T. H. Breen, *The Lockean Moment: The Language of Rights on the Eve of the American Revolution* (Oxford, 2001).

50. James Smither (engraver), *The Patriotic American Farmer. J-n D-k-ns-n Esqr. Barrister at Law* ([Philadelphia], 1768).

51. For the lone contemporary illustration, see [John Norman?], *The Grand Convention*, woodcut from the title page of *Weatherwise's Federal Almanack* (Boston, 1787), in Richard B. Bernstein and Kym S. Rice, *Are We to Be a Nation? The Making of the Constitution* (Cambridge, Mass., 1987), 154–55.

52. See George Washington to the President of Congress, "In Convention, September 17, 1787," in *The Report of the Constitutional Convention* (Philadelphia, 1787), broadside.

53. [David Ramsay], "Civis, To the Citizens of South Carolina," *Columbian Herald* (Charleston), February 4, 1788, in *DHRC*, 16:22.

54. "An Old Whig" IV, *Philadelphia Independent Gazetteer*, October 27, 1787, in *DHRC*, 13:500–501; "Vox Populi," *Massachusetts Gazette*, November 6, 1787, in *DHRC*, 4:223.

55. *The Federalist*, ed. Jacob E. Cooke (Middletown, Conn., 1961), 469, 238. See also Diary of Gouverneur Morris, in *Life and Writings of Gouverneur Morris*, ed. Jared Sparks, 3 vols. (Boston, 1832), 1:311 (1789).

56. Madison, *PJM*, 9:356 and 10:213.

57. In the greatly enlarged 1787 French edition of *Letters from an American Farmer* (rarely examined today), J. Hector St. John de Crèvecoeur recounted the origin and establishment of an imaginary community of English, French, German, Irish, and Scottish settlers called "Socialburg" located in northwestern New York state; see *Lettres d'un cultivateur américain*, 3 vols. (Paris, 1787), 3:56–96. For squatters and the Land Ordinance, see Peter S. Onuf, *Statehood and Union: A History of the Northwest Ordinance* (Bloomington, Ind.,

1987), 21–43. Other popular stories also focused on the lone inhabitants of caves, especially the "Panther Narrative," which first appeared as "A surprising account of the discovery of a lady who was taken by the Indians in the year 1777, and after making her escape, she retired to a lonely cave, where she lived nine years," in *Bickerstaff's Almanack, for the Year of Our Lord, 1788* (Norwich, Conn., [1787]), and was reprinted at least ten times before 1801.

58. *A wonderful Discovery of a HERMIT! Who lived upwards of 200 Years* (n.p., 1786).

59. *An Account of the Wonderful Old Hermit's Death and Burial* ([Boston], 1787).

60. "John Humble," "Address of the Lowborn," *Independent Gazetteer* (Philadelphia), October 29, 1787, in *DHRC*, 2:205.

61. *The Picture Exhibition* (Albany, 1790), broadside. The image derives from a woodcut illustration of the Old Hermit printed in Springfield, Massachusetts, in 1786.

62. Thomas Spence claimed he coined the phrase "rights of man" a decade before Paine when "inspired by the independence of a hermit living in a cave by the sea, he inscribed on the cave wall, 'Ye Landlords vile, who man's peace marr/ Come levy rents here if you can/Your stewards and lawyers I defy;/And live with all the RIGHTS OF MAN'"; see Gregory Claeys, *Thomas Paine: Social and Political Thought* (Boston, 1989), 107 n. 10. I thank Alfred F. Young for this citation. For narratives of people-making, see Rogers M. Smith, *Stories of Peoplehood: The Politics and Morals of Political Membership* (Cambridge, England, 2003).

63. *Daily Advertiser* (New York), September 2, 1789.

64. The voice of an antislavery hermit chastised readers in the 1790s, warning that "there shall arise wars and revolts; the savages in the west, and the slaves in the south shall do unto you as you have done unto them." The text probably appeared first in German in 1792 and went through at least twelve editions in English over the next decade; see *Remarkable Prophecy, of a Certain Hermit, Who . . . was discovered last Spring, by Doctor Peter Snyder* (n.p., [1793?]), 9.

65. On reading history out of (rather than into) literary texts, see Jacqueline Goldsby, *A Spectacular Secret: Lynching in American Life and Literature* (Chicago, 2006).

Chapter Six

1. Massachusetts Constitution (1780), preamble; James Madison, "Memorial and Remonstrance against Religious Assessments," June 20, 1785, in *PJM*, 8:297; Continental Congress, Declaration of Independence, July 4, 1776.

2. Thomas Wilson to Archibald Stuart, November 4, 1787, in *DHRC*, 8:145.

3. Virginia Declaration of Rights (1776), art. 16.

4. William Williams, *American Mercury* (Hartford), February 11, 1788, in *Debates on the Constitution*, ed. Bernard Bailyn, 2 vols. (New York, 1993), 2:193–94.

5. Rush to Adams, June 15, 1789, in Benjamin Rush, *Letters*, ed. L. H. Butterfield, 2 vols. (Princeton, 1951), 1:517.

6. Madison Resolution, June 8, 1789, in *Creating the Bill of Rights: The Documentary Records from the First Federal Congress*, ed. Helen E. Veit, Kenneth R. Bowling, and Charlene Bangs Bickford (Baltimore, 1991), 12. New Hampshire, Virginia, and New York had requested protections for religious freedom; only Virginia (following Article 16 of the state Declaration of Rights) mentioned "our Creator."

7. See "Forum: God and the Enlightenment," *American Historical Review* 108, no. 4 (October 2003): 1057–1104; Henry F. May, *The Enlightenment in America* (New York, 1976), 3–101; Robert A. Ferguson, "The American Enlightenment, 1750–1820," in Sacvan Bercovitch, ed., *The Cambridge History of American Literature*, 8 vols. (Cambridge, England, 1994–2002), 1:390–425.

8. See Vernon Louis Parrington, *Main Currents in American Thought* (New York, 1930), and Robert A. Ferguson, "The Dialectic of Liberty," *Reading the Early Republic* (Cambridge, Mass., 2004), 51–83. On the Great Awakening and the Revolution, see Alan Heimert, *Religion and the American Mind from the Great Awakening to the Revolution* (Cambridge, Mass., 1966), and Patricia U. Bonomi, *Under the Cope of Heaven: Religion, Society, and Politics in Colonial America* (New York, 1986).

9. Jon Butler, *Awash in a Sea of Faith: Christianizing the American People* (Cambridge, Mass., 1990). On the absence of God in the Constitution, see Susan Jacoby, *Freethinkers: A History of American Secularism* (New York, 2004); Gertrude Himmelfarb, *The Roads to Modernity: The British, French, and American Enlightenments* (New York, 2004), esp. 204–5; Frank Lambert, *The Founding Fathers and the Place of Religion in America* (Princeton, 2003), 246–53; and Isaac Kramnick and R. Laurence Moore, *The Godless Constitution: The Case against Religious Correctness* (New York, 1996).

10. I take the phrase from Ruth H. Bloch, "The Social and Political Base of Millennial Literature in Late Eighteenth-Century America," *American Quarterly* 40 (September 1988): 393.

11. The decade aggregations conform to Mark Noll's account of "evangelical decline" between 1760 and 1790; the peaks and depressions correspond with Ruth Bloch's description of the rise and fall of millennialism in the revolutionary era and its revival in the 1790s. See Noll, *America's God: From Edwards to Lincoln* (New York, 2003), 161, and Ruth Bloch, *Visionary Republic: Millennial Themes in American Thought, 1756–1800* (Cambridge, England, 1985).

12. On press and pulpit, see Frank Lambert, *Inventing the "Great Awakening"* (Princeton, 1999), 214 (table 6.1).

13. Readex Digital Collections, Early American Imprints, Series I, Evans

(1639–1800). I do not distinguish between titles (separate publications) and imprints and do not measure word frequency within imprints. The optical character recognition (OCR) technology is not always accurate, and I have checked the results of electronic searches as well as I could. The best index may be title pages, if only because they are easily verifiable.

14. However, "Supreme Being" doubled in absolute use in every decade from the 1750s (present in 15 texts) to the 1780s (134 texts) and then almost quadrupled (to 501 texts) in the 1790s. The 233 proclamations for days of thanksgiving made by New England colonies and later states as well as the Continental Congress from 1676 to 1800 give some indication of the significance of the various terms (and order of appearance): "God" appeared ninety-three times, beginning in 1676; "providence" appeared eighty-seven times, beginning in 1696; "Christ" appeared thirty-two times, beginning in 1745; "religion" appeared thirty-four times, beginning in 1757; "creator" appeared" fifteen times, beginning in 1759; "deity" appeared once in 1775; and "Supreme Being" appeared three times, all in Rhode Island, beginning in 1794.

15. G. Thomas Tanselle, "Some Statistics on American Printing," in Bernard Bailyn and John B. Hench, eds., *The Press and the American Revolution* (Worcester, Mass., 1980), 315–63, esp. 329 (table 2B); Noll, *America's God*, 163 (table 9.2).

16. For cautions about bibliographic subject fields, see "Appendix 1: Connecticut Imprints," in Christopher Grasso, *A Speaking Aristocracy: Transforming Public Discourse in Eighteenth-Century Connecticut* (Chapel Hill, 1999), 487–90, esp. 487 n. 1.

17. Analysis of almanacs, juvenile literature, and novels confirms the major trend of higher percentages in the 1750s giving way to lower ones in the revolutionary era and beginning to revive in the 1790s, but only the almanac had a generic stability in the second half of the eighteenth century.

18. The category of "sermons" contains individual sermons on a variety of occasions (artillery day, election day, fast day, ordination, etc.) as well as collections of sermons. I am grateful to Christopher Grasso for helping me to see why sermons may not have been a genre in the eighteenth century.

19. On this general distinction, see Mechal Sobel, *Teach Me Dreams: The Search for Self in the Revolutionary Era* (Princeton, 2000).

20. On correlating print and event, see Emmanuel le Roy Ladurie, Anette Smedley-Weill, and André Zysberg, "French Book Production from 1454: A Quantitative Analysis," *Library History* 15, no. 2 (November 1999): 83–98.

21. The essays in Christian Smith, ed., *The Secular Revolution: Power, Interests, and Conflict in the Secularization of American Public Life* (Berkeley, 2003), date "secularization" to the 1870s, but for the problems of defining and dating "the secular," see Talal Asad, *Formations of the Secular: Christianity, Islam, Modernity* (Stanford, 2003).

22. See David A. Bell, *The Cult of the Nation in France: Inventing Nationalism, 1680–1800* (Cambridge, Mass., 2001).

23. John Adams to Samuel Chase, July 9, 1776, in *LDC*, 4:415.

24. August 20, 1776, in *Journals of the Continental Congress, 1774–1789*, ed. Worthington Chauncey Ford et al., 34 vols. (Washington, D.C., 1904–37), 4:689.

25. Report on a Seal for the United States, with Related Papers [August 20, 1776], in *PTJ*, 1:494–97.

26. On the emblem, see John Barrell, *The Political Theory of Painting from Reynolds to Hazlitt: "The Body of the Public"* (New Haven, 1986), 27–33; and David H. Solkin, *Painting for Money: The Visual Arts and the Public Sphere in Eighteenth-Century England* (New Haven, 1992), 63–65, 203–5.

27. Shaftesbury, "The Judgment of Hercules," *Characteristicks of Men, Manners, Opinions, Times*, 2nd ed., 3 vols. ([London], 1714), 3:355–56.

28. John Adams to Abigail Adams, August 14, 1776, in *Adams Family Correspondence*, ed. L. H. Butterfield et al., 8 vols. to date (Cambridge, Mass., 1963–), 2:ix–x, 97 n. 4.

29. Report of the Seal Committee, August 20, 1776, in *Journals of the Continental Congress*, 4:690. The *Journals* report that the "Goddess Justice" had replaced the soldier, but a copy of the report in the hand of John Lovell does not reflect the change (see 690 n. 1).

30. James Hutson, *Religion and the Founding of the American Republic* (Washington, D.C., 1998), 50.

31. See the reproduction of the manuscript in Hutson, *Religion and the Founding*, 50; see also a transcript in *Journals of the Continental Congress*, 4:690 n. 1. On Franklin as the source of the phrase "Rebellion to Tyrants is Obedience to God," see *PTJ*, 1:677–79.

32. *Adams Family Correspondence*, ed. Butterfield et al., 2:96.

33. For the most recent commentary, see Hutson, *Religion and the Founding*, 51.

34. *The Papers of Alexander Hamilton*, ed. Harold C. Syrett, Jacob E. Cooke, et al., 27 vols. (New York, 1961–87), 1:122.

35. *PJA*, 1:111–12; James Hutson, *The Founders on Religion* (Princeton, 2005), 196.

36. John Dickinson, *Letters of Fabius, in 1788 . . . and on the present Situation of Public Affairs* (Wilmington, 1797), 184n; see also Hutson, *The Founders on Religion*, 196.

37. For the alteration between draft and approved text, see Jack N. Rakove, *Declaring Rights: A Brief History with Documents* (Boston, 1998), 77. Julian P. Boyd and Pauline Maier agree that Mason's draft had little effect on Jefferson's phrasing; see Boyd, *The Declaration of Independence: The Evolution of the Text* (Princeton, 1945), 24–25, and Maier, *American Scripture: Making the Declaration of Independence* (New York, 1997), 126.

38. *PTJ*, 1:423 and 427 n. 2.

39. Boyd, *Declaration of Independence*, 67.

40. In a bid to win a government printing contract in 1785, Isaac Collins of Trenton printed a specimen of the Declaration in which he capitalized the words "God" and "Creator," but other contemporary printings did not; see *Proposals Made by Isaac Collins, for Printing a New Edition of the Journals of Congress* ([Trenton, 1785]), 2; Rough Draft in Boyd, *Declaration of Independence*, 27; Declaration of Causes of Taking Up Arms, in *A Decent Respect to the Opinions of Mankind: Congressional State Papers, 1774–1776*, ed. James H. Hutson (Washington, D.C., 1975), 91, 96.

41. Pennsylvania Constitution (1776), art. 2; North Carolina Declaration of Rights (1776), art. 19.

42. New Hampshire Constitution (1783), arts. 3 and 4.

43. Maryland Constitution (1776), art. 33.

44. Vermont Constitution (1777), chap. 1, sec. 3.

45. Massachusetts Constitution (1780), art. 2.

46. See Bernard Schwartz, *The Roots of the Bill of Rights*, 5 vols. (New York, 1980), 2:370.

47. See *The Popular Sources of Political Authority: Documents on the Massachusetts Constitution of 1780*, ed. Oscar and Mary Handlin (Cambridge, Mass., 1966), 29–33.

48. South Carolina Constitution (1778), art. 38.

49. New Jersey Constitution (1776), art. 18.

50. New York Constitution (1777), art. 38.

51. John Jay, "Charge to the Ulster Grand Jury," September 9, 1777, in Hutson, *The Founders on Religion*, 135.

52. Delaware Declaration of Rights (1776), sec. 3.

53. Maryland Constitution (1776), art. 33.

54. Georgia Constitution (1777), art. 56.

55. See the 1779 warning-out order, reproduced in Katherine E. Conlin, "Warning Out in Windsor, 1779–1817," *Vermont History* 23, no. 3 (July 1955): 246.

56. See the action on the petition of listers of the town of Windsor, February 22 and 26, 1783, in *State Papers of Vermont: Journal of the House of Assembly*, 3, no. 2 (Rutland, Vt., 1918–): 168, 178. For Thomson's presentation of his bill for "supplying this house with coal, candles, &c.," see February 22, 1781, *State Papers of Vermont: Journal of the House of Assembly*, 3, no. 1, at 206–7.

57. William G. McLoughlin, *New England Dissent, 1630-1883: The Baptists and the Separation of Church and State*, 2 vols. (Cambridge, Mass., 1971), 2:798.

58. For Leland on certificates in 1791, see McLoughlin, *New England Dissent*.

59. "A Vermontean," *Vermont Journal*, July 21, 1784.

60. The lawsuit between Joseph Thomson and the East Windsor Church is described as a cause celebre in Elisha Ransom, "An Appeal to the Public," *Vermont Journal*, July 5, 1785.

61. By 1787, there were eleven members; by 1790, seventy-five members. The church lacked its own meeting house until 1802, and had a difficult time compensating its minister. Cited in Henry Crocker, *History of the Baptists in Vermont* (Bellows Falls, Vt., 1913), 241–44; see also John Peak, *Memoir of Elder John Peak* (Boston, 1832).

62. "Just published for, and sold by, Deacon Joseph Thomson, at Windsor, a Letter on Toleration, by Mr. John Locke. A few Copies of the above Letter, may be had at this Office" (an advertisement in *Spooner's Vermont Journal*, January 26 and February 9, 1789).

63. Other possible editors of Thomson's edition include Baptists Elisha Ransom (Thomson's former minister in Woodstock) and John Peak (Thomson's current minister). Peak had little education, and he records in his autobiography that he had initially believed that the Baptists in Vermont would not ordain him; once ordained in 1787 he set to reading a list of books, including Locke's *Essay Concerning Human Understanding* and Hugh Blair's *Lectures on Rhetoric*, in order to compensate for his "want of learning and theological information." See Peak, *Memoir*, 63.

64. John Locke, *A Letter Concerning Toleration*, 4th ed. (Windsor, Vt., 1788), title page. For the source of the epigraph, see Richard Price, *Observations on the Importance of the American Revolution* (London, 1784), 23, 29.

65. Locke, *Letter Concerning Toleration*, 60, 43.

66. Locke, "Letter Concerning Toleration," in David Wootton, ed., *Political Writings of John Locke* (New York, 1993), 426; see also Thomson's edition, 57.

67. Locke, *Letter Concerning Toleration*, iv.

68. On Madison and Locke, see *PJM*, 8:297.

69. "Notes for a Speech Favoring Revision of the Virginia Convention of 1776," June 14 or 21, 1784, in *PJM*, 8:77–78.

70. "Memorial and Remonstrance," June 20, 1785, in *PJM*, 8:299–304.

71. On the Westmoreland petition, see *PJM*, 8:297–98.

72. South Carolina Constitution (1778), art. 38.

73. Thomas Paine, *Common Sense*, ed. Edward Larkin (Toronto, 2004), 74.

74. McLoughlin, *New England Dissent*, 1:92.

75. John Norton, *The Heart of New England Rent* (Cambridge, 1659), cited in McLoughlin, *New England Dissent*, 1:93–94. This paragraph relies on McLoughlin's account of the different understandings of conscience in early New England.

76. William Vesey, *A Sermon Preaced . . . at the Funeral of the Right Honourable John Lord Lovelace . . .* ([New York], 1709), 8.

77. Nathaniel Appleton, *The Clearest and Surest Marks of Our Being so Led*

by the Spirit of God as to Demonstrate that We Are the Children of God (Boston, 1743), 99.

78. Hester Chapone, *Letters on the Improvement of the Mind. Addressed to a Young Lady*, 2 vols. (Worcester, 1783), 1:34–35. The passage was also reprinted in J. Hamilton Moore, *The Gentleman and Lady's Monitor* (New York, 1790), 277.

79. [Samuel Spring], *A Friendly Dialogue . . . upon the Nature of Duty* (Newbury-Port, Mass., 1784), 77, 80.

80. [Jonathan Mitchell Sewall], *An Oration, delivered . . . on the Fourth of July, 1788* (Portsmouth, N.H., 1788), 11.

81. Lycurgus III, *XIV Sermons on the Characters of Jacob's Fourteen Sons* (Philadelphia, 1789), 12.

82. *The Hapless Orphan . . . By an American Lady*, 2 vols. (Boston, 1793), 2:87.

83. See Rhys Isaac, *The Transformation of Virginia, 1740–1790* (Chapel Hill, 1982), 273–95.

84. J. G. A. Pocock, "Religious Freedom and the Desacralization of Politics: From the English Civil Wars to the Virginia Statute," in *The Virginia Statute for Religious Freedom: Its Evolution and Consequences in American History*, ed. Merrill D. Peterson and Robert C. Vaughn (New York, 1988), 61 (and see 61–66).

85. See *PTJ*, 2:548n.

86. Jefferson's *Autobiography*, cited in *PTJ*, 2:552 n. 3. Boyd notes that "there is no record in the Journals [of Congress] of this particular amendment" (ibid.).

87. See *PTJ*, 2:550–52.

88. See *Acte de la République de Virginie, qui établit la liberté de Religion* ([Paris, 1786]).

89. Richard Price dropped the claim that it was in God's "Almighty power" to propagate religion by coercions on mind and body. [Richard Price], *Act for establishing Religious Freedom, passed in the Assembly of Virginnia [sic], in the beginning of the Year, 1786* (London, [1786]).

90. See Madison to Jefferson, January 22, 1786, in *PJM*, 8:474, 481 n. 5.

91. On the circulation of the Virginia statute by Baptists in New England, see McLoughlin, *New England Dissent*, 1:619 n. 1, and 2:1008. McLoughlin finds the first printing in Massachusetts in the *Independent Chronicle* (Boston), April 20, 1780, and notes that the town of Bellingham proposed the Virginia bill as an alternative to Article III of the proposed state constitution (1:619 n. 1).

92. *Loudon's New-York Packet*, February 9, 1786, repeated the list of Virginia enactments from the Philadelphia paper but did not reprint the act.

93. *A Memorial and Remonstrance* (Worcester, Mass., 1786), 2.

94. *The American Recorder and Charleston Advertiser* (Charleston, S.C.), February 17, 1786, and March 3, 1786.

95. "A Citizen of Philadelphia" [Swanwick], "Consideration on an Act of the Legislature of Virginia," *Columbian Herald*, May 29, June 1, June 5, June 8, and June 12, 1786. Curiously the paper did not delete Swanwick's comments about slavery. On the evolution of religious freedom in South Carolina, see *The Dawn of Religious Freedom in South Carolina*, ed. James Lowell Underwood and W. Lewis Burke (Columbia, S.C., 2006).

96. For Swanwick's biography, see Roland M. Baumann, "John Swanwick: Spokesman for 'Merchant-Republicanism' in Philadelphia, 1790–1798," *Pennsylvania Magazine of History and Biography* 97, no. 2 (April 1973): 131–82, esp. 138–41.

97. Swanwick's poem, "Occasioned by the sickness and death of Mrs. Luica Magaw," is included in Samuel Magaw, *Notes on the Last Illness, and Death, of a Most Beloved Friend* (Philadelphia, 1790), 3–4. For the 1786 sermon, see Samuel Magaw, *A Sermon Delivered . . . on the 4th of July, 1786* (Philadelphia, 1786).

98. [John Swanwick], *Considerations on an Act of the Legislature of Virginia, Entitled, An Act for the Establishment of Religious Freedom* (Philadelphia, 1786), iii–vi, 1.

99. Ibid., 4, 6–7, 19, 21–24.

100. Ibid., 24–25.

101. Ibid., 8–9, 11.

102. Madison, "Memorial and Remonstrance," in *PJM*, 8:299.

103. Robert Whitehill at Pennsylvania Convention, December 12, 1787, *Debates*, ed. Bailyn, 1:871.

104. Joseph Barrell to Nathaniel Barrell, December 20, 1787, in *Debates*, ed. Bailyn, 1:588.

105. James Madison, *Federalist* 37, in *The Federalist*, ed. Jacob E. Cooke (Middletown, Conn., 1961), 238.

106. [James Winthrop], "Agrippa, no. XII," *Massachusetts Gazette* (Boston), January 15, 1788, in *Debates*, ed. Bailyn, 1:764.

107. "K." [Franklin], to the Editor, *Federal Gazette* (Philadelphia), April 8, 1788, in *Debates*, ed. Bailyn, 2:401.

108. Jefferson to Madison, December 20, 1787, in *Debates*, ed. Bailyn, 1:210.

109. Henry, Virginia Convention, June 12, 1788, in *Debates*, ed. Bailyn, 2:677.

110. Madison, Virginia Convention, June 12, 1788, in *Debates*, ed. Bailyn, 2:690.

111. Virginia Convention, June 17, 1788, in *Debates*, ed. Bailyn, 2:715.

112. Virginia Convention, June 25, 1788, in *Debates*, ed. Bailyn, 2:752–53.

113. Virginia Convention, June 6, 1788, in *Debates*, ed. Bailyn, 2:618.

114. *Federalist* 51, in *Debates*, ed. Bailyn, 2:166.

115. William G. McLoughlin, *Soul Liberty: The Baptists' Struggle in New England, 1630–1833* (Hanover, N.H., 1991), 249. McLoughlin's work is directed

against the misunderstanding that holds that separation of church and state "as we know it today came primarily, if not entirely, from the rationalistic spirit of the Enlightenment" (ix).

116. Crèvecoeur, cited in Jon Butler, "Why Revolutionary America Wasn't a 'Christian Nation,'" in James Hutson, *Religion and the New Republic: Faith in the Founding of America* (Lanham, Md., 2000), 187.

117. Madison Resolution, June 8, 1789, in *Creating the Bill of Rights*, 11–12.

118. House Committee Report, July 28, 1789, in *Creating the Bill of Rights*, 29.

119. Copy in the Ruggles Collection, Newberry Library, Chicago.

120. House of Representative Debates, August 14, 1789, in *Daily Advertiser*, August 15, 1789, in *Creating the Bill of Rights*, 128–29. See also the report of this day's debates in *Gazette of the United States*, August 19, 1789, in ibid., 132–33.

121. *The Congressional Register*, August 13, 1789, in *Creating the Bill of Rights*, 105–6 (and see 105, 125, 120).

122. Ibid., in *Creating the Bill of Rights*, 106–7 (and see 106, 120, 118).

Epilogue

1. Robert C. Smith, "Liberty Displaying the Arts and Sciences: A Philadelphia Allegory by Samuel Jennings," *Winterthur Portfolio* 2 (1965): 89.

2. Montesquieu, *The Spirit of the Laws*, trans. Thomas Nugent, 2 vols. (1750; New York, 1949), 1:35 (bk. III, chap. 6).

3. Adams to James Lloyd, March 29 and 30, 1815, in *The Works of John Adams*, ed. Charles Francis Adams, 10 vols. (Boston, 1850–56), 10:149–50.

4. Simon Bolivar, "Address Delivered at the Second National Congress of Venezuela in Angostura" (February 15, 1819), in Miguel Schor, "Constitutionalism through the Looking Glass of Latin America," *Texas International Law Journal* 41 (Winter 2006): 16–17.

Index

abolition of slavery, 3, 172, 207–9
Account of the Wonderful Old Hermit's Death and Burial, 236–38, 237 fig. 18
Ackerman, Bruce, 315n114
Act for Establishing Religious Freedom (Virginia). *See* Virginia Act for Establishing Religious Freedom
Act for the Abolition of Slavery (Rhode Island), 208
Act for the Gradual Abolition of Slavery (Pennsylvania), 3, 304n3
Act to Enable Towns . . . to Erect Proper Houses for Public Worship (Vermont), 269
Act to Prohibit the Importation of Slaves (United States), 209
Adams, Abigail: painting and, 138–41; Pope's *Essay on Man* and, 28, 33; Shays' Rebellion and, 34; Seal of the United States and, 259–60
Adams, John: constitutional history and, 15; as constitutional "physician," 238; *Defence* mocked, 238; *Defence of the Constitutions of the United States of America,* 28, 34, 132, 140; depicted by Trumbull, 230; on end of slavery in Massachusetts, 210–11; on form versus administration, 31, 34, 36; on function of Continental Congress, 45; God in Constitution and, 244; on Latin American constitutionalism, 299–300; Massachusetts Constitution and, 33, 63, 241; miniature paintings of, 140–41; on Paine's *Common Sense,* 41, 131; painting and, 138–41; on political architects, 64–66; Pope's *Essay on Man* and, 27–28; on refinement in politics, 108; on representation as "portrait in miniature," 16, 128–34; rights and, 262; Seal of the United States and, 258–61; Shays' Rebellion and, 34; sons of a political liability, 78; *Spectator* and, 102–3; Stevens criticizes, 72; *Thoughts on Government,* 31, 66, 128–32; transcribes draft Declaration of Independence, 263; on writing as painting, 153
Adams, John Quincy: on Paine's *Rights of Man,* 71, 121–22; Shays' Rebellion and, 34; visual proportionality and, 140
Adams, Samuel, 310n38
Adams, Willi Paul, 307n11, 331n105
Addison, Joseph, 102–3, 106, 115
Address on Slavery (Rush), 190
Address to the Negroes in the State of New-York (Hammon), 203
administration, political, versus form, 27–36
aesthetics, 87, 95; politics and, 8, 97–107, 177–78. *See also* taste
Africa, views of culture in, 205
African-American writers, word "God" and, 253
age of constitutions, 18, 299–301
"Agrippa" (Winthrop), 288
Akers, Charles W., 338n56
Algerine Spy in Philadelphia (Markoe), 110, 113
Allen, Danielle S., 309n16

Allen, Ethan, 28
Allen, Ira, 28
Allen, Theodore, 336n29
almanacs, as stable genre, 350n17
Amar, Akhil Reed, 305n19, 305n20
amendments to the Constitution, 244–45,
   291–95; debate over incorporating or
   appending to 1787 text, 293–95
American Bibliography (Evans), 251
American Magazine (Boston), reprints
   Ralph's "Essay on Taste," 103–4
American Magazine (Philadelphia),
   Smith's "Hermit" essays in, 220–21
American Museum (Philadelphia), 227
American Recorder (Charleston, S.C.),
   reprints Swanwick on religious free-
   dom, 282
American Revolution: central political phi-
   losophy of, 291; civil slavery and, 176;
   iconography of, 2–4, 55–59, 231–32; po-
   litical culture of, 8, 59
American Selection of Lessons in Reading
   (Webster), 158
Amherst, Mass., Shay's Rebellion in, 93
Amory, Hugh, 343n1
Analytical Review (London), 151
Anderson, Jennifer, 304n6
And look thro' Nature, up to Nature's God
   (Trumbull), 228–30, 229 fig. 15
Anecdote for Great Men, 70–71
Ankersmit, F. R., 128, 319n17, 326n13
Anti-Federalists: access of to print, 20;
   adopt Adams's definition of represen-
   tation, 132–33; architectural metaphors
   of, 81–85; Bill of Rights and, 234; burn
   Wilson and McKean in effigy, 35; cite
   text of Constitution more frequently
   than Federalists, 24–25; *Columbian
   Magazine* and, 83–84; on Constitution
   as cure worse than disease, 239; on *The
   Federalist,* 21; on form versus administration, 35; Franklin compares to ancient Jews, 288; on "Godless" Constitution, 242–43; in Massachusetts, 35;
   metaphors of for representation, 126–
   27; in New York, 21; in Pennsylvania,
   35; reprint Federalist pieces, 21; on resemblance in representation, 133–34;
   satires on, 59–60, 288; second convention and, 118–19; sympathy and, 127,

164; theory of representation, 126–27,
   133–34; in Virginia, 289–91. *See also*
   "Agrippa" (Winthrop); "Brutus"
   (Anti-Federalist); "Cornelius" (Anti-
   Federalist); Dallas, Alexander James;
   "DeWitt, John" (Anti-Federalist);
   "Federal Farmer" (Anti-Federalist);
   "Federal Republican" (Anti-Federal-
   ist); Gerry, Elbridge; Henry, Patrick;
   "Impartial Examiner" (Anti-Federal-
   ist); Mason, George; "Poplicola" (Anti-
   Federalist)
Appleton, Nathaniel, 197, 278
Aptheker, Herbert, 340n89
architects, political, 62, 64, 65
architecture, political, 63–71, 79–85
Aristotle, 46
Arminius, Jacobus, 272
Armitage, David, 334n4, 334n5
Armonica, 112
Arnauld, Antoine, 327n36
art, late eighteenth-century theories of,
   117–18
artfulness of runaway slaves, 189
Articles of Confederation: architectural
   metaphors for, 63, 79–80; Congress impotent under, 73–75; Constitution's
   union "more perfect" than, 20, 117;
   function of, 45; Shays' Rebellion and,
   94; Swanwick on, 286–87; term limits in, 44
Asad, Talal, 350n21
Ashton, Samuel, 161
atheists, 272–73

Backus, Isaac, 68, 269, 290
Bailyn, Bernard, 321n48, 326n20, 335n11,
   335n16, 350n15
Banneker, Benjamin, 208–9
Barkan, Leonard, 309n11
Barlow, Joel: on constitutionalism of
   Manco Capac, 107; legal dissertation of,
   108; "On the Genealogy of the Tree of
   Liberty," 59; *Vision of Columbus,* 107
Barnard, John, 51, 52–53
Barnes, Elizabeth, 344n11
Barrell, John, 351n26
Barrell, Joseph, 288
Bartram, John, 28
Bartram, William, 28

Bayle, Pierre, 278
Beattie, James, 190
beauty, 116, 118; as foundation for politics, 121
"Behold! A Fabric now to Freedom rear'd" (Trenchard), 81–84, 82 fig. 8
Belchertown, Mass.: Dickinson's oration on taste and government delivered in, 94–95; votes against Constitution, 88
Belknap, Jeremy, 182, 209–13
Bell, Archibald, 194
Bell, David A., 257, 351n22
Bell, Robert, 61, 62, 312n56
Bellion, Wendy, 324n95
Benezet, Anthony, 196, 207–8, 285
Bercovitch, Sacvan, 349n7
Berlin, Ira, 335n13
Bernstein, Richard B., 347n51
Bestes, Peter, 198
Bhabha, Homi, 335n12, 337n42
Bible, Geneva, 260
Bickford, Charlene Bangs, 349n6
Biddle, Edward, 310n37
Bill Establishing a Provision for Teachers of the Christian Religion (Virginia), 274
Bill for Establishing Religious Freedom (Virginia): Jefferson's draft, 274–75, 280–82, 290. See also Virginia Act for Establishing Religious Freedom
Bill of Rights (Federal): Anti-Federalists campaign for, 234; debates on amendments in First Federal Congress, 291–95; Federalists campaign against, 227–28; Jefferson on lack of, 289
Blackburn, Robin, 336n29
Blackstone, William, 72, 226
Blair, Hugh, 104, 106, 285, 321n43
Blake, William, 193, 195
Bloch, Ruth, 96, 319n15, 343n8, 349n10, 349n11
Blyth, Benjamin, 138
body politic: anatomy of, 45, 47, 53–54; architectural metaphors and, 63, 64; classical and medieval images of, 46–47; constitutional "physicians" and, 238; Constitution and, 119; diversity over homogeneity and, 50; Hobbes on, 47–48, 54; Huntington on, 44–47; Mayflower Compact and, 55; metaphor de-

valued in eighteenth century, 16, 41, 54–55; New England and, 55, 309n17; Paul and, 50; Perkins on, 49; Pufendorf on, 54; Puritans on, 48–52; Winthrop on, 49; Wise on, 53–54
Bogin, Ruth, 334n7, 342n113
Bolingbroke, Henry St. John, Lord, 27
Bolívar, Simón 301
Bonomi, Patricia, 246, 317n133, 349n8
Bouton, Terry, 304n9
Bowling, Kenneth R., 349n6
Boyd, Julian P., 351n37
Boy with a Flying Squirrel (Copley), 192–93
Brackenridge, Hugh Henry, 79, 158
Bradford, Thomas and William (printing firm), 57, 62
Bradfords, Thomas, 155
Brant, Joseph, 227
Breen, T. H., 321n47, 327n45, 335n17, 347n49
Brekke, Linzy A., 322n61
Brewer, John, 319n16
Brigham, David R., 323n94, 330n97
British Architect (Swan), 61
British Constitution, 39–41, 53, 71–72
Brown, Charles Brockden, 28, 149
Brown, Mather, 138, 140, 142
Brown, William Hill, 160
Brückner, Martin, 309n16
Bruns, Roger, 338n46
"Brutus" (Anti-Federalist), 133, 135, 164
Bryan, George, 304n3
Buckminster, Joseph, 67, 69
Burckhardt, Jacob, 9–10, 304n11
Burgett, Bruce, 317n130, 344n8
Burgh, James, 327n32
Burke, Aedanus, 162
Burke, Edmund: on constitutions, 39; Paine and, 39, 226; Reflections on the Revolution in France, 72; "salutary neglect" and, 193; Sublime and Beautiful, 98, 100–101, 106; Sublime and Beautiful in America, 347n45; Vindication of Natural Society, 101
Burlamaqui, Jean Jacques, 226
Bushman, Richard L., 96, 319n15
Butler, Jon, 246, 349n9, 356n116

Caeser, James W., 304n15
Calvert, Karin, 329n79

Campbell, James, 79
"Cantata for the Fourth of July, 1788,"
    77–78
Capac, Manco, Barlow on constitutional-
    ism of, 107–8
Carey, John, 151, 154, 160, 162
Carey, Mathew, 150–51
Carter, Robert, III, 185
Carter, Robert, IV, and Wheatley, 185
Caygill, Hoard, 319n19
Chaplin, Joyce E., 309n15, 309n17
Chapone, Hester, 278
Characteristicks (Shaftesbury), 258–59
Charleston Evening Gazette, 150–51
Chartier, Roger, 319n16, 326n16, 344n9
Chase, Samuel, 136, 258
"Chatterton, Augustus" (pseud.), 108
Chauncy, Charles, 181
Childs, Francis, 157
Chippendale, Thomas, 304n4
Choice, The (Pomfret), 221–22
"Christ," word in eighteenth-century
    American imprints, 249, 252 chart 2
Chytry, Josef, 319n19
Cicero, 113
civil slavery. *See* political slavery
Claeys, Gregory, 348n62
Clark, J. C. D., 335n18
Clarke, Samuel, 278
Clérisseau, Charles-Louis, 194
Clive, John, 321n48
closet, and decision-making, 234–35
closet politicians, 234
Clymer, George, 294
Coke, Edward, 72, 233 fig. 17
Cokesbury College, 77
Collection of Designs in Architecture
    (Norman), 61
College of Philadelphia, 171
Collier, Christopher, 343n2
Collins, Isaac, 352n40
Colman, Benjamin, 66–67
Columbian Herald (Charleston, S.C.), 282
Columbian Magazine (Philadelphia),
    82–84, 110, 119
Common Sense (Paine): Adams criti-
    cizes, 41, 66, 131; coronation of charter
    in, 63–64, 313n61; *Leviathan* and, 230;
    on purpose of government, 60; repre-
    sentation and, 131; "Rising Sun" arm-

chair and, 4; solitude in, 224–25; source
    for free exercise of religion clauses in
    state constitutions, 277; translated into
    Spanish, 300
compromise, strategies of, 5–7
Congressional Register (Lloyd), 151, 156;
    Lloyd's shorthand notes for, 152 fig. 12
Conjectures on Original Composition
    (Young), 195
Connecticut Wits, 243
"Connection of Civil Government with
    Manners and Taste" (Dickinson),
    88–89, 94–97
conscience, 277–79. *See also* "religion": re-
    ligious freedom
*Considerations on . . . An Act for the Es-
    tablishment of Religious Freedom*
    (Swanwick), 282–87
constitution: changing meaning of the
    word, 39, 44, 238; human body and,
    10, 44
Constitutional Convention. *See* Federal
    Convention
constitutional fit, 11–13
constitutional history: cultural history and,
    15, 18–26; popular literature and, 240;
    sources for, 14, 20–26
constitutional interpretation, 18–26.
    See also originalism; structuralism;
    textualism
constitutionalism: in revolutionary Europe,
    300; in revolutionary Latin America,
    300–301; since 1987, 301; written con-
    stitutions, 25
constitutionality, 273–76
"constitutional taste," 88, 95, 97, 107
Constitution of the United States: Amer-
    ican Revolution and, 7–8; antidemo-
    cratic character of, 8; Art. 1, sec. 2,
    125–26, 206; Art. I, sec. 9, 206; Art.
    IV, sec. 2, 206; Art. V, 295; Art. VII, 5;
    barely ratified, 20; beauty of original
    text, 293–95; cultural origins of, 8, 299;
    as fulfillment of American Revolution,
    7; "Godless," 242–45; as living organ-
    ism, 19; "necessary and proper" clause
    of, 25; new Preamble proposed for,
    291–95; politics as marriage metaphor
    and, 75–76; Preamble of, 292; religious
    language in, 243–44; signing of, 1, 5–6;

slavery and, 205–6; as static document, 19; style of, 24, 115; taste in ratification of, 114–19; Washington's transmittal letter for, 232–33, 292

Continental Congress: function of, 45; impotence of, 73–77; votes independence, 169–70

contractualism, 51, 76

Cooke and Co. (miniature painters), 144

Cooper, David, 208

Copley, John Singleton: Adams compares Mercy Otis Warren to, 153; *Boy with a Flying Squirrel* as imperial allegory, 192–93; paints Adams, 139–40, 141; Wilkes and, 339n65

copyright: clause in Constitution, 114; of transcripts of political debates, 154–56, 332n126

"Cornelius" (Anti-Federalist), 36

Cott, Nancy F., 343n8

Cotton, John, 277

"County Convention for the Redress of Grievances of Courts," 93

Cowper, William, 77

Cox and Berry (booksellers), 191

Coxe, Tench, 110, 314n99

Craven, Wesley, 327n44

"creator": in Declaration of Independence, 263–64; in Virginia Declaration of Rights, 242, 244; word in eighteenth-century American imprints, 249, 252 chart 2

Crèvecoeur, J. Hector St. John de, 290, 347n57, 356n116

Crisp, Stephen, 161

cultural determinists, 13

cultural history: constitutional history and, 15, 18–26; quantitative analysis and, 14

cultural origins of constitutions, 8–9, 11–14

cultural study of law, 25–26, 305n25

culture: eighteenth-century meaning, 92; manners, customs, tastes, and, 11, 92; modern analytic meaning, 11; politics and, 301

customs, Montesquieu on, 91–92, 107

Dagget, David, 110

Dahl, Robert A., 304n9

Daily Advertiser (New York), 156

Dallas, Alexander James: as Anti-Federalist, 83; as editor of *Columbian Magazine,* 83–84; as reporter of speeches and debates during ratification, 155, 161

Dana, James, 208

Daniels, Peter T., 330n100

Darnton, Robert, 315n111

Dartmouth, Earl of, 184

Dartmouth College, 88–89, 91–92, 94

Davidson, Cathy N., 343n8

Davidson, Robert, 111

Davis, David Brion, 336n26

Davis, Thomas J., 340n89

Dayton, Cornelia Hughes, 343n8

de Baeque, Antoine, 311n45, 315n111

Debates in the Several State Conventions (Elliot), 158

Debates of the Convention of the State of Pennsylvania (Lloyd), 156

Declaration of Independence: artificial government and, 10–11; changing meanings of, 172–74, 207–9; constitutionalized in Madison's proposed first amendment, 291–92; equality and, 172–74, 207–9; God and, 241–42; Jefferson's draft of, 263–64; "Nature's God" and, 246; "sacred" rights in, 262; slavery and, 171–74, 207–9; sovereignty and, 11, 172–73; Spanish translation of, 300; unalienable rights and, 11; Virginia Declaration of Rights and, 215, 263–64

Declaration of Independence (Durand after Trumbull), 231 fig. 16

Declaration of Independence (Hicks), 231

Declaration of Independence (Trumbull), 230–31

Declaration of the Causes of Taking up Arms, 207

Defoe, Daniel, 225

"deity," word in eighteenth-century American imprints, 249, 252 chart 2

Delaware Constitution (1776), 264, 268, 276

De Lolme, Jean Louis, 72, 307n7

Democratic Republicans, 209

Demosthenes, 113

de Retz, Cardinal (Jean Francois de Gondi), 346n43

Desdemona, 316n117

Detweiler, Philip F., 334n4

"DeWitt, John" (Anti-Federalist), 133–35
Dickinson, Emily, 318n12
Dickinson, John: in Continental Congress, 310n37; at Federal Convention, 125; footnotes and, 232; *Letters from a Farmer in Pennsylvania,* 28, 125, 180, 221, 232; on origin of rights, 262; on political slavery, 180; Pope's *Essay on Man* and, 28; retirement and, 221; Smither's image of, 233 fig. 17
Dickinson, Moses, 94
Dickinson, Nathan, Jr., 93
Dickinson, Samuel Fowler, 88–90, 93–97, 98, 318n12
Dickinson College, 111
Dickson, Harold, 144
dictators, 164–65
digitized texts, 14, 349n13
Dillon, Elizabeth Maddox, 344n8
Discourse on . . . the Body Politic (Huntington), 43–46, 54
Discourses on Art (Reynolds), 193, 195
diversity, 50, 291
Documentary History of the Ratification of the Constitution, 20
Douglass, Frederick, 209
Douthwaite, Julia, 344n11
Dragonetti, Giacinto, as visual source for Paine, 313n61
DuBos, Abbé, 102
Dunlap, John, 57, 334
Dunlap, William, 145
Dunmore, Lord, 171
Dunn, Richard, 316n115
Durand, Asher, 231
DuSimitiere, Pierre Eugene, 258, 260

Eagleton, Terry, 319n17
Eco, Umberto, 327n36
Edling, Max M., 315n106
Egan, Jim, 309n17
Elements of Criticism (Kames), in America, 106
Elliot, Jonathan, 151, 153, 158
Ellison, Julie, 344n8
Eltis, David, 182, 336n29
Encyclopedia Britannica, 149
enlightenment, 246
Eppes, John Wayles, 166, 333n165
equality: in Declaration of Independence,

172–74, 207–9; mental, 174, 186–90, 207; political, 174, 207
"Equality—A Political Romance," 227
erection, language of, 63, 64–67, 313n65
Essay on Man (Pope): popularity in United States, 28–30, 306n2, 307n3; responses to couplet on political form and administration, 27–36; Trumbull and, 228
Essay on Taste (Gerard), 101, 104
"Essay on Taste" (Ralph), 103–4, 106
Essex *Result,* 134–35
Evans, Charles, 251
Evans, Griffith, 76
Examination into the Leading Principles of the Constitution (Webster), 114–19
Exodus, 260–61
Eze, Emmanuel Chukwudi, 337n35

Farber, Daniel A., 305n20
Farrand, Max, 22, 303n1
"Fashion" (Madison), 109
Fashion, and politics, 109–11
Fashion before Ease (Gillray), 40–41, 40 fig. 4
"Fate of Beauty," 121
Fea, John, 337n34
Federal Convention: debates representation, 123–27; debates what signing Constitution means, 1–2, 5–6; Madison's notetaking practices at, 163–64; narrative histories of, 124, 165; nonsigners at, 6–7, 7 fig. 3; notes of debates at, 124–25; orations and sermons delivered while Convention sits, 67–68; speeches from published during ratification, 34–35, 157–58, 160; "unanimity" at, 5–6; visual representations of, 232. See also *Notes of Debates at the Federal Convention* (Madison)
"Federal Farmer" (Anti-Federalist), 36, 327n31
Federalist, The (Hamilton, Madison, and Jay): Anti-Federalists on, 21; architectural metaphors in, 64; circulation of, 24; on closet theorists, 234; on decisions made behind closed doors, 234–35; delays discussion of Constitution, 21; early articulations of no. 10, 125, 235; "foundation" in, 81; on God's hand in unanimity at Federal Convention, 288;

Jefferson's modified copy of, 293; localism and "great national discussion," 20; minority rights and, 235; "natural" representation in, 137; no. 1 (Hamilton), 20, 122; no. 10 (Madison), 25, 108, 125, 127, 136, 164, 235, 290; no. 35 (Hamilton), 137; no. 37 (Madison), 288; no. 51 (Madison), 25, 290; no. 69 (Hamilton), 234; originalist and textualist interpretations, source for, 24–25; Pope's *Essay on Man* and, 36; public voice and, 108, 127, 136, 164; rarely cites text of Constitution, 24–25; refinement in, 108–9; "reflection and choice" in, 122; religious diversity and faction in, 290–91; slave insurrections and, 206

Federalists: architectural metaphors of, 64, 79–81; avoid citing text of Constitution, 24–25; on beauty of Constitution, 21, 113–18; create bogus Anti-Federalist essays, 21; on divine agency in proposed Constitution, 287–88; on expertise of legislators, 135–37; on form versus administration, 35; on impotence of Confederation, 73–74; metaphors of for representation, 126–27; reprint Anti-Federalist essays, 21

Federal Procession (Philadelphia), 60, 81

"Federal Republican" (Anti-Federalist), 118–21

feelings: political form and, 32; rights and, 121

Fenno, John, 151

Ferguson, Adam, 95

Ferguson, Robert A., 14, 246, 323n90, 349n7, 349n8

Ferry, Luc, 319n17, 319n19, 320n23

First Amendment, 245, 276

Fischer, David Hackett, 311n39, 312n46, 334n5

Fithian, Philip Vickers, 185, 337n34

Flaherty, David H., 343n7

Fliegelman, Jay, 316n116, 321n43, 332n138, 337n43, 339n58

Folwell, John, 2–5, 304n4

Fordyce, James, 112

Forham, Kate Langdon, 309n12

form, political: versus administration, 27–36; eligibility to judge, 31–33

Foucault, Michel, 312n54

foundations, 81

Four Letters on Interesting Subjects (Paine?), 39, 66, 72

"Frame of Government of the Province of Pennsylvania" (Penn), 66

framing, language of, 115–16

Franklin, Benjamin: on Anti-Federalists and ancient Jews, 288; constitutional origins and, 15; at Federal Convention, 1–8, 34, 124; final speech at Federal Convention frequently reprinted, 35; music and, 112; painted by Trumbull, 230; Pope's *Essay on Man* and, 27, 35; proposes signing Constitution by "unanimous Consent of the States present," 5–6, 8; Ralph and, 103; on "Rising Sun" armchair, 1–2, 2 fig. 1, 7 fig. 3; Seal of the United States and, 258–61; *Spectator* and, 102; Swanwick and, 285

Franklin College, 68

free exercise of religion, 268, 270–71, 276–77. *See also* Paine, Thomas; Virginia Act for Establishing Religious Freedom; Virginia Declaration of Rights (1776)

Freeman, Sambo, 198

Fredrickson, George, 177, 335n10, 335n13

French and Indian War, 254, 256

French Revolution, 173

Freneau, Philip, 222–23

Fry, John, 110

Fuseli, Henry, 312n61

Gage, Thomas, 59

García de Sena, Manuel, 300

Gates, Henry Louis, Jr., 337n35, 338n56, 339n69

Gazette of the United States (New York), 151

genius of the people, 11, 33–34, 299, 304n10

Georgia Constitution (1777), 268, 276

Gerard, Alexander, 101, 104, 106

Gerry, Elbridge: at Federal Convention, 6, 124; in House of Representatives, 292; refuses to sign Constitution, 6

Gettysburg Address (Lincoln), 173

Gibney, Simon, 169

Gillray, James, 40

God: as architect, 67–68; as author of natural rights, 261–64

"God": absence of word in Constitution, 242–45; in Declaration of Independence, 241; in Massachusetts Constitution, 241; in "Memorial and Remonstrance," 241; natural rights and, 256–57, 257 chart 4; in state constitutions, 244; word in eighteenth-century British American imprints, 246–57, 248 charts 1A–B, 252 chart 2, 255 chart 3, 257 chart 4; word in revolutionary United States, 18, 246, 254–57

Godbeer, Richard, 344n8

Goldford, Dennis J., 305n19

Goldsby, Jacqueline, 348n64

gonorrhea, as "constitutional" problem, 78

Goodman, Dean, 344n9

Goodrich, Elizur, 68, 111

Gordon-Reed, Annette, 317n133

Gossman, Lionel, 304n12

Gould, Stephen Jay, 335n13

government: best forms of, 11–13, 34; erotic images of, 59–62; form of not ordained by God, 52; freedom and, 60; genius of the people and, 11, 34; of laws and not of men, 8, 30–31, 36, 63; as master noun of eighteenth-century political thought, 95; "natural" when suited to population, 11; purpose of, 60–61; society and, 60–61

Government the Pillar of the Earth (Colman), 66–67

Grasso, Christopher, 325n10, 343n2, 350n16

Graves, Robert, 161

Great Awakening, 247, 249

Green, Jacob, 207

Greene, Jack P., 311n45, 314n96, 316n116

Group, The (Warren), and *Leviathan* as prop, 230

Gulliver's Travels (Swift), 159

Habermas, Jurgen, 218

hair work (miniatures), 145

Hall, David D., 331n108, 343n1

Hall, Prince, 210–11

Hambrick-Stowe, Charles E., 331n108

Hamilton, Alexander: architectural metaphors of, 64; *Farmer Refuted,* 230; at Federal Convention, 5, 125; *The Federalist,* 20, 24, 36, 118, 122, 137, 234; Hobbes and, 230; notetaking and, 125; part and whole and, 118; Pope's *Essay on Man* and, 27, 36; rights and, 58, 227, 261–62

Hamilton, Dr. Alexander, 62

Hammon, Jupiter, 17; *Address to the Negroes in the State of New-York,* 203; slave petitioners and, 203

Hancock, John, 61, 231

Handlin, Mary, 352n47

Handlin, Oscar, 352n47

Harrington, James, 30–31

Harris, Neil, 330n90

Harvard College, 196, 205

Haulman, Kate, 322n61

Haynes, Lemuel, 173–75, 207

Heimert, Alan, 349n8

Hench, John B., 350n15

Henry, Patrick, 197, 289

Hercules, Choice of, 258–60

"Hermit, The" (Smith), 220–21

"Hermitess; Or, Fair Secluder," 220

"Hermit of Saba" (Freneau), 222

hermits: in print culture, 220, 236, 344n12; in wax exhibits, 239–40

"Hermit's Soliloquy," 217–19

Hertz, Neil, 311n46

Higginbotham, A. Leon, 341n93

Higginson, John, 51, 53

Himmelfarb, Gertrude, 349n9

Hirschman, Albert O., 220, 345n14

History of Jamaica (Long), 186–87

Hobbes: American Revolution and, 228–30; architectural metaphors and, 65; body politic and, 53–54; *Leviathan,* 47–48, 48 fig. 6, 54, 228–30; Madison and, 48; political science and, 11; Pufendorf and, 54, 228–30; on state as a work of art, 10, 47–48; Wise and, 54

Holbrook, Felix, 198

Holton, Woody, 305n19

Hooper, William, 31, 130

Hopkins, Samuel, 197

Hopkinson, Francis, 60, 80, 155, 221

Horton, James Oliver, 341n89

Horton, Lois E., 341n89

House of Representatives: debates amendments to the Constitution, 244, 291–95; recording of debates in, 161–62; representation in, 123–27, 166

Hubbard, William, 50

Hume, David: aesthetics and, 98–100; ar-

chitectural metaphors and, 65; on form versus administration, 30; "Idea of a Perfect Commonwealth," 65; on intelligence of Africans, 186, 190; Lee and, 204; on government of laws not men, 30–31; "Of National Characters," 186, 190; "Of the Standard of Taste," 98, 99–100; "On the First Principles of Government," 99; on Pope's *Essay on Man,* 27, 30; "That Politics May be Reduced to a Science," 30–31
Humphreys, Daniel, 155
Humphreys, David, 74
Hunt, Lynn, 177, 311n45, 315n111, 335n9
Huntington, Joseph, 43–46, 69
Huntington, Samuel, 43
Hutcheson, Francis, 102
Hutson, James H., 305n22, 325n3, 325n6, 351n30, 356n116

imitation: cultural, 186–90; neoclassical, 191–95
"Impartial Examiner" (Anti-Federalist), 136
impotence: of Continental Congress, 73; in divorce cases, 74
Independent Whig, 278
individualism, 17, 223–35
"Influence of Opinion" (Webster), 91, 99
Inquiry into the Beauties of Painting (Webb), 103
intention, 22–3
interpretation, constitutional. *See* constitutional interpretation
invention, 192
Isaac, Rhys, 324n100, 354n83
Isani, Mukhtar Ali, 337n32
Ishmael (runaway slave), 169–71, 170 fig. 13, 334n1
"Island of Matrimony," 220
Israel, ancient, United States compared with, 43

Jackson, William, 125
Jacobson, Norman, 309n16
Jacoby, Susan, 349n9
James, Joseph, 156
James Peale Painting a Miniature (Peale), 146–48, 147 fig. 11
Jay, John, 267

Jefferson, Thomas: as author of Declaration of Independence, 173, 242; as author of Declaration of the Causes of Taking up Arms, 207; Banneker and, 208–9; Bill for Establishing Religious Freedom and, 274–75, 280–82, 285–86, 290; on closet politicians, 234; constitutional origins and, 15; on Continental Congress, 45; copy of *The Federalist* and, 293; on hermitage for Monticello, 222; on intelligence of blacks, 187–88; Madison and, 73, 161; no son of a political advantage, 78; *Notes on the State of Virginia,* 17, 148, 187–88, 204, 281; painting and, 138–39; Pope's *Essay on Man* and, 28; receives transcripts of speeches, 155, 161; runaway slave advertisement of, 189; Seal of the United States and, 258–61; slavery and, 189, 206; Trumbull depicts, 230–31
"Jesus", word in eighteenth-century American imprints, 249, 252 chart 2
John of Salisbury, 46
Johnson, Samuel, 160, 172, 184, 191
Johnston, Zachariah, 289
Joie, Chester, 198
Jordan, Winthrop, 335n13, 336n26, 340n77
Journal of the Proceedings of the Congress (1774), 55–58, 56 fig. 7
Judgment of Hercules (Gribelin after Mattheis), 258–59, 259 fig. 21
"Justice" (abolitionist), 208
juvenile literature, rise of, 350n17

Kahn, Paul, 306n25
Kahn, Victoria, 304n14
Kames, Lord (Henry Home): *Elements of Criticism,* 106; on "voting" on taste, 104, 106, 319n18
Kaminski, John 20, 304n3
Kammen, Michael, 311n45
Kant, Immanuel: on Africans, 186; on art, 118; *Observations on the Feeling of the Beautiful and Sublime,* 186; on Pope's *Essay on Man,* 27, 30
Kerber, Linda, 343n8
Kilburn, Lawrence, 142–43
King, Rufus, 124, 126, 132
Klein, Lawrence E., 319n16
Knapp, Samuel Lorenzo, 158
Knight, Janice, 316n115

Knott, Sarah, 312n56
Kramer, Larry D., 305n19
Kramnick, Isaac, 96, 319n15, 349n9

Ladurie, Emmanuel le Roy, 350n20
Lamb, Jonathan, 344n11
Lambee, Bristol, 198
Lambert, Frank, 349n9, 349n12
Landes, Joan, 344n9
Land Ordinance (1785), 236
Langhorne, John, 183, 191, 194, 197
Lansing, John, 5, 125
Laquer, Thomas, 343n6
lawgivers, 297–99
Law of Nature and Nations (Pufendorf), 54
law-takers, 298–99
lawyers, popular images of, 93–94
Lectures on American Literature
    (Knapp), 158
Lectures on Rhetoric (Blair), 104
Lee, Arthur, and Pope, 33; and slavery,
    196, 204
Lee, Richard Henry, 66, 327n31
legislative omnipotence, 72–73
Leland, John, 269, 290
Leonard, Thomas C., 343n4
Letter Concerning Toleration (Locke),
    15, 274; Vermont edition, 270–73, 271
    fig. 22
Letters from a Farmer in Pennsylvania
    (Dickinson), 28, 125, 180, 221, 232
*Letters on the Improvement of the Human
    Mind* (Chapone), 278
Leviathan (Hobbes), 47–48, 54; Ameri-
    can Revolution and, 228–30; Madison's
    copy of, 48 fig. 6
Levinson, Sanford, 304n9
Lewis, Jan, 343n8
liberty: phallic images of, 59; proximity to
    slavery, 169; temples for, 73
Liberty ("Hermit in New-Jersey"), 221
liberty cap, 58–59
liberty tree, 59
likeness: in miniature painting, 127,
    137–48; political representation and,
    130, 137; in transcription of speech, 127
Lincoln, Abraham, 173
Linebaugh, Peter, 311n41
Lipovetsky, Gilles, 319n17
literary property. *See* copyright
Livingston, Robert R., 73, 230

Lloyd, Thomas, 23, 148–52, 155–59, 162
Locke, John: architectural metaphors of,
    65; body politic and, 134; civil slavery
    and, 180; contractualism of, 51; Dickin-
    son and, 95; eighteenth-century politi-
    cal science and, 11; *Letter Concerning
    Toleration*, 15, 270–74; pedagogy of,
    188; sensationalism of, 102, 193; social
    compact and, 95; on state as a work of
    art, 10; Thompson and, 270–74
Lofgren, Charles A., 305n20
Long, Edward, 186–87
Longinus, 106
Looby, Christopher, 325n10
Loughran, Trish, 305n23
Lovell, Margaretta M., 327n45
Lunch, Joseph M., 305n20
Lundberg, David, 324n94
Lutz, Donald S., 307n7, 313n69
Lycurgus, 299
Lyman, Joseph, 110
Lyons, Clare A., 334n1

Machiavelli, 47
Mack, Mr. (miniature painter), 143
Madison, James: on "Almighty hand" in
    the Federal Convention, 288; amend-
    ments and, 244–45, 289, 291–95; on
    closet theorists, 234; constitutional ori-
    gins and, 15; "Fashion," 109; at Federal
    Convention, 1–2, 124–26, 163; *The Fed-
    eralist*, 24, 25, 108, 125, 127, 136, 164,
    235, 288, 290; on free exercise of reli-
    gion, 268, 270–71; on government as re-
    flection on human nature, 61; on impo-
    tency of Confederation, 73; *Leviathan*
    and, 48 fig. 6; "Memorial and Remon-
    strance," 241, 274–76, 287, 290; mis-
    quotes Virginia Declaration of Rights,
    275–76; *Notes of Debates in the Fed-
    eral Convention*, 1–2, 2 fig. 1, 7, 7 fig. 3,
    17, 22, 124–25, 148, 163–64, 333n165; as
    note-taker, 1–2, 163, 165–66; on parch-
    ment barriers, 25, 305n24; on Pope's *Essay
    on Man* and, 28; public voice and, 108,
    127, 136, 164; on religion and diversity,
    290–91; representation and, 124–26; on
    rights of conscience, 245; slavery and,
    206; *Spectator* and, 103; on transcribed
    speeches, 161–62; "Vices of the Politi-
    cal System," 235; Virginia Act for Es-

tablishing Religious Freedom and, 280–81; on volume of legislation, 227; Washington's First Inaugural and, 78

Madison Papers (Library of Congress), 1–2, 6, 22, 166

Mad Tom in a Rage, 41, 42 fig. 5

Magaw, Lucia, 283

Magaw, Samuel, 283

Magna Charta: as confirming rather than creating rights, 58, 227; Paine and, 277; in revolutionary writings, 232, 311n41; visual representations of, 56 fig. 7, 58–59, 232, 233 fig. 17

Maier, Pauline, 334n4, 342n1, 351n37

manners: government and, 88–93, 95–97, 107; morals and, 91–92; slavery and, 188

Marienstras, Elise, 311n45

Marin, Louis, 327n36

Markoe, Peter, 110, 113

marriage, as metaphor for politics, 74–77

Marshall, John, 28

Martinich, A. P., 309n15

Maryland Constitution (1776), 265, 268

Mason, George: at Federal Convention, 6, 125; "Memorial and Remonstrance" and, 274; Pope's *Essay on Man* and, 28; refuses to sign Constitution, 6; Virginia Declaration of Rights and, 28, 125, 215, 263–64, 267, 351n37

Massachusetts Constitution (1780): acknowledges "Great Legislator of the Universe," 241; architectural metaphors in, 66; body politic in, 55; cannot ensure good administration, 33; creates "a government of laws and not of men," 31, 63; religion and, 266, 269; slavery and, 174, 176, 210–13

Massachusetts Historical Society, 182, 209

Massachusetts Magazine (Boston), 220

May, Henry, 324n94, 349n7

Mayflower "Compact" (1620), 55

McDonald, Robert M. S., 334n5

McKean, Thomas, 35

McLoughlin, William G., 352n57, 353n74, 354n91, 355n115

Meigs, Josiah, 217

Melish, Janne Pope, 341n89

"Memorial and Remonstrance" (Madison), 241, 274–76, 287, 290; misquotations in, 275–76; reprinted in Massachusetts, 282

Mengs, Anton, 193

Methodism, 82

Milton, John, 199

miniature painting, 137–48

monarchism, 13

Monroe, James, 28, 73

Montesquieu: aesthetics and, 98; Bolívar on, 301; on climate, 95; on cultural origins of constitutions, 12–13, 107; on manners and morals, 91–92, 107; religion and, 285, 301; *Spirit of the Laws*, 12–13, 77, 91–92, 107; "Taste," 101–2, 104

Monthly Review (London): read in Virginia, 185; on Wheatley, 183

Monticello, 222

Moore, R. Laurence, 349n9

More, Thomas, 227

Morgan, Edmund S., 182, 315n114, 320n20, 326n14, 336n26

Moritz, Karl Philipp, 118

Morris, Gouverneur: additions to Madison's *Notes* and, 166; on closet politicians, 234; at Federal Convention, 5–6, 166; Morris, Robert, 283; and "style" of Constitution, 5

Moses, 43, 44, 260–61, 299

Murray, Judith Sargent, 220

Murrin, John, 317n137

musical instruments, appropriateness for women, 111–12

Narrative of . . . Mrs. Mary Rowlandson, 249, 251 fig. 20

Nash, Gary, 304n3, 334n3, 336n27

nationalism, 257

nation building, 79

natural rights, 216–17, 226; and God, 256–57, 257 chart 4

nature, politics and, 11, 304n15

"nature's God," 246, 262

Nederman, Cary J., 309n12

Nelson, Dana D., 316n120, 337n39

Nemerov, Alexander, 345n15

neoclassicism, 177–79, 190–95

neo-roman political theory, 179–80

Newberry Library, 356n119

New Hampshire Bill of Rights (1783), 265

New Hampshire Constitution (1783), 92

New Haven Gazette, 217–18

New Jersey Constitution (1776), 267

Newman, Richard S., 334n3
Newman, Simon, 334n1
"New Roof, The" (Hopkinson), 80
New York Constitution (1777), 150, 267, 276
Nicole, Pierre, 327n36
Niobe (Wilson), 199–200
Noll, Mark, 250–51, 350n15
Norman, John, 61
North Carolina Assembly, 73
North Carolina Constitution (1776), 265
Norton, John, 277
Norton, Mary Beth, 316n115, 343n8
Notes of Debates in the Federal Convention (Madison), 1–2, 7, 17, 22, 124–25, 148, 163–64, 333n165; final page in facsimile of 1840, 2 fig. 1; final page in manuscript, 7 fig. 3; later revisions, 165–66
Notes on the State of Virginia (Jefferson), 17, 148, 187–88, 204, 281
novels, 350n17
Numa, 299
Nugent, Thomas, 91

Oakes, James, 336n27
Observations on Government, 71
Observations on the Importance of the American Revolution (Price), 270–71
Observations on the Plan . . . submitted to the Federal Convention (Pinckney), 157
Occom, Samson, 198
Olson, Lester C., 311n39
O'Neill, Jonathan, 305n20
"On the Equality of the Sexes" (Murray), 220
On the Imitation of the Painting and Sculpture of the Greeks (Winckelmann), 191
Onuf, Peter S., 347n57
opinion, 91, 99, 176, 210–12; in religion, 279–80
originalism, 19, 22–24, 305n19, 305n20
Othello (Shakespeare), 76, 316n117
Otis, James: philology of, 194–95; on rights, 58, 227, 311n41; *Rights of the British Colonies Asserted and Proved,* 195, 223–25; *Rudiments of Latin Prosody,* 194–95; on slavery, 196, 227; on solitude, 17, 223–25, 226

Outlines of a Constitution for North and South Columbia (Thornton), 300
Ovid, 199, 202

Paine, Thomas: Act for the Gradual Abolition of Slavery and, 304n3; as clerk to Pennsylvania Assembly, 3; *Common Sense,* 4, 41, 60, 63–64, 66, 131, 224–25, 230, 277, 300, 313n61; constitutional origins and, 15; on constitutions as property of nation, 16; Dragonetti and, 312n61; and free exercise of religion, 277; on government, 60–61; on law as king, 63–64, 312n61; representation and, 131, 326n22; *Rights of Man,* 39, 71–72, 122, 173, 227; satires of, 40–42, 40 fig. 4, 42 fig. 5; on solitude, 17, 224–25, 226; on written constitutions, 39, 41
Painter, Nell Irvin, 342n112
painters, miniature, 127, 137–48
"Painting in the Creek Taste" (Romans), 95, 96 fig. 9
"Panther Narrative," 348n57
parchment barriers, 25, 305n24
Park, Helen, 324n94, 324n100
Parliament, 159
Parrington, Vernon L., 349n8
Paterson, Orlando, 335n11
Patriotic American Farmer (Smither), 232, 233 fig. 17
Paul, 50, 278–79
Peak, John, 353n63
Peale, Charles Willson: exhibition of Italian paintings, 112, 283; Federal Procession and, 81, 83, 330n97; *James Peale Painting a Miniature,* 146–48, 147 fig. 11; mezzotint of Washington, 141; miniature painting and, 143, 144; transcripts and, 153
Peale, James, 146–47
Peale, Raphaelle, 143
Pelham, Henry, 192
Pemberton, Ebenezer, 148
Penn, John, 130
Penn, William, 66, 299
Penn's Treaty with the Indians (West), 230
Pennsylvania Constitution (1776), 2, 32, 150, 244; religion and, 264, 276, 284
Pennsylvania Declaration of Rights (1776), 225–26, 276

Pennsylvania Evening Herald (Philadelphia): prints legislative debates, 150; reprints Virginia Act for Establishing Religious Freedom, 282

Pennsylvania Evening Post (Philadelphia), prints vote on independence beside runaway slave notice, 169–71, 170 fig. 13

Pennsylvania General Assembly, debates calling ratification convention, 79

Pennsylvania Herald (Philadelphia), 155

Pennsylvania State House: Federal Convention in, 1–5, 34; redecoration of, 2–3

people, 241, 243

Perkins, William, 49–50

Peterson, Merril D., 334n4, 354n84

petitions, slave, 197–99, 201, 203, 205, 341n94

phallic images of liberty, 59, 77

"Philosophical History of the Advancement of Nations" (Wheelock), 89–93

Philosophical Solitude (Livingston), 222

physiognotrace, 330n97

pillars, ratification images of, 79, 84

Pinckney, Charles, 73, 77, 123, 126, 157–58, 304n10

Pitkin, Hanna Fenichel, 128, 135, 325n12, 326n13, 327n37

Plato, 46, 113

"Pleasures of the Imagination" (Addison), 102

Pocock, J. G. A., 95–97, 280, 319n15, 335n17, 346n27, 354n84

Pole, J. R., 311n45, 326n14, 327n34

Policraticus (John of Salisbury), 46

Polite Philosopher, 112–13, 118

political determinists, 13

political science, 10–14, 16, 87, 89–93, 97–102. *See also* political thought

political slavery, 176–85, 336n23; racial slavery and, 15, 181–82, 203–5

political theory, becomes political science, 11–12

political thought: aesthetics and, 98–99; popular literature and, 235–40. *See also* political science

politics, as marriage, 74–77

Pomfret, John, 221–22

Ponte, Alessandra, 312n59

Poovey, Mary, 100, 319n17, 320n22, 344n10

Pope, Alexander: "Eloisa to Abelard," 76, 316n117; *Essay on Man,* 27–36, 306n2; Wheatley and, 194, 199

Popkin, Richard, 337n35

"Poplicola" (Anti-Federalist), 36

popular literature, political thought and, 235–40

Powell, H. Jefferson, 305n20

Pretty Story Written in . . . 2774 (Hopkinson), 221

Price, Richard: describes political slavery, 180–81, 204; modifies Virginia Statute of Religious Freedom, 281, 354n89; *Observations on the Importance of the American Revolution,* 270–71

print marketplace, 21, 305n23

privacy, 17, 60, 218–19; and gender, 343n8

Proceedings and Debates of the General Assembly of Pennsylvania (Lloyd), 156

"providence," word in eighteenth-century American imprints, 249, 252 chart 2

providentialism, 253, 311n40

Prown, Jules David, 339n66

public opinion, 32, 210–12

public sphere, 217

public voice, 165

publishing, religious and non-religious, 250–53

"Publius" (Federalist), 21, 24–25, 36, 235

Pufendorf, Samuel, 54

Pybus, Cassandra, 334n3

Pye, Christopher, 309n16

Quakers, and antislavery, 172, 196

quantitative intellectual history, 247, 349n10

Quarles, Benjamin, 336n30, 340n89

Quincy, Josiah, 132, 188–89, 326n25

racism, 17; and language of rights, 177–79

"Raising, The" (Hopkinson), 80

Rakove, Jack N., 304n15, 305n19, 305n20, 305n22, 316n124, 324n95, 325n3, 326n15, 327n31, 335n11, 342n1, 351n37

Ralph, James, 103–4, 106

Ramage, John, 145

Ramsay, David, 234

Randolph, Edmund: on Confederation, 73; at Federal Convention, 6; on firm government, 77; on ratification procedure, 117; refuses to sign Constitution, 6; at Virginia Ratifying Convention, 289

Randolph, Peyton, 44

Ransom, Elisha, 269, 353n63

ratification: as discussion, 21–22; popular images of, 79, 84; taste and, 113–22

ratifying conventions: in Connecticut, 20; in Delaware, 20; in Georgia, 20; in Maryland, 20; in Massachusetts, 20, 23, 288; in New Hampshire, 20; in New Jersey, 20; in New York, 20, 23, 132, 217; in North Carolina, 20; in Pennsylvania, 20, 35, 154, 161, 287; in Rhode Island, 20; in South Carolina, 20; in Virginia, 20, 23, 289; transcripts of 23–24, 160

Rawley, James, 338n48

reason, politics and, 32

Records of the Federal Convention (Farrand), 22

refinement, 95, 107–9, 322n59

reflection: choice and, 122; as mental category, 187

Reid, John Philip, 334n4

relativism, political, 12–13

"religion": religious freedom, 264–87; in South Carolina, 355n95; in Vermont, 268–73; in Virginia, 274–75, 279–87, 290; word in eighteenth-century American imprints, 249, 252 chart 2, 257. *See also* Virginia Act for Establishing Religious Freedom

religion, and politics, 287–91. *See also* conscience; free exercise of religion; "religion": religious freedom

religious publishing, 250–52

reparations for slavery, 213

representation, 123–67; actual, 129, 131; "aesthetic," 128; conceptions of in revolutionary America, 23; "descriptive" or "mimetic," 128; image (portrait metaphor) and, 16, 126, 128–37; metaphors for, 127; "natural," 137; "true," 136–37; virtual, 129, 131, 326n14; voice (transcript metaphor) and, 15, 17, 125–26, 148–66

republicanism, 13, 40–41

"Retirement" (Freneau), 222

retirement, and solitude, 219, 221–22

Reynolds, Joshua, 142, 191, 193; *Discourses,* 193

Richards, Leonard L., 318n1

Rigal, Laura, 317n143

rights: as antecedent to earthly government, 262; as better felt than explained, 121; of charter, 256; circulation of, 206–7; of conscience, 245, 264–68; of Englishmen, 256; God and, 256–57, 257 chart 4, 261–64; language of, 17, 171, 207; of man, 91, 348n62; of nations, 122; natural, 216–17, 226; as products of governments, 226–28; race and, 17, 169–213; "sacred," 256–57, 262; sacrifice of, 232–33; slavery and, 169–213; visual representations of, 231–32; written on heart, 58

Rights of Man (Paine), 39, 71–72, 122, 173, 227

Riker, William H., 305n21

"Rising Sun" armchair (Folwell), 1–5, 4 fig. 2

Roberts, Jennifer L., 339n65

Robertson, David, 160

Robinson, William H., 338n55

Robinson Crusoe (Defoe), 225

Rocafuerte, Vincente, 300

Roche, Daniel, 315n111

Roediger, David, 336n29

Romans, Bernard, 95–96

romanticism, 187, 194

Rosenblum, Nancy L., 304n15

Rousseau, Jean-Jacques 10, 113, 187, 304n13; *On the Social Contract,* 195

Rowlandson, Mary, 249, 250 fig. 19, 251 fig. 20

Royal Magazine (London), 200

Rush, Benjamin: *Address on Slavery,* 190; on Dallas's transcripts of debates, 161; on divine agency in Constitution, 287; "Godless" Constitution and, 244; Pope's *Essay on Man* and, 28, 32; on rights, 121; as "Sidney," 32; solitude and, 218, 225; *Thoughts upon Female Education,* 110–12, 283

Saladino, Gaspare, 20

Sandoz, Ellis, 313n77

Sandy (runaway slave), 189

Saussure, Ferdinand de, 135

Saxton, Alexander, 336n29

Scalia, Antonin, 306n25

Schama, Simon, 334n3

Schimmelman, Janice, 320n34, 324n94, 339n57, 347n45
School of Wisdom, 144
Schor, Miguel, 356n4
Schwartz, Bernard, 352n46
Scruggs, Charles, 339n70
Seal of the United States, 258–61
secularization, political, 8, 245–46, 257
Selby, John E., 342n1
sermons: declining mentions of "God" in, 252–53; as genre, 350n18
Sermons to Young Women (Fordyce), 112
Shaftesbury, Third Earl of (Anthony Ashley Cooper), 118, 228, 258–59
Shays' Rebellion, 34, 88, 93
Sher, Richard B., 312n56
Sherman, Roger, 230, 293–95
Sherry, Susanna, 305n20
Shields, David S., 319n16, 344n8
Shklar, Judith N., 337n33
shorthand, 148–58; manuals, 153–54; reporters, 15, 23–24, 127, 148–58, 152 fig. 12
"Sidney" (Rush?), 32–33
Siemers, David J., 305n21
silhouettes, 330n97
Silverman, Kenneth, 328n54
Skinner, Quentin, 179, 308n3, 309n14, 310n31, 335n8, 335n14
slave petitions for freedom, 197–99, 201, 203, 205, 341n94
slavery: Constitution and, 1, 3, 8, 17, 166, 206; language of rights and, 169–213; legislative solutions for, 211–13; Massachusetts Constitution and, 182, 209–13; as paradox, 182; reparations for, 213; Vermont Constitution and, 216, 226; Virginia Declaration of Rights and, 216. *See also* political slavery
slaves, runaway, 169–72, 334n3
Smith, Adam, 95, 224
Smith, Billy G., 334n3
Smith, Christian, 350n21
Smith, Daniel Blake, 337n44
Smith, Melancton, 132–33, 327n31
Smith, Robert C., 356n1
Smith, Rogers, 304n15; "stories of peoplehood," 239, 348n62
Smith, Samuel Stanhope: *Essay on the Causes of the Variety of Complex-*

ion and Figure in the Human Species, 189–90; lectures on politics, 12
Smither, James, 232–33
Sobel, Mechal, 337n42, 350n19
sociability, 217–18
"Socialburg," imaginary community of described by Crèvecoeur, 347n57
"Social Compact" (Federalist), 217
social contract, 164
society: renunciation of, 221; state of, 216
Society for Political Inquiries, Rush addresses, 343n5
Society for Promoting the Abolition of Slavery (Pennsylvania), 208
Society for the Encouragement of Manufactures and the Useful Arts (Pennsylvania), 110
Society for the Relief of Free Negroes Unlawfully Held in Bondage (Pennsylvania), 172
Society of St. George (New York), 71
Society of the Cincinnati: in Pennsylvania, 79; in Massachusetts, 121
Soderlund, Jean R., 304n3, 334n3
solitude, 219–25; individualism and, 225–35; retirement and, 219, 221–22
Solkin, David, 339n59, 351n26
Solon: as lawgiver, 299; as model for framers of constitutions, 12
Sophia (runaway slave), 333n1
South Carolina Constitution (1778), 266–67
Soveraignty and Goodness of God (Rowlandson), 249, 250 fig. 19
sovereignty, in Declaration of Independence, 172–73
Spacks, Patricia Meyer, 343n6
Spectator, The (Addison and Steele), 102–3, 221, 278
spectatorship, 116–17
Spence, Thomas, 348n62
Spirit of the Laws (Montesquieu), 77, 91–92, 101–2
Staiti, Paul, 327n45
Stamp Act, 192–93, 215
state: as artificial, 8–11; as "impersonal," 41, 64; metaphors for, 15–16; Puritans and, 51; society and, 107
state as a work of art, 8–11, 51, 65, 298
state of nature, 10, 217, 230, 235

Stern, Julia, 328n50, 344n11
Stevens, John, 72
St. George, Robert Blair, 324n100, 328n45
Stockton, Julia, 28
Storing, Herbert J., 326n30
Story, Joseph, 219, 344n11
Stourzh, Gerard, 313n64
Strong, Simeon, 94
structuralism, 19–22
Stuart, William, 75–76
Substance of a Speech Delivered by James
    Wilson (Dallas), 155, 160
Sugar Act, 58, 196
"Supreme being," word in eighteenth-cen-
    tury American imprints, 350n14
Swan, Abraham, 61, 197
Swanwick, John: Considerations on . . . An
    Act for the Establishment of Religious
    Freedom, 282–87; Peale's exhibition of
    Italian paintings and, 15, 283; "Poem,
    On the Prospect of seeing the fine Arts
    flourish in America," 106–7; Thoughts
    on Education, 111–12
Swift, Jonathan, 115
sympathy, power of, 219

Tanselle, G. Thomas, 250–51, 254, 350n15
Task, The (Cowper), 77
taste: consent and, 98; "constitutional
    taste," 88, 95, 97; as master noun of
    eighteenth-century aesthetics, 95; poli-
    tics and, 16, 87, 97–107; provincial writ-
    ers and, 105–7; satirized, 104–5; rati-
    fication of Constitution and, 113–22;
    unification of society and, 106–7
"Taste under the Influence of Wisdom"
    (Thackara), 119, 120 fig. 10
Tate, Thad W., 343n2
Taylor, Joshua C., 330n88
Tetley, William Birchell, 145
textualism, 24–25, 306n25
Thackara, James, 120
thanksgiving proclamations, 350n14
Thaxter, John, 33
Thelen, David, 334n4
Thomas, Isaiah, 282
Thomas, William, 171
Thompson, Charles, 310n37
Thompson, Joseph, 15, 268–73
Thornton, William, 300

toleration, 268, 270–71, 276–77
Towne, Benjamin, 169–71
transcripts of debates, 15, 23–24, 124–25,
    127; market for, 23
Trenchard, James, 81–84
Trevett v. Weeden, 113, 158
Trumble, Francis, 3
Trumbull, John (painter), 139, 228–31
Trumbull, John (poet), 331n112
Truth, Sojourner, 206–7
"Truth and Taste," 119
Tuck, Richard, 309n15
Tucker, St. George, 182, 209–10
Tucker, Thomas Tudor, 292–93

Ulrich, Laurel Thatcher, 343n8
unanimity: Franklin's attempt to obtain
    in signing of Constitution, 5–6; lack of
    during "founding period," 6
Universal Magazine (London), 185
Upton, Dell, 318n143, 345n22
Utopia (More), 227

Varnum, James Mitchell, 113, 158
Veit, Helen E., 349n6
venereal disease, 66, 78, 317n132
Vermont Constitution (1777): religion and,
    265, 268, 273, 276; slavery and, 216,
    226, 282
vice, allegory of, 258–59
Virginia Act for Establishing Religious
    Freedom, 15, 279–87. See also Bill
    for Establishing Religious Freedom
    (Virginia)
Virginia Almanac, 110
Virginia Constitution (1776), 33, 244
Virginia Declaration of Rights (1776), 28,
    125, 207, 263; circulation and influence
    of, 215–16; committee draft, 215–17;
    "Creator" in, 242, 244, 263; religion
    and, 264, 267, 274–76, 277, 280
Virginia Gazette (Williamsburg), 189
Virginia House of Burgesses, 215
"Virginia Plan" (Madison), 123, 157
virtue, 95–97; allegory of, 258–59
Voltaire, 9, 104
voting, in politics and aesthetics, 87

Wahrman, Dror, 344n10
Waldstreicher, David, 334n3

Walpole, Robert, 29–30
Walters, John, 143
Warburton, William, 29–30
Warner, Michael, 305n19, 313n64, 343n4
Warren, James, 131
Warren, Mercy Otis, 153, 230
Washington, George: "Circular Letter," 69;
    as dedicatee of Paine's *Rights of Man,*
    40; at Federal Convention, 1, 5, 35; First
    Inaugural (rejected), 74, 78; as lawgiver,
    297–98; Pope's *Essay on Man* and, 27;
    retirement and, 222; transmittal letter
    for Constitution, 232–33, 292
"Washington Giving the Laws to Amer-
    ica," 297–98, 298 fig. 23
wax exhibits, 239–40
Webb, Daniel, 103
Webster, Daniel: "The Influence of Opin-
    ion," 91, 99; and Pope, 28
Webster, Noah: *American Selection of Les-
    sons in Reading and Spelling,* 158; on
    Confederation, 73; on Constitution as
    a painting, 16, 114–19; copyright and,
    114; *Examination into the Leading
    Principles of the Constitution,* 114–19;
    on false taste, 109; on libertinism, 61;
    organicism of, 71; on political mimesis,
    192; on representation, 135–36
West, Benjamin, 142, 153, 192–93; *Penn's
    Treaty with the Indians,* 230
Westmoreland County Petition, 276
Whatley, Thomas, 326n14
Wheatley, Phillis: British reviews of,
    183–86, 336n32; elegies of, 200–201;
    Jefferson on, 187; neoclassicism and,
    178; "Niobe in Distress for Her Chil-
    dren," 198–202; "On Being Brought
    from Africa to America," 185; *Poems
    on Various Subjects,* 176, 182–86, 189,
    192, 196, 202; political poetry, 338n48;
    political thought of, 15; Pope and, 28,
    194, 199; slave petitions and, 196–203;
    Virginia readers of, 185
Wheelock, Eleazor, 89
Wheelock, John, 89–93
White, Graham, 187–88, 337n41
White, Shane, 187–88, 337n41
Whitehill, Robert, 287–88
Whole Art of Tachygraphy (Graves and
    Ashton), 161

Wilkes, John, 339n65
Williams, Abraham, 50, 51–52
Williams, Francis, 187
Williams, Raymond, 345n16
Williams, Roger, 277
Williams, William, 242–43
Wilson, James: bills of rights and, 289;
    burned in effigy, 35; on Confederation,
    73; constitutional origins and, 15; deliv-
    ers Franklin's speeches, 5, 124; at Fed-
    eral Convention, 5, 123–26; lectures
    on law, 225; on representation, 123–26,
    132; solitude and, 17, 225–26; speech
    transcribed by Dallas, 155; "statehouse
    speech," 153, 289
Wilson, Richard, 199–200
Winckelmann, Johann Joachim, 191
Winterer, Caroline, 339n62
Winthrop, James, 211, 288
Winthrop, John: "Model of Christian
    Charity," 49–50, 53, 70; on politics as
    marriage, 74–75
Wise, John, 52, 53–54
Wojtowicz, Richard, 334n3
Wolf, Edwin, 311n39
women: and miniature painting, 146; and
    politics of consumption, 33, 109–13
women writers, and "God," 253
Wonderful Discovery of a Hermit, 235–39
Wood, Gordon S., 96, 311n40, 315n114,
    319n15, 319n18, 326n14, 326n30,
    335n17, 336n24, 343n1
Woodmansee, Martha, 339n59
Woollett, William, 200
Wooton, David, 353n66
Wright, William, 169
written constitutions, 25, 72, 164

Yates, Robert, 5, 124
Young, Alfred F., 305n19, 312n46, 335n17,
    348n62
Young, Edward, 195
Young Ladies Academy (Philadelphia),
    111–12, 283

Zagarri, Rosemary, 343n8
Zoffany, Johann, 142
Zuckert, Michael P., 304n14